Lecture Notes in Computer Scie

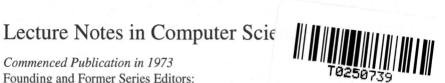

Commenced Publication in 1973
Founding and Former Series Editors:
Gerhard Goos, Juris Hartmanis, and Jan van Leeuwen

Editorial Board

Gavin Bierman   Christoph Koch (Eds.)

Database Programming Languages

10th International Symposium, DBPL 2005
Trondheim, Norway, August 28-29, 2005
Revised Selected Papers

 Springer

Volume Editors

Gavin Bierman
Microsoft Research
JJ Thomson Avenue, Cambridge CB3 0FB, UK
E-mail: gmb@microsoft.com

Christoph Koch
Universität des Saarlandes
Lehrstuhl für Informationssysteme
Postfach 15 11 50, 66041 Saarbrücken, Germany
E-mail: koch@infosys.uni-sb.de

Library of Congress Control Number: 2005937142

CR Subject Classification (1998): H.2, H.3, E.2, D.3.3, H.4

ISSN   0302-9743
ISBN-10   3-540-30951-9 Springer Berlin Heidelberg New York
ISBN-13   978-3-540-30951-2 Springer Berlin Heidelberg New York

Springer is a part of Springer Science+Business Media

springeronline.com

© Springer-Verlag Berlin Heidelberg 2005
Printed in Germany

Typesetting: Camera-ready by author, data conversion by Scientific Publishing Services, Chennai, India
Printed on acid-free paper   SPIN: 11601524   06/3142   5 4 3 2 1 0

Preface

The 10th International Symposium on Database Programming Languages, DBPL 2005, was held in Trondheim, Norway in August 2005. DBPL 2005 was one of 11 meetings to be co-located with VLDB (the International Conference on Very Large Data Bases).

DBPL continues to present the very best work at the intersection of database and programming language research. DBPL 2005 accepted 17 papers out of a total of 63 submissions; an acceptance rate of 27%. Every submission was reviewed by at least three members of the program committee. In addition, the program committee sought the opinions of 51 additional referees, selected because of their expertise on particular topics. The final selection of papers was made during the last week of June. All authors of accepted papers submitted corrected versions, which were collected in an informal proceedings and distributed to the attendees of DBPL 2005. As is traditional for DBPL, this volume was produced after the meeting and authors were able to make improvements to their papers following discussions and feedback at the meeting.

The invited lecture at DBPL 2005 was given by Giuseppe Castagna entitled "Patterns and Types for Querying XML Documents"; an extended version of the lecture appears in this volume. Given the topic of this invited lecture, we invited all attendees of the Third International XML Database Symposium (XSym 2005), also co-located with VLDB, to attend. Continuing this collaboration, we organized with the co-chairs of XSym 2005 a shared panel session to close both meetings. The invited panel discussed "Whither XML, c. 2005?" and consisted of experts on various aspects of XML: Gavin Bierman (Microsoft Research), Peter Buneman (University of Edinburgh), Dana Florescu (Oracle), H.V. Jagadish (University of Michigan) and Jayavel Shanmugasundaram (Cornell University). We are grateful to the panel and the audience for a stimulating and good-humored discussion.

We owe thanks to a large number of people for making DBPL 2005 such a great success. First, we are grateful to the hard work and diligence of the 21 distinguished researchers who served on the program committee. We also thank Peter Buneman, Georg Lausen and Dan Suciu, who offered us much assistance and sound counsel. Svein Erik Bratsberg provided flawless local organization. Chani Johnson gave us much help in mastering the subtleties of the Microsoft Research Conference Management Tool. It was a great pleasure to organize a shared panel and invited lecture with Ela Hunt and Zachary Ives; the co-chairs of XSym 2005. Finally, we acknowledge the generous financial support of Microsoft Research.

September 2005   Gavin Bierman and Christoph Koch

Organization

Program Co-chairs

Gavin Bierman   Microsoft Research Cambridge, UK
Christoph Koch   University of Saarland, Germany

Program Committee

Marcelo Arenas	University of Toronto, Canada
Omar Benjelloun	Stanford University, USA
Sara Cohen	Technion, Israel
James Cheney	University of Edinburgh, UK
Alin Deutsch	University of California, San Diego, USA
Alain Frisch	INRIA Rocquencourt, France
Philippa Gardner	Imperial College, London, UK
Giorgio Ghelli	University of Pisa, Italy
Torsten Grust	University of Konstanz, Germany
Jan Hidders	University of Antwerp, Belgium
Haruo Hosoya	Tokyo University, Japan
Sergey Melnik	Microsoft Research, USA
Tova Milo	Tel Aviv University, Israel
Gerome Miklau	University of Washington, USA
Frank Neven	University of Limburg, Belgium
Alexandra Poulovassilis	Birkbeck College, London, UK
Francesco Scarcello	University of Calabria, Italy
Michael Schwartzbach	BRICS, Denmark
Alan Schmitt	INRIA Rhône-Alpes, France
Nicole Schweikardt	Humboldt University, Berlin, Germany
David Toman	University of Waterloo, Canada

Additional Referees

Fabrizio Angiulli	William Cook
Alessandro Artale	Giovanni Conforti
Pablo Barcelo	Thierry Coupaye
Leo Bertossi	Nick Crasswell
José Blakeley	Wlodzimierz Drabent
Claus Brabrand	Wolfgang Faber
Gilad Bracha	Nate Foster
Cristiano Calcagno	Eric Fusy
Dario Colazzo	Vladimir Gapeyev

Sponsoring Institution

Microsoft Research

Table of Contents

Patterns and Types for Querying XML Documents

Giuseppe Castagna

CNRS, École Normale Supérieure de Paris, France

Abstract. Among various proposals for primitives for deconstructing XML data two approaches seem to clearly stem from practice: path expressions, widely adopted by the database community, and regular expression patterns, mainly developed and studied in the programming language community. We think that the two approaches are complementary and should be both integrated in languages for XML, and we see in that an opportunity of collaboration between the two communities. With this aim, we give a presentation of regular expression patterns and the type systems they are tightly coupled with. Although this article advocates a construction promoted by the programming language community, we will try to stress some characteristics that the database community, we hope, may find interesting.

1 Introduction

Working on XML trees requires at least two different kinds of language primitives: (*i*) deconstruction/extraction primitives (usually called patterns or templates) that pinpoint and capture subparts of the XML data, and (*ii*) iteration primitives, that iterate over XML trees the process of extraction and transformation of data.

Concerning iteration primitives, there are many quite disparate proposals: in this category one can find such different primitives as the FLWR (i.e., for-let-where-return) expressions of XQuery [7], the `filter` primitive of XDuce [40, 39], the `xtransform` primitive of CDuce [4], the `iterate` primitive of Xtatic [31], the select-from-where of Cω [6] and CQL [5], the select-where of Lorel [1] and loto-ql [51], while for other languages, for instance XSLT [22], the iterator is hard-coded in the semantics itself of the language.

Concerning deconstructing primitives, instead, the situation looks clearer since, among various proposals (see the related work section later on), two different and complementary solutions clearly stem from practice: path expressions (usually XPath paths [21], but also the "dot" navigations of Cω or Lorel [1], caterpillar expressions [12] and their "looping" extension [33]) and regular expression patterns [41].

Path expressions are navigational primitives that pinpoint where to capture data subcomponents. XML path expressions (and those of Cω and Lorel in particular) closely resemble the homonimic primitives used by OQL [23] in the context of OODB query languages, with the difference that instead of sets of objects they return sets or sequences of XML elements: more precisely all elements that can be reached by following the paths at issue. These primitives are at the basis of standard languages such as XSLT and XQuery.

More recently, a new kind of deconstruction primitive was proposed: regular expression patterns [41], which extends by regular expressions the pattern matching primitive

G. Bierman and C. Koch (Eds.): DBPL 2005, LNCS 3774, pp. 1–26, 2005.

as popularised by functional languages such as ML and Haskell. Regular expression patterns were first introduced in the XDuce programming language and are becoming more and more popular, since they are being adopted by such quite different languages as ℂDuce [4] (a general purpose extension of the XDuce language) and its query language ℂQL [5], Xtatic [31] (an extension of C#), Scala [54] (a general purpose Java-like object-oriented language that compiles to Java bytecode), XHaskell [45] as well as the extension of Haskell proposed by Broberg *et al.* [11].

The two kinds of primitives are not antagonist, but rather orthogonal and complementary. Path expressions implement a "vertical" exploration of data as they capture elements that may be at different depths, while patterns perform a "horizontal" exploration of data since they are able to perform finer grained decomposition on sequences of elements. The two kinds of primitives are quite useful and they complement each other nicely. Therefore, it would seem natural to integrate both of them in a query or programming language for XML. In spite of this and of several theoretical works on the topic (see the related work section), we are aware of just two running languages in which both primitives are embedded (and, yet, loosely coupled): in ℂQL [5] it is possible to write select-from-where expressions, where regular expression patterns are applied in the from clause to sequences that are returned by XPath-like expressions (see the example at the end of Section 2.3); Gapeyev and Pierce [32] show how it is possible to use regular expression patterns with an all-matches semantics to encode a subset of XPath and use this encoding to add XPath to the Xtatic programming language.

The reason for the lack of study of the integration of these two primitives may be due to the fact that each of them is adopted by a different community: regular patterns are almost confined to the programming language community while XPath expressions are pervasive in the database community.

The goal of this lecture is to give a brief presentation of the regular pattern expressions style together with the type system they are tightly coupled with, that is the *semantic subtyping*-based type systems [19, 29]. We are not promoting the use of these to the detriment of path expressions, since we think that the two approaches should be integrated in the same language and we see in that a great opportunity of collaboration between the database and the programming languages communities. Since the author belongs to latter, this lecture tries to describe the pattern approach addressing some points that, we hope, should be of interest to the database community as well. In particular, after a general overview of regular expression patterns and types (Section 2) in which we show how to embed patterns in a select-from-where expression, we discuss several usages of these semantic subtyping based patterns/types (henceforward, we will often call them "semantic patterns/types"): how to use these patterns and types to give informative error messages (Section 3.2), to dig out errors that are out of reach of previous type checker technologies (Section 3.3) and how the static information they give can be used to define very efficient and highly optimised runtimes (Section 3.4); we show that these patterns permit new logical query optimisations (Section 3.5) and can be used as building blocks to allow the programmer to fine-grainedly define new iterators on data (Section 3.6); finally, the techniques developed for the semantic patterns and types can be used to define optimal data pruning and other optimisation techniques (Section 3.7–3.8)

Related Work. In this work we focus on data extraction primitives coming from the *practice* of programming and query languages manipulating XML data. Thus, we restrict our attention to the primitives included in full-featured languages with a stable community of users. There are however many other proposals in the literature for deconstructing, extracting, and querying XML data.

First and foremost there are all the languages developed from logics for unranked trees whose yardstick in term of expressiveness is the Monadic Second Order Logic. The list here would be too long and we invite the interested reader to consult the excellent overview by Leonid Libkin on the subject [44]. In this area we want to single out the work on composition of monadic queries in [26], since it looks as a promising step toward the integration of path and pattern primitives we are promoting in this work: we will say more about it in the conclusion. A second work that we want to distinguish is Neven and Schwentick's ETL [49], where regular expressions over logical formulæ allow both horizontal and vertical exploration of data; but, as the authors themselves remark, the gap with a usable pattern language is very important, especially if one wants to define non-unary queries typical of Hosoya's regular expressions patterns.

Based on logics also are the query languages developed on or inspired to Ambient Logic, a modal logic that can express spatial properties on unordered trees, as well as to other spatial logics. The result is a very interesting mix of path-like and pattern-like primitives (cf. the dot notation and the spatial formulæ with capture variables that can be found in TQL) [24, 13, 16, 14, 15, 17].

In the query language research, we want to signal the work of Papakonstantinou and Vianu [51] where the loto-ql query language is introduced. In loto-ql it is possible to write select x where p, where p is a pattern in the form of tree which uses regular expressions to navigate both horizontally and vertically in the input tree, and provides bindings of x.

2   A Brief Introduction to Patterns and Types for XML

In this section we give a short survey of patterns and types for XML. We start with a presentation of pattern matching as it can be found in functional languages (Section 2.1), followed by a description of "semantic" types and of pattern-based query primitives (Section 2.2); a description of regular expression patterns for XML (Section 2.3) and their formal definition (Section 2.4) follow, and few comments on iterators (Section 2.5) close the section. Since we introduce early in this section new concepts and notations that will be used in the rest of the article, we advise also the knowledgeable reader to consult it.

2.1   Pattern Matching in Functional Languages

Pattern matching is used in functional languages as a convenient way to capture subparts of non-functional[1] values, by binding them to some variables. For instance, imagine that

---

[1] We intend *non-functional* in a strict sense. So non-functional values are integer and boolean constants, pair of values, record of values, etc., but not λ-abstractions. Similarly a non-functional type is any type that is not an arrow type.

e is an expression denoting a pair and that we want to bind to *x* and *y* respectively to the first and second projection of *e*, so as to use them in some expression *e'*. Without patterns this is usually done by two `let` expressions:

```
let x = first(e) in
let y = second(e) in e'
```

With patterns this can be obtained by a single let expression:

```
let (x,y) = e in e'
```

The pattern (x,y) simply reproduces the form of the expected result of *e* and variables indicate the parts of the value that are to be captured: the value returned by *e* is *matched* against the pattern and the result of this matching is a *substitution*; in the specific case, it is the substitution that assigns the first projection of (the result of) *e* to *x* and the second one to *y*.

If we are not interested in capturing all the parts that compose the result of *e*, then we can use the wildcard "_" in correspondence of the parts we want to discard. For instance, in order to capture just the first projection of *e*, we can use the following pattern:

```
let (x,_) = e in ...
```

which returns the substitution that assigns the result of *first*(*e*) to *x*. In general, a pattern has the form of a value in which some sub-occurrences are replaced by variables (these correspond to parts that are to be captured) and other are replaced by "_" (these correspond to parts that are to be discarded). A value is then matched against a pattern and if they both have the same structure, then the matching operation returns the substitution of the pattern variables by the corresponding occurrences of the value. If they do not have the same structure the matching operation *fails*. Since a pattern may fail—and here resides the power of pattern matching—it is interesting to try on the same value several different patterns. This is usually done with a `match` expression, where several patterns, separated by |, are tried in succession (according to a so-called "first match" policy). For instance:

```
match e with
  | (_,_) -> true
  | _ -> false
```

first checks whether *e* returns a pair in which case it returns `true`, otherwise it returns `false`. Note that, in some sense, matching is not very different from a type case. Actually, if we carefully define the syntax of our types, in particular if we use the same syntax for constructing types and their values, then the `match` operation *becomes* a type case: let us write (*s*,*t*) for the product type of the types *s* and *t* (instead of the more common $s \times t$ or $s * t$ notations) and use the wildcard "_" to denote the super-type of all types (instead of the more common Top, $\mathbb{1}$, or $\top$ symbols), then the match expression above is indeed a type case (if the result of *e* is in the product type (_,_) —the type of all products—, then return true else if it is of type top—all values have this type—, then return false). We will see the advantages of such a notation later on, for the time being just notice that with such a syntactic convention for types and values, a pattern is a (non-functional) type in which some variables may appear.

Remark 1. *A pattern is just a non-functional type where some occurrences may be variables.*

The matching operation is very useful in the definition of functions, as it allows the programmer to define them by cases on the input. For instance, imagine that we encode lists recursively *à la* lisp, that is, either by a nil element for the empty list, or by pairs in which the left projection is the head and the right projection the tail of the list. With our syntax for products and top this corresponds to the recursive definition List = 'nil | (_,List): a list is either 'nil (we use a back-quote to denote constants so to syntactically distinguish them in patterns from variables) or the product of any type and a list. We can now write a tail recursive function[2] that computes the length of a list[3]

```
fun length ((List,Int) -> Int)
  | ('nil , n) -> n
  | ((_,t), n) -> length(t,n+1)
```

which is declared (see Footnote 3 for notation) to be of type (List,Int) -> Int, that is, it takes a pair composed of a list and an integer and returns an integer. More precisely, it takes the list of elements still to be counted and the number of elements already counted (thus length(a,0) computes the length of the list a). If the list is 'nil, then the function returns the integer captured by the pattern variable n, otherwise it discards the head of the list (by using a wildcard) and performs a recursive call on the tail, captured in t, and on n+1. Note that, as shown by the use of 'nil in the first pattern, patterns can also specify values. When a pattern contains a value v, then it matches only values in which the value v occurs in the same position. Remark 1 is still valid even in the case that values occur in patterns, since we can still consider a pattern as a type with variables: it suffices to consider a value as being the denotation of the singleton type that contains that value.

---

[2] A function is *tail recursive* if all recursive calls in its definition occur at the end of its execution flow (more precisely, it is tail recursive if the result of every call is equal to result of its recursive calls): this allows the compiler to optimise the execution of such functions, since it then becomes useless to save and restore the state of recursive calls since the result will be pushed on the top of the stack by the last recursive call.

[3] We use two different syntaxes for functions. The usual notation is standard: for instance, the identity function on integers will be written as fun id(x :Int):Int = x. But if we want to feed the arguments of a function directly to a pattern matching, then the name of the function will be immediately followed by the type of the function itself. In this notation the identity for integers is rather written as fun id(Int->Int) x -> x. This is the case for the function length that follows, which could be equivalently defined as

```
fun length (x :(List,Int)):Int =
match x with
  | ('nil , n) -> n
  | ((_,t), n) -> length(t,n+1)
```

2.2 Union, Intersection, and Difference Types

In order to type-check `match` expressions, the type-checker must compute unions, intersections, and differences (or, equivalently, negations) of types: let us denote these operations by | for the union, & for the intersection, and \ for the difference. The reason why the type-checker needs to compute them can be better understood if we consider a type as a set of values, more precisely as the set of values that have that type: $t = \{v \mid v$ value of type $t\}$[4]. For instance, the product of the singleton type `'nil` and of the type `Int`, denoted by `('nil,Int)`, will be the set of all pairs in which the first element is the constant `'nil` and the second element is an integer. Notice that we already implicitly did such an hypothesis at the end of the previous section, when we considered a singleton type as a type *containing* just one value.

As we did for types, it is possible to associate also patterns to sets of values (actually, to types). Specifically, we associate to a pattern p the type $\lceil p \rfloor$ defined as the set of values for which the pattern does not fail: $\lceil p \rfloor = \{v \mid v$ matches pattern $p\}$. Since we use the same syntax for type constructors and value constructors, it results quite straightforward to compute $\lceil p \rfloor$: it is the type obtained from p by substituting "_" for all occurrences of variables: the occurrences of values are now interpreted as the corresponding singleton types.

Let us check whether the function `length` has the type `(List,Int)` $\rightarrow$ `Int` it declares to have. The function is formed by two branches, each one corresponding to a different pattern. To know the type of the first branch we need to know the set of values (i.e., the type) that can be bound to n; the branch at issue will be selected and executed only for values that are arguments of the function—so that are in `(List,Int)`—and that are accepted by the pattern of the branch—so that are in $\lceil$`('nil,n)`$\rfloor$ which by definition is equal to `('nil,_)`—. Thus, these are the values in the intersection `(List,Int)&('nil,_)`. By distributing the intersection on products and noticing that `List&'nil= 'nil` and `Int&_= Int`, we deduce that the branch is executed for values in `('nil,Int)` and thus n is (bound to values) of type `Int`. The second branch returns a result of type `Int` (the result type declared for the function) provided that the recursive call is well-typed. In order to verify it, we need once more to compute the set of values for which the branch will be executed. These are the arguments of the function, minus the values accepted by the first branch, and intersected with the set of values accepted by the pattern of second branch, that is: `((List,Int)/('nil,_)) & ((_,_),_)`. Again, it is easy to see that this type is equal to `((_,List),Int)` and deduce that variable t is of type `List` and the variable n is of type `Int`: since the arguments have the expected types, then the application of the recursive call is well typed. The type of the result of the whole function is the union of the types of the two branches: since both return integers the union is integer. Finally, notice also that the match is *exhaustive*, that is, for every possible value that can be fed to the match, there exists at least one pattern that matches it. This holds true because the set of all arguments of the the function (that is, its domain) is contained in the union of the types accepted by the patterns.

---

[4] Formally, we are not defining the types, we are giving their semantics. So a type "is interpreted as" or "denotes" a set of values. We prefer not to enter in such a distinction here. See [19] for a more formal introduction about these types.

More generally, to deduce the type of an expression (for the sake of simplicity we use a match expression with just two patterns)

$$\texttt{match } e \texttt{ with } p_1\texttt{->}e_1 \quad | \quad p_2\texttt{->}e_2$$

one must: (i) deduce the type t of e, (ii) calculate the type t_1 of e_1 in function of the values in $t\&\langle p_1\rangle$, (iii) calculate the type t_2 of e_2 in function of the values in $(t\backslash\langle p_1\rangle)\&\langle p_2\rangle$ and, finally, (iv) check whether the match is exhaustive that is, $t \leq \langle p_1 \rangle | \langle p_2 \rangle$: the type of the expression is then the union $t_1 | t_2$.

The example with match clearly shows that for a precise typing of the programs the type-checker needs to compute unions, intersections, and differences of types. Of course, the fact that the type-checker needs to compute unions, intersections, and negations of types does not mean that we need to introduce these operations in the syntax of the types (namely, in the type system): they could be meta-operations whose usage is confined to the type-checker. This is for instance the choice of XDuce (or of XQuery whose types borrow many features from XDuce's ones), where only union types are included in the type system (they are needed to define regular expression types), while intersections and negations are meta-operations computed by the subtyping algorithm.

We defend a choice different from XDuce's one and think that unions, intersections, and differences must be present at type level since, we argue, having these type constructors in the type system is useful for programming[5]. This is particularly true for programs that manipulate XML data—as we will see next— in particular if we completely embrace the "pattern as types" analogy of Remark 1. We have seen that in the "pattern as types" viewpoint, the pattern ('nil,_) is matched by all values that *have type* ('nil,_). This pattern is built from two very specific types: a singleton type and the "_" type. In order to generalise the approach, instead of using in patterns just singleton and "_" types, let us build patterns using as building blocks generic types. So, to give some examples, let us write patterns such as (x,Int) which captures in x the first projection of the matched value only if the second projection is an integer; if we want to capture in y also the second projection, it suffices to use an intersection: (x,y&Int) as to match an intersection a value must match both patterns (the variable to capture and Int to check the type); if the second projection of the matched value is an integer, then (x,y&Int)|(_,x&y) will capture in x the first projection and in y the second projection, otherwise both variables will capture the second projection.

We can then write the pattern (x & (Car&(Guarantee|(_\Used)))) that captures in x all cars that, if they are used have a guarantee (these properties being expressed by the types Car, Guarantee, and Used, the type _\Used being equivalent to ¬Used) and use it to select the wanted items in a catalogue by a select-from-where expression. We have seen at the very beginning of Section 2.1 that patterns can be used instead of variables in let bindings. The idea underlying CQL [5] is to do the same with the bindings in the

---

[5] From a theoretical point of view the XDuce's choice is justified by the fact that XDuce types are closed with respect to boolean operations. This is no longer true if, as in CDuce, one also has function types. However, the point we defend here is that it is useful in practice to have all the boolean operations in the syntax of types, even in the presence of such closure properties.

from clause of a select-from-where. So if `catalogue` denotes a sequence of items, then we can select from it the cars that if used then have a guarantee, by

```
select x from
    (x & (Car&(Guarantee|(_\Used)))) in catalogue
```

As customary, the select-from-where iterates on all elements of `catalogue`; but instead of capturing every element, it captures only those elements that match the pattern, and then binds the pattern variables to their corresponding subparts. These variables are then used in the select and in the subsequent "from" and "where" clauses to form the result. In some sense, the use of patterns in the from clauses corresponds to a syntactic way to force the classic logical optimisation of remounting projections, where here the projection is on the values that match the pattern (we say more about it in Section 3.5). The general form of the select-from-where we will consider here is then the one of CQL, namely:

```
select e from
    p in e',...,p in e'
where e''
```

where p are patterns, e' expressions that denote sequences, and e'' a boolean expression. The select iterates on the e' sequences capturing the variables in the patterns only for the elements that match the respective pattern and satisfy the condition e''. Note that the usual select-from-where syntax as found in SQL is the special case of the above where all the patterns are variables. The same of course holds true also for the FLWR expressions of XQuery, which are nothing but a different syntax for the old select expression (the let binding would appear in the e expression following the select).

The select-from-where expressions we just introduced is nothing but a query-oriented syntax for *list comprehensions* [56], which are a convenient way to define a new list in terms of another list. As discussed by Trinder and Wadler [55] a list comprehension is an expression of the form $[e \mid p \leftarrow e'; c]$ where e is a list expression, p a pattern, e' a generic expression, and c a boolean condition; it defines the list obtained by evaluating e' in the environment produced by matching an element of the result of e against p provided that in the same environment the condition c holds. It is clear that the expression above is just a different syntax for `select e' from p in e where c`, and that the general case with several from clauses is obtained by nesting list comprehensions in e'.

2.3   Regular Expression Patterns

If we want to use patterns also to manipulate XML data, then the simple and somehow naive approach is to define XML patterns as XML values where capture variables and wildcards may occur. To the best of our knowledge, this was first proposed in the programming language community by XMλ [47] and in the database community by XML-QL [25] (whose query primitive is a simpler version of the pattern-based select-from-where introduced in the previous section). This corresponds to extend the classic "patterns as values with variables (and wildcards)" analogy of functional languages to XML data. However, in the previous sections we introduced a more expressive analogy, the one of "patterns as *types* with capture variables" as stated in Remark 1. Since values denote singleton types, then the latter analogy extends the former one, and so it is in principle more expressive. The gain in expressiveness obtained by using the second analogy becomes clear also in practice as soon as we deal with XML, since the types for XML can be more richly combined than those of classic functional languages. Indeed, XML types are usually defined by regular expressions. This can be best shown by using the paradigmatic example of bibliographies expressed by using the CDuce (and CQL) type syntax:

```
type Bib    = <bib>[Book*]
type Book   = <book year=String>[Title (Author+|Editor+) Price?]
type Author = <author>[Last First]
type Editor = <editor>[Last First]
type Title  = <title>[PCDATA]
type Last   = <last>[PCDATA]
type First  = <first>[PCDATA]
type Price  = <price>[PCDATA]
```

The declarations above should not pose any problem to the reader familiar with XML, DTD, and XML Schema. The type Bib classifies XML-trees rooted at tag bib that delimits a possibly empty list of books. These are elements with tag book, an attribute year, and containing a sequence formed exactly by one element title, followed by either a non empty list of author elements, or a non empty list of editor elements, and ended by an optional element price. Title elements are tagged by title and contain a sequence of characters, that is, a string (in XML terminology "parsed character data", PCDATA). The other declarations have similar explanations.

We used the CDuce syntax (which slightly differs from the XDuce's one for tags and attributes) foremost because it is the syntax we are most familiar with, but also because CDuce currently possesses the richest type and pattern algebras among the languages that use regular expression patterns.

The declarations above give a rather complete presentation of CDuce types. There are XML types, that are formed by a tag part and a sequence type (denoted by square brackets). The content of a sequence type is described by a regular expression on types, that is, by the juxtaposition, the application of *, +, ? operators, and the union | of types. Besides these types there also are all the type constructors we saw earlier in this section, namely: (*i*) values which are considered singleton types, so for instance "Buneman" is the type that contains only the string "Buneman", (*ii*) intersection of types, denoted by $s\&t$ that contains all the values that have both type s and type t, (*iii*) difference "\" of types, so that <book year=String\"1999">[Title (Author+|Editor+) Price?] is the type of all books *not* published in 1999, (*iv*) the "_" type, which is the type of all values and is also noted Any, and its complement the Empty type.

According to Remark 1, patterns are the above types enriched with capture variables. With respect to XMλ's approach of "patterns as values with capture variables", this approach yields regular expression patterns. For instance, <bib>[(x::Book)*] is a pattern that captures in x the sequence of all books of a bibliography. Indeed, the * indicates that the pattern x::Book must be applied to every element of the sequence delimited by <bib>. When matched against an element, the pattern x::Book captures this element in the sequence x, provided that the element is of type Book[6]. Patterns can then be used in match expressions:

```
match biblio with   <bib>[ (x::Book)* ] -> x
```

This expression matches biblio against our pattern and returns x as result, thus it makes nothing but stripping the <bib> tag from biblio. Note that if we knew that biblio has type Bib, then we could have used the pattern   <bib>[(x::_)*] (or, equivalently, <bib>[(x::Any)*]), since we statically know that all elements have type Book.

Besides capture variables there is just one further difference between patterns and types, namely the union operator |, which is commutative for types while it obeys a first match policy in patterns. So for instance the following expression returns the sequence of all books published in 1999:

```
match biblio with <bib>[( (x::<book year="1999">_) | _ )*] -> x
```

Again, the pattern ((x::<book year="1999">_) | _) is applied to each element of the sequence. This pattern first checks whether the element has the tag <book year="1999"> whatever its sequence of elements is, and if such is the case it captures it in x; otherwise it matches the element against the pattern "_", which always succeeds without capturing anything (in this way it discards the element). Note that, if we had instead used <bib>[(x::<book year="1999">_)*] this pattern would have succeeded only for bibliographies composed only by books published in 1999, and failed otherwise.

As we said in the introduction, an extraction primitive must be coupled with iterator primitives to apply the extraction all over the data. There are several kinds of iterators in CDuce, but for the sake of the presentation we will use the one defined in the query sub-language CQL, that is the select-from-where defined in the previous section. So, for example, we can define a function that for each book in a sequence extracts all titles, together with relative authors or editors.

```
fun extract(x : [Book*]) : [ [Title (Author+|Editor+)]* ] =
    select (flatten[z y]) from
        <book ..>[ z::Title  y::(Author|Editor)+  _* ] in x
```

The function extract takes a possibly empty sequence of books and returns a possibly empty sequence of sequences that start by a title followed by a non-empty uniform sequence of authors or editors. The operator flatten takes a sequence of sequences and returns their concatenation, thus flatten[z y] is nothing but the concatenation of the sequences z and y. The select-from-where applies the pattern before the in keyword to each element of the sequence x and returns flatten[z y] for every element matching the pattern. In particular, the pattern captures the title in the sequence variable z, the sequence of authors or editors in the sequence variable y, and uses ".." (the wildcard that matches any set of attributes) to discard the year attribute. Had we wanted to return a sequences of pairs (title,price), we would have written

---

[6] The reader may have noticed that we used both x&t and x::t. The double semicolon indicates that the variable x captures *sequences* of t elements: while the first x is of type t the second one is of type [t*]. Since inside regular expression patterns, variables capture sequences, then only the latter can be used (see the formal syntax at the beginning of Section 2.4).

```
fun extract2(x : [Book*]) : [ (Title,Price)* ] =
    select (t,p) from
        <book ..>[ t&Title _* p&Price ] in x
```

where we used "&" instead of ":" to denote that variables capture single elements rather than sequences (see Footnote 6).

Both examples show one of the advantages of using patterns, that is the ability to capture different subparts of a sequence of elements (in the specific case the title and the authors/editors) in a single pass of the sequence.

The select-from-where expression is enough to encode XPath-like navigation expressions. In $\mathbb{C}$Duce/$\mathbb{C}$QL one can use the expression e/t, which is syntactic sugar for `flatten(select x from <_ ..>[(x::t|_)*] in e)` and returns all children of type t of elements of the sequence e. We can compose these expressions to obtain an XPath-like expression. For instance, if `bibs` denotes a sequence of bibliographies (i.e., it is of type [Bib*]), then `bibs/Book/(Author|Editor)` returns the sequence of all authors and editors appearing in the bibliographies. In order to match more closely the semantics of XPath, we will often write `bibs/<book ..>_/(<author ..>_|<editor ..>_)`, since this kind of expression checks only tags while, in principle, the previous path expression checks the whole type of the elements (not just the tag). As a matter of fact, by using the static type of `bibs`, $\mathbb{C}$Duce compiles the first expression into the second one, as we will explain in Section 3.4. Similarly, the expression $e/@id$ is syntactic sugar for `select x from <_ id=x ..> in e`, which returns all the values of the attribute id occurring in the children of elements in e. One can combine select-from-where and path expressions and write queries such as

```
select name from
    <book year="2005">[Title  a::Author+  <price>p] in bibs/Book,
    name in a/<last>(String\"anonymous")
where int_of(p) << 100
```

which returns the sequence of last name elements of the authors of all the books in `bibs` published this year for which a list of authors is given, a price lower than 100 is specified, and the last name is different from "anonymous". The reader is invited to verify that the query would be far more cumbersome if we had to write it either using only patterns or, as it would be for XQuery, using only paths (in this latter case we also would need many more nested loops). A pattern-based encoding of XPath completely different from the one presented here has been proposed by Gapeyev and Pierce [32].

2.4 Pattern and Type Algebras

Patterns and types presented in the previous sections are summarised below:

Types
$$t ::= b \mid t|t \mid t\&t \mid t\backslash t \mid (t,t) \mid <t\ \ell=t\ldots\ell=t>t \mid [R] \mid \text{Empty} \mid \text{Any}$$

Type regular expressions
$$R ::= t \mid R\,R \mid R|R \mid R* \mid R+ \mid R?$$

Patterns

$$p ::= x \mid t \mid p\&p \mid p \mid p \mid (p,p) \mid <p \; \ell=p \; \ldots \; \ell=p> p \mid [r]$$

Pattern regular expressions

$$r ::= p \mid x :: r \mid r \mid r \mid r \, r \mid r+ \mid r* \mid r?$$

where b ranges over basic types, that is Char, Int, etc., as well as singleton types (denoted by values). As a matter of fact, most of the syntax above is just syntactic sugar. These types and patterns can indeed be expressed in a much more compact system, composed only the very simple constructors we started from: basic and product types and their boolean combination. In this short section we will deal with more type-theoretic aspects and give an outline of the fact that all the patterns and types above can be expressed in the system defined as follows.

Definition 1. *A type is a possibly infinite term produced by the following grammar:*

$$t ::= b \mid (t_1, t_2) \mid t_1 | t_2 \mid t_1 \& t_2 \mid \neg t \mid 0 \mid 1$$

with two additional requirements:
1. *(regularity) the term must be a regular tree (it has only a finite number of distinct sub-terms);*
2. *(contractivity) every infinite branch must contain an infinite number of pair nodes (t_1, t_2).*

A pattern is a type in which (possibly infinitely many) occurrences of finitely many capture variables may appear anywhere provided that
1. *no variable occurs under a negation,*
2. *patterns forming an intersection have distinct sets of occurring variables,*
3. *patterns forming an union have the same sets of occurring variables.*   □

In the definition b ranges again overs basic types and 0 and 1 respectively represent the Empty and Any types. The infiniteness of types/patterns accounts for recursive types/patterns. Of course these types must be machine representable, therefore we impose a condition of regularity (in practice, this means that we can define types by recursive equations, using at most as many equations as distinct subtrees). The contractivity condition rules out meaningless terms such as $X = \neg X$ (that is, an infinite unary tree where all nodes are labelled by $\neg$). Both conditions are standard when dealing with recursive types (e.g. see [2]). Also pretty standard are the conditions on the capture variables for patterns: it is meaningless to capture subparts that do not match (one rather captures parts that match the negation); in intersections both patterns must be matched so they have to assign distinct variables, while in union patterns just one pattern will be matched so always the same variables must be assigned whichever alternatives is chosen.

Definition 1 formalises the intuition given in Remark 1 and explains why in the introduction we announced that patterns and types we were going to present were closely connected.

These types and patterns (which are the *semantic subtyping* based ones hinted at in the introduction) are enough to encode all the regular expression types and patterns we used in Section 2.3 (actually, they can do much more than that): sequences can be encoded *à la* Lisp by pairs, pairs can also be used to encode XML types, while regular expression types are encoded by recursive patterns. For instance, if we do not consider attributes, the type

```
type Book = <book>[Title (Author+|Editor+) Price?]
```

can be encoded as $Book = (\text{`}book, (Title, X|Y))$, $X = (Author, X|(Price, \text{`}nil)|\text{`}nil)$ and $Y = (Editor, Y|(Price, \text{`}nil)|\text{`}nil)$, where $\text{`}book$ and $\text{`}nil$ are singleton (basic) types. More details about the encoding, such as the use of non-linear capture variables to match sequences and the use of record patterns to match attributes, as well as the formal definition of pattern matching are given elsewhere [4].

The core syntax of the semantic types and patterns is very simple and this turns out to be quite useful in the formal treatment of the system. The other characteristic that makes life easier is that the boolean combinators on types are interpreted set theoretically: types are sets of values and intersection, union, and difference of types are interpreted as the corresponding operators on these sets (this is the essence of the semantic subtyping approach). Although this simplifies significantly both the theoretical development (types can be transformed by using the classical set-theoretic laws, e.g. De Morgans's, etc.) and the practice (e.g. for a programmer it is easier to understand subtyping in terms of set containment, than in terms of an axiomatisation), the development of the underlying theory is quite complex (see for instance [19, 37, 35, 34, 38, 30, 29, 39]). Fortunately, this complexity is hidden from the programmer: all (s)he has to know is that types are set of values and subtyping is set inclusion. Such theoretical complexity is the counterpart of the expressiveness of the system; expressiveness that is manifest in the simplicity of the query language: value constructors (constants, pairs, and XML values), operators for basic types (e.g. arithmetic and boolean operators), the `flatten` operator, and the pattern-based select-from-where (i.e., list comprehensions) constitute the complete definition of the $\mathbb{C}$QL query language [5]. We are in the presence of few primitives that permit to query complex data in XML format: of course the power comes from the use of patterns in the select-from-where expressions.

2.5 Iterators

In the introduction we said that in order to manipulate XML data besides extraction primitives we also need iterators. Therefore, let us spend a final word about them. In the previous section we used just one iterator, the select-from-where expression. This iterator is very simple but not very expressive: it cannot transform complex trees but just query them (it returns sequences not whole trees) and it applies just one pattern to each element of the scanned sequences (while we have seen that the power of pattern matching resides in the possibility of trying several alternative patterns on the same element). Of course, a select-from-where is meant to be so: it is a query primitive, not a transformation primitive. Therefore it was designed to be simple and not very expressive in order to be easily optimisable (see Section 3.5). But if we want to define concisely more complex transformations, then the language has to provide more powerful built-in operators. For instance, the $\mathbb{C}$Duce language provides three different iterators: the `map` constructor, whose syntax is `map e with` $p_1\text{->}e_1 \mid \ldots \mid p_n\text{->}e_n$, which applies the specified matching alternatives to each element of the sequence e and returns the sequence of results; the `transform` constructor which acts like map but filters out elements that are not matched; the `xtransform` constructor which performs the same operation but on trees, leaving unmatched subtrees unmodified. Of course, the same behaviour could be obtained by programming these operators by using functions but, as we explain in Section 3.6, we would not obtain the same precision of type checking as we obtain by hard-coding them as primitive constructions of the language.

3 Eight Good Reasons to Use Regular Expression Patterns and Types in Query Languages

As its title clearly states, in this section we try to advocate the use of regular expression patterns and of the union, intersection, and negation types we introduced in the previous section. A first reason to be interested in this approach is that its theoretical core is very compact (which does not mean "simple"): we have seen that an expressive query language can be simply obtained by adding list comprehensions to the types and patterns of Definition 1. Rather than concentrating on the theoretical aspects, in the rest of this work we will focus on more practical issues. We already said that we are not promoting the use of regular expressions to the detriment of path expressions, but we would like to invite the database and programming language community to share their skills to find a suitable way to integrate the two mechanisms. Since the author belongs to latter community this paper has described up to now the pattern approach and will now try to address some points which, hopefully, should interest the database community as well: we apologise in advance for the naiveties that might slip in such a *démarche*.

3.1 Classic Usage

The most obvious usages of the type system presented here are those typical of every type system: e.g. static detection of type errors, partial correctness, and database schema specification. In this respect, semantic types do not differ significantly from other type systems and we will no spend much time on this aspect.

The only point that is worth noticing is that union, intersection, and difference types, form quite a natural specification language to express schema constraints. This looks particularly interesting from the database perspective, in particular for the definition of different views. Notwithstanding that the specification of complex views requires complex queries, union intersection and negation types constitute a powerful specification language for simple views. Defining views by restriction or extension looks like a natural application of boolean combinators of types. To give a naive example define the following types

```
type WithPrice = <_ ..>[_* Price _*]
type ThisYear = <_ year="2005">_
```

The first is the type of every element (whatever its tag and attributes are) that has at least a child element of type `Price`, the second types every element (whatever its tag and its content is) that has an attribute year equal to "2005". We can then use the type `<bib>[((Biblio&ThisYear)\WithPrice)*]` to specify a view of our bibliography containing only those books published in 2005 that do not have a price element.

3.2   Informative Error Messages

The use of boolean combinators for types is quite useful in producing informative error messages at compile time. When type checking fails it is always because the type-checker was expecting an expression of some type s and found instead an expression of a type t that is not a subtype of s. Showing the two types s and t is not always informative enough to help the programmer to find the error, especially in case of XML data where s and t can be quite complex (just think of the type describing XHTML documents). Thanks to boolean combinators of types we can compute the difference of these two types, $t \backslash s$, inductively generate a sample value belonging to this difference, and return it to the programmer. This value is a witness that the program is ill-typed, and the generation of just enough of the sample value to outline the error usually allows the programmer to rapidly localise the problem.

To give a practical example of this fact, imagine we want to define a function that returns the list of books of a given year, stripped of the Editors and Price elements. Consider the following solution:

```
fun onlyAuthors (year :Int , books :[Book*]) :[Book*] =
    select <book year=y> (flatten[ t a ]) from
        <book year=y>[ (t::Title | a::Author | _)+] in books
    where int_of(y) = year
```

The idea is that for each book the pattern captures the year in y, the title in the sequence variable t, and the sequence of authors in a. Then, the expression preceding the from clauses rebuilds the book by concatenating the sequences stored in t and a, provided that the year is the one specified at the argument of the function. The function above is not well-typed and the CDuce compiler returns the following error message

```
Error at chars 81-95:
    select <book year=y> ( flatten[ t a ]) from
This expression should have type:
[ Title Editor+ | Title Editor+ Price | Title Author+ | Title Author+ Price ]
but its inferred type is:
[ Title Author+ | Title ]
which is not a subtype, as shown by the sample:
[ <title>[ ] ]
```

The sample value at the end of the message shows at once the origin of the problem: the expression flatten[t a] outlined in the error message (i.e., the expression at chars 81-95) may return a sequence that contains just a title, but no author or editor. This allows the programmer to understand that the problem is that a may denote the empty sequence (the case in which a book specifies a list of editors) and, according to the intended semantics of the program, make her/him correct the error by modifying either the return type of the function (i.e., [(<book year=String>[Title Author*])*]), or the pattern (typically, a pattern like <book year=y>[t::Title a::Author+ _*]).

Of course in such a simple example the expected and inferred types would have been informative enough: it is easy to see that the former type in the error message is equivalent to [Title (Author|Editor)+ Price?] while the latter is [Title Author*] and hence to arrive to the same conclusion. But in practice types are seldom so simple and from our experience in programming with CDuce we have found that sample values in error messages play an essential role in helping the programmer to rapidly spot where bugs lie. We invite the reader to verify this claim by trying the CDuce online interpreter at www.cduce.org.

3.3 Error Mining

Patterns and types are powerful enough to spot some subtle errors that elude current type checking technology. Suppose we had programmed the function extract of Section 2.3 as follows

```
fun extract(x : [Book*]) : [ [Title (Author+|Editor+)]* ] =
   select (flatten[z y]) from
       <book ..>[ z::Title  y::(<author>_|<edtor>_)+  _* ] in x
```

Note that despite the typo we outlined in bold in the program, the function above is well-typed: no typing rule is violated and the pattern is not a useless one since it can still match authors. However, all the books with editors would be filtered out from the result. Since there are cases in which the pattern matches, a possible static emptiness check of the result (as, for instance, recommended in Section 4, "Static Type Analysis" subsection of the XQuery 1.0 and XPath 2.0 Formal Semantics[7] of would not uncover the error. Such an error can only be detected by examining the result and verifying that no book with editors appear. This kind of error is not the exclusive resort of patterns, but can happen also with paths. For instance, if we want to extract each title together with the relative price, from our bibliographic collection bibs we can write

```
bibs/<book ..>_/(<title>_|<prize>_)
```

which contains an error, as prize occurs instead of price. But since the result is not always empty no warning is raised. Again, the error is hidden by the fact that the pattern is partially correct: it does find some match, even if, locally, <prize>_ never matches, hence is incorrect. Once more, as price is optional, by looking at the query output, when seeing only titles, we do not know whether prices are not present in that database or something else went wrong.

These errors can be roughly characterised as the presence of dead code in extraction primitives, that is, the presence of subcomponents (of the patterns or paths) that have no chance to match data. The presence of such errors is very likely in writing programs that process typed XML data, since programmers tend to specify only the part of the schema that is strictly necessary to recover desired data. To that end they make extensive usage of wildcards and alternations that are an important (but not exclusive) source of this kind of errors.

The consequence of these errors is that some desired data may end up not contributing to partial and/or final results, without having the possibility of becoming aware of this problem at compile time. So, this problem may be visible only by carefully observing the results of the programs. This makes error detection quite difficult and the subsequent debugging very hard. And it is made even harder by the fact that, as argued

---

[7] See http://www.w3.org/TR/2005/WD-xquery-semantics-20050915/#processing_ static.

in [18], such errors are not just created by typos—as shown here—but they may be of more conceptual nature.

It has been shown [18] that the errors of this kind can be formally characterised and statically detected by using the set-theoretic operators of the types and patterns we presented here. In particular given a type t and a pattern p, it is not difficult to characterise the parts of p which are used for at least one value v in t (and hence the dead parts that are never used). This is done by applying a rewriting system to the pair (t, p) which decomposes the matching problem for each subcomponent of p, by applying the set-theoretic properties of the semantic types and patterns. So for instance $(t, p_1|p_2)$ is rewritten into (t, p_1) and $(t \& \neg \langle p_1 \rangle, p_2)$; the set of sub-patterns of p that may be used when matching values of type t is formed by all patterns p' such that (t, p) rewrites in zero or more steps into (t', p') and $t' \& \langle p' \rangle = 0$.

Finally, the implementation of such a technique in the current type-checkers of, among others, Xtatic, CDuce, and XDuce, does not produce any noticeable overhead, since the rewriting can be performed by the normal type inference process itself. Further details are available elsewhere [18].

3.4 Efficient Execution

The benefits of semantic patterns/types are not confined to the static aspects of XML programming. On the contrary they are the key ingredient that makes languages as CDuce and Xtatic outperform the fastest XML processors. The idea is quite simple: by using the static type information and the set-theoretic properties of the semantic patterns/types one can compile data queries (e.g. the patterns) so that they perform a minimum number of checks. For instance, if we look in an XML tree for some given tag and the type of the tree tells us that this tag cannot occur in the left subtree, then we will skip the exploration of this subtree and explore only the right one. As a more concrete example consider the following definitions (see Footnote 3 for notation)

```
type A = <a>[A*]
type B = <b>[B*]

fun check( A|B -> Int ) A -> 1 |  B -> 0
```

The type A types all the XML trees where only the <a> tags occurs, the type B does the same for <b>, while the function check returns either 1 or 0 according to whether its argument is of type A or B. A naive compilation schema would yield the following behaviour for the function: first check whether the first pattern matches the argument, by checking that all the elements of the argument are <a>; if this fails, try the second branch and do all these tests again with <b>. The argument may be run through completely several times. There are many useless tests: since we statically know that the argument is forcedly either of type A or of type B, then the check of the root tag is enough. It is thus possible to use the static type information to compile pattern matching so that it not only avoids backtracking but it also avoids checking whole parts of the matched value. In practice check will be compiled as

```
fun check( A|B -> Int ) <a>_ -> 1 |  _ -> 0
```

As a second example consider the query at the end of Section 2.3. By using the information that bibs has static type [Bib*], it will be compiled as:

```
select name from
    <_ year="2005">[ _   a::Author+   <price>p ] in bibs/_,
    name in a/<last>(_\"anonymous")
where int_of(p) << 100
```

While in both cases the solutions are easy to find, in general computing the optimal solution requires fully exploiting intersections and differences of types. These are used to reduce the problem of generating an optimal test to that of deciding to which summand of a union of pairwise disjoint types the values of a given static type belong to. To find the solution, the algorithm—whose description is outside the scope of this paper (see the references below)—descends deep in the static type starting from its root and accumulates enough information to stop the process as soon as possible. The information is accumulated by generating at each step of the descent a new union of pairwise distinct types, each type corresponding to a different branching of the decision procedure.

This algorithm was first defined and implemented for CDuce and it is outlined in [4] (whose extended version contain a more detailed description). The tree-automata theory underlying has been formally described [28] and generalised [30]. Levin and Pierce have adapt this technique to Xtatic and extend it with heuristics (their work is included in these proceedings [43]).

We just want to stress that this compilation schema is semantic with respect to types, in the sense that the produced code does not depend on the syntax of the types that appear in patterns, but only on their interpretation as sets of values. Therefore there is no need to simplify types—for instance by applying any of the many type equivalences—before producing code, since such simplifications are all "internalised" in the compilation schema itself.

The practical benefits of this compilation schema have been shown [5] by using XMark [52] and the XQuery Use Cases [20] to benchmark CDuce/ CQL against Qizx [27] and Qexo [9] two of most efficient XQuery processors (these are several orders of magnitude faster than the reference implementation of XQuery, Galax [3]). The results show that in main memory processing CQL is on the average noticeably faster than Qizx and Qexo, especially when computing intensive queries such as joins. Furthermore, since the execution times of CQL benchmarks always include the type-checking phase, this also shows that the semantic types presented here are algorithmically tractable in practice.

3.5   Logical Optimisation of Pattern-Based Queries

We already remarked at the end of Section 2.2 that the usual select-from-where as found in SQL and the for-expressions of XQuery are both special cases of our pattern-based select-from-where expressions, in which all patterns are variables. Hence, all classic logical optimisations defined for the former apply also to the pattern-based case. However, the use of patterns introduces a new class of pattern-specific optimisations [5] that being orthogonal to the classical optimisations bring a further gain of performance. These optimisations essentially try to transform the from clauses so as to capture in a single pattern as much information as possible. This can be obtained essentially in three ways: (*i*) by merging into a single pattern two different patterns that work on a common sequence, (*ii*) by transforming parts of the where clauses into patterns, and (*iii*) by transforming path expressions into nested pattern-based selections and then merging the different selects before applying the previous optimisations. As an example consider

```
select <book>[t]  from
   b in bibs/<book>_ ,
   p in [b]/<price>_ ,
   t in [b]/<title>_ ,
   y in [b]/@year
where (p = <price>"69.99") and (y="1990")
```

which is a query written in a XQuery style (the from clauses use path expressions on right of the in keyword and single variables on its left), and that returns all the titles of books published in 1990 whose price is "69.99" (this essentially is the query Q1 of the XQuery Use Cases). After applying pattern-specific optimisations it will be transformed into

```
select <book>[t]  from
   <bib>[b::Book*] in bibs,
   <book year="1990">[ t&Title  _+  <price>"69.99" ] in b
```

which is intuitively better performing since it computes less nested loops.

The benchmarks mentioned above [5] show that these pattern-specific optimisations in most cases bring a gain in performance, and in no case degrading it.

3.6   Pattern Matches as Building Blocks for Iterators

In the introduction we said that in order to work with XML data one needs two different primitives: deconstructors and iterators. Although patterns belong to the first class of primitives, thanks to an idea of Haruo Hosoya, they are useful to define iterators, as well. More precisely, they allow the programmer to define her/his own iterators. This is very important in the context of XML processing for two reasons: (*i*) the complex structure of data makes virtually impossible for a language to provide a set of iterators covering, in a satisfactory way, all possible cases[8] and (*ii*) an iterator programmed using the existing primitives of the language would be far less precisely typed than the same built-in operator and would thus require a massive usage of casting operations.

We have seen that by defining regular expressions over patterns we can perform data extraction along sequences of elements. But patterns play a passive role with respect to the elements of the sequence: they can capture (part of) them but do not compute any transformation. Haruo Hosoya noticed that if instead of using patterns as basic blocks of regular expressions one uses pattern matching branches of the form "$p \to e$", then it is possible to define powerful iterators that he dubs *filters* [36] and that are included in the recent versions of XDuce. The idea is that as regular expressions over

---

[8] No formal expressiveness concern here: just programming experience where the need of a new iterator that would fit and solve the current problem appears over and over.

patterns describe the way the patterns are matched against the elements of a sequence, in the same way regular expressions over match branches "$p \rightarrow e$" describe the way to apply the transformation described by the branch to the elements of a sequence provided that they match p. For instance, the filter[9] `filter[(x&Int -> x+1)*]` applied to [1 2 3] returns [2 3 4], while `filter[( x&Int->x+1 | x&Bool->not(x) )*]` transforms [1 'true 'true 2] into [2 'false 'false 3]. To show a filter in our paradigmatic example consider the following `translate` filter

```
type Titre = <titre>[PCDATA]
type Auteur = <auteur edt=("oui"|"non")>[Last First]

let translate = filter[
      ( <title> x -> <titre> x
      | <author> x -> <auteur edt="non"> x
      | <editor> x -> <auteur edt="oui"> x
      | x -> x )*]
```

which transforms title elements to their French translation, author and editor elements into "auteur" elements, and leaves other elements unchanged. This filter can then be applied to the content of a book element to obtain new elements which will have type `<book year=String>[Titre Auteur+ Price]`.

More generally, filters provide a unique mechanism to implement several primitives. For instance, `match` e `with` $p_1\rightarrow e_1$ | ... | $p_n\rightarrow e_n$ is just syntactic sugar for the application `filter[`$p_1\rightarrow e_1$ | ... | $p_n\rightarrow e_n$`]`(`[`e`]`), while a filter such as `filter[(`$p_1\rightarrow e_1$ | ... | $p_n\rightarrow e_n$`)*]`(e) corresponds to the `transform` iterator of CDuce we hinted at in Section 2.5. Filters can also encode the `xtransform` iterator of Section 2.5 (this is a little clumsier, since it requires the use of recursive filters). The typing of XDuce filters is less precise than the one of map, transform and xtransform, but in exchange filters can do more as they can process several elements at a time while map, transform and xtransform can just process a single element per iteration (see [36] for details).

We already explained that the reason why we need to give the programmer the possibility to define iterators is that built-in iterators cannot cover all possible cases and that iterations implemented via functions would not be typed precisely enough. To see why consider the filter `translate` we defined before, and notice that the type-checker must be able to deduce that when this filter is applied to a sequence of type `[Title (Author+|Editor+) Price?]`, then the result has type `[Titre Auteur+ Price?]`, while when the same filter is applied to a sequence of type `[Author* Editor]` the type-checker must deduce a result type `[Auteur+]`. This kind of polymorphism goes beyond the possibilities of parametric polymorphism of, say, ML or System F, which can be applied only to homogeneous lists. Here instead the result type is obtained by performing an abstract execution of the iterator on the type of the input. In practice, what the type-checker does is to execute the iterator on the DTD of the input in order to precisely map the transformation of each element of the input tree in the resulting output tree. This justifies the use of a specific syntax for defining iterators, since this sub-language instructs the type-checker to perform this abstract execution, makes it possible, and ensures its termination.

---

[9] We use for filters a syntax slightly different from the one of XDuce.

The expressive power of Hosoya's filters is limited, as they rely on regular expressions. The kind of processing that these filters permits is, roughly, that of the map operator in functional languages. But, for instance, they are not able to express the function that reverses a list. Also, type inference is less precise than that of map, transform, and xtransform, and it is further penalised in the presence of recursion. To obviate all these problems Kim Nguyễn has proposed a more radical approach [50]. He proceeds along the ideas of Haruo Hosoya and takes as basic building blocks the pattern matching branches, but instead of building his filters by defining regular expressions on these building blocks, Nguyễn's filters are obtained by applying the grammar of Definition 1 to them. His filters are then regular trees generated by the following grammar:

$$ f ::= e \mid p \rightarrow f \mid (f,f) \mid f \mid f \mid f;f $$

where e ranges over expressions and p over patterns. Their semantics is quite natural. When a filter formed by just an expression is applied, then the expression is executed. If the filter $p \rightarrow f$ is applied to e, then the filter f applied to e is executed in the environment obtained by matching p against the result of e (failure of this matching makes the whole filter fail); if (f_1, f_2) is applied to a pair, then each f_i is applied to the corresponding element of the pair and the pair of the results is returned; the alternation applies the first filter to the argument and if this fails it applies the second one; finally, the sequencing applies the second filter to the result of the application of the first filter to the argument. Note that with respect to the grammar in Definition 1, sequencing plays the role of the intersection. Furthermore, as in Definition 1 there cannot be any capture variable under a negation, so there is no negation filter in Nguyễn's filters. A limited form of recursion ensures the termination of the type-checking and of the execution of Nguyễn's filters.

As simple as they are, Nguyễn's filters have many of the sought properties: they are expressive enough to encode list reversal, while the encodings of map, transform, and xtransform have same precise typing as in CDuce. The algorithmic properties of their type system are (at the moment of writing) still a matter of study.

3.7 Type and Pattern-Based Data Pruning for Memory Usage Optimisation

XML data projection (or pruning) is one of the main optimisation techniques recently adopted in the context of main-memory XML query-engines [46, 10]. The underlying idea is very simple but useful at the same time. In short, given a query q over a document d, subtrees of d not necessary for evaluating q are pruned, thus obtaining a smaller document d'. Then q is executed over d', hence avoiding the need to allocate and process nodes that will never be reached by navigational specifications in q. As has been shown [46, 10], in general, XML navigation specifications expressed in queries tend to be very selective. Hence, significant improvements due to pruning can be actually obtained, either in terms of query execution time or in term of memory usage (it is worth observing that for main-memory XML query engines, very large documents can not be queried without pruning).

The work we have described in Section 3.4 already provides optimal data pruning for pattern matching. Even if the actual implementation relies on automata, we have seen that it essentially consists in computing a set of equivalent minimal patterns. The "minimality" is given by the presence of "_" wildcards that denote parts of the data that need not to be checked. It is clear that the set of the parts denoted by "_" and not in the scope of any capture variable constitutes an optimal set of data to be pruned.

Of course, extending the technique developed for the compilation of patterns to general and more complex queries (i.e. not just consisting of simple pattern matching) requires further work. But this does not seems a far-reached objective: once more set-theoretic operations should came to rescue, as the process should essentially reduce to the computation of the intersections of the various optimal patterns met in the query, and its distribution with respect to the data stored in secondary memory, so that to individuate its optimal pruning set.

3.8   Type-Based Query Optimisation

Let us conclude this overview by a somewhat vague but nevertheless important remark. The type system presented in this work is very precise.

Concerning data description the XML components of Xtatic, XDuce, and CDuce's type systems are already more expressive than DTDs and XML Schemas. This holds true from a formal point of view (see [48] for a formal taxonomy) but, above all, in practice, too.[10] For the practical aspect let us take a real life example and consider the Internet Movie Database [42] whose XML Schema cab be found elsewhere [8]: thanks to singleton types and boolean combinators, CDuce types can express integrity constraints such as the fact that the type attribute of show elements can only be either "Movie" or "TV Series", and that only in the former case the show element can contain a box_office element, and only in the latter case it can contain a season element.

But the real boost with these new types is when typing queries and transformations, since semantic types are far more precise than the type-systems of current languages for XML. We have already seen in Section 3.6 the stringent requirements for typing iterators: the type-checker must be able to compute the precise modifications performed on each element the iterator meets. For instance the system presented here will deduce for bibs/Book/(Title|Author|Editor) the type [(Title (Author+|Editor+))*] while, at best, the corresponding XPath expression will be typed by the XQuery type system as [(Title|Author|Editor)*], which is far less precise. A further example of precision of the type system is the typing of pattern variables which is *exact*, in the sense that the type inferred by the type-checker for a pattern variable is exactly the set of values that may be assigned to that variable at run-time. The precision of the type system is also witnessed by the practice, since in languages that use these semantic types and patterns, downward casts are essentially confined to external data, while internal data (that is, data generated by the program) have sufficiently precise types that no cast is needed. Such precision gives a lot of information about the queries at hand and, as in the case of the pruning presented in the previous section, it should and could be possible to use this information for the optimisation of secondary memory queries. DTDs and XML Schemas have already been used to optimise access to XML data in secondary storage (in particular they were used to map XML into relations, e.g., [8, 53]), but for

---

[10] To tell the truth, some fancier aspects of XML Schema, such as integrity of IDREFs are not captured. But this goes beyond the possibility of any static type system.

semantic types/patterns this is a research direction that, as far as we know, has not yet been explored.

4 Conclusion

With this presentation of regular patterns and types for XML we hope to have convinced the reader that they constitute primitives worthy of consideration. To that end we described various problems that can be solved with the help of regular patterns and types. Apart from the interest of each problem, what really seems important is that regular patterns and types constitute a unique and general framework to understand and solve such a disparate disparate problems. Despite that, we do not believe that regular patterns are *the* solution: as we said repeatedly, we think one should aim at a tight integration, or even a unification, of path and pattern extraction primitives. We have discussed a query language, $\mathbb{C}$QL, and hinted at an object-oriented language, Xtatic, in which both primitives coexist (even if one is defined in terms of the other), but the solutions proposed for these languages are far from being satisfactory since the two primitives are essentially disconnected. We aim at a deeper integration of the approaches in which, say, we could build paths over patterns (so as to capture intermediate results) or define regular expression patterns on paths (so as to perform pattern extractions at different depths) ... or maybe both. In this perspective the work on the composition of monadic queries [26] that we cited in the related work section of the Introduction, looks quite promising. The idea is simple and elegant and consists in concatenating monadic queries so that the set of the nodes resulting from one query are the input nodes of the query that follows it. Actually, the concatenation (noted by a dot and denoting composition) is not performed among single queries but among unions and intersections of queries. This yields the following composition formalism $\phi ::= q \mid q.\phi \mid \phi \wedge \phi \mid \phi \vee \phi$ (where q ranges over particular monadic queries, called *parametrised queries*) that closely resembles to a mix of paths and pattern primitives.

All these considerations concern the extraction primitives, but the need of mixing horizontal and vertical navigation concerns iterators, as well. For instance, Hosoya's filters are inherently characterised by an horizontal behaviour: it is easier to use a path to apply a filter at a given depth, than to program the latter recursively so that it can autonomously perform the vertical navigation. Such a problem may be less felt in Nguyễn's filters, but we are afraid that using them to program a mix of vertical and horizontal iterations would be out of reach of the average programmer.

As a matter of fact, this last consideration probably holds for patterns already: it is true that it is easier to write a path than a pattern, and even if the use of the more sophisticated features of XPath is not for the fainthearted programmer, nevertheless simple queries are simpler in XPath. So if we want the use of regular expression patterns to spread outside the community of functional programmers, it will be necessary to find alternative ways to program them, for instance by developing QBE-style query interfaces. This will be even more urgent for a formalism integrating both pattern and path navigational primitives. It looks as a promising topic for future work.

Acknowledgements. I want to warmly thank Gavin Bierman for several suggestions and for proof-reading the paper. Véronique Benzaken, Peter Buneman, Dario Colazzo,

Cédric Miachon, Ioana Manolescu, and Matthieu Objois provided useful feedback on this work. Part of it was prepared while I was visiting Microsoft Research in Cambridge and it greatly benefited of the interesting discussions and stimulating environment that I enjoyed during my stay. Thus let me warmly thank Microsoft Research for its support and the MSR Cambridge Lab for its "unmatchable" hospitality. This work was partially supported by the RNTL project "GraphDuce" and by the ACI project "Transformation Languages for XML: Logics and Applications".

References

1. S. Abiteboul, D. Quass, J. McHugh, J. Widom, and J. Wiener. The Lorel query language for semistructured data. *International Journal on Digital Libraries*, 1(1):68–88, 1997.
2. Roberto M. Amadio and Luca Cardelli. Subtyping recursive types. *ACM Transactions on Programming Languages and Systems*, 15(4), September 1993.
3. Bell-labs. *Galax.* http://db.bell-labs.com/galax/.
4. V. Benzaken, G. Castagna, and A. Frisch. CDuce: an XML-friendly general purpose language. In *ICFP '03, 8th ACM International Conference on Functional Programming*, pages 51–63, Uppsala, Sweden, 2003. ACM Press.
5. V. Benzaken, G. Castagna, and C. Miachon. A full pattern-based paradigm for XML query processing. In *PADL 05, 7th International Symposium on Practical Aspects of Declarative Languages*, number 3350 in LNCS, pages 235–252. Springer, January 2005.
6. Gavin Bierman, Erik Meijer, and Wolfram Schulte. The essence of data access in Cω. In *Proc. of ECOOP '2005, European Conference on Object-Oriented Programming*, volume 3586 of *Lecture Notes in Computer Science*. Springer, 2005.
7. S. Boag, D. Chamberlin, M. Fernandez, D. Florescu, J. Robie, J. Siméon, and M. Stefanescu. *XQuery 1.0: An XML Query Language*. W3C Working Draft, http://www.w3.org/TR/xquery/, May 2003.
8. P. Bohannon, J. Freire, J. Haritsa, M. Ramanath, P. Roy, and J. Simeon. LegoDB: customizing relational storage for XML documents. In *VLDB '02, 28th Int. Conference on Very Large Databases*, pages 1091–1094, 2002.
9. P. Bothner. Qexo - the GNU Kawa implementation of XQuery. http://www.gnu.org/software/qexo/.
10. Stéphane Bressan, Zoé Lacroix, Ying Guang Li, and Anna Maddalena. Prune the XML before you search it: XML transformations for query optimization. *DataX Workshop*, 2004.
11. Niklas Broberg, Andreas Farre, and Josef Svenningsson. Regular expression patterns. In *ICFP '04: 9th ACM SIGPLAN International Conference on Functional programming*, pages 67–78, New York, NY, USA, 2004. ACM Press.
12. A. Brüggemann-Klein and D. Wood. Caterpillars, context, tree automata and tree pattern matching. In *Proceedings of DLT '99: Foundations, Applications and Perspectives*. World Scientific Publishing Co., 2000.
13. C. Calcagno, P. Gardner, and U. Zarfaty. Context logic and tree update. In *POPL '05, 32nd ACM Symposium on Principles of Programming Languages*. ACM Press, 2005.
14. L. Cardelli, P. Gardner, and G. Ghelli. A spatial logic for querying graphs. In *29th International Colloquium on Automata, Languages, and Programming*, volume 2380 of *Lecture Notes in Computer Science*. Springer-Verlag, 2002.
15. L. Cardelli, P. Gardner, and G. Ghelli. Manipulating trees with hidden labels. In *6th International Conference on Foundations of Software Science and Computational Structures*, volume 2620 of *Lecture Notes in Computer Science*. Springer-Verlag, 2003.

16. L. Cardelli and G. Ghelli. Tql: A query language for semistructured data based on the ambient logic. *Mathematical Structures in Computer Science*, 14:285–327, 2004.

17. Luca Cardelli, Philippa Gardner, and Giorgio Ghelli. A spatial logic for querying graphs. In *ICALP '02, 29th International Colloquium on Automata, Languages and Programming*, pages 597–610. Springer-Verlag, 2002.

18. G. Castagna, D. Colazzo, and A. Frisch. Error mining for regular expression patterns. In *ICTCS 2005, Italian Conference on Theoretical Computer Science*, number 3701 in Lecture Notes in Computer Science. Springer, 2005.

19. G. Castagna and A. Frisch. A gentle introduction to semantic subtyping. In Proceedings of *PPDP '05, the 7th ACM SIGPLAN International Symposium on Principles and Practice of Declarative Programming*, ACM Press (full version) and *ICALP '05, 32nd International Colloquium on Automata, Languages and Programming*, Lecture Notes in Computer Science n. 3580, Springer (summary), Lisboa, Portugal, 2005. Joint ICALP-PPDP keynote talk.

20. D. Chamberlin, P. Fankhauser, D. Florescu, M. Marchiori, and J. Robie. XML Query Use Cases. Technical Report 20030822, World Wide Web Consortium, 2003.

21. J. Clark and S. DeRose. *XML Path Language (XPath)*. W3C Recommendation, `http://www.w3.org/TR/xpath/`, November 1999.

22. James Clark. *XSL Transformations (XSLT)*. W3C Recommendation, `http://www.w3.org/TR/xslt/`, November 1999.

23. Sophie Cluet. Designing OQL: allowing objects to be queried. *Inf. Syst.*, 23(5):279–305, 1998.

24. G. Conforti, G. Ghelli, A. Albano, D. Colazzo, P. Manghi, and C. Sartiani. The query language TQL. In *Proc. of the 5th WebDB, Madison, Wisconsin, USA*, pages 19–24, 2002.

25. A. Deutsch, M. F. Fernandez, D. Florescu, A. Y. Levy, and D. Suciu. "XML-QL: A Query Language for XML". In *WWW The Query Language Workshop (QL)*, 1998.

26. E. Filiot. Composition de requêtes monadiques dans les arbres. Master's thesis, Master Recherche de l'Université des Sciences et Technologies de Lille, 2005.

27. X. Franc. Qizx/open. `http://www.xfra.net/qizxopen`.

28. A. Frisch. Regular tree language recognition with static information. In *Proc. IFIP Conference on Theoretical Computer Science (TCS)*, Toulouse, 2004. Kluwer.

29. A. Frisch, G. Castagna, and V. Benzaken. Semantic Subtyping. In *LICS '02, 17th Annual IEEE Symposium on Logic in Computer Science*, pages 137–146. IEEE Computer Society Press, 2002.

30. Alain Frisch. *Théorie, conception et réalisation d'un langage de programmation fonctionnel adapté à XML*. PhD thesis, Université Paris 7, December 2004.

31. Vladimir Gapeyev and Benjamin C. Pierce. Regular object types. In *ECOOP '03, European Conference on Object-Oriented Programming*, 2003.

32. Vladimir Gapeyev and Benjamin C. Pierce. Paths into patterns. Technical Report MS-CIS-04-25, University of Pennsylvania, October 2004.

33. E. Goris and M. Marx. Looping caterpillars. In *LICS '05, 20th Annual IEEE Symposium on Logic in Computer Science*. IEEE Computer Society Press, 2005.

34. H. Hosoya. *Regular Expression Types for XML*. PhD thesis, The University of Tokyo, 2001.

35. H. Hosoya. Regular expressions pattern matching: a simpler design. Unpublished manuscript, February 2003.

36. H. Hosoya. Regular expression filters for XML. In *Programming Languages Technologies for XML (PLAN-X)*, 2004.

37. H. Hosoya, A. Frisch, and G. Castagna. Parametric polymorphism for XML. In *POPL '05, 32nd ACM Symposium on Principles of Programming Languages*. ACM Press, 2005.

38. H. Hosoya and M. Murata. Validation and boolean operations for attribute-element constraints. In *Programming Language Technologies for XML (PLAN-X)*, 2002.

39. H. Hosoya and B. Pierce. XDuce: A typed XML processing language. *ACM Transactions on Internet Technology*, 3(2):117–148, 2003.

40. H. Hosoya and B.C. Pierce. XDuce: A typed XML processing language. In *WebDB2000, 3rd International Workshop on the Web and Databases*, 2000.

41. H. Hosoya and B.C. Pierce. Regular expression pattern matching for XML. In *POPL '01, 25th ACM Symposium on Principles of Programming Languages*, 2001.

42. Internet Movie Database. `http://imdb.com`.

43. Michael Y. Levin and Benjamin C. Pierce. Type-based optimization for regular patterns. In *DBPL '05, Database Programming Languages*, August 2005.

44. L. Libkin. Logics for unranked trees: an overview. In *ICALP '05, 32nd International Colloquium on Automata, Languages and Programming*, number 3580 in LNCS. Springer, 2005.

45. K. Zhuo Ming Lu and M. Sulzmann. An implementation of subtyping among regular expression types. In *Proc. of APLAS'04*, volume 3302 of *LNCS*, pages 57–73. Springer, 2004.

46. Amélie Marian and Jérôme Siméon. Projecting XML elements. In *29th Int. Conference on Very Large Databases (VLDB '03)*, pages 213–224, 2003.

47. Erik Meijer and Mark Shields. XMλ: A functional language for constructing and manipulating XML documents. (Draft), 1999.

48. M. Murata, D. Lee, and M. Mani. Taxonomy of XML schema languages using formal language theory. In *Extreme Markup Languages*, 2001.

49. F. Neven and T. Schwentick. Expressive and efficient pattern languages for tree-structured data. In *PODS '00: 19th ACM Symposium on Principles of Database Dystems*, pages 145–156. ACM Press, 2000.

50. Kim Nguyễn. Une algèbre de filtrage pour le langage ℂDuce. DEA *Programmation*, Université Paris 11, September 2004. Available at `http://www.lri.fr/~kn/main.pdf`.

51. Yannis Papakonstantinou and Victor Vianu. Dtd inference for views of xml data. In *PODS '00: Proceedings of the nineteenth ACM SIGMOD-SIGACT-SIGART symposium on Principles of database systems*, pages 35–46, New York, NY, USA, 2000. ACM Press.

52. Albrecht Schmidt, Florian Waas, Martin L. Kersten, Michael J. Carey, Ioana Manolescu, and Ralph Busse. XMark: A benchmark for XML data management. In *Proceedings of the Int'l. Conference on Very Large Database Management (VLDB)*, pages 974–985, 2002.

53. J. Shanmugasundaram, K. Tufte, C. Zhang, G. He, D. DeWitt, and J. Naughton. Relational databases for querying XML documents: Limitations and opportunities. In *VLDB '99, 25th Int. Conference on Very Large Databases*, pages 302–314, 1999.

54. M. Odersky *et. al.* An overview of the Scala programming language. Technical Report IC/2004/64, École Polytechnique Fédérale de Lausanne, 2004. Latest version at `http://scala.epfl.ch`.

55. P. Trinder and P. Wadler. Improving list comprehension database queries. In *Proc. of TENCON '89, Bombay, India (November 1989), 186-192.*, 1989.

56. P. Wadler. List comprehensions. In *The Implementation of Functional Programming Languages* by S. Peyton Jones (chapter 7). Prentice Hall, 1987. Available on-line at `http://research.microsoft.com/Users/simonpj/Papers/slpj-book-1987`.

Dual Syntax for XML Languages

Claus Brabrand, Anders Møller*, and Michael I. Schwartzbach

BRICS**, University of Aarhus, Denmark
{brabrand, amoeller, mis}@brics.dk

Abstract. XML is successful as a machine processable data interchange format, but it is often too verbose for human use. For this reason, many XML languages permit an alternative more legible non-XML syntax. XSLT stylesheets are often used to convert from the XML syntax to the alternative syntax; however, such transformations are not reversible since no general tool exists to automatically parse the alternative syntax back into XML.

We present *XSugar*, which makes it possible to manage dual syntax for XML languages. An XSugar specification is built around a context-free grammar that unifies the two syntaxes of a language. Given such a specification, the XSugar tool can translate from alternative syntax to XML and vice versa. Moreover, the tool statically checks that the transformations are reversible and that all XML documents generated from the alternative syntax are valid according to a given XML schema.

1 Introduction

XML has proven successful as a machine processable data interchange format. There exist numerous APIs for processing XML data in general purpose programming languages and also many specialized XML processing languages, such as XSLT and XQuery. Realizing the benefits of using XML, an increasing number of new languages, ranging from loosely structured document-oriented languages to purely data-oriented ones, use an XML syntax. The XML format, however, is verbose and not always ideal for human use. Yet, in many of these new languages, documents are intended to be read and written directly by humans. For this reason, many languages have *two* syntaxes—an XML syntax intended for machine processing and interchange, and an alternative non-XML syntax for human use. This necessitates automated translation in one or both directions.

As a representative example, consider the language RELAX NG [8]. It is a schema language for XML, but we are not interested in the semantics of RELAX NG documents here, only in their syntax. The original language definition specifies an XML syntax, and a later separate specification provides a compact non-XML syntax [7]. A main goal of providing the non-XML syntax is to maximize readability. As an example (taken from the RELAX NG documentation),

---

* Supported by the Carlsberg Foundation contract number 04-0080.

** Basic Research in Computer Science (www.brics.dk), funded by the Danish National Research Foundation.

G. Bierman and C. Koch (Eds.): DBPL 2005, LNCS 3774, pp. 27–41, 2005.

consider the following tiny RELAX NG document written using the XML syntax:

```
<element name="addressBook"
         xmlns="http://relaxng.org/ns/structure/1.0">
  <zeroOrMore>
    <element name="card">
      <element name="name">
        <text/>
      </element>
      <element name="email">
        <text/>
      </element>
    </element>
  </zeroOrMore>
</element>
```

In the non-XML syntax, this document looks as follows:

```
element addressBook {
  element card {
    element name { text },
    element email { text }
  }*
}
```

The former can be manipulated by standard XML tools, whereas the latter is more friendly towards human beings. The XML syntax may be formalized by an XML schema language, such as DTD (or RELAX NG itself). The main structure of the non-XML syntax may be formalized using, for example, EBNF.

With the two syntaxes in place, we need to be able to transform documents between them. For RELAX NG, there are numerous implementations of such converters. Converting from the XML syntax to the non-XML syntax, a common approach is to use an XSLT stylesheet. In the other direction, there are no obvious choices, so typically, one resorts to programming the conversion in a general purpose programming language, for example Java or Python.

This raises a number of problems: The translations in the two directions are made as two entirely different programs, often even using two different programming languages. This requires lots of tedious programming. Also, it makes maintenance difficult in case the syntax evolves. Since the programming languages being used are typically Turing complete (even XSLT is so), it is generally difficult to reason about their correctness. Specifically,

- there is no guarantee that the translations are *reversible* in the sense that translating a document in one direction and then back again will result in the original document (modulo whitespace or similar irrelevant details); and
- there is no guarantee that the translation into the XML syntax always produces documents that are *valid* according to a schema description.

These problems are not specific to the RELAX NG example. Similar situations occur for many other languages, however, RELAX NG is among the more complicated ones.

To attack these problems, we first make an interesting observation: Considering the grammars for the two syntaxes (one given by an XML schema, the other by an EBNF grammar), they commonly have a similar overall structure. The variations mainly occur at the level of individual grammar productions where the two syntaxes may vary in the order of production constituents, choices of literals, and whitespace and other ignorable parts. Notably, there are typically no drastic reorganizations when converting one way or the other. In the remainder of this paper, we exploit this in the design of *XSugar*, a system for managing dual syntax of XML languages.

1.1 Contributions

Our contributions are the following:

- We describe the XSugar language and show how it can be used for concisely specifying two-way translations between XML and non-XML syntax.
- We identify conditions for reversibility and outline an approach for conservatively checking these conditions.
- Based on previous results on static analysis of XML transformations [5, 6, 12], we show that it is possible to statically guarantee validity of output for the translation to XML.
- Using a prototype implementation, we evaluate the approach on a number of real-world examples: RELAX NG, XFlat [17], BibTeXML [11], and XSugar itself.

We imagine various possible usage scenarios of XSugar: Non-XML languages can easily be given an alternative XML syntax for enhancing data interchange; XML-based languages may be given a more human readable non-XML syntax; and, as in the case of RELAX NG, for languages where both syntaxes already exist, XSugar may be used to concisely specify the relation between the two.

1.2 Related Work

Several other projects and technologies are aimed at providing alternative syntax for XML languages. While they have overlapping goals with XSugar, none of them simultaneously consider general two-way translations and static guarantees of validity.

XSLT is often used for translating XML documents into other representations; however, stylesheets are not reversible, so these representations cannot in general be parsed back into XML.

The Presenting XML project [16] provides a domain-specific language for programming transformations between XML and flat files. However, translations are not reversible and, thus, two separate specifications must be maintained for a given dual syntax. The XFlat project [17] has largely the same approach as XSugar, as it allows translations between flat file formats and XML, specified by a single XFlat schema. However, it is restricted to files consisting of sequences of records, rather than general context-free syntax. Section 5.1 contains a more detailed comparison. The PADS project [10] translates data into other representations, including XML. It is focused on streams of data items, which are described using a sophisticated calculus that include dependent types and computations—thus going beyond context-free parsing. PADS also differs from XSugar in that its translations are not automatically reversible. The paper [15] presents a framework for programming reversible translations between two XML languages, but does not consider the case of parsing or generating alternative syntax.

Several projects, such as [9, 2, 13], suggest an alternative syntax for XML itself, independently of any particular XML language. Such work is only superficially similar to our work, since this alternative syntax is fixed while our is different for each application domain. Program inversion [1] attacks reversibility in a general context, but does not provide a solution to our particular problem.

2   The XSugar Language

We describe the XSugar language by a small example and then explain how to translate between XML- and non-XML syntax based on an XSugar specification.

2.1   Example: Student Information

Assume that we have an XML representation of *student information* as described by the following DTD:

```
<!ELEMENT students (student*)>
<!ELEMENT student (name,email)>
<!ATTLIST student sid CDATA #REQUIRED>
<!ELEMENT name (#PCDATA)>
<!ELEMENT email (#PCDATA)>
```

All elements belong to the namespace http://studentsRus.org/. Additionally, the values of name, email, and sid are required to satisfy some extra syntactic requirements, which we describe later. A valid document is the following:

```
<students xmlns="http://studentsRus.org/">
  <student sid="19701234">
    <name>John Doe</name>
    <email>john_doe@notmail.org</email>
  </student>
  <student sid="19785678">
    <name>Jane Dow</name>
    <email>dow@bmail.org</email>
  </student>
</students>
```

There is also an alternative non-XML syntax for this document:

```
John Doe (john_doe@notmail.org) 19701234
Jane Dow (dow@bmail.org) 19785678
```

That is, each student corresponds to one line. The name is written first, then
the email address in parentheses, and finally the ID. Notice that the ordering of
the constituents differs from the XML version.

With XSugar, we can concisely specify the connection between the two
syntaxes:

```
xmlns = "http://studentsRus.org/" ;

Alpha   = [a-zA-Z_] ;
Name    = <Alpha>+(" "<Alpha>+)* ;
Email   = <Alpha>+"@"<Alpha>+("."<Alpha>+)+ ;
Id      = [0-9]{8} ;
NL      = "\r"*"\n" ;

file : [persons p] = <students>[persons p]</students> ;

persons : [person p] [NL] [persons more] = _ [person p] _ [persons more];
        : = _ ;

person : [Name name] _ ( [Email email] ) _ [Id id] =
           <student sid=[Id id]> _
             <name>[Name name]</name> _
             <email>[Email email]</email> _
           </student> ;
```

The first line declares the namespace associated with the empty prefix. The next
five lines define some *regular expressions*, which are used for describing syntactic
tokens. For example, Name matches one or more blocks of Alpha characters,
separated by space characters. The remaining lines define *grammar productions*,
each having the form

$$nonterminal : \alpha = \beta ;$$

(If the nonterminal is omitted, the one from the preceding production is assumed.) The α part is generally a sequence of *items* of the form [T name]
or [T], where T is either a nonterminal or a regular expression name, and
of literals such as (and) above. Additionally, the special character _ is used
for describing whitespace, which we return to later. The β part consists of an
XML template, which is a fragment of well-formed XML that may contain items
in place of attribute values (as sid=[Id id] in the example) and in element
content (as [Email email], for example). Also the nonterminal or regular expression name associated with a given item name must be the same in α and β.
We use the convention that regular expression names start with a capital letter,
and nonterminals start with a lower case letter. Special characters (such as =
and ;) can be escaped with a backslash notation or Unicode escapes as in Java.
XML character references can also be used in XML templates.

Notice that if we ignore the β part in every production and the *name* part in every item, an XSugar specification S is essentially an ordinary BNF-like context-free grammar S_α (where the first occurring nonterminal is the start nonterminal). This grammar specifies the non-XML syntax of the language. Conversely, we obtain a grammar S_β for the XML syntax by ignoring the α parts. Notice that literals and unnamed items correspond to information that has no counterpart in the opposite grammar. For both grammars, we require all nonterminals to be productive. For later use, we assume that the productions in S are implicitly indexed in order of occurrence.

As an extension of the notion of grammars presented above, we also allow *unordered* productions: In a production where the delimiter :& appears in place of :, the α part is unordered, meaning that it matches any permutation of the constituents. We show a use of unordered productions in Section 5.4.

2.2   Transforming Via Unifying Syntax Trees

An XSugar specification S additionally defines a translation from the non-XML syntax to the XML syntax and vice versa. This translation goes via a *unifying syntax tree* (UST), which abstracts away the ordering of the constituents of each grammar production and also ignores parts corresponding to literals and unnamed items. More precisely, a UST is an unordered labeled tree of nodes where each node is either a *terminal node* or a *nonterminal node*. A terminal node is a leaf that is labeled with a string. A nonterminal node is labeled with a nonterminal, each edge to a child node is labeled with an item name, and every node has at most one outgoing edge with a given item name. Moreover, every nonterminal node is labeled with an index, which we will need later. As an example, the UST corresponding to the example student information document is shown in Figure 1.

Assume that we want to transform a text x from the non-XML syntax to the XML syntax. This is done in two steps: (1) we first *parse* the text x according to S_α, yielding a UST u; (2) we then *unparse* u relative to S_β yielding the resulting XML document. The other direction—translating from XML syntax to non-XML syntax—is symmetric. The processes of parsing and unparsing with USTs are described in the following.

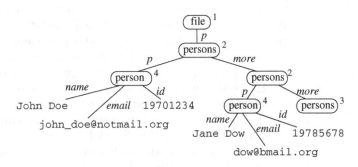

Fig. 1. UST for the student information document

Parsing. Given a text x and a grammar $\mathcal{S}_i$ (where i is either α or β, depending on which direction we are translating), we construct the UST u as follows. First, we run an ordinary context-free-grammar parser on x and $\mathcal{S}_i$, yielding an ordinary parse tree t. (If $\mathcal{S}_i$ is ambiguous, t is chosen arbitrarily among the possibilities; we discuss ambiguity further in Section 3.) From this parse tree, we construct the UST u as follows:

- Every parse tree node corresponding to a named regular expression item in $\mathcal{S}_i$ becomes a terminal node labeled with the corresponding string.
- Every parse tree node corresponding to a named nonterminal item in $\mathcal{S}_i$ becomes a nonterminal node. Its label is the nonterminal, and its index is the index of the associated grammar production of the parse tree node. For each named item in the production, a child edge with that name is made to the UST node of the corresponding child node in the parse tree.

Note that all parse tree nodes corresponding to literals or unnamed items are ignored in the construction.

The whitespace marker _ is implicitly defined as an abbreviation of the unnamed regular expression item [OPT_WHITESPACE] where OPT_WHITESPACE is the regular expression [\t\r\n]* (that is, strings of whitespace characters). Similarly, __ refers to WHITESPACE, which represents *nonempty* strings of whitespace.

In case x is an XML document and $i = \beta$, we initially *normalize* both x and $\mathcal{S}_\beta$ in a process that resembles XML canonicalization [3]: (1) whitespace inside tags (but outside attribute values) is reduced to a minimum; (2) the attributes in each start tag are sorted lexicographically and attribute values are enclosed by double quotes; (3) the short form of empty elements is expanded (for instance, <p/> becomes <p></p>); (4) character encoding is set to UTF-8; (5) character and entity references are expanded where possible; (6) XML comments, XML declarations, and DOCTYPEs are removed; and (7) in every start tag, all namespace declarations that are used in the tag are inserted explicitly, and prefixes are renamed to coincide with those chosen in $\mathcal{S}$.

Unparsing. Given a UST u and an XSugar specification $\mathcal{S}$ where u has been generated from either $\mathcal{S}_\alpha$ or $\mathcal{S}_\beta$, we construct an ordinary parse tree t as a concretization of u relative to $\mathcal{S}_i$ as follows, starting at the root of u:

- A terminal node in u becomes a parse tree leaf node labeled with the same string.
- A nonterminal node with index k becomes a parse tree node labeled with the same nonterminal. For each component in the production with index k in $\mathcal{S}_i$ in order, a corresponding subtree is constructed depending on the component kind:
    - for a named item, the subtree is constructed recursively from the child UST node with that name;
    - for an unnamed regular expression item, the subtree is a leaf node labeled with an arbitrary string matching the regular expression (for example, a shortest one);

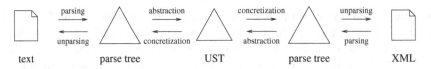

Fig. 2. The transformation process

- for an unnamed nonterminal item, the subtree is chosen as an arbitrary parse tree derivable from the corresponding nonterminal in $\mathcal{S}_i$; and
- for a literal, the subtree is a leaf node labeled with the literal string.

Notice that unnamed items are handled by picking arbitrary representatives. This makes sense since such items describe information that only occurs in one of the two syntaxes.

Once we have the parse tree t, the resulting text x is simply the concatenation of the text in the leaves. One technical issue remains: We escape and unescape special XML characters to ensure that, for example, the character < in non-XML corresponds to < in XML.

Figure 2 shows the complete transformation process with parsing, abstraction, concretization, and unparsing.

3   Reversibility

Having two syntaxes for a document poses a problem in that one would like to maintain a document in only one of the two syntaxes. However, since the two syntaxes are to represent the same logical information, the ideal solution would be to be able to move freely between them without loss of information. This imposes some static demands on XSugar specifications.

In order to achieve this goal, a specification needs to be *reversible* meaning that a roundtrip to the other syntactic alternative and back should yield the exact same document, modulo XML normalization. In practice, however, this is too strong a property to work with due to ignorable information, such as whitespace and comments, and unordered productions. For that reason, it is convenient to work with a weaker reversibility property that takes such things into account.

The notion of ignorable information is precisely what is captured by the unnamed items in an XSugar specification, which in this way explicitly annotates certain information as ignorable. Such information is not to be recorded and injected into the other syntactic alternative; as explained above the parser discards such information and the unparser in turn invents representatives. Similarly, when unparsing an unordered production, the order is chosen as the one provided in the XSugar specification.

Since the transformations are conducted in the same way for both syntaxes, we only need to be able to check that (1) parsing/unparsing to and from ordinary parse trees is bijective modulo ignorable information and unordered productions and (2) abstraction/concretization to and from USTs is bijective modulo ignorable information.

The parsing/unparsing check is equivalent to deciding whether a context-free grammar is ambiguous modulo ignorable constituents, which is of course undecidable. However, we deal with this issue by relying on a static analysis based on regular approximations of context-free grammars [4]. The analysis conservatively approximates the decision problem in that if it says that a grammar is unambiguous then this is indeed the case, but for certain grammars, the analysis will be unable to give a definitive answer. This is reminiscent of the LR(k) and LALR(k) ambiguity checks in Yacc/Bison, but with built-in support for ignorable constituents and unordered productions. Unambiguity is, aside from reversibility issues, a desirable property for a grammar, so that there can be no misunderstandings as to how a string is interpreted by a parser.

As for the second check, recall that all UST tree nodes are annotated with their production indices and all edges to subtrees are labeled with item names. This means that we simply have to check that all named items are used exactly once on the other side, so that no non-ignorable information is ever thrown away by the abstraction.

4   Static Validation

Consider the typical situation where an XML language, described by some schema formalism, has been given an alternative syntax. An obvious *validation* check is that the translations of alternative documents will always result in valid XML documents.

XSugar performs a *static analysis* that conservatively approximates this check. When the analysis reports success, it is guaranteed that syntactically correct input always results in valid output.

The dual validation check only makes sense if the alternative syntax is already described by a different context-free grammar. As shown in Section 5.2, this is the case for RELAX NG, where the original grammar must be rewritten to allow the XSugar translation. However, the inclusion test between context-free grammars is of course undecidable, and we are not aware of useful approximation algorithms.

We may also consider *coverage* checks, which for the XML to non-XML direction means that every XML document described by the external schema can be parsed by the XSugar grammar. This is an interesting problem that at present is left for future work. The dual coverage check is just the opposite inclusion check between the two context-free grammars. Note that it will often be the case that the alternative syntax is simply defined by the XSugar specification. In that situation, both the non-XML to XML coverage checks and the XML to non-XML validation checks become trivial.

Our static analysis is based on previous results [5, 6, 12], where the concept of *summary graph* is used to model sets of XML documents. We have an algorithm that is able statically to check that every document described by a summary

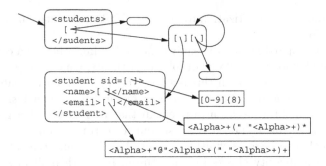

Fig. 3. Summary graph for the student information example

graph is valid according to a DSD2 schema [14]. Through embeddings, this technique also works for DTD and XML Schema.

From an XSugar specification, it is simple to extract a summary graph that describes all XML documents that can be generated by the β productions: Each right-hand side becomes a summary graph node, items become gaps, and the edges reflect the possible derivations of nonterminal and terminal items. For the student information example, the resulting summary graph looks as shown in Figure 3. The static validation is then performed by checking this summary graph against the given XML schema [6]. This is further exemplified in Section 5.3.

5 Evaluation

We have implemented a fully functional prototype of the XSugar tool, which is available for download from `http://www.brics.dk/xsugar/`. The underlying parser is a variation of Earley's algorithm that builds a UST directly without the intermediate ordinary parse tree, has explicit support for regular expression items, and allows the unordered productions explained in Section 2.1. The tool also performs the static validation described in Section 4, by means of the summary graph validator component from the JWIG project [6].

In the following, we present a range of examples showing how XSugar may be used for concrete XML languages. Each example highlights certain features of the XSugar tool. The complete source of the these XSugar specifications are available at the URL mentioned above, along with examples of input and output documents.

5.1 XFlat

The XFlat system [17] allows translations between flat file formats and XML, specified by a single XFlat schema. As an example, the translation between these two formats

```
123456789,"Doe, John",100000.00
444556666,"Average, Joe",53000.00
```

```
<employees>
 <employee>
  <ssn>123456789</ssn><name>Doe, John</name><salary>100000.00</salary>
  </employee>
 <employee>
  <ssn>444556666</ssn><name>Average, Joe</name><salary>53000.00</salary>
  </employee>
</employees>
```

is specified by the following XFlat schema:

```
<XFlat Name="employees_schema" Description="Schema for CSV flat file">
  <SequenceDef Name="employees" Description="employees flat file">
    <RecordDef Name="employee" FieldSep="," RecSep="\N" MaxOccur="0">
      <FieldDef Name="ssn" NullAllowed="No"
                MinFieldLength="9" MaxFieldLength="11"
                DataType="Integer" MinValue="0" QuotedValue="Yes"/>
      <FieldDef Name="name" NullAllowed="No" QuotedValue="Yes"/>
      <FieldDef Name="salary" NullAllowed="No"
                DataType="Float" MinValue="0" QuotedValue="Yes"/>
    </RecordDef>
  </SequenceDef>
</XFlat>
```

Each such schema may systematically be translated into an equivalent XSugar description, which for the above example looks as follows:

```
SSN =   [0-9]{9,11} ;
Name1 = [^",]* ;
Name2 = [^"]* ;
Salary = [0-9]+("."[0-9]+)? ;

file : [employees es] = <employees> _ [employees es] _ </employees> ;

employees : [employee e] [employees es] = [employee e] _ [employees es] ;
          : = ;

employee  : [SSN x] , [name y] , [Salary z] \n =
              <employee> _
                <ssn> _ [SSN x] _ </ssn> _
                <name> _ [name y] _ </name> _
                <salary> _ [Salary z] _ </salary> _
              </employee> ;

name : [Name1 y] = [Name1 y] ;
     : \" [Name2 y] \" = [Name2 y] ;
```

The XSugar version differs from the XFlat version in one respect. The XFlat translation from XML to flat file format is ambiguous, since quotes around fields are optional, unless the field value contains a comma. In our version, quotes are only added when they are necessary.

In other respects, the XSugar tool is more general. First, it may handle context-free syntax. Second, even in the niche of flat files, it may perform more general translations. For example, an XSugar translator could parse up the first and last names and swap their order within the field, which is not possible using XFlat.

5.2   Relax NG

As mentioned in the introduction, the RELAX NG schema language allows an alternative syntax, which may be captured by an XSugar specification. The α-grammar is relatively close to the one given in the RELAX NG specification, but some massaging was required to accommodate the local translations that XSugar supports. For example, the official EBNF for the compact syntax contains the following productions:

```
pattern ::=   ...
            | pattern ("," pattern)+
            | pattern ("&" pattern)+
            | pattern ("|" pattern)+
            | pattern "?"
            | pattern "*"
            | pattern "+"
```

In the translation, maximal non-empty sequences of patterns separated by , must be enclosed by <group> tags, those separated by & by <interleave> tags, and those separated by | by <choice> tags. Furthermore, the three operators must satisfy an operator precedence hierarchy. This translation is only possible in XSugar, if the grammar is made more explicit in the following manner:

```
pattern ::=        cpattern
cpattern ::=       gpattern "|" crestpattern
                 | gpattern
crestpattern ::=   gpattern "|" crestpattern
                 | gpattern
gpattern ::=       ipattern "," grestpattern
                 | ipattern
grestpattern ::=   ipattern "," grestpattern
                 | ipattern
ipattern ::=       upattern "&" irestpattern
                 | upattern
irestpattern ::=   upattern "&" irestpattern
                 | upattern
upattern ::=       bpattern
                 | bpattern "?"
                 | bpattern "*"
                 | bpattern "+"
bpattern ::=       ...
```

Here, the operator precedences are expressed in the usual manner by introducing extra nonterminals, and the grammar is further unfolded to allow us to distinguish between the first and the rest of maximal sequences. These techniques may in general be necessary, but this particular example requires by far the most complex unfoldings that we have yet encountered.

On the RELAX NG site, the translation from compact to ordinary syntax is defined by an XSLT stylesheet of 894 lines. The inverse translation is defined by a Python script of 1,478 lines. In all, that implementation stacks up to 2,372 lines of code, while the XSugar description is only 123 lines (a factor of 1:19). On top of this succinctness, the XSugar solution is easier to maintain and delivers all the safety guarantees discussed in Sections 3 and 4.

5.3 BibTeXML

The BibTeXML project [11] provides an XML-syntax for the popular BibTeX bibliography format. The XML format is quite complex and is described in 400 lines of DTD notation. This dual syntax is also a larger example of an XSugar specification, totaling 750 lines.

The example is noticeable in two respects. First, it involves some fairly detailed parsing and translation. For example, a list of authors may be separated by the word **and**, and first and last names may be written either directly or in reverse order separated by commas. In the translation to XML, each author must be enclosed by a separate **author** element and the names must be normalized. This is obtained by the following dual syntax:

```
PART = ([^",{}&<>~ \n\t]+) & ~([Aa][Nn][Dd]) ;
AND = [Aa][Nn][Dd] ;

authors : [name n] = <bibxml:author> _ [name n] _ </bibxml:author> ;
        : [name n] [AND] [authors as] =
            <bibxml:author> _ [name n] _ </bibxml:author> _ [authors as] ;

name : [parts ps] = [parts ps] ;
     : [parts last] _ , _ [parts first] = [parts first] __ [parts last];

parts : [PART p] = [PART p] ;
      : { [PART p] } = [PART p] ;
      : "~" =   ;
      : \n = " " ;
      : [PART p] [parts ps] = [PART p] [parts ps] ;
      : _ = ;
```

Second, a BibTeX file allows an arbitrary mix of fields, whereas the XML version requires (for some reason) a specific order. This is a situation where the unordered productions are useful:

```
ARTICLE = [Aa][Rr][Tt][Ii][Cc][Ll][Ee] ;
ID = [^ \n\t]+ ;

article : @[ARTICLE] _ { _ [ID id] _ , _ [articlefields fs] _ } =
```

```
   <bibxml:entry id=[ID id]>
     <bibxml:article> _
        [articlefields fs] _
     </bibxml:article> _
   </bibxml:entry> ;

articlefields :& [author author] [title title] [journal journal]
               [year year] [volume volume] ... =
               [author author] _ [title title] _ [journal journal] _
               [year year] _ [volume volume] _ ... _ ;
```

Note that only the non-XML production is unordered in this case.

In both these situations, the BibTeX format is more liberal than the Bib-TeXML format. Thus, the translation from BibTeXML to BibTeX will automatically choose a normalized representation.

Static validation of the generated XML documents is for this substantial example performed in 6 seconds (on a standard PC). The analysis discovered 4 true errors in the definition of the BiBTeX translation (despite our best efforts at defining it correctly), which were subsequently corrected. No false errors were reported.

5.4 XSugar

The final example applies XSugar to itself, by providing an XML syntax inspired by XSLT. Apart from the amusement of self-application, this example demonstrates the use of another feature. The production for the dual syntax for literal XML elements looks as follows:

```
element : "<" _ [qname q] _ [attributes as] _ ">"
             _ [xml x] _
          "</" _ [qname q] _ ">" =
          <xsg:element name=[qname q]> _
            [attributes as] _ [xml x] _
          </xsg:element> ;
```

We extend the XSugar language by allowing the identifier q to appear twice in the rule for the non-XML syntax. When translating from XML to non-XML syntax, the corresponding string is copied to the two locations, and in the other direction the parser checks that the two USTs generate the same output (and picks either one of them). This ability to match subterms for equality during parsing of course means that we go beyond context-free languages, while maintaining the functionality and guarantees of the XSugar tool. Yet, it is straightforward to incorporate this extension in the implementation.

6 Conclusion

We have presented the XSugar system, which allows specification of languages with dual syntax—one of which is XML-based—and provides translations in both directions. Moreover, we have presented techniques for statically checking reversibility of an XSugar specification and validity of the output in the direction that generates XML. Finally, we have conducted a number of experiments by applying the system to various existing languages with dual syntax. Of course, XSugar does not support all imaginable transformations; however, all dual syntaxes that we have encountered fit into our model. We conclude that XSugar provides sufficient expressiveness and useful static guarantees, and at the same time allows concise specifications making it a practically useful system.

References

1. Sergei Abramov and Robert Glück. Principles of inverse computation and the universal resolving algorithm. In *The essence of computation: complexity, analysis, transformation*, pages 269–295. Springer-Verlag, 2002.
2. Nitesh Ambastha and Tahir Hashmi. Xqueeze, 2005. `http://xqueeze.` source-forge.net/.
3. John Boyer. Canonical XML Version 1.0, March 2001. W3C Recommendation. `http://www.w3.org/TR/xml-c14n`.
4. Claus Brabrand and Anders Møller. Analyzing ambiguity of context-free grammars, 2005. In preparation.
5. Claus Brabrand, Anders Møller, and Michael I. Schwartzbach. Static validation of dynamically generated HTML. In *Proc. ACM SIGPLAN-SIGSOFT Workshop on Program Analysis for Software Tools and Engineering, PASTE '01*, pages 221–231, June 2001.
6. Aske Simon Christensen, Anders Møller, and Michael I. Schwartzbach. Extending Java for high-level Web service construction. *ACM Transactions on Programming Languages and Systems*, 25(6):814–875, November 2003.
7. James Clark. RELAX NG compact syntax, November 2002. OASIS. `http://relaxng.org/compact.html`.
8. James Clark and Makoto Murata. RELAX NG specification, December 2001. OASIS. `http://www.oasis-open.org/committees/relax-ng/`.
9. Clear Methods, Inc. ConciseXML, 2005. `http://www.concisexml.org/`.
10. Kathleen Fisher et al. PADS: Processing Arbitrary Data Streams, 2005. `http://www.padsproj.org/`.
11. Vidar Bronken Gundersen and Zeger W. Hendrikse. BibTeXML, 2005. `http://bibtexml.sourceforge.net/`.
12. Christian Kirkegaard, Anders Møller, and Michael I. Schwartzbach. Static analysis of XML transformations in Java. *IEEE Transactions on Software Engineering*, 30(3):181–192, March 2004.
13. Sean McGrath. *XML processing with Python*. Prentice Hall, 2000.
14. Anders Møller. Document Structure Description 2.0, December 2002. BRICS, Department of Computer Science, University of Aarhus, Notes Series NS-02-7. Available from `http://www.brics.dk/DSD/`.
15. Shin-Cheng Mu, Zhenjiang Hu, and Masato Takeichi. Bidirectionalising HaXML, 2005.
16. Daniel Parker. Presenting XML, 2005. `http://presentingxml.sourceforge.net/`.
17. Unidex Inc. XFlat, 2005. `http://www.unidex.com/xflat.htm`.

Exploiting Schemas in Data Synchronization

J. Nathan Foster[1], Michael B. Greenwald[2], Christian Kirkegaard[3],
Benjamin C. Pierce[1], and Alan Schmitt[4]

[1] University of Pennsylvania
{jnfoster, bcpierce}@cis.upenn.edu
[2] Bell Labs, Lucent Technologies
greenwald@lucent.com
[3] BRICS, University of Aarhus
ck@brics.dk
[4] INRIA Rhône-Alpes
Alan.Schmitt@polytechnique.org

Abstract. Increased reliance on optimistic data replication has led to
burgeoning interest in tools and frameworks for *synchronizing* disconnected updates to replicated data. We have implemented a generic synchronization framework, called Harmony, that can be used to build state-
based synchronizers for a wide variety of tree-structured data formats. A
novel feature of this framework is that the synchronization process—in
particular, the recognition of conflicts—is driven by the schema of the
structures being synchronized. We formalize Harmony's synchronization
algorithm, state a simple and intuitive specification, and illustrate how it
can be used to synchronize trees representing a variety of specific forms
of application data, including sets, records, and tuples.

1   Introduction

Optimistic replication strategies are attractive in a growing range of settings
where weak consistency guarantees can be accepted in return for higher availability and the ability to update data while disconnected. These uncoordinated
updates must later be *synchronized* (or *reconciled*) by automatically combining
non-conflicting updates while detecting and reporting conflicting updates.

Our long-term aim is to develop a generic framework that can be used to build
high-quality synchronizers for a wide variety of application data formats with
minimal effort. As a step toward this goal, we have designed and built a prototype synchronization framework called Harmony, focusing on the important
special cases of unordered and rigidly ordered data (including sets, relations,
tuples, records, feature trees, etc.), with only limited support for list-structured
data such as structured documents. An instance of Harmony that synchronizes
multiple calendar formats (Palm Datebook, Unix ical, and iCalendar) has been
deployed within our group; we are currently developing Harmony instances for
bookmark data (handling the formats used by several common browsers, including Mozilla, Safari, and Internet Explorer), address books, application preference
files, drawings, and bibliographic databases.

G. Bierman and C. Koch (Eds.): DBPL 2005, LNCS 3774, pp. 42–57, 2005.

The Harmony system has two main components: (1) a domain-specific programming language for writing *lenses*—bi-directional transformations on trees—which we use to convert low-level (and possibly heterogeneous) concrete data formats into a high-level *synchronization schema*, and (2) a generic synchronization algorithm, whose behavior is controlled by the synchronization schema.

The synchronization schema actually guides Harmony's behavior in two ways. First, by choosing an appropriate synchronization schema (and the lenses that transform concrete structures into this form and back), users of Harmony can control the *alignment* of the information being synchronized: the same concrete format might be transformed to different synchronization schemas (for example, making different choices of keys) to yield quite different synchronization semantics; this process is illustrated in detail in Section 6. Second, during synchronization, the synchronization schema is used to identify *conflicts*—situations where changes in one replica must *not* be propagated to the other because the resulting combined structure would be ill-formed.

Our language for lenses has been described in detail elsewhere [7]; in the present paper, our focus is on the synchronization algorithm and the way it uses schema information. The intuition behind this algorithm is simple: we try to propagate changes from each replica to the other, validate the resulting trees according to the expected schema, and signal a conflict if validation fails. However, this process is actually somewhat subtle: there may be many changes to propagate from each replica to the others, leading to many possible choices of *where* to signal conflicts (i.e., which subset of the changes to propagate). To ensure progress, we want synchronization to propagate as many changes as possible while respecting the schema; at the same time, to avoid surprising users, we need the results of synchronization to be predictable; for example, small variations in the inputs should not produce large variations in the set of changes that are propagated. A natural way of combining these design constraints is to demand that the results of synchronization be *maximal*, in the sense that, if there is *any* well-formed way to propagate a given change from one replica to the other that does not violate schema constraints, then that change *must* be propagated.

Our main technical contribution is a simple one-pass, recursive tree-walking algorithm that does indeed yield results that are maximal in this sense for schemas satisfying a locality constraint called *path consistency* (a semantic variant of the *consistent element declaration* condition in W3C Schema).

After establishing some notation in Section 2, we explore the design space further, beginning in Section 3 with some simple synchronization examples. Section 4 focuses on difficulties that arise in a schema-aware algorithm. Section 5 presents the algorithm itself. Section 6 illustrates the behavior of the algorithm using a simple address book schema. Related work is discussed in Section 7.

2   Data Model

Internally, Harmony manipulates structured data in an extremely simple form: unordered, edge-labeled trees; richer external formats such as XML are encoded in terms of unordered trees. We chose this simple data model on pragmatic grounds: the reduction in the overall complexity of the Harmony system far outweighs the cost of manipulating ordered data in encoded form.

We write $\mathcal{N}$ for the set of character strings and $\mathcal{T}$ for the set of unordered, edge-labeled trees whose labels are drawn from $\mathcal{N}$ and where labels of the immediate children of nodes are pairwise distinct. We draw trees sideways: in text, each pair of curly braces denotes a tree node, and each "$\mathbf{x} \mapsto ...$" denotes a child labeled $\mathbf{x}$—e.g., $\{\mathtt{Pat} \mapsto \mathtt{111\text{-}1111},\ \mathtt{Chris} \mapsto \mathtt{222\text{-}2222}\}$. When an edge leads to an empty tree, we omit the final childless node—e.g., "$\mathtt{111\text{-}1111}$" above actually stands for "$\{\mathtt{111\text{-}1111} \mapsto \{\}\}$."

A tree can be viewed as a partial function from names to trees; we write $t(n)$ for the immediate subtree of t labeled with the name n and $dom(t)$ for its domain—i.e. the set of the names of its children. The concatenation operator, $\cdot$, is only defined for trees t and t' with disjoint domains; $t \cdot t'$ is the tree mapping n to $t(n)$ for $n \in dom(t)$, to $t'(n)$ for $n \in dom(t')$. When $n \notin dom(t)$, we define $t(n)$ to be $\bot$, the "missing tree." By convention, we take $dom(\bot) = \emptyset$. To represent conflicts during synchronization, we enrich the set of trees with a special pseudo-tree $\mathcal{X}$, pronounced "conflict." We define $dom(\mathcal{X}) = \{n_{\mathcal{X}}\}$, where $n_{\mathcal{X}}$ is a special name that does not occur in ordinary trees. We write $\mathcal{T}_{\bot}$ for $\mathcal{T} \cup \{\bot\}$ and $\mathcal{T}_{\mathcal{X}}$ for the set of extended trees that may contain $\mathcal{X}$ as a subtree.

A *path* is a sequence of names. We write $\bullet$ for the empty path and p/q for the concatenation of p and q; the set of all paths is written $\mathcal{P}$. The *projection* of t along a path p, written $t(p)$, is defined in the obvious way: (1) $t(\bullet) = t$, (2) $t(n/p) = (t(n))(p)$ if $t \neq \mathcal{X}$ and $n \in dom(t)$, (3) $t(n/p) = \bot$ if $t \neq \mathcal{X}$ and $n \notin dom(t)$, and (4) $t(p) = \mathcal{X}$ if $t = \mathcal{X}$.

A tree is included in another tree, written $t \sqsubset t'$, iff any missing or conflicting path in t' is missing in t: $\forall p \in \mathcal{P}.\ (t'(p) = \bot \lor t'(p) = \mathcal{X}) \implies t(p) = \bot$.

Our synchronization algorithm is formulated using a semantic notion of *schemas*—a schema S is a set of trees $S \subseteq \mathcal{T}$. We write $S_{\bot}$ for the set $S \cup \{\bot\}$. In Section 6 we also define a syntactic notion of schema that is used for describing sets of trees in our implementation. However, the algorithm does not rely on this particular notion of schema.

3   Basics

Harmony's synchronization algorithm takes two[1] replicas $a, b \in \mathcal{T}_{\bot}$ and a common ancestor $o \in \mathcal{T}_{\mathcal{X}}$ and yields new replicas in which all non-conflicting updates are merged. Suppose that we have a tree representing a phone book, $o = \{\mathtt{Pat} \mapsto \mathtt{111\text{-}1111},\ \mathtt{Chris} \mapsto \mathtt{222\text{-}2222}\}$. Now suppose we make two replicas of this structure, a and b and separately modify one phone number in each so that $a = \{\mathtt{Pat} \mapsto \mathtt{111\text{-}1111},\ \mathtt{Chris} \mapsto \mathtt{888\text{-}8888}\}$ and $b = \{\mathtt{Pat} \mapsto \mathtt{999\text{-}9999},\ \mathtt{Chris} \mapsto \mathtt{222\text{-}2222}\}$. Synchronization takes these structures and produces structures $a' = b' =$

---

[1] We focus on the two-replica case. Our algorithm generalizes straightforwardly to synchronizing n replicas, but the more realistic case of a network of possibly *disconnected* replicas poses additional challenges (see [8] for our progress in this area).

$\{$Pat $\mapsto$ 999-9999, Chris $\mapsto$ 888-8888$\}$ that reflect all the changes in a and b with respect to o.

Loose Coupling. Harmony is a *state-based* synchronizer: only the current states of the replicas (plus the remembered state o) are supplied to the synchronizer, rather than the sequence of operations that produced a and b from o. Harmony is designed to require only *loose coupling* with applications: it manipulates application data in external, on-disk representations such as XML trees. The advantage of the loosely coupled (or *state-based*) approach is that we can use Harmony to synchronize off-the-shelf applications that were implemented without replication in mind. By contrast, many synchronizers manipulate a trace of the operations that the application has performed on each replica, and propagate changes by undoing and/or replaying operations. This approach requires tight coupling between the synchronizer and application programs.

Conflicts and Persistence. During synchronization, it is possible that some of the changes made to the two replicas are in conflict and cannot be merged. For example, suppose that, beginning from the same original o, we change both Pat's and Chris's phone numbers in a and, in b, delete the record for Chris entirely, yielding replicas $a = \{$Pat $\mapsto$ 123-4567, Chris $\mapsto$ 888-8888$\}$ and $b = \{$Pat $\mapsto$ 111-1111$\}$. Clearly, there is no single phone book that incorporates both changes to Chris: we have a *conflict*. At this point, we must choose between two evils. On one hand, we can weaken users' expectations for the *persistence* of their changes to the replicas—i.e., we can decline to promise that synchronization will never back out changes that have explicitly been made to either replica. For example, here, we might back out the deletion of Chris: $a' = b' = \{$Pat $\mapsto$ 123-4567, Chris $\mapsto$ 888-8888$\}$. The user would then be notified of the lost changes and given the opportunity to re-apply them if desired. Alternatively, we can keep persistence and instead give up *convergence*—i.e., we can allow the replicas to remain different after synchronization, propagating just the non-conflicting change to Pat's phone number letting $a' = \{$Pat $\mapsto$ 123-4567, Chris $\mapsto$ 888-8888$\}$ and $b' = \{$Pat $\mapsto$ 123-4567$\}$, and notifying the user of the conflict.[2] In Harmony, we choose persistence and sacrifice convergence.

Local Alignment. Another fundamental consideration in the design of any synchronizer is *alignment*—i.e., the mechanism that identifies which parts of each replica represent "the same information" and should be synchronized with each other. Synchronization algorithms can be broadly grouped into two categories, according to whether they make alignment decisions *locally* or *globally*. Synchronizers that use global heuristics for alignment—e.g., the popular Unix tool diff3, Lindholm's 3DM [12], the work of Chawathe et al [4], and FCDP [11]—make a "best guess" about what operations the user performed on the replicas by comparing the *entire* current states with the last common state. This works

---

[2] An industrial-strength synchronization tool will not only notify the user of conflicts, but may also assist in bringing the replicas back into agreement by providing graphical views of the differences, applying special heuristics, etc. We omit discussion of this part of the process, focusing on the synchronizer's basic, "unattended" behavior.

well in many cases (where the best guess is clear), but in boundary cases these algorithms can make surprising decisions. To avoid these issues, our algorithm employs a simple, local alignment strategy that associates the subtrees under children with the same name with each other. The behavior of this scheme should be easy for users to understand and predict. The cost of operating *completely* locally is that Harmony's ability to deal with ordered data is limited, as we discuss in Section 6. An important avenue for future work is hybridizing local and global alignment techniques to combine their advantages.

Lenses. The local alignment scheme described above works well when the replicas are represented in a format that naturally exposes the structure of the data to be synchronized. For example, if the replicas represent address books, then a good representation is as a bush where an appropriate *key field*, providing access to each contact, is at the root level. The key fields, which uniquely identify a contact, are often drawn from some underlying database:

$$\left\{ \begin{array}{l} \texttt{92373} \mapsto \{\texttt{name} \mapsto \{\texttt{first} \mapsto \texttt{Megan, last} \mapsto \texttt{Smith}\}, \texttt{home} \mapsto \texttt{555-6666}\} \\ \texttt{92374} \mapsto \{\texttt{name} \mapsto \{\texttt{first} \mapsto \texttt{Pat, last} \mapsto \texttt{Jones}\}, \texttt{home} \mapsto \texttt{555-2222}\} \end{array} \right\}$$

Using the alignment scheme described above, the effect during synchronization will be that entries from the two replicas with the same UID are synchronized with each other. Alternatively, if UIDs are not available, we can synthesize a UID by lifting information out of each record—e.g., we might concatenate the `name` data and use it as the top-level key field: $\{\texttt{Megan:Smith} \mapsto \{\texttt{home} \mapsto \texttt{555-6666}\}, \texttt{Pat:Jones} \mapsto \{\texttt{home} \mapsto \texttt{555-2222}\}\}$.

It is unlikely, however, that the address book will be represented concretely (e.g., as an XML document) using either of these formats. To bridge this gap, the Harmony system includes a domain-specific language for writing bi-directional transformations [7], which we call *lenses*. By passing each replica through a lens, we can transform the replicas from concrete formats into appropriately "pre-aligned" forms. After synchronization, our language guarantees that the updated replicas are transformed back into the appropriate concrete formats using the other side of the same lens (i.e., lenses can be thought of as *view update translators* [2]). Lenses also facilitate synchronization of heterogeneous formats. Since each replica is passed through a lens both before and after synchronization, it does not much matter if the replicas are represented in the same format or not. We can apply a different lens on each side to bring replicas stored using different concrete representations into the same format for synchronization.

4   The Role of Schemas

We impose two core requirements on synchronization, which we call *safety* and *maximality* and describe informally here (the long version has precise definitions).

Safety. The safety requirement encompasses four sanity checks: (1) a synchronizer must not "back out" any changes made at a replica since the last synchronization (because we favor persistence over convergence); (2) it should only copy data from one replica to the other, never "make up" content on its own; (3) it must halt at conflicting paths, leaving the replicas untouched below; (4), it must produce results that belong to the same schema as the originals.

Schema Conflicts. Our algorithm (unlike other state-based synchronizers) is designed to preserve structural invariants. As an example of how schema invariants can be broken, consider a run of the algorithm sketched above where $o = \{\text{Pat} \mapsto \{\text{Phone} \mapsto \{333\text{-}4444 \mapsto \{\}\}\}\}$, $a = \{\text{Pat} \mapsto \{\text{Phone} \mapsto \{111\text{-}2222 \mapsto \{\}\}\}\}$, and $b = \{\text{Pat} \mapsto \{\text{Phone} \mapsto \{987\text{-}6543 \mapsto \{\}\}\}\}$. The subtree labeled 333-4444 has been deleted in both replicas, and remains so in both a' and b'. The subtree labeled 111-2222 has been created in a, so we can propagate the creation to b'; similarly, we can propagate the creation of 987-6543 to a', yielding $a' = b' = \{\text{Pat} \mapsto \{\text{Phone} \mapsto \{111\text{-}2222 \mapsto \{\}, 987\text{-}6543 \mapsto \{\}\}\}\}$. But this would be wrong. Pat's phone number was *changed* in different ways in the two replicas: what's wanted is a conflict. If the phonebook schema only allows a single number per person, then the new replica is not well formed!

We avoid these situations by providing the schema as an input to the synchronizer. The synchronizer signals a conflict (leaving its inputs unchanged) whenever merging the changes at a particular point yields an ill-formed structure.

Locality and Schemas. Because alignment in our algorithm is local, we cannot expect the algorithm to enforce global invariants expressed by arbitrary schemas; we need a corresponding restriction to schemas that permits them to express only local constraints on structure. As an example of a schema that expresses a *non*-local invariant, consider the following set of trees: $\{\{\}, \{n \mapsto x, m \mapsto x\}, \{n \mapsto y, m \mapsto y,\}, \{n \mapsto \{x, y\}, m \mapsto y\}, \{n \mapsto x, m \mapsto \{x, y\}\}\}$.

Now consider synchronizing two replicas belonging to this set with respect to an empty archive: $o = \{\}$, with $a = \{n \mapsto x, m \mapsto x\}$, and $b = \{n \mapsto y, m \mapsto y\}$. A local algorithm that aligns each replica by name will recursively synchronize the associated subtrees below n and m. However, it is not clear what *schema* to use for these recursive calls, because the set of trees that can validly appear under n depends on the subtree under m and vice versa. We might try the schema that consists of all the trees that can appear under n (and m): $\{x, y, \{x, y\}\}$. With this schema, the synchronizer computes the tree $\{x, y\}$ for both n and m. However, these trees cannot be assembled into a well-formed tree: $\{n \mapsto \{x, y\}, m \mapsto \{x, y\}\}$ does not belong to the schema. The "most synchronized" well-formed results are $a' = \{n \mapsto x, m \mapsto \{x, y\}\}$ and $b' = \{n \mapsto \{x, y\}, m \mapsto y\}$, but there does not seem to be any way to find them without backtracking.

The global invariant expressed by this schema—at most one of n or m may have $\{x, y\}$ as a subtree—cannot easily be preserved by a local algorithm. To avoid such situations, we impose a restriction on schemas, *path consistency*, that is analogous to the restriction on tree grammars embodied by W3C Schema. Intuitively, a schema is path consistent if any subtree that appears at some path in one tree can be validly "transplanted" to the same location in any other tree in the schema. This restriction ensures that the sub-schema used to synchronize a single child is consistent across the schema; i.e., the set of trees that may validly appear under a child only depends on the path from the root to the node and does not depend on the presence (or absence) of other parts of the tree.

To define path consistency precisely, we need a little new notation. First, the notion of projection at a path is extended pointwise to schemas—that is, for a schema $S \subseteq \mathcal{T}$ and path $p \in \mathcal{P}$, we have $S(p) = \{t(p) \mid t \in S \wedge t(p) \neq \perp\}$. Note that the projection of a schema at any path is itself a schema.

Next, we define what it means to transplant a subtree from one tree to another at a given path. Let t be a tree and p a path such that $t(p) \in \mathcal{T}$. We define the *update* of t at p with t', written $t[p \mapsto t']$, inductively on the structure of p as: $t[\bullet \mapsto t'] = t', t[n/p \mapsto t'] = \{n \mapsto t(n)[p \mapsto t'], m \mapsto t(m) \mid m \in dom(t) \setminus \{n\}\}$. A schema S is *path consistent* if, whenever t and t' are in S, it is the case that, for every path p, the result of updating t along p with $t'(p)$ is also in the schema. Formally, a schema S is path consistent iff, for all $t, t' \in S$ and $p \in \mathcal{P}$, we have $t(p) \neq \perp \wedge t'(p) \neq \perp \implies t[p \mapsto t'(p)] \in S$.

Maximality. Of course, safety alone is too weak: an algorithm that returns both replicas unchanged is trivially safe! We therefore say that a run of a synchronizer is *maximal* just in case it propagates all the changes of every other safe run. Our specification is that every run must be both safe and maximal.

This brings us to one final complication that arises in schema-aware synchronization algorithms: on some inputs, there *aren't any* safe, maximal runs belonging to the schema. Consider a run of the synchronizer on input trees $o = \{v\}$, $a = \{w, y, z\}$, and $b = \{w, x\}$, with respect to the schema $\{\{v\}, \{w, x\}, \{w, x, y\}, \{w, x, z\}, \{w, y, z\}.\}$ On the b side, there are three safe results belonging to the schema, $\{w, x\}$, $\{w, x, y\}$, and $\{w, x, z\}$, but none is maximal. Notice that, since $\{w, x, y, z\}$ does not belong to the schema, we cannot include both y and z in b' (without backing out the addition of x). Indeed, for every safe b', there is a path p where $b'(p) \neq a'(p)$, but, for a different choice of b', the trees at that path are equal. To ensure that synchronization always has a maximal result, we stipulate that a *schema domain conflict* occurs whenever propagating *all* of the (otherwise non-conflicting) additions and deletions of children at a node yields an ill-formed result. On the above trees, our algorithm yields a schema domain conflict at the root since it cannot add y and z to a'.

5   Algorithm

The synchronization algorithm is depicted in Figure 1. Its structure is as follows: we first check for trivial cases (replicas being equal to each other or unmodified), then we check for *delete/create conflicts*, and in the general case we recurse on each child label and check for *schema domain conflicts* before returning the results. In practice, synchronization will be performed repeatedly, with additional updates applied to one or both of the replicas between synchronizations. To support this, the algorithm constructs a new archive. Its calculation is straightforward: we use the synchronized version at every path where the replicas agree and insert a conflict marker $\mathcal{X}$ at paths where they conflict.

$sync(S, o, a, b) =$
   if $a = b$ then (a, a, b) – *equal replicas: done*
   else if $a = o$ then (b, b, b) – *no change to a*
   else if $b = o$ then (a, a, a) – *no change to b*
   else if $o = \mathcal{X}$ then (o, a, b) – *unresolved conflict*
   else if $a = \perp$ and $b \sqsubset o$ then (a, a, a) – *a deleted more than b*
   else if $a = \perp$ and $b \not\sqsubset o$ then $(\mathcal{X}, a, b)$ – *delete/create conflict*
   else if $b = \perp$ and $a \sqsubset o$ then (b, b, b) – *b deleted more than a*
   else if $b = \perp$ and $a \not\sqsubset o$ then $(\mathcal{X}, a, b)$ – *delete/create conflict*
   else   – *proceed recursively*
     let $(o'(k), a'(k), b'(k)) = sync(S(k), o(k), a(k), b(k))$
       $\forall k \in dom(a) \cup dom(b)$
    in if $(dom(a') \notin doms(S))$ or $(dom(b') \notin doms(S))$
      then $(\mathcal{X}, a, b)$ – *schema domain conflict*
      else (o', a', b')

Fig. 1. Synchronization Algorithm

Formally, the algorithm takes as inputs a path-consistent schema S, an archive o, and two current replicas a and b; it outputs a new archive o' and two new replicas a' and b'. We require that both a and b belong to $S_\perp$. The input archive may contain the special conflict tree $\mathcal{X}$. The algorithm also relies on one piece of new notation: $doms(S)$ stands for the *domain-set* of S, the set of all domains of trees in S—i.e., $doms(S) = \{dom(t) \mid t \in S\}$.

In the case where a and b are identical, they are immediately returned, and the new archive is set to their value. If one of the replicas is unchanged (equal to the archive), then all the changes in the other replica can safely be propagated, so we simply return three copies of it as the result replicas and archive. Otherwise, both replicas have changed, in different ways. If one replica is missing, then we check whether all the changes in the other replica are also deletions; if so, we consider the larger deletion (throwing away the whole tree at this point) as subsuming the smaller; otherwise, we have a *delete/create conflict* and we simply return the original replicas.

Finally, in the general case, the algorithm recurses: for each k in the domain of either current replica, we call *sync* with the corresponding subtrees, $o(k)$, $a(k)$, and $b(k)$ (any of which may be $\perp$), and the sub-schema $S(k)$; we collect up the results of these calls to form new trees o', a', and b'. If either of the new replicas is ill-formed (i.e., its domain is not in the domain-set of the schema), then we have a schema domain conflict and the original replicas are returned unmodified. Otherwise, the synchronized results are returned.

Theorem 1. Let $S \subseteq \mathcal{T}$ be a path-consistent schema. If $a, b \in S_\perp$ and the run $sync(S, o, a, b)$ evaluates to o', a', b', then the run is both *safe* and *maximal*.

6   Case Study: Address Books

We now present a brief case study, illustrating how schemas can be used to guide the behavior of our generic synchronizer on trees of realistic complexity. The examples use an address book schema loosely based on the vCard standard.

Schemas. We begin with a concrete notation for writing schemas. Schemas are given by mutually recursive equations of the form X = S, where S is generated by the following grammar: S ::= {} | n[S] | !(F)[S] | *(F)[S] | S,S | S|S.

Here n ranges over names in $\mathcal{N}$ and F ranges over finite sets of names. The first form of schema, {}, denotes the singleton set containing the empty tree; n[S] denotes the set of trees with a single child named n where the subtree under n is in S; the wildcard schema !(F)[S] denotes the set of trees with *any single child* not in F, where the subtree under that child is in S; the other wildcard schema, *(F)[S] denotes the set of trees with *any number of children* not in F where the subtree under each child is in S. The set of trees described by $S_1|S_2$ is the union of the sets described by S_1 and S_2, while S_1,S_2 denotes the set of trees $t_1 \cdot t_2$ where t_1 belongs to S_1 and t_2 to S_2. Note that, as trees are unordered, the "," operator is commutative (e.g., n[X],m[Y] and m[Y],n[X] are equivalent). We abbreviate n[S]|{} as n?[S], and likewise !(∅)[S] as ![S] and *(∅)[S] as *[S].

All the schemas we write are path consistent. This can be checked syntactically: if a name appears twice in a node, like m in m[X],n[Y]|m[X],o[Z], the subschemas associated with each occurrence of the name are textually identical.

Address Book Schema. Here is a typical contact (the notation $[t_1; \ldots; t_n]$, which represents a list encoded as a tree, is explained below):

$$o = \left\{ \begin{array}{l} \texttt{name} \mapsto \big\{\texttt{first} \mapsto \texttt{Meg, other} \mapsto [\texttt{Liz; Jo], last} \mapsto \texttt{Smith}\big\} \\ \texttt{email} \mapsto \big\{\texttt{pref} \mapsto \texttt{ms@c.edu, alts} \mapsto \texttt{meg@s.com}\big\} \\ \texttt{home} \mapsto \texttt{555-6666, work} \mapsto \texttt{555-7777} \\ \texttt{org} \mapsto \big\{\texttt{orgname} \mapsto \texttt{City U, orgunit} \mapsto \texttt{CS Dept}\big\} \end{array} \right\}$$

There are two sorts of contacts—"professional" contacts, which contain mandatory work phone and organization entries, plus, optionally, a home phone, and "personal" ones, which have a mandatory home phone and, optionally, a work phone and organization information. Contacts are not explicitly tagged with their sort, so some contacts, like the one for Meg shown above, belong to both sorts. Each contact also has fields representing name and email data. Both sorts of contacts have natural schemas that reflects their record-like structures.

The schema C describes both sorts of contacts (using some sub-schemas that we will define below): C = name[N],work[V],home?[V],org[O],email[E] | name[N],work?[V],home[V],org?[O],email[E]. The trees appearing under the home and work children represent simple string values—i.e., trees with a single child leading to the empty tree; they belong to the V schema, V = ![{}]. The name edge leads to a tree with a record-like structure containing mandatory first and last fields and an optional other field. The first and last fields lead to values belonging to the V schema. The other field leads to a list of alternate names such as middle names or nicknames, stored (for the sake of the example) in some particular order. Because our actual trees are unordered, we use a standard "cons cell" representation to encode ordered lists: $[t_1; \ldots; t_n]$ is encoded as $\{\texttt{head} \mapsto t_1 , \texttt{tail} \mapsto \{\ldots \mapsto \{\texttt{head} \mapsto t_n , \texttt{tail} \mapsto \texttt{nil} \}\ldots\}\}$. Using this representation of lists, the schema N is defined as $\texttt{N = first[V],other?[VL],last[V]}$, where VL describes lists of values: $\texttt{VL = head[V],tail[VL] | nil[\{\}]}$. The email address data for a contact is either a single value, or a set of addresses with one distinguished "preferred" address. The E schema describes these structures using a union of a wildcard to represent single values (which excludes pref and alts to ensure path consistency) and a record-like structure with fields pref and alts to represent sets of addresses: $\texttt{E = !(pref, alts)[\{\}] | pref[V],alts[VS]}$, where $\texttt{VS = *[\{\}]}$ describes the trees that may appear under alts—bushes with any number of children where each child leads to the empty tree. These bushes are a natural encoding of sets of values. Finally, organization information is represented by a structure with orgname and orgunit fields, each leading to a value, as described by this schema: $\texttt{O = orgname[V],orgunit[V]}$.

The Need For Schemas. To illustrate how and where schema conflicts can occur, let us see what can go wrong when *no* schema information is used. We consider four runs of the synchronizer using the universal schema $\texttt{Any = *[Any]}$, each showing a different way in which schema-ignorant synchronization can produce mangled results. In each case, the archive, o, is the tree shown above.

Suppose, first, that the a replica is obtained by deleting the work and org children, making the entry personal, and that the b replica is obtained by deleting the home child, making the entry professional:

$$a = \left\{ \begin{array}{l} \texttt{name} \mapsto \left\{ \begin{array}{l} \texttt{first} \mapsto \texttt{Meg} \\ \texttt{other} \mapsto [\texttt{Liz; Jo}] \\ \texttt{last} \mapsto \texttt{Smith} \end{array} \right\} \\ \texttt{email} \mapsto \left\{ \begin{array}{l} \texttt{pref} \mapsto \texttt{ms@c.edu} \\ \texttt{alts} \mapsto \texttt{meg@s.com} \end{array} \right\} \\ \texttt{home} \mapsto \texttt{555-6666} \end{array} \right\} \qquad b = \left\{ \begin{array}{l} \texttt{name} \mapsto \left\{ \begin{array}{l} \texttt{first} \mapsto \texttt{Meg} \\ \texttt{other} \mapsto [\texttt{Liz; Jo}] \\ \texttt{last} \mapsto \texttt{Smith} \end{array} \right\} \\ \texttt{email} \mapsto \left\{ \begin{array}{l} \texttt{pref} \mapsto \texttt{ms@c.edu} \\ \texttt{alts} \mapsto \texttt{meg@s.com} \end{array} \right\} \\ \texttt{work} \mapsto \texttt{555-7777} \\ \texttt{org} \mapsto \left\{ \begin{array}{l} \texttt{orgname} \mapsto \texttt{City U} \\ \texttt{orgunit} \mapsto \texttt{CS Dept} \end{array} \right\} \end{array} \right\}$$

Although a and b are both valid address book contacts, the trees that result from synchronizing them with respect to the Any schema are not, since they have the structure neither of personal nor of professional contacts:

$$a' = b' = \left\{ \begin{array}{l} \texttt{name} \mapsto \{\texttt{first} \mapsto \texttt{Meg, other} \mapsto [\texttt{Liz; Jo}], \texttt{last} \mapsto \texttt{Smith} \} \\ \texttt{email} \mapsto \{\texttt{pref} \mapsto \texttt{ms@c.edu, alts} \mapsto \texttt{meg@s.com, }\} \end{array} \right\}$$

Now suppose that the replicas are obtained by updating the trees along the path name/first, replacing Meg with Maggie in a and Megan in b. (From now on, for the sake of brevity we only show the parts of the tree that are different from o and elide the rest.) $o(\texttt{name/first}) = \texttt{Meg}$, $a(\texttt{name/first}) = \texttt{Maggie}$, and $b(\texttt{name/first}) = \texttt{Megan}$. Synchronizing with respect to the Any schema yields results where *both* names appear under first: $a'(\texttt{name/first}) = b'(\texttt{name/first}) = \{\texttt{Maggie, Megan}\}$. These results are ill-formed because they do not belong to the V schema, which describes trees that have a *single* child.

Next consider updates to the email information where the a replica replaces the set of addresses in o with a single address, and b updates both pref and alts children in b: $o(\texttt{email}) = \{\texttt{pref} \mapsto \texttt{ms@c.edu}, \texttt{alts} \mapsto \texttt{meg@s.com} \}$, $a(\texttt{email}) = \{\texttt{meg@s.com}\}$, and $b(\texttt{email}) = \{\texttt{pref} \mapsto \texttt{meg.smith@cs.c.edu}, \texttt{alts} \mapsto \texttt{ms@c.edu}\}$. Synchronizing these trees with respect to Any propagates the addition of the edge labeled meg@s.com from a to b' and yields conflicts on both pref and alts children, since both have been deleted in a but modified in b. The results after synchronizing are thus: $a'(\texttt{email}) = \texttt{meg@s.com}$ and $b'(\texttt{email}) = \{\texttt{meg@s.com}, \texttt{pref} \mapsto \texttt{meg.smith@cs.c.edu}, \texttt{alts} \mapsto \texttt{ms@c.edu}\}$. The second result, b', is ill-formed because it contains three children, whereas all the trees in the email schema E have either one or two children.

Next consider changes to the list of names along the path name/other. Suppose that a removes both Liz and Jo, but b only removes Jo: $o(\texttt{name/other}) = [\texttt{Liz}; \texttt{Jo}]$, $a(\texttt{name/other}) = []$, and $b(\texttt{name/other}) = [\texttt{Liz}]$. Comparing the a replica to o, both head and tail are deleted and nil is newly added. Examining the b replica, the tree under head is identical to corresponding tree in o but deleted from a. The tree under tail is different from o but deleted from a. Collecting all of these changes, the algorithm yields these results: $a'(\texttt{name/other}) = \texttt{nil}$ and $b'(\texttt{name/other}) = \{\texttt{tail} \mapsto \texttt{nil}, \texttt{nil}\}$. Here again, the second result, b', is ill-formed: it has children tail and nil, which is not a valid encoding of a list.

Situations like these—invalid records, multiple children where a single value is expected, and mangled lists—provided the initial motivation for equipping a straightforward "tree-merging" synchronization algorithm with schema information. Fortunately, in all of these examples, the step that breaks the structural invariant can be detected by a simple, local, domain test. In the first example, where the algorithm removed the home, work, and org children, the algorithm tests if $\{\texttt{name}, \texttt{email}\}$ is in $doms(\texttt{C})$. Similarly, in the second example, where both replicas changed the first name to a different value, the algorithm tests if $\{\texttt{Maggie}, \texttt{Megan}\}$ is in $doms(\texttt{V})$. In the example involving the tree under email, the algorithm tests if the domain $\{\texttt{meg@s.com}, \texttt{pref}, \texttt{alts}\}$ is in $doms(\texttt{E})$. Finally, in the example where both replicas updated the list of other names, it tests whether $\{\texttt{tail}, \texttt{nil}\}$ is in $doms(\texttt{VL})$. All of these local tests fail and so the synchronizer halts with a schema domain conflict at the appropriate path in each case, ensuring that the results are valid according to the schema.

Next we further explore the strengths (and weaknesses) of our algorithm by studying its behavior on the structures used in address books.

Values. The simplest structures in our address books, string values, are represented as trees with a single child that leads to the empty tree and described by ![{}]. When we synchronize two non-missing trees using this schema, there are three possible cases: (1) if either of a or b is identical to o then the algorithm set the results equal to the other replica; (2) if a and b are identical to each other but different to o then the algorithm preserves the equality; (3) if a and b are both different from o and each other then the algorithm reaches a schema domain conflict. That is, the algorithm enforces *atomic* updates to values.

Sets. Sets can be represented as bushes—nodes with many children, each labeled with the key of an element in the set— e.g., for sets of values, this structure is described by the schema *[{}]. When synchronizing two sets of values, the synchronization algorithm *never* reaches a schema conflict; it always produces a valid result, combining the additions and deletions of values from a and b. For example, given these three trees representing value sets: $o = \{\texttt{meg@s.com}\}$, $a = \{\texttt{ms@c.edu, meg.smith@cs.c.edu}\}$, and $b = \{\texttt{meg@s.com, meg.smith@cs.c.edu}\}$ The synchronizer propagates the deletion of $\texttt{meg@s.com}$ and the addition of two new children, $\texttt{ms@c.edu}$ and $\texttt{meg.smith@cs.c.edu}$, yielding $a' = b' = \{\texttt{ms@c.edu, meg.smith@cs.c.edu}\}$, as expected.

Records. Two sorts of record structures appear in the address book schema. The simplest records, like the one for organization data ($\texttt{orgname[V]}$,$\texttt{orgunit[V]}$), have a fixed set of mandatory fields. Given two trees representing such records, the synchronizer aligns the common fields, which are *all* guaranteed to be present, and synchronizes the nested data one level down. It never reaches a schema domain conflict at the root of a tree representing such a record. Other records, which we call *sparse*, allow some variation in the names of their immediate children. For example, the contact schema uses a sparse record to represent the structure of each entry; some fields, like $\texttt{org}$, may be mandatory or optional (depending on the presence of other fields). As we saw in the preceeding section, on some inputs—namely, when the updates to the replicas cannot be combined into a tree satisfying the constraint expressed by the sparse record schema—the synchronizer yields a schema conflict but preserves the sparse record structure.

Lists. Lists present special challenges, because we would like the algorithm to detect updates both to elements and to their relative position. On lists, our local alignment strategy matches up list elements by *absolute* position, leading to surprising results on some inputs. We illustrate the problem and propose a more sophisticated encoding of lists that reduces the chances of confusion.

On many runs of the synchronizer, updates to lists can be successfully propagated from one replica to the other. If either replica is identical to the archive, or if each replica modifies a disjoint subset of the elements of the list (leaving the list spine intact), then the synchronizer merges the changes successfully. There are some inputs, however, where synchronizing lists using the local alignment strategy and simple cons cell encoding produces strange results. Consider a run on the following inputs: $o = [\texttt{Liz; Jo}]$, $a = [\texttt{Jo}]$ and $b = [\texttt{Liz; Joanna}]$. Considering the changes that were made to each list from a high-level—a removed the head and b renamed the second element—the result calculated for b' is surprising: $[\texttt{Jo; Joanna}]$. The algorithm does not recognize that $\texttt{Jo}$ and $\texttt{Joanna}$ should be aligned. Instead, it aligns pieces of the list by absolute position, matching $\texttt{Jo}$ with $\texttt{Liz}$ and $\texttt{nil}$ with $[\texttt{Joanna}]$.

It is not surprising that our algorithm doesn't have an intuitive behavior when its inputs are lists. In general, detecting changes in relative position in a list requires global reasoning but our algorithm is essentially local. In order to avoid these problematic cases, we can use an alternative schema, which we call the *keyed list schema*, for lists whose relative order matters. Rather than embedding the elements under a spine of cons cells, one can lift up the value at each position into the spine of the list. For example, in the extended encoding, the list a from above is represented as the tree $a = \{\text{Jo} \mapsto \{\text{head} \mapsto \{\}, \text{tail} \mapsto \text{nil}\}\}^3$. The schema for keyed lists of values is: `KVL = !(nil)[head[{}],tail[KVL]] | nil`. During synchronization, elements of the list are identified by the value above each cons cell; synchronization proceeds until a trivial case applies (unchanged or identical replicas), or when the two replicas disagree on the domain of an element, resulting in a schema domain conflict. In the problematic example, the algorithm terminates with a conflict at the root. Keyed lists combine an alternate representation of lists with an appropriate schema to ensure that the local algorithm has reasonable (if conservative) behavior.

Conclusion. The examples in this section demonstrate that schemas are a valuable addition to a synchronization algorithm: (1) we are guaranteed valid results in situations where a schema-blind algorithm would yield mangled results; (2) by selecting an appropriate encoding and schema for application data, we can tune the behavior of the generic algorithm to work well with a variety of structures. While building demos using our prototype implementation, we have found that this works well with rigidly structured data (e.g., values and records) and unstructured data (e.g., sets of values), but so far has limited utility when used with ordered and semi-structured data (e.g., lists and documents). In the future, we hope to extend our algorithm to better handle ordered data.

7   Related Work

In the taxonomy of optimistic replication strategies in the survey by Saito and Shapiro [22], Harmony is a multi-master state-transfer system, recognizing subobjects and manually resolving conflicts. Harmony is further distinguished by some distinctions not covered in that survey: it is generic, loosely coupled from applications, able to synchronize heterogeneous representations, and is usable both interactively and *unsupervised*. Supporting unsupervised runs (where Harmony does as much work as it can, and leaves conflicts for later) requires our synchronizer's behavior to be intuitive and easy to predict.

IceCube [10] is a generic operation-based reconciler that is parameterized over a specific algebra of operations appropriate to the application data being synchronized and by a set of syntactic/static and semantic/dynamic ordering constraints on these operations. Molli et al [15], have also implemented a generic operation-based reconciler, using the technique of *operational transformation*.

---

[3] For keyed lists of values, we could drop the child **head**, which always maps to the empty tree. However, we can also form keyed lists of arbitrary trees, not just values.

Their synchronizer is parameterized on transformation functions for all operations, which must obey certain conditions. Bengal [6] records operations to avoid scanning the entire replica during update detection. Like Harmony, Bengal is a loosely-coupled synchronizer. It can extend any commercial database system that uses OLE/COM hooks to support optimistic replication. However, it is not generic because it only supports databases, it is not heterogeneous because reconciliation can only occur between replicas of the same database, and it requires users to write *conflict resolvers* if they want to avoid manually resolving conflicts. FCDP [11] is a generic, state-based reconciler parameterized by ad-hoc translations from heterogeneous concrete representations to XML and back again. There is no formal specification and reconciliation takes place at "synchronization servers" that are assumed to be more powerful machines permanently connected to the network. FCDP fixes a specific semantics for ordered lists—particularly suited for document editing. This interpretation may sometimes be problematic, as described in the long version of this paper. File system synchronizers (such as [23,16,1,18]) and PDA synchronizers (such as Palm's HotSync), are not generic, but they do generally share Harmony's state-based approach. An interesting exception is DARCS [21], a hybrid state-/operation-based revision control system built on a "theory of patches."

Harmony, unlike many reconcilers, does not guarantee convergence in the case of conflicts. Systems such as Ficus [19], Rumor [9], Clique [20], Bengal [6], and TAL/S5 [15] converge by making additional copies of primitive objects that conflict and renaming one of the copies. CVS embeds markers in the bodies of files where conflicts occurred. In contrast, systems such as Harmony and IceCube [10] do not reconcile objects affected by conflicting updates.

Harmony's emphasis on schema-based pre-alignment is influenced by examples we have found in the context of data integration where heterogeneity is a primary concern. Alignment, in the form of schema-mapping, has been frequently used to good effect (c.f. [17,14,3,5,13]). The goal of alignment, there, is to construct views over heterogeneous data, much as we transform concrete views into abstract views with a shared schema to make alignment trivial for the reconciler. Some synchronizers differ mainly in their treatment of alignment. For example, the main difference between Unison [1] (which has almost trivial alignment) and CVS, is the comparative alignment strategy (based on the standard Unix tool `diff3`) used by CVS. At this stage, Harmony's core synchronization algorithm is deliberately simplistic, particularly with respect to ordered data. As we develop an understanding of how to integrate more sophisticated alignment algorithms in a generic and principled way, we hope to incorporate them into Harmony. Of particular interest are `diff3` and its XML based descendants: Lindholm's 3DM [12], the work of Chawathe et al [4], and FCDP [11].

Acknowledgements. The Harmony project was begun in collaboration with Zhe Yang. Trevor Jim, Jonathan Moore, Owen Gunden, Malo Denielou, and Stéphane Lescuyer have collaborated with us on many aspects of Harmony's design and implementation. Conversations with Martin Hofmann, Zack Ives, Nitin Khandelwal, Sanjeev Jhanna, Keshav Kunal, William Lovas, Kate Moore, Cyrus

Najmabadi, Stephen Tse, Steve Zdancewic, and comments from the anonymous referees helped sharpen our ideas. Harmony is supported by the National Science Foundation under grant ITR-0113226, *Principles and Practice of Synchronization*. Nathan Foster is also supported by an NSF GRF.

References

1. S. Balasubramaniam and B. C. Pierce. What is a file synchronizer? In *Fourth Annual ACM/IEEE International Conference on Mobile Computing and Networking (MobiCom '98)*, Oct. 1998. Full version available as Indiana University CSCI technical report #507, April 1998.
2. F. Bancilhon and N. Spyratos. Update semantics of relational views. *TODS*, 6(4):557–575, 1981.
3. C. Beeri and T. Milo. Schemas for integration and translation of structured and semi-structured data. In *ICDT'99*, 1999.
4. S. S. Chawathe, A. Rajamaran, H. Garcia-Molina, and J. Widom. Change detection in hierarchically structured information. In *Proceedings of the ACM SIGMOD International Conference on the management of Data*, pages 493–504, Montreal, Quebec, 1996.
5. A. Doan, P. Domingos, and A. Y. Halevy. Reconciling schemas of disparate data sources: A machine-learning approach. In *SIGMOD Conference*, 2001.
6. T. Ekenstam, C. Matheny, P. L. Reiher, and G. J. Popek. The Bengal database replication system. *Distributed and Parallel Databases*, 9(3):187–210, 2001.
7. J. N. Foster, M. B. Greenwald, J. T. Moore, B. C. Pierce, and A. Schmitt. Combinators for bi-directional tree transformations: A linguistic approach to the view update problem. In *ACM SIGPLAN–SIGACT Symposium on Principles of Programming Languages (POPL), Long Beach, California*, 2005.
8. M. B. Greenwald, S. Khanna, K. Kunal, B. C. Pierce, and A. Schmitt. Agreement is quicker than domination: Conflict resolution for optimistically replicated data. Submitted for publication; available electronically, 2005.
9. R. G. Guy, P. L. Reiher, D. Ratner, M. Gunter, W. Ma, and G. J. Popek. Rumor: Mobile data access through optimistic peer-to-peer replication. In *Proceedings of the ER '98 Workshop on Mobile Data Access*, pages 254–265, 1998.
10. A.-M. Kermarrec, A. Rowstron, M. Shapiro, and P. Druschel. The IceCube approach to the reconciliation of diverging replicas. In *proceedings of the 20th annual ACM SIGACT-SIGOPS Symposium on Principles of Distributed Computing (PODC '01)*, Aug. 26-29 2001. Newport, Rhode Island.
11. M. Lanham, A. Kang, J. Hammer, A. Helal, and J. Wilson. Format-independent change detection and propoagation in support of mobile computing. In *Proceedings of the XVII Symposium on Databases (SBBD 2002)*, pages 27–41, October 14-17 2002. Gramado, Brazil.
12. T. Lindholm. XML three-way merge as a reconciliation engine for mobile data. In *Proceedings of MobiDE '03*, pages 93–97, September 19 2003. San Diego, CA.
13. J. Madhavan, P. A. Bernstein, and E. Rahm. Generic schema matching with Cupid. In *The VLDB Journal*, pages 49–58, 2001.
14. T. Milo and S. Zohar. Using schema matching to simplify heterogeneous data translation. In *VLDB'98*, 1998.
15. P. Molli, G. Oster, H. Skaf-Molli, and A. Imine. Using the transformational approach to build a safe and generic data synchronizer. In *Proceedings of ACM Group 2003 Conference*, November 9–12 2003. Sanibel Island, Florida.

16. T. W. Page, Jr., R. G. Guy, J. S. Heidemann, D. H. Ratner, P. L. Reiher, A. Goel, G. H. Kuenning, and G. Popek. Perspectives on optimistically replicated peer-to-peer filing. *Software – Practice and Experience*, 11(1), December 1997.
17. E. Rahm and P. A. Bernstein. A survey of approaches to automatic schema matching. *VLDB Journal*, 10(4):334–350, 2001.
18. N. Ramsey and E. Csirmaz. An algebraic approach to file synchronization. In *Proceedings of the 8th European Software Engineering Conference*, pages 175–185. ACM Press, 2001.
19. P. L. Reiher, J. S. Heidemann, D. Ratner, G. Skinner, and G. J. Popek. Resolving file conflicts in the ficus file system. In *USENIX Summer Conference Proceedings*, pages 183–195, 1994.
20. B. Richard, D. M. Nioclais, and D. Chalon. Clique: a transparent, peer-to-peer collaborative file sharing system. In *Proceedings of the 4th international conference on mobile data management (MDM '03)*, Jan. 21-24 2003. Melbourne, Australia.
21. D. Roundy. The DARCS system, 2004. `http://abridgegame.org/darcs/`.
22. Y. Saito and M. Shapiro. Replication: Optimistic approaches. Technical Report HPL-2002-33, HP Laboratories Palo Alto, Feb. 8 2002.
23. M. Satyanarayanan, J. J. Kistler, P. Kumar, M. E. Okasaki, E. H. Siegel, and D. C. Steere. Coda: A highly available file system for a distributed workstation environment. *IEEE Transactions on Computers*, C-39(4):447–459, Apr. 1990.

Efficiently Enumerating Results
of Keyword Search⋆

Benny Kimelfeld and Yehoshua Sagiv

The Selim and Rachel Benin School of Engineering and Computer Science,
The Hebrew University of Jerusalem,
Edmond J. Safra Campus,
Jerusalem 91904, Israel

Abstract. Various approaches for keyword search in different settings
(e.g., relational databases, XML and the Web) actually deal with the
problem of enumerating K-fragments. For a given set of keywords K, a
K-fragment is a subtree T of the given data graph, such that T contains
all the keywords of K and no proper subtree of T has this property. There
are three types of K-fragments: rooted, undirected and strong. This paper describes the first provably efficient algorithms for enumerating K-
fragments. Specifically, for all three types of K-fragments, algorithms are
given for enumerating all K-fragments with polynomial delay. For rooted
K-fragments and acyclic data graphs, an algorithm is given for enumerating with polynomial delay in the order of increasing weight (i.e., the
ranked order), assuming that K is of a fixed size. Finally, an efficient
algorithm is described for enumerating K-fragments in a heuristically
ranked order.

1   Introduction

The advent of the World-Wide Web and the proliferation of search engines
have transformed keyword search from a niche role to a major player in the
information-technology field. Modern database languages should have both
querying and searching capabilities. In recent years, different approaches for
developing such capabilities have been investigated.

DBXplorer [1], BANKS [2] and DISCOVER [6] are systems that implement
keyword search in relational databases. XKeyword [7] is an extension of the techniques used in DISCOVER to keyword search in XML. The "backward search"
algorithm used in BANKS is improved in [10] to a "bidirectional search." Keyword search in a different context is discussed in [13], where the main idea is to
retrieve and organize Web pages by "information units."

The above approaches to keyword search consider different settings and use
a variety of techniques. At the core, however, they all deal with similar graph
problems and solve them heuristically. While these heuristics may perform well
in practice, they either lack a clear upper bound or have an exponential upper

---

⋆ This work was supported by the Israel Science Foundation (Grant No. 96/01).

G. Bierman and C. Koch (Eds.): DBPL 2005, LNCS 3774, pp. 58–73, 2005.

bound (even if there are only a few results). The goal of this paper is to provide provably efficient algorithms (rather than heuristics) for solving the underlying graph problems.

A formal framework for keyword search that captures all of the above approaches is presented in [11]. In this framework, data are represented as a graph that has two types of nodes: *structural nodes* and *keyword nodes*. When searching a data graph G for a set of keywords K, the results are K-*fragments*, where each K-fragment is a subtree of G that contains the keywords of K and has no proper subtree that also contains K. Actually, there are three types of K-fragments: *rooted* (i.e., directed), *undirected* and *strong*, where the latter is an undirected K-fragment, such that all its keyword nodes are leaves.

Typically, results of a keyword search are either strong K-fragments [1, 3, 5, 6, 7, 13] or rooted K-fragments [2, 10, 3]; in some cases [1, 3], however, undirected K-fragments have to be enumerated. Some systems [1, 6, 7] use the schema to extract (by increasing size) all the join expressions that may potentially yield results and then evaluate these expressions over the database (but for a given database, many of these expressions may generate no result at all). In other systems [2, 10, 13], the data graph is processed directly. In either case, an algorithm for enumerating K-fragments is used. Usually, the goal is to enumerate results by increasing size (or weight). For the sake of efficiency, some systems [2, 10, 13] enumerate in an "almost" ranked order (but without any guarantee by how much the actual order may deviate from the ranked order). However, even in these systems, an upper bound on the running time is either missing or exponential (even if there is only a small number of K-fragments).

In this paper, we give efficient algorithms for enumerating K-fragments. Since the output of an enumeration algorithm can be exponential in the size of the input, we use the yardstick of enumeration with *polynomial delay* as an indication of efficiency. We show that all rooted, undirected or strong K-fragments can be enumerated with polynomial delay. We also consider the problem of enumerating by increasing weight. Specifically, we show that if the size of K is fixed, then all rooted K-fragments of an acyclic data graph can be enumerated by increasing weight with polynomial delay. Note that a known NP-complete problem [4] implies that this result can hold only if the size of K is assumed to be fixed. Making this assumption is realistic and in line with the notion of data complexity [14], which is commonly used for measuring the complexity of query evaluation.

In summary, the main contribution of this paper is in giving, for the first time, provably efficient algorithms for enumeration problems that need to be solved in many different settings of keyword search. These settings include relational databases, XML and the Web.

This paper is organized as follows. Section 2 defines basic concepts and notations. The notion of enumeration algorithms, their complexity measures, and threaded enumerators are discussed in Section 3. Our algorithms are described in Sections 4, 5 and 6. In Section 7, we present a heuristics for enumerating in sorted order. We conclude and discuss future work in Section 8. Due to a lack of space, proofs are not given, but they are available in [12].

2 Preliminaries

2.1 Data Graphs

A *data graph* G consists of a set $\mathcal{V}(G)$ of *nodes* and a set $\mathcal{E}(G)$ of *edges*. There are two types of nodes: *structural* nodes and *keyword* nodes (or *keywords* for short). $\mathcal{S}(G)$ denotes the set of structural nodes and $\mathcal{K}(G)$ denotes the set of keyword nodes. Unless explicitly stated otherwise, edges are directed, i.e., an edge is a pair (n_1, n_2) of nodes. Keywords have only incoming edges, while structural nodes may have both incoming and outgoing edges. Hence, no edge can connect two keywords. These restrictions mean that $\mathcal{E}(G) \subseteq \mathcal{S}(G) \times \mathcal{V}(G)$. The edges of a data graph G may have *weights*. The weight function w_G assigns a positive weight $w_G(e)$ to every edge $e \in \mathcal{E}(G)$. The weight of the data graph G, denoted $w(G)$, is the sum of the weights of all the edges of G, i.e., $w(G) = \sum_{e \in \mathcal{E}(G)} w_G(e)$.

A data graph is *rooted* if it contains some node r, such that every node of G is reachable from r through a directed path. The node r is called a *root* of G. (Note that a rooted data graph may have several roots.) A data graph is *connected* if its underlying undirected graph is connected.

As an example, consider the data graph G_1 depicted in Figure 1. (This data graph represents a part of the Mondial[1] XML database.) In this graph, filled circles represent structural nodes and keywords are written in italic font. Note that the structural nodes of G_1 have *labels*, which are ignored in this paper. The data graph G_1 is rooted and the node labeled with **continent** is the only root.

We use two types of data *trees*. A *rooted tree* is a rooted data graph, such that there is only one root and for every node u, there is a unique path from the root to u. An *undirected tree* is a data graph that is connected and has no cycles, when ignoring the directions of the edges.

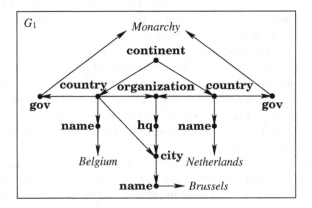

Fig. 1. A data graph G_1

---

[1] http://www.dbis.informatik.uni-goettingen.de/Mondial/

We say that a data graph G' is a *subgraph* of the data graph G, denoted $G' \subseteq G$, if $\mathcal{V}(G') \subseteq \mathcal{V}(G)$, $\mathcal{E}(G') \subseteq \mathcal{E}(G)$ and each edge in G' has the same weight in both G and G'. Rooted and undirected *subtrees* are special cases of subgraphs.

For a data graph G and a subset $U \subseteq \mathcal{V}(G)$, we denote by $G - U$ the induced subgraph of G that consists of the nodes of $\mathcal{V}(G) \setminus U$ and all the edges of G between these nodes. If $u \in \mathcal{V}(G)$, then we may write $G - u$ instead of $G - \{u\}$.

If G_1 and G_2 are subgraphs of G, we use $G_1 \cup G_2$ to denote the subgraph that consists of all the nodes and edges that appear in either G_1 or G_2; that is, the graph G' that satisfies $\mathcal{V}(G') = \mathcal{V}(G_1) \cup \mathcal{V}(G_2)$ and $\mathcal{E}(G') = \mathcal{E}(G_1) \cup \mathcal{E}(G_2)$.

Given a data graph G, a subset $U \subseteq \mathcal{V}(G)$ and an edge $e = (v, u) \in \mathcal{E}(G)$, we use $U^{\pm e}$ to denote the set $(U \setminus \{u\}) \cup \{v\}$.

Given two nodes u and v in a data graph G, we use $u \leadsto_G v$ to denote that v is reachable from u through a directed path in G.

A rooted (respectively, undirected) subtree T of a data graph G is *reduced* w.r.t. a subset U of the nodes of G if T contains U, but no proper rooted (respectively, undirected) subtree of T contains U.

2.2 Keyword Search

A *query* is simply a finite set K of keywords. Given a data graph G, a *rooted K-fragment* (abbr. RKF) is a rooted subtree of G that is reduced w.r.t. K. Similarly, an *undirected K-fragment* (abbr. UKF) is an undirected subtree of G that is reduced w.r.t. K. A *strong K-fragment* (abbr. SKF) is a UKF, such that all the keywords are leaves. Note that an RKF is also an SKF and an SKF is also a UKF. Figure 2 shows three K-fragments of G_1, where K is the query $\{Belgium, Netherlands\}$. F_3 is a UKF, F_2 is an SKF and F_1 is an RKF.

In some approaches to keyword search (e.g., [1, 5, 6, 7, 13]), the goal is to solve the *SKF problem*, that is, to enumerate all SKFs for a given K. In other

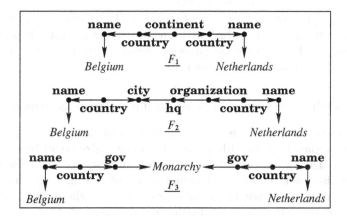

Fig. 2. Fragments of G_1

approaches (e.g., [2, 10]), the goal is to solve the *RKF problem*. The *UKF problem* arises in some cases [1, 3] that are different from keyword search as defined here.

3   Enumeration Algorithms

3.1   Threaded Enumerators

In order to construct efficient enumeration algorithms, we employ threaded enumerators that enable one algorithm to use the elements enumerated by another algorithm (or even by itself, recursively) as soon as these elements are generated, rather than waiting for termination.

Formally, an *enumeration algorithm* E generates, for a given input x, a sequence $E_1(x), \ldots, E_{N(x)}(x)$. Each element $E_i(x)$ is produced by the operation **print**$(\cdot)$. We say that $E(x)$ *enumerates* the set S if $\{ E_1(x), \ldots, E_{N(x)}(x) \} = S$ and $E_i(x) \neq E_j(x)$ for all $1 \leq i < j \leq N(x)$.

Sometimes one enumeration algorithm E uses another enumeration algorithm E', or may even use itself recursively. An important property of an enumeration algorithm is the ability to start generating elements as soon as possible. This property is realized by employing *threaded enumerators* that enable E to use each element generated by E' when that element is created, rather than having to wait until E' finishes its enumeration. A specific threaded enumerator TE is constructed by the command $TE := \mathbf{new}[E](x)$, where E is some enumeration algorithm and x is an input for E. The elements $E_1(x), \ldots, E_{N(x)}(x)$ are enumerated by repeatedly executing the command **next**$[TE]$. The ith execution of **next**$[TE]$ generates the element $E_i(x)$ if $1 \leq i \leq N(x)$; otherwise, if $i > N(x)$, the *null* element, denoted $\perp$, is generated. We assume that $\perp$ is not an element in the output of $E(x)$. An enumeration algorithm E, with input x, may use a threaded enumerator recursively, i.e, a threaded enumerator for $E(x')$, where x' is usually different from x. Note that threaded enumerators are basically *coroutines* and the operations **print** and **next**$[\,]$ correspond to the traditional operations *exit* and *resume*, respectively.

As an example, consider the pseudo code of the algorithm REDUCEDSUB-TREES, presented in Figure 4. In Line 21, a threaded enumerator is constructed for the algorithm RSEXTENSIONS (shown in Figure 5(a)). Line 18 is an example of a recursive construction of a threaded enumerator.

3.2   Measuring the Complexity of Enumeration Algorithms

Polynomial time complexity is not a suitable yardstick of efficiency when analyzing an enumeration algorithm, since the output size could be exponential in the input size. In [9], several definitions of efficiency for enumeration algorithms are discussed. The weakest definition is *polynomial total time,* that is, the running time is polynomial in the combined size of the input and the output. Two stronger definitions consider the time that is needed for generating the

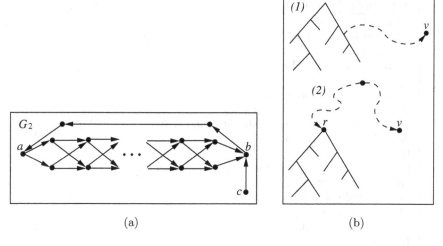

Fig. 3. (a) A data graph G_2 **(b)** Extensions: *(1)* by a directed simple path, *and (2)* by a reduced subtree

ith element, after the first $i-1$ elements have already been created. *Incremental polynomial time* means that the ith element is generated in time that is polynomial in the combined size of the input and the first $i-1$ elements. The strongest definition is *polynomial delay,* that is, the ith element is generated in time that is polynomial only in the input size. For characterizing space efficiency, we use two definitions. Note that the amount of space needed for writing the output is ignored—only the space used for storing intermediate results is measured. The usual definition is *polynomial space,* that is, the amount of space used by the algorithm is polynomial in the input size. *Linearly incremental polynomial space* means that the space needed for generating the first i elements is bounded by i times a polynomial in the input size. Note that an enumeration algorithm that runs with polynomial delay uses (at most) linearly incremental polynomial space. All the algorithms in this paper, except for one version of the heuristics of Section 7, run with polynomial delay. The algorithms of the next two sections use polynomial space.

4   Enumerating Rooted K-Fragments

4.1   The Algorithm

In this section, we describe an algorithm for enumerating RKFs. Our algorithm solves the more general problem of enumerating reduced subtrees. That is, given a data graph G and a subset $U \subseteq \mathcal{V}(G)$, the algorithm enumerates, with polynomial delay, the set $\mathcal{RS}(G, U)$ of all rooted subtrees of G that are reduced w.r.t. U. Hence, to solve the RKF problem, we execute the algorithm with $U = K$, where K is the given set of keywords.

```
ReducedSubtrees(G, U)
1: if |U| = 1 then
2:     print(G₀), where 𝒱(G₀) = U and E(G₀) = ∅
3:     exit
4: if 𝓡𝓢(G, U) = ∅ then
5:     exit
6: choose an arbitrary node u ∈ U
7: if ∀v ∈ U \ { u }, u ↛_G v then
8:     W := {w | (w, u) is an edge of G and 𝓡𝓢(G − u, U^{±(w,u)}) ≠ ∅}
9:     for all w ∈ W do
10:        U_w := U^{±(w,u)}
11:        TE := new [ReducedSubtrees](G − u, U_w)
12:        T := next[TE]
13:        while T ≠ ⊥ do
14:            print(T ∪ (w, u))
15:            T := next[TE]
16: else
17:     let v ∈ U be a node s.t. u ≠ v and u ⤳_G v
18:     TE₁ := new [ReducedSubtrees](G, U \ { v })
19:     T := next[TE₁]
20:     while T ≠ ⊥ do
21:        TE₂ := new [RSExtensions](G, T, v)
22:        T' := next[TE₂]
23:        while T' ≠ ⊥ do
24:            print(T')
25:            T' := next[TE₂]
26:        T := next[TE₁]
```

Fig. 4. Enumerating $\mathcal{RS}(G, U)$

If U has only two nodes, the enumeration is done by a rather straightforward algorithm, PairRS(G, u, v), that is given in Figure 5(b). The problem is more difficult for larger sets of nodes, because for some subsets $U' \subseteq U$, the set $\mathcal{RS}(G, U')$ might be much larger than the set $\mathcal{RS}(G, U)$. For example, for the graph G_2 of Figure 3(a), $\mathcal{RS}(G_2, \{ a, b, c \})$ has only one subtree, whereas the size of $\mathcal{RS}(G_2, \{ a, b \})$ is exponential in the size of G_2.

In the algorithm ReducedSubtrees(G, U) of Figure 4, every intermediate result, obtained from the recursive calls in Lines 11 and 18, can be extended into at least one distinct element of $\mathcal{RS}(G, U)$. Thus, the complexity is not worse than polynomial total time. Next, we describe this algorithm in detail. In Lines 1–3, the algorithm ReducedSubtrees(G, U) terminates after printing a single tree that has one node and no edges, if $|U| = 1$. In Lines 4–5, the algorithm terminates if $\mathcal{RS}(G, U)$ is empty. Note that $\mathcal{RS}(G, U) = \emptyset$ if and only if there is no node w of G, such that all the nodes of U are reachable from w. An arbitrary node $u \in U$ is chosen in Line 6 and if the test of Line 7 is true, then u is a leaf in every tree of $\mathcal{RS}(G, U)$. If so, Line 9 iterates over all nodes w, such that (w, u) is an edge of G and $\mathcal{RS}(G - u, U^{\pm(w,u)}) \neq \emptyset$. All the trees of $\mathcal{RS}(G - u, U^{\pm(w,u)})$ are enumerated in Lines 11–15. The edge (w, u) is added to each of these trees and the result is printed in Line 14.

If the test of Line 7 is false, then Line 17 arbitrarily chooses a node $v \in U$ ($v \neq u$) that is reachable from u. All the trees of $\mathcal{RS}(G, U \setminus \{v\})$ are enumerated starting at Line 18. Each of these trees can be extended to a tree of $\mathcal{RS}(G, U)$ in two different ways, as illustrated in Figure 3(b). For each $T \in \mathcal{RS}(G, U \setminus \{v\})$, all extensions T' of T are enumerated starting at Line 21 by calling RSEXTENSIONS(G, T, v). These extensions are printed in Line 24. Next, we explain how RSEXTENSIONS(G, T, v) works.

Given a node $v \in U$ and a subtree $T \in \mathcal{RS}(G, U \setminus \{v\})$ having a root r, the algorithm RSEXTENSIONS(G, T, v) of Figure 5(a) enumerates all subtrees T', such that T' contains T and $T' \in \mathcal{RS}(G, U)$. In Lines 5–12, T is extended by directed simple paths. Each path P is from a node u ($u \neq r$) of T to v, and u is the only node in both P and T. These paths are enumerated by the algorithm PATHS(G, u, v) of Figure 6. The extensions of T by these paths are printed in Line 11. In Lines 13–19, T is extended by reduced subtrees $\hat{T}$ of G, such that each $\hat{T}$ is reduced w.r.t. $\{r, v\}$ and r is the only node in both T and $\hat{T}$. Note that the root of the new tree is the root of $\hat{T}$. The trees $\hat{T}$ are generated by the algorithm PAIRRS(G, u, v) of Figure 5(b) that enumerates, for a given graph G and two nodes u and v, all subtrees of G that are reduced w.r.t. $\{u, v\}$. The extensions of T by the trees $\hat{T}$ are printed in Line 18. The following theorem shows the correctness of REDUCEDSUBTREES; the proof is given in [12].

Theorem 1. *Let G be a data graph and U be a subset of the nodes of G. The algorithm* REDUCEDSUBTREES(G, U) *enumerates* $\mathcal{RS}(G, U)$.

Interestingly, the algorithm remains correct even if Line 6 and the test of Line 7 are ignored, and only the **else** part (i.e., Lines 17–26) is executed in all cases, where in Line 17 v can be any node in U. However, the complexity is no longer polynomial total time, since the enumerator TE_1 may generate trees T that cannot be extended by RSEXTENSIONS(G, T, v). For example, consider the graph G_2 of Figure 3(a) and let $U = \{a, b, c\}$. If we choose $v = c$, then all directed paths from a to b will be generated by TE_1. However, none of these paths can be extended to a subtree of $\mathcal{RS}(G_2, U)$. If, on the other hand, only the **then** part (i.e., Lines 8–15) is executed, then the algorithm will not be correct.

4.2   Complexity Analysis

To show that the algorithm REDUCEDSUBTREES enumerates with polynomial delay, we have to calculate the computation cost between successive **print** commands. Formally, let E be an enumeration algorithm and suppose that $E(x)$ enumerates the sequence $E_1(x), \ldots, E_N(x)$. For $1 < i \leq N$, the *ith interval* starts immediately after the printing of $E_{i-1}(x)$ and ends with the printing of $E_i(x)$. The *first interval* starts at the beginning of the execution of $E(x)$ and ends with the printing of $E_1(x)$. The *$(N+1)$st interval* starts immediately after

```
RSEXTENSIONS(G, T, v)
 1: let r be the root of T
 2: if v ∈ V(T) then
 3:    print(T)
 4:    exit
 5: for all u ∈ V(T) \ { r } do
 6:    Ḡ := G − (V(T) \ { u })
 7:    if u ⤳_Ḡ v then
 8:       TE := new [PATHS](Ḡ, u, v)
 9:       P := next[TE]
10:       while P ≠ ⊥ do
11:          print(T ∪ P)
12:          P := next[TE]
13: G_r := G − (V(T) \ { r })
14: if RS(G_r, { r, v }) ≠ ∅ then
15:    TE := new [PAIRRS](G_r, r, v)
16:    T̂ := next[TE]
17:    while T̂ ≠ ⊥ do
18:       print(T ∪ T̂)
19:       T̂ := next[TE]
```

```
PAIRRS(G, u, v)
 1: if u = v then
 2:    print(G_0), where V(G_0) = U and
          E(G_0) = ∅
 3:    exit
 4: if u ⤳_G v then
 5:    TE := new [PATHS](G, u, v)
 6:    T := next[TE]
 7:    while T ≠ ⊥ do
 8:       print(T)
 9:       T := next[TE]
10: W := {w ∈ V(G) | (w, u) ∈ E(G)∧
          RS(G − u, { w, v }) ≠ ∅}
11: for all w ∈ W do
12:    TE := new [PAIRRS](G−u, w, v)
13:    T := next[TE]
14:    while T ≠ ⊥ do
15:       print(T ∪ (w, u))
16:       T := next[TE]
```

(a)   (b)

Fig. 5. (a) Enumerating subtree extensions (b) Enumerating $RS(G, \{ u, v \})$

```
PATHS(G, u, v)
 1: if u = v then
 2:    let P the path containing u only
 3:    print(P)
 4:    exit
 5: W := {w ∈ V(G) | w ⤳_{G−u} v and (u, w) ∈ E(G)}
 6: for all w ∈ W do
 7:    TE := new [PATHS](G − u, w, v)
 8:    P := next[TE]
 9:    while P ≠ ⊥ do
10:       print(P ∪ (u, w))
11:       P := next[TE]
```

Fig. 6. Enumerating all simple paths from u to v

the printing of $E_N(x)$ and ends when the execution of $E(x)$ terminates. The *ith delay* of $E(x)$ is the execution cost of the ith interval. The cost of each line in the pseudo code of E, other than a **next** command, is defined as usual. If $E(x)$ uses a threaded enumerator TE' of $E'(x')$, the cost of the jth execution of **next**[TE'] is $1 + C$, where C is the jth delay of $E'(x')$. (Note that this a recursive definition.) The *ith space usage* of $E(x)$ is the amount of space used for printing the first i elements $E_1(x), \ldots, E_i(x)$. Note that the $(N+1)$st space usage is equal to the total space used by $E(x)$ from start to finish.

It is not easy to compute directly the ith delay of REDUCEDSUBTREES, since the threaded enumerators that are used recursively lead to complex recursive equations. Therefore, for each enumeration algorithm involved in the execution of REDUCEDSUBTREES, we compute the *basic ith delay* that is defined as the cost of the ith interval, assuming that each **next** command has a unit cost (instead of the true cost of $1 + C$ as described above). Moreover, we actually compute an upper bound B that is greater than every basic ith delay of every enumeration algorithm involved. It can be shown that $O(|U| \cdot |\mathcal{E}(G)|)$ is such an upper bound.

An upper bound on the ith delay of REDUCEDSUBTREES can be obtained by multiplying B and the number of **next** commands in the ith interval of REDUCEDSUBTREES, including **next** commands of threaded enumerators that are created recursively. It is not easy to show that the number of such **next** commands is polynomial in the size of the input. For example, by removing the non-emptiness tests (e.g., those in Lines 4 and 8 of Figure 4 and Line 14 of Figure 5(a)), the algorithm remains correct but the number of **next** commands is no longer polynomial. The complexity of REDUCEDSUBTREES is summarized in the following theorem and the detailed analysis is given in [12].

Theorem 2. *Let K be a query of size k and G be a data graph with n nodes and m edges. Consider the execution of REDUCEDSUBTREES(G, K). Suppose that $F_1, \ldots, F_N$ are the K-fragments that are printed and let $|F_i|$ denote the number of nodes in F_i. Then,*

- *The first delay is $O\left(mk|F_1|\right)$;*
- *For $1 < i \leq N$, the ith delay is $O\left(mk(|F_i| + |F_{i-1}|)\right)$;*
- *The $(N+1)$st delay is $O\left(mk|F_N|\right)$; and*
- *The ith space usage is $O\left(mn\right)$.*

Corollary 1. *The RKF problem can be solved with polynomial delay and polynomial space.*

A simple optimization that can be applied to the algorithm is to first remove irrelevant nodes. A node v is considered *irrelevant* if either no keyword of K can be reached from v or v cannot be reached from any node u, such that all the keywords of K are reachable from u. We implemented the algorithm REDUCED-SUBTREES and tested it on the data graph of the Mondial XML document (ID references were replaced with edges). We found that usually the running time was improved by an order of magnitude due to this optimization. Also note that the space usage can be reduced to $O(m)$ by implementing the algorithm so that different threaded enumerators share data structures.

5   Enumerating Strong and Undirected K-Fragments

Enumerating SKFs is simpler than enumerating RKFs. It suffices to choose an arbitrary keyword $k \in K$ and recursively enumerate all the strong $(K \setminus \{k\})$-fragments. Each strong $(K \setminus \{k\})$-fragment T is extended to a strong K-fragment by adding all simple undirected paths P, such that P starts at some structural node u of T, ends at k and passes only through structural nodes that are not in T. These paths are enumerated by an algorithm that is similar to $\text{PATHS}(G, u, v)$. In order to enumerate UKFs, the algorithm for enumerating SKFs should be modified so that the generated paths may include, between u and k, both structural and keyword nodes that are not in T (note that u itself may also be a keyword). The complete algorithms for enumerating SKFs and UKFs are described in [12].

Theorem 3. *The SKF and UKF problems can be solved with polynomial delay and polynomial space.*

The algorithms of this and the previous section can be easily parallelized by assigning a processor to each threaded enumerator that executes a recursive call for a smaller set of nodes (e.g., in Line 18 of REDUCEDSUBTREES). The processor that does the recursive call sends the results to the processor that generated that call. The latter extends these results to fragments with one more keyword of K. Note that there is no point in assigning a processor to each threaded enumerator that is created in Line 11 of REDUCEDSUBTREES, since the extension process that follows this line can be done quickly (i.e., by adding just one edge).

6   Enumerating Rooted K-Fragments in Sorted Order

In this section, we present an efficient algorithm for enumerating RKFs by increasing weight, assuming that the query is of a fixed size and the data graph is acyclic. As in the unordered case, we solve this problem by solving the more general problem of enumerating reduced subtrees by increasing weight. Thus, the input is an acyclic data graph and a subset of nodes. Note that a related, but simpler problem is that of enumerating the k shortest paths (e.g., [8]).

We use $\preceq$ to denote a topological order on the nodes of G. The maximal element of a nonempty set W is denoted as $\max_{\preceq} W$. Given the input G and U, the algorithm generates one or more reduced subtrees w.r.t. every set of nodes W, such that $|W| \leq |U|$, and stores them in the array $T[W, i]$, where $T[W, 1]$ is the smallest, etc. Values are assigned to $T[W, i]$ in sorted order, and the array $\mathcal{I}[W]$ stores the largest i, such that the subtree $T[W, i]$ has already been created. If $T[W, i] = \perp$ $(i \geq 1)$, it means that the graph G has $i - 1$ subtrees that are reduced w.r.t. W.

Consider an edge e entering $\max_{\preceq} W$. A sorted sequence of reduced subtrees w.r.t. W can be obtained by adding e to each subtree $T[W^{\pm e}, i]$. Let $\{T[W^{\pm e}, i] \cup e\}$ denote this sequence. The complete sequence $\{T[W, i]\}$ is generated by merging all the sequences $\{T[W^{\pm e}, i] \cup e\}$ of edges e that enter $\max_{\preceq} W$. We use $\mathcal{N}[W, e]$ to denote the smallest j, such that the subtree $T[W^{\pm e}, j] \cup e$ has not yet been merged into the sequence $T[W, i]$.

The algorithm is shown in Figure 7. Subtrees are assigned to $T[W, i]$ in Line 14 of GENERATE. It can be shown that $i = \mathcal{I}[W] + 1$ whenever this line is reached. Let $e_1, \ldots, e_m$ be all the edges entering $\max_{\preceq} W$. The reduced subtree w.r.t. W that is assigned to $T[W, i]$ is chosen in Line 13 and is a minimal

SORTEDRS(G, U)
1: INITIALIZE($|U|$)
2: $i := 1$
3: **while** $\mathcal{T}[U, i] \neq\perp$ **do**
4:    print($\mathcal{T}[U, i]$)
5:    $i := i + 1$
6:    GENERATE(U, i)

INITIALIZE(K)
1: **for all** subsets $W \subseteq \mathcal{V}(G)$, where $1 \leq |W| \leq K$, in the $\preceq_s$ order **do**
2:    $\mathcal{I}[W] := 0$
3:    $u := \max_{\prec} W$
4:    **for all** edges $e = (v, u)$ in G **do**
5:      $\mathcal{N}[W, e] := 1$
6:    GENERATE($W, 1$)

NEXTSUBTREE(W, e)
1: $l := \mathcal{N}[W, e]$
2: **if** $\mathcal{T}[W^{\pm e}, l] \neq\perp$ **then**
3:    **return** $\mathcal{T}[W^{\pm e}, l] \cup e$
4: **else**
5:    **return** $\perp$

GENERATE(W, i)
1: **if** $\mathcal{I}[W] \geq i$ **then**
2:    **return**
3: **if** $|W| = 1$ **then**
4:    $\mathcal{T}[W, 1] := T_0$, where $\mathcal{V}(T_0) = W$ and $\mathcal{E}(T_0) = \emptyset$
5:    $\mathcal{T}[W, 2] :=\perp$
6:    $\mathcal{I}[W] = 2$
7:    **return**
8: $u := \max_{\prec} W$
9: **if** $\{v \mid (v, u) \in \mathcal{E}(G)\} = \emptyset$ **then**
10:    $\mathcal{T}[W, 1] :=\perp$
11:    $\mathcal{I}[W] := 1$
12:    **return**
13: let $e = (v, u) \in \mathcal{E}(G)$ be such that $w(\text{NEXTSUBTREE}(W, e))$ is minimal
14: $\mathcal{T}[W, i] :=$ NEXTSUBTREE(W, e)
15: **if** NEXTSUBTREE(W, e)$\neq\perp$ **then**
16:    GENERATE($W^{\pm e}, \mathcal{N}[W, e] + 1$)
17:    $\mathcal{N}[W, e] := \mathcal{N}[W, e] + 1$
18: $\mathcal{I}[W] := i$

Fig. 7. Enumerating $\mathcal{RS}(G, U)$ by increasing weight

subtree among $\mathcal{T}[W^{\pm e_1}, \mathcal{N}[W, e_1]] \cup e_1, \ldots, \mathcal{T}[W^{\pm e_m}, \mathcal{N}[W, e_m]] \cup e_m$, which are obtained by calling NEXTSUBTREE. Clearly, all the subtrees $\mathcal{T}[W^{\pm e_j}, \mathcal{N}[W, e_j]]$ ($1 \leq j \leq m$) should have been generated before $\mathcal{T}[W, i]$. For that reason, if $\mathcal{T}[W^{\pm e_k}, \mathcal{N}[W, e_k]] \cup e_k$ is the subtree that has just been assigned to $\mathcal{T}[W, i]$, then in Line 16 the subtree $\mathcal{T}[W^{\pm e_k}, \mathcal{N}[W, e_k] + 1]$ is generated. Note that $\mathcal{T}[W^{\pm e_k}, \mathcal{N}[W, e_k] + 1] =\perp$ may hold after executing Line 16; it happens if $|\mathcal{RS}(G, W^{\pm e_k})| < \mathcal{N}[W, e_k] + 1$. (Note that $w(\perp) = \infty$.) It is also possible that $\mathcal{T}[W^{\pm e_k}, \mathcal{N}[W, e_k] + 1]$ may have already been created before executing Line 16; hence, the test in Line 1 of GENERATE.

The enumeration algorithm SORTEDRS(G, U) starts by calling the algorithm INITIALIZE($|U|$) in order to compute $\mathcal{T}[W, 1]$ for every nonempty subset W, such that $|W| \leq |U|$. The loop in Line 1 of INITIALIZE traverses the sets W in the $\preceq_s$ order, where $W_1 \preceq_s W_2$ if $\max_{\prec} W_1 \preceq \max_{\prec} W_2$. After initialization, the subtrees $\mathcal{T}[U, i]$ are generated in sorted order. The algorithm terminates when $\mathcal{T}[U, i] =\perp$. The following theorem states the correctness of SORTEDRS. The crux of the proof (given in [12]) is in showing that each of the arrays $\mathcal{T}$, $\mathcal{I}$, and $\mathcal{N}$ holds the correct information described above.

Theorem 4. *Let G be an acyclic data graph and U be a subset of the nodes of G. SORTEDRS(G, U) enumerates $\mathcal{RS}(G, U)$ by increasing weight.*

Theorem 5. *Let K be a query of size k and G be an acyclic data graph with n nodes and m edges. In the execution of* SORTEDRS(G, K),

- *The first delay is $O\left(mn^k\right)$;*
- *For $i > 1$, the ith delay is $O(m)$;*
- *The ith space usage is $O\left(n^{k+2} + in^2\right)$.*

Corollary 2. *If queries are of a fixed size and data graphs are acyclic, then the sorted RKF problem can be solved with polynomial delay.*

Note that in practice, for each set W, the array $T[W, i]$ should be implemented as a linked list. In addition, $\mathcal{N}[W, e]$ should store a pointer to the list $T[W^{\pm e}, i]$. This does not change the running time and it limits the amount of space just to the size of the subtrees that are actually explored for W.

7 A Heuristics for Sorted Enumerations

Usually, the goal is enumeration by increasing weight. There are two approaches for achieving this goal. In [1, 6, 7], the enumeration is by increasing weight, but the worst-case upper bound on the running time is (at best) exponential. In [2, 10, 13], a heuristic approach is used to enumerate in an order that is likely to be close to the sorted order. Note that there is no guarantee by how much the actual order may deviate from the sorted order. The upper bound on the running time is exponential [13] or not stated [2, 10]. In comparison, the algorithms of Sections 4 and 5 imply that enumeration by increasing weight can be done in polynomial total time (even if the size of the query is unbounded) simply by first generating all the fragments and then sorting them. None of the current systems achieves this worst-case upper bound.

Generating and then sorting would work well when there are not too many results. Next, we outline an efficient heuristics (for queries of unbounded size) that enumerates in an order that is likely to be close to the sorted order. The general idea is to apply the algorithms of Sections 4 and 5 in a neighborhood of the data graph around the keywords of K, starting with the neighborhood comprising just the keywords of K and then enlarging this neighborhood in stages.

The heuristics for building the successive neighborhoods is based on assigning a cost $C(n)$ to each node n and then adding the nodes, one at a time, in the order of increasing cost. $C(n)$ could be, for example, the sum of (or maximal value among) the distances between n and the keywords of K. Alternatively, $C(n)$ could be a number that is at most twice the weight of a minimal undirected subtree that contains all the keywords of K and n. Note that in either case, $C(n)$ can be computed efficiently.

For a given neighborhood, we should generate all the K-fragments that are included in this neighborhood. However, in order to avoid generating the same K-fragment for two distinct neighborhoods, we only generate the K-fragments that contain v, where v is the most-recently added node. One way of doing it is by applying directly the algorithms of Sections 4 and 5, and printing only those K-fragments that contain the node v. This would result in an enumeration that runs in incremental polynomial time. To realize enumeration with polynomial delay, we should have algorithms that can enumerate, with polynomial delay, K-fragments that contain a given node $v \notin K$ (note that v must be an interior node). We can show that such algorithms exist for enumerating SKFs and UKFs. For RKFs, we can show existence of such an algorithm if the data graph is acyclic; for cyclic data graphs, no such algorithm exists, unless P=NP. The proof of these results is beyond the scope of this paper.

8   Conclusion and Related Work

Different systems for keyword search [1, 2, 10, 6, 7, 13] essentially solve the problem of enumerating K-fragments. We have identified three types of K-fragments (i.e., RKFs, SKFs and UKFs) and there are four types of enumerations (as illustrated in Figure 8): *unsorted, heuristically sorted, approximately sorted* and *sorted*. Three of these types are discussed in this paper. The fourth type, namely enumeration in an *approximate* order, is defined in [11]. The most desirable type is enumeration in sorted order and, in this paper, we have given an algorithm that does it with polynomial delay provided that the data graph is acyclic and the K-fragments are rooted. An efficient enumeration in sorted order is possible, however, only if queries have a fixed size. The most efficient enumeration algorithms are those that enumerate in an arbitrary order. In this paper, we have given algorithms for enumerating all three types of K-fragments with polynomial delay when the order of the results is not important. Note that by first enumerating and then sorting, it follows that enumeration in sorted order can be done in polynomial total time (without assuming that queries have a fixed size). We have also shown how our algorithms for enumerating in an arbitrary order can be the basis for developing efficient algorithms that enumerate in a heuristic order, that is, an order that is likely to be close to the sorted order, but without any guarantee. Our algorithms for enumerating in a heuristic order run with polynomial delay, except for the case of enumerating RKFs of a cyclic data graph where the algorithm runs in incremental polynomial time. In comparison, some of the existing systems [6, 7, 1] have implemented algorithms that enumerate in sorted order while other systems [2, 10, 13] have implemented algorithms that

Fig. 8. Efficiency vs. Sorted-Order Tradeoff

enumerate in a heuristic order. All these algorithms require exponential time in the worst case (i.e., they are not in polynomial total time) even if queries have a fixed size.

The results of this paper can be extended in two ways. First, for queries of a fixed size, all types of K-fragments can be enumerated by increasing weight with polynomial delay; however, for RKFs the polynomial delay is not as good as the polynomial delay of the algorithm SORTEDRS of Section 6, which applies only to acyclic data graphs. The second extension is enumeration in an *approximate order* [11], which can be done with polynomial delay even if queries are of unbounded size. A brief overview of these extensions, including running times, is given in [11]; the full details will be described in a future paper. Note that the heuristics of Section 7 does not satisfy the notion of an approximate order, but it yields better delays than those of the algorithms for enumerating in an approximate order.

In this paper, results of keyword search are subtrees that connect the given keywords. In [3], results are sets of semantically related nodes that contain the keywords. These two approaches are different, because the existence of a semantic relationship between some nodes entails more than just connectivity. However, as shown in [3], the algorithms of this paper can be used for finding semantically related nodes and, in some cases, they are even more efficient than other approaches for finding such nodes.

References

[1] S. Agrawal, S. Chaudhuri, and G. Das. DBXplorer: enabling keyword search over relational databases. In *SIGMOD Conference*, page 627, 2002.

[2] G. Bhalotia, A. Hulgeri, C. Nakhe, S. Chakrabarti, and S. Sudarshan. Keyword searching and browsing in databases using BANKS. In *ICDE*, pages 431–440, 2002.

[3] S. Cohen, Y. Kanza, B. Kimelfeld, and Y. Sagiv. Interconnection semantics for keyword search in xml. In *CIKM*, 2005.

[4] M. R. Garey, R. L. Graham, and D. S. Johnson. The complexity of computing Steiner minimal trees. *SIAM Journal on Applied Mathematics*, 32:835–859, 1977.

[5] V. Hristidis, L. Gravano, and Y. Papakonstantinou. Efficient IR-style keyword search over relational databases. In *HDMS*, 2003.

[6] V. Hristidis and Y. Papakonstantinou. DISCOVER: Keyword search in relational databases. In *VLDB*, pages 670–681, 2002.

[7] V. Hristidis, Y. Papakonstantinou, and A. Balmin. Keyword proximity search on XML graphs. In *ICDE*, pages 367–378, 2003.

[8] V. M. Jiménez and A. Marzal. Computing the K shortest paths: A new algorithm and an experimental comparison. In *Algorithm Engineering*, pages 15–29, 1999.

[9] D. S. Johnson, M. Yannakakis, and C. H. Papadimitriou. On generating all maximal independent sets. *Information Processing Letters*, 27:119–123, March 1988.

[10] V. Kacholia, S. Pandit, S. Chakrabarti, S. Sudarshan, R. Desai, and H. Karambelkar. Bidirectional expansion for keyword search on graph databases. In *VLDB*, pages 505–516, 2005.

[11] B. Kimelfeld and Y. Sagiv. Efficient engines for keyword proximity search. In *WebDB*, pages 67–72, 2005.

[12] B. Kimelfeld and Y. Sagiv. Efficiently enumerating results of keyword search, 2005. Available at Kimelfeld's home page (http://www.cs.huji.ac.il/~bennyk/).

[13] W. S. Li, K. S. Candan, Q. Vu, and D. Agrawal. Retrieving and organizing Web pages by "information unit". In *WWW*, pages 230–244, 2001.

[14] M. Y. Vardi. The complexity of relational query languages (extended abstract). In *STOC*, pages 137–146, 1982.

Mapping Maintenance in XML P2P Databases*

Dario Colazzo[1] and Carlo Sartiani[2]

[1] LRI - Université Paris Sud - France
`dario.colazzo@lri.fr`
[2] Dipartimento di Informatica - Università di Pisa - Italy
`sartiani@di.unipi.it`

Abstract. Unstructured p2p database systems are usually characterized by the presence of *schema mappings* among peers. In these systems, the detection of *corrupted* mappings is a key problem. A corrupted mapping fails in matching the target or the source schema, hence it is not able to transform data conforming to a schema S_i into data conforming to a schema S_j, nor it can be used for effective query reformulation.

This paper describes a novel technique for maintaining mappings in XML p2p databases, based on a *semantic* notion of mapping correctness.

1 Introduction

The *peer-to-peer* computational model (p2p) is nowadays massively used for sharing and querying data dispersed over the Internet. Peer-to-peer data sharing systems can be classified in two main categories. *Structured* p2p systems [1] [2] distribute data across the network according to a hash function, so to form a distributed hash table (DHT); systems in this class allows for a fast retrieval of data ($O(logn)$, where n is the number of peers in the system), at the price of very limited query capabilities (key lookup queries and, in some systems, range queries). *Unstructured* systems, instead, leave peers free to manage their own data, and feature rich query languages like, for instance, XQuery [3]. Queries are executed by flooding the network and traversing the whole system.

Most unstructured p2p database systems (see [4], [5], and [6] for instance) are characterized by the presence of *schema mappings* among peers. A schema mapping (e.g., a set of Datalog rules) describes how to translate data conforming to a source schema S_i into data conforming to a target schema S_j (or to a projection of S_j), and it can be used to reformulate, according to the *Global As View* (GAV) and *Local As View* (LAV) paradigms [7, 8], queries on S_i into queries over S_j, and *vice versa*. Schema mappings, hence, allow the system to retrieve data that are semantically similar but described by different schemas.

A main problem in mapping-based systems is the maintenance of schema mappings, and, in particular, the detection of *corrupted* mappings. A corrupted mapping fails in matching the target or the source schema, hence it is not able to transform data conforming to a source schema S_i into data conforming to the target schema S_j. The presence

---

* Dario Colazzo was funded by the RNTL-GraphDuce project and by the ACI project "Transformation Languages for XML: Logics and Applications". Carlo Sartiani was funded by the FIRB GRID.IT project and by Microsoft Corporation under the BigTop project.

G. Bierman and C. Koch (Eds.): DBPL 2005, LNCS 3774, pp. 74–89, 2005.

of such mappings can affect query processing: since queries are processed by flooding the network and by repeatedly applying reformulation steps, a corrupted mapping may make the data of some peers unreachable; moreover, optimization techniques based on mapping pre-combination can be vanished by the presence of corrupted mappings.

Nowadays, mapping maintenance is performed manually by the site administrator, and quick responses to sudden mapping corruptions are not possible. To the best of our knowledge, the only proposed technique for automatically maintaining mappings, in the context of XML p2p database systems, has been described in [9]. This technique is based on the use of a type system capable of checking the correctness of a query, in a XQuery-like language [10], wrt a schema, i.e., if the structural requirements of the query are matched by the schema. By relying on this type system, a distributed type-checking algorithm verifies that, at each reformulation step, the transformed query matches the target schema, and, if an error is raised, informs the source of the target peers that there is an error in the mapping.

The technique described in [9] has two main drawbacks. First, it is not *complete*, since wrong rules that are not used for reformulating a given query cannot be discovered. Second, the algorithm requires that a query were reformulated by the system before detecting a possible error in the mapping; this implies that the algorithm cannot directly check for mapping correctness, but, instead, it checks for the correctness of a mapping wrt a given reformulation algorithm. Hence, mapping correctness is not a *query-independent*, *semantics-based* property, but is strongly related to the properties of the reformulation algorithm.

Our Contribution. This paper describes a novel technique for maintaining mappings in XML p2p database systems. As for [9], the technique relies on a type system for an XML query language: while in [9] we exploited the type system to check for the correctness of a query wrt a given schema, in the spirit of [10], in this paper we develop a slightly different type system focused on type inference. The main idea is to compare the inferred type of each mapping query with the target schema, so to verify the adherence of the mapping to this schema.

Unlike [9], the proposed technique is independent from queries, does not require a prior query reformulation, and it is *complete*, i.e., any error in a mapping will be discovered.

The paper proposes a *semantic* notion of mapping correctness based on a *simulation-like* form of type projection. Type projection brings the essence of the relational projection to XML, and it can be safely reduced to standard type-checking among *weakened* types, as shown in Section 5. To minimize false-negatives, we provide quite precise type inference techniques, inspired by those proposed in [10].

The proposed technique can be used in unstructured p2p database systems as well as in structured systems, like [11], that combine the DHT paradigm with mappings.

Paper Outline. The paper is structured as follows. Section 2 describes a reference scenario for our technique, and briefly introduce the system model and the query language. Section 3, then, defines our notions of mapping validity (no wrong rules wrt the source schema) and mapping correctness (no wrong rules wrt the target schema). Section 4 describes the type system we use for inferring query types. Section 5, next, shows how the definitions of Section 3 can be turned in an operational technique with the assistance of our type system. Section 6, then, discusses some related work. In Section 7, finally, we draw our conclusions.

2   Motivating Scenario

We describe our technique by referring to a sample XML p2p database system inspired by Piazza [4]. The system is composed of a dynamic set of peers, capable of executing queries on XML data, and connected through *sparse point-to-point* schema mappings.

Each peer publishes some XML data (db), that may be empty, in which case the peer only submits queries to the system. Furthermore, each peer has two distinct schema descriptions. The first one, U (the *peer schema*), describes how local data are organized. The second one, V (the *peer view*), is a view over U, and has a twofold role. First, it works as input interface for the peer, so that queries sent to peer p_i should respect p_i view of the world. Second, it describes the peer *view* of the world, i.e., the virtual view against which queries are posed: each peer poses queries against its peer view, since it assumes that the outer world adopts this schema.

The peer schema and the peer view are connected through a schema mapping (in the following we will use the expression "schema mapping" to denote any mapping between types). The mapping can be defined according to the *Global As View* (GAV) approach, or to the *Local As View* (LAV) approach. Our approach is based on GAV mappings, where the target schema is described in terms of the source schema; nevertheless, this approach applies to LAV mappings too, since, as noted in [12], a LAV mapping from p_i to p_j can be interpreted as a GAV mapping from p_j to p_i.

In addition to (possibly empty) data and schema information, each peer contains a set, possibly a singleton, of *peer mappings* $\{m_{ij}\}_j$. A peer mapping m_{ij} from peer p_i to peer p_j is a set of queries that show how to translate data belonging to the view of p_i (V_i) into data conforming to a projection of the view of p_j (V_j).

Mapping queries are expressed in the same query language used for posing general queries: this language, called μXQ, is roughly equivalent to the FLWR core of XQuery, and will be described in Section 3. These mappings link peers together, and form a sparse graph; queries are then executed by exploring the transitive closure of such mappings.

Systems conforming to this architecture rely on schema mappings to process and execute queries. The correctness of the query answering process for a given query depends on the properties of the reformulation algorithm as well as on the correctness of the mappings involved in the transformation: indeed, if the mapping fails in matching the target schema, the transformed query will probably fail as well.

The evolution of the system, namely the connection of new nodes and the disconnection of existing nodes, as well as the changes in peer data and schemas, can dramatically affect the quality of schema mappings and, in particular, lead to the corruption of existing mappings. This will reflect on query answering and on existing optimization techniques for p2p systems, such as the mapping composition approach described in [13].

The following Example illustrates the basic concepts of the query language, provides an intuition of the mapping correctness notion (described in Section 3), and shows how mapping incorrectness can reflect on query answering.

Fig. 1. Bibliographic p2p network

Example 1. Consider a bibliographic data sharing system, whose topology is shown in Figure 1.

Assume that Pisa and New York use the following views.

```
PisaBib = bib[(Author)*]
Author = author[Name, Affiliation, Paper*]
Name = name[String]
Affiliation = affiliation[String]
Paper = paper[Title, Year]
Title = title[String]
Year = year[Integer]

NYBib = bib[(Article|Book)*]
Article = article[Author*,Title,Year, RefCode]
Author = author[String]
Title = title[String]
Year = year[Integer]
Book = book[Author*,Title,Year, RefCode]
RefCode = refCode[String]
```

Suppose now that Pisa uses the following queries to map its view into the view of New York.

```
NYBibliography <-
Q₁($input): for $y in $input/year return $y
Q₂($input): for $t in $input/title return $t
Q₃($input): for $p in $input//paper,
                  $t in $p/title
            return article[ Q₂($p), Q₁($p),
                            for $aut in $input/author,
                                $pap in $aut/paper
                                $title in $pap/title
                            where $title = $t
                            return author[$aut/name/text()]]
Q₄($input): for $bib in /bib return bib[Q₃($bib)]
```

This mapping transforms data conforming to a large fragment of the PisaBib schema (only affiliation elements are discarded) into data conforming to a fraction of the NYBib schema. This is a quite common situation in data integration and p2p data sharing systems, since usually only a fraction of semantically related heterogeneous schemas can be reconciled. Since this mapping is not a function from PisaBib to NYBib (it does not produce refCode elements), standard result analysis based on subtyping cannot be used to check its correctness.

Consider query Q_3 in the Pisa → NY mapping. The outer for clause iterates over paper element, and binds the $p and $t variables to paper and title elements respectively. The outer `return` clause produces the results of the query; in this case, a nested query changing the nesting of **author** and **paper** elements is invoked. The correlation of the nested query with the outer query is given by the inner `where` clause, which filters the variable bindings of the inner query.

As it can be noted, this mapping is *correct* since it transforms a data instance conforming to `PisaBib` into a data instance conforming to a projection of `NYBib`.

Assume now that New York slightly changes its view: in particular, the site administrator changes the way author names are represented: instead of a simple **author** element, information about author's first name and second name is inserted into the **author** element: `Author = author[first[String],second[String]]`.

This change in the target schema makes the Pisa → NY mapping incorrect. Indeed, a `PisaBib` data instance is transformed in a data instance having *simple content* **author** elements, while the new New York view requires more complex **author** elements.

The incorrectness of the Pisa → NY schema mapping reflects on query answering. Indeed, consider the query shown in Figure 2 (a). This query, submitted by a user in Pisa, asks for all articles written by Mary F. Fernandez. The query is first executed locally in Pisa. Then, the system reformulates the query so to match New York view; this reformulation is performed by directly composing the query with the mapping from Pisa to New York, relying again on standard algorithms for query unfolding [14, 13][1].

At the end of the reformulation process, the reformulated query, shown in Figure 2 (b), is then sent to the New York site. Unfortunately, the transformed query does not match the new view of New York, so the Pisa user cannot gather results from the New York site.

```
articles_Fernandez[
for $aut in $bib/author,
    $pap in $aut/paper,
    $t in $pap/title,
    $n in $aut/name
let $mf := ''Mary F. Fernandez''
where $n = $mf
return article[$t, $pap/year]
```

```
articles_Fernandez[
for $a in $bib/article,
    $aut in $a/author
let $mf := ''Mary F. Fernandez''
where $aut = $mf
return article[$a/title, $a/year]
```

(a) Pisa user query   (b) Transformed Pisa user query

Fig. 2. Reformulation of a user query

3   Mapping Validity and Correctness

In this Section we describe the notions of mapping validity (no wrong rules wrt the source schema) and mapping correctness (no wrong rules wrt the target schema). These notions are central to our approach, and allow for the definition of an operational checking technique, as shown in Section 5.

---

[1] We show a minimal transformed query, obtained by minimizing the original transformed query and by deleting all redundant subqueries.

To define mapping properties, we have to formally present the query language used for expressing both user queries and mapping rules, as well as the type language used for describing schemas and views.

3.1 Query Language

User queries and mapping rules are expressed in the μXQ query language [10], whose grammar is shown in Table 1. μXQ is a minimal core language for XML data, roughly equivalent to the FLWR core of XQuery. We impose two further restrictions wrt this grammar: first, we forbid the navigation of the result of a nested query by the outer query; second, we restrict the predicate language to the conjunction, disjunction, or negation of variable comparisons. These restrictions, also present in Piazza, allow for a better handling of errors at the price of a modest decrease in the expressive power of the language.

The semantics of the language and the required auxiliary functions are shown in Tables 2 and 3. There, ρ is a substitution assigning a forest to each free variable in the query; also, dos is a shortcut for descendant-or-self. All the rest is self explicative.

Note that our data model is unordered, so that we consider a tree $l[f_1, f_2]$ as equivalent to $l[f_2, f_1]$. As in Piazza, this assumption is motivated by the non feasibility of imposing a global document order over XML data dispersed over a p2p network.

Table 1. μXQ grammar

$$
\begin{aligned}
Q \quad &::= () \mid b \mid l[Q] \mid Q, Q \mid \overline{x}\ \texttt{child} :: NodeTest \mid \overline{x}\ \texttt{dos} :: NodeTest \\
&\mid \texttt{for}\ \overline{x}\ \texttt{in}\ Q\ \texttt{return}\ Q \mid \texttt{let}\ x ::= Q\ \texttt{return}\ Q \\
&\mid \texttt{for}\ \overline{x}\ \texttt{in}\ Q\ \texttt{where}\ P\ \texttt{return}\ Q \mid \texttt{let}\ x ::= Q\ \texttt{where}\ P\ \texttt{return}\ Q \\
NodeTest &::= 1 \mid \texttt{node()} \mid \texttt{text()} \\[4pt]
P \quad &::= \texttt{true} \mid \chi\ \delta\ \chi \mid \texttt{empty}(\chi) \mid P\ \texttt{or}\ P \mid \texttt{not}\ P \mid (P) \\
\chi \quad &::= \overline{x} \mid x \\
\delta \quad &::= = \mid <
\end{aligned}
$$

Table 2. μXQ semantics

$$
\begin{aligned}
[\![b]\!]_\rho &\triangleq b & [\![x]\!]_\rho &\triangleq \rho(x) \\
[\![\overline{x}]\!]_\rho &\triangleq \rho(\overline{x}) & [\![()]\!]_\rho &\triangleq () \\
[\![Q_1, Q_2]\!]_\rho &\triangleq [\![Q_1]\!]_\rho, [\![Q_2]\!]_\rho & [\![l[Q]]\!]_\rho &\triangleq l[[\![Q]\!]_\rho]
\end{aligned}
$$

$$
[\![\overline{x}\ \texttt{child} :: NodeTest]\!]_\rho \triangleq childr([\![\overline{x}]\!]_\rho) :: NodeTest
$$

$$
[\![\overline{x}\ \texttt{dos} :: NodeTest]\!]_\rho \triangleq dos([\![\overline{x}]\!]_\rho) :: NodeTest
$$

$$
[\![\texttt{let}\ x ::= Q_1\ \texttt{return}\ Q_2]\!]_\rho \triangleq [\![Q_2]\!]_{\rho, x \mapsto [\![Q_1]\!]_\rho}
$$

$$
[\![\texttt{for}\ \overline{x}\ \texttt{in}\ Q_1\ \texttt{return}\ Q_2]\!]_\rho \triangleq \prod_{t \in trees([\![Q_1]\!]_\rho)} [\![Q_2]\!]_{\rho, \overline{x} \mapsto t}
$$

$$
[\![\texttt{let}\ x ::= Q_1\ \texttt{where}\ P\ \texttt{return}\ Q_2]\!]_\rho \triangleq \text{if } P(\rho, x \mapsto [\![Q_1]\!]_\rho) \text{ then } [\![Q_2]\!]_{\rho, x \mapsto [\![Q_1]\!]_\rho} \text{ else } ()
$$

$$
[\![\texttt{for}\ \overline{x}\ \texttt{in}\ Q_1\ \texttt{where}\ P\ \texttt{return}\ Q_2]\!]_\rho \triangleq \prod_{t \in trees([\![Q_1]\!]_\rho)} (\text{if } P(\rho, \overline{x} \mapsto t) \text{ then } [\![Q_2]\!]_{\rho, \overline{x} \mapsto t} \text{ else } ())
$$

Table 3. Auxiliary functions

$dos(b)$	$\triangleq b$	$childr(b)$	$\triangleq ()$
$dos(l[f])$	$\triangleq l[f], dos(f)$	$childr(l[f])$	$\triangleq f$
$dos(())$	$\triangleq ()$	$dos(f, f')$	$\triangleq dos(f), dos(f')$
$b :: l$	$\triangleq ()$	$l[f] :: l$	$\triangleq l[f]$
$() :: l$	$\triangleq ()$	$(f, f') :: l$	$\triangleq f :: l, f' :: l$
$m[f] :: l \quad \triangleq ()$	$m \neq l$		
$b :: node()$	$\triangleq ()$	$() :: node()$	$\triangleq ()$
$m[f] :: node() \triangleq m[f]$		$(f, f') :: node() \triangleq f :: node(), f' :: node()$	
$b :: text()$	$\triangleq b$	$() :: text()$	$\triangleq ()$
$m[f] :: text() \triangleq ()$		$(f, f') :: text() \triangleq f :: text(), f' :: text()$	

3.2 Type Language

We adopt, essentially, XDuce's type language [15], with two exceptions. First, we exclude (vertical) recursive types. This is motivated by the fact that FLWR queries are not powerful enough to transform trees with arbitrary depth, hence we can restrict the type language to types that describe trees with limited and finite depth. As we will see, this restriction will allow us to introduce rather precise type-inference techniques, that will minimize false negatives returned while checking for mapping correctness.

Second, we consider commutative product types. In other words, we do not assume any order on sequence types, so that $T, U \sim U, T$. This is motivated by the fact that in distributed environments is almost impossible to reach a common agreement about ordering, so some peer may assume that title elements precede author elements in the document order, while other peers may assume the contrary. Hence, we must adopt types that abstract from ordering. This aspect will affect the notions of type projection as well.

Following XDuce notation, types are defined as follows:

Types $\qquad T ::= () \mid B \mid l[T] \mid T, T \mid T \mid T \mid T*$

Base Type $\quad B ::= \texttt{String}$

Here, $()$ is the type for the empty sequence value; B denotes the type for base values (without loss of generality, we only consider string base values); types T, U and $T \mid U$ are, respectively, product and union types, while $T*$ is the type for repetition. In the following, an element type with empty content $l[()]$ will always be abbreviated as $l[]$.

Type semantics is standard: $[\![\_]\!]$ is the minimal function from types to sets of forests that satisfies the following monotone equations:

$$[\![()]\!] \triangleq \{()\} \qquad [\![B]\!] \triangleq \{b \mid b \text{ is a string}\} \qquad [\![l[T]]\!] \triangleq \{l[f] \mid f \in [\![T]\!]\}$$

$$[\![T_1 \mid T_2]\!] \triangleq [\![T_1]\!] \cup [\![T_2]\!] \qquad [\![T_1, T_2]\!] \triangleq \{f_1, f_2 \mid f_i \in [\![T_i]\!]\} \qquad [\![T*]\!] \triangleq [\![T]\!]^*$$

In the following we will use $f : T$ as shortcut for $f \in [\![T]\!]$. Type semantics induces the following subtyping relation:

$$T < U \iff_{\text{def}} [\![T]\!] \subseteq [\![U]\!]$$

3.3 Correctness of Schema Mappings

In this Section, we introduce and formalize our notion of mapping correctness. The notion is *semantic* and is not related to any particular type system.

Definition 1 (Mapping). *A mapping m from the peer view of p_i to the peer view of p_j is a set of queries $m = \{q_k\}_k$ on data (possibly) conforming to p_i's view and returning data (possibly) conforming to p_j's view.*

The previous definition states that a mapping is just a set of queries that may match the source and/or the target schema. Unlike [16], where mappings must match both the target and the source schema, we do not impose constraints on mappings. This allows for capturing mappings that are imprecise or that become incorrect because of a change in the system status.

The following definition introduces the notion of mapping validity.

Definition 2 (Mapping Validity). *A mapping $m = \{q_k\}_k$ from p_i's view to p_j's view $(\mathcal{V}_i \to \mathcal{V}_j)$ is valid if and only if, for each query q_k, q_k is correct wrt $\mathcal{V}_i$, in the sense that, for each non-empty subquery q of q_k, there exists a data instance d of $\mathcal{V}_i$ such that, when evaluated on d, q will return a non-empty result.*

Mapping validity implies that a valid mapping must be correct wrt the source schema, i.e., it matches the structure and the constraints of the source schema. We adopt the query correctness notion described in [18, 10] and [9]. Mapping validity[2] allows for identifying mappings that are *obsolete*, i.e., that contain rules referring to fragments of the source schema that have been changed or deleted. From now on, we will assume that each mapping is valid, and focus on the detection of errors wrt the target schema.

Definition 3 (Mapping Correctness). *A mapping $m = \{q_k\}_k$ from p_i's view to p_j's view $(\mathcal{V}_i \to \mathcal{V}_j)$ is correct if and only if, for each query q_k, for each data instance d_h conforming to $\mathcal{V}_i$, there exists a data instance d_l conforming to $\mathcal{V}_j$, such that, $q_k(d_h) \precsim d_l$, where $\precsim$ is defined as shown in Definition 4.*

Definition 4 (Value Projection). *The value projection relation $\precsim$ is the minimal relation such that:*

$$
\begin{array}{ll}
() \precsim f & f_1, f_2 \precsim f_3, f_4 \quad \text{if } (f_1 \precsim f_3 \wedge f_2 \precsim f_4) \\
b_1 \precsim b_2 & f_1 \precsim f_3 \qquad \text{if } \exists f_2 : f_1 \precsim f_2 \wedge f_2 \precsim f_3 \\
f \precsim f, () & l[f_1] \precsim l[f_2] \quad \text{if } f_1 \precsim f_2 \\
f_1, f_2 \precsim f_2, f_1 &
\end{array}
$$

The above definitions state that a mapping from $\mathcal{V}_i$ to $\mathcal{V}_j$ is correct if and only, for each rule in the mapping, the result of each query on $\mathcal{V}_i$ is mapped, according to the $\precsim$ relation, into a value conforming to $\mathcal{V}_j$. $\precsim$ is an *injective* simulation relation among values, inspired by the projection operator of the relation data model. Intuitively, $d_1 \precsim d_2$ if there exists a subterm d_3 in d_2 such that d_3 matches d_1; this is very close (up to simulation) to the relational projection, where $r_1 = \pi_A r_2$ if r_1 is equal to the fragment of r_2 obtained by

---

[2] Validity can be checked by algorithms proposed in [18][10][9]; these algorithms are polynomial in most practical cases.

discarding non-A attributes. This notion of projection for XML trees is a generalization of that introduced in [17], where leaf values are taken into account too.

Our correctness notion is *semantic*, in the sense that it depends on the semantics of queries and types rather than on a set of type-checking rules; this implies that errors are independent from the type-checking rules, so that our correctness notion can be adopted in any context and with any type language.

4 Type System

Our type system is a variation of the type systems shown in [18][10][9]. While those type systems focus on the detection of errors in a query wrt a source schema, this type system focuses on type inference.

4.1 Judgments and Type Rules

To infer the output type of a μXQ query, we adopt rules, shown in Tables 4 and 5, that prove judgments of the form $\Gamma \vdash Q : T$, where the environment Γ provides information about the types of Q free variables, while T is an upper bound for all possible values returned by Q, when evaluated under a valid substitution, that is an assignment of free variables that respects type constraint in Γ. Variable environments and valid substitutions are defined below.

Variable Environments $\Gamma ::= () \mid x : T, \Gamma \mid \overline{x} : T, \Gamma$

Table 4. Query Type Rules

(TYPEEMPTY)	(TYPEATOMIC)	(TYPEVAR)
$\dfrac{WF(\Gamma \vdash () : ())}{\Gamma \vdash () : ()}$	$\dfrac{WF(\Gamma \vdash b : B)}{\Gamma \vdash b : B}$	$\dfrac{\chi : T \in \Gamma \; WF(\Gamma \vdash \chi : T)}{\Gamma \vdash \chi : T}$

(TYPEELEM)	(TYPEFOREST)
$\dfrac{\Gamma \vdash Q : T}{\Gamma \vdash l[Q] : l[T]}$	$\dfrac{\Gamma \vdash Q_i : T_i \quad i = 1, 2}{\Gamma \vdash Q_1, Q_2 : T_1, T_2}$

(TYPELETWHERESPLITTING)
$$\dfrac{\Gamma \vdash Q_1 : T_1 \quad Split(T_1) = \{A_1, \ldots, A_n\} \quad \Gamma, x : A_i \vdash P \quad \Gamma, x : A_i \vdash Q_2 : U_i \quad i = 1 \ldots n}{\Gamma \vdash \mathtt{let}\ x ::= Q_1\ \mathtt{where}\ P\ \mathtt{return}\ Q_2 : U_1 \mid \ldots \mid U_n \mid ()}$$

(TYPEFORWHERE)
$$\dfrac{\Gamma \vdash Q_1 : T_1 \quad \Gamma \vdash \overline{x}\ \mathtt{in}\ T_1 \rightarrow Q_2\ \mathtt{where}\ P : T_2}{\Gamma \vdash \mathtt{for}\ \overline{x}\ \mathtt{in}\ Q_1\ \mathtt{where}\ P\ \mathtt{return}\ Q_2 : T_2 \mid ()}$$

(TYPELETSPLITTING)	(TYPEFOR)
$\dfrac{\Gamma \vdash Q_1 : T_1 \quad Split(T_1) = \{A_1, \ldots, A_n\} \quad \Gamma, x : A_i \vdash Q_2 : U_i \quad i = 1 \ldots n}{\Gamma \vdash \mathtt{let}\ x ::= Q_1\ \mathtt{return}\ Q_2 : U_1 \mid \ldots \mid U_n}$	$\dfrac{\Gamma \vdash Q_1 : T_1 \quad \Gamma \vdash \overline{x}\ \mathtt{in}\ T_1 \rightarrow Q_2\ \mathtt{where}\ \mathtt{true} : T_2}{\Gamma \vdash \mathtt{for}\ \overline{x}\ \mathtt{in}\ Q_1\ \mathtt{return}\ Q_2 : T_2}$

Table 5. Query Type Rules: Rules for Iteration, Child and Dos

---

(TYPEINEMPTY)

$$\frac{WF(\Gamma \vdash \overline{x} \text{ in } () \;\rightarrow\; Q \text{ where } P : ())}{\Gamma \vdash \overline{x} \text{ in } () \;\rightarrow\; Q \text{ where } P : ()}$$

(TYPEINUNION)

$$\frac{\Gamma \vdash \overline{x} \text{ in } T_i \;\rightarrow\; Q \text{ where } P : T_i' \quad i = 1, 2}{\Gamma \vdash \overline{x} \text{ in } T_1 \mid T_2 \;\rightarrow\; Q \text{ where } P : T_1' \mid T_2'}$$

(TYPEINTREE)

$$\frac{(T = m[T'] \vee T = B) \quad Split(T) = \{A_1, \ldots, A_n\}}{\Gamma, \overline{x} : A_i \vdash P \quad \Gamma, \overline{x} : A_i \vdash Q : U_i \quad i = 1 \ldots n}{\Gamma \vdash \overline{x} \text{ in } T \;\rightarrow\; Q \text{ where } P : U_1 \mid \ldots \mid U_n}$$

(TYPEINCONC)

$$\frac{\Gamma \vdash \overline{x} \text{ in } T_i \;\rightarrow\; Q \text{ where } P : T_i' \quad i = 1, 2}{\Gamma \vdash \overline{x} \text{ in } T_1, T_2 \;\rightarrow\; Q \text{ where } P : T_1', T_2'}$$

(TYPEINSTAR)

$$\frac{\Gamma \vdash \overline{x} \text{ in } T \;\rightarrow\; Q \text{ where } P : U}{\Gamma \vdash \overline{x} \text{ in } T* \;\rightarrow\; Q \text{ where } P : U*}$$

(TYPECHILD)

$$\frac{WF(\Gamma \vdash \overline{x} \text{ child} :: NodeTest : U)}{\overline{x} : T \in \Gamma \wedge (T = m[T''] \vee T = B)}{T' = \text{ if } T = m[T''] \text{ then } T'' \text{else } ()}{\vdash T' :: NodeTest \Rightarrow U}{\Gamma \vdash \overline{x} \text{ child} :: NodeTest : U}$$

(TYPEDOS)

$$\frac{WF(\Gamma \vdash \overline{x} \text{ dos} :: NodeTest : U)}{\overline{x} : T \in \Gamma \wedge (T = m[T''] \vee T = B)}{\{U_1, \ldots, U_n\} = \text{Trees}(T')}{U' = (U_1 \mid \ldots \mid U_n)*}{\vdash U' :: NodeTest \Rightarrow U}{\Gamma \vdash \overline{x} \text{ dos} :: NodeTest : U}$$

A variable environment Γ is well-formed if no variable is defined twice, and if every for-variable $\overline{x}$ (i.e., a variable bound by a $\mathtt{for}$ clause) is associated to a tree type ($l[T']$ or B).

Definition 5 (Valid Substitutions $\mathcal{R}(\Gamma)$). *For any well-formed environment Γ, we define the set of valid substitutions wrt Γ as follows:*

$$\mathcal{R}(\Gamma) = \{\rho \mid \chi \mapsto f \in \rho \Rightarrow (\chi : T \in \Gamma \wedge f \in [\![T]\!])\}$$

A first basis for a good level of precision is given by a particular technique we use to infer types for $\mathtt{for}$ queries. Given a query $\mathtt{for}\ \overline{x}\ \mathtt{in}\ Q_1\ \mathtt{return}\ Q_2$, in order to infer a type for it, the rules first infer a type T_1 for Q_1, and then they simulate a sort of abstract iteration over T_1, in order to type the body Q_2. This is done by means of the auxiliary judgment $\Gamma \vdash \overline{x} \text{ in } T_1 \;\rightarrow\; Q_2 : T_2$[3].

For example, if $T_1 = S_1, S_2$, to type $\mathtt{for}\ \overline{x}\ \mathtt{in}\ Q_1\ \mathtt{return}\ Q_2$ we recursively prove $\Gamma \vdash \overline{x} \text{ in } S_i \;\rightarrow\; Q_2 : S_i'$, for $i = 1, 2$, and then combine the results to obtain $T_2 = S_1', S_2'$. The recursive process is still purely structural for union and * types, and stops when a tree type is finally encountered.

Similar comments hold for queries with $\mathtt{where}$ conditions, where we use an auxiliary judgment $\Gamma \vdash \overline{x} \text{ in } T \;\rightarrow\; Q \text{ where } P : T$. Type correctness of $\mathtt{where}$ clauses is proved by rules over judgments $\Gamma \vdash P$ which are quite standard (and omitted in this abstract for reasons of space).

---

[3] This technique was first formalized in [19], where no properties about the system were proved.

More in details, case analysis for iterations is performed by (TYPEIN_) rules. In particular, termination is ensured by rule (TYPEINTREE), which stops the case-analysis, since a tree type $T=B$ or $T=m[T']$ is reached, inserts the assumption $\overline{x} : T$ in Γ, starts the analysis of the where condition P, and falls back to standard type-checking. Observe here that we use an operator $Split(T)$; for the moment just assume that $Split(T) = \{T\}$. Later we will modify this operator in order to improve precision of type inference. Rule (TYPELETSPLITTING) is standard, since we are assuming that $Split(T) = \{T\}$.

Rule (TYPECHILD) requires the type of $\overline{x}$ to be a tree type $m[T']$, and uses $\vdash T' ::$ $NodeTest \Rightarrow U$ to restrict the content type T' to the tree types with structure satisfying $NodeTest$. Rules to prove judgments $\vdash T' :: NodeTest \Rightarrow U$ are straightforward, and their meaning is stated in the following lemma.

Lemma 1 (Type Filtering Checking). *For any T* :

$$\vdash T :: NodeTest \Rightarrow U \iff \llbracket U \rrbracket = \{f :: NodeTest \mid f \in \llbracket T \rrbracket\}$$

Rule (TYPEDOS) is similar, and is strictly inspired by the technique adopted in the current W3C XQuery type system. Instead of using the content type T', it extracts all the node types $\{U_1, \ldots, U_n\}$ that are reachable from T, using the function $\mathrm{Trees}(T)$ defined later, and defines a new type $U' = (U_1 \mid \ldots \mid U_n)*$. U' is the type of any forest that contains only nodes whose type is one of the U_i's, hence is an appropriate type for the forest of all descendants of a tree of type T. The type of $\overline{x}$ dos $:: NodeTest$ is obtained by restricting U' to the tree types with structure satisfying $NodeTest$.

We can now define the auxiliary function $\mathrm{Trees}(T)$:

Definition 6 (Subtrees Type Extraction).

$$
\begin{aligned}
Trees(()) &\triangleq \emptyset & Trees(T, U) &\triangleq Trees(T) \cup Trees(U) \\
Trees(B) &\triangleq \{B\} & Trees(T*) &\triangleq Trees(T) \\
Trees(l[T]) &\triangleq \{l[T]\} \cup Trees(T) & Trees(T \mid U) &\triangleq Trees(T) \cup Trees(U)
\end{aligned}
$$

Lemma 2 (Soundness of DOS). *For any T* :

$$\{U_1, \ldots, U_n\} = Trees(T) \wedge U = (U_1 \mid \ldots \mid U_n)* \Rightarrow \forall f \in \llbracket T \rrbracket. \, dos(f) \in \llbracket U \rrbracket$$

4.2   Soundness of the Type System

We provisionally assumed that $Split(T) = \{T\}$, which results in a completely standard LET-RETURN type rule. This is sufficient to obtain the canonical 'soundness' property (Theorem 1): types are upper bounds for the set of all possible results.

Theorem 1 (Upper Bound). *For any well-formed Γ and query Q:*

$$\Gamma \vdash Q : U \wedge \rho \in \mathcal{R}(\Gamma) \Rightarrow \llbracket Q \rrbracket_\rho \in \llbracket U \rrbracket$$

The proof of this theorem is essentially the same as the one given in [18] [10], since considered XPath-like paths do not match the horizontal structure of sequences, so their typing does not depend on ordering.

This theorem is crucial to guarantee soundness of mapping correctness checking. Indeed, if Q is a mapping from $\mathcal{S}_i$ to $\mathcal{S}_j$, and $\Gamma \vdash Q : U$, then thanks to the above theorem, we can compare U wrt $\mathcal{S}_j$ in order to verify whether the semantics of Q conforms to $\mathcal{S}_j$. In the next section we will formalize how this comparison can be done in order to agree to the notion of mapping correctness (Definition 3).

The system cannot be made complete: as for any type system based on regular expression types, the presence of queries that may produce sets of trees that are not regular languages makes completeness impossible. However, we will see later how the precision of the type system may be improved, and why more precision is desirable in our context.

5 Correctness Checking

Definitions 3 and 4 describe our notion of mapping correctness, but they cannot directly be used to check whether a mapping is correct or not. To obtain a constructive definition, we need to switch from values to types.

Definition 7 (Type Projection). *Given two type T_1 and T_2, we say that T_1 is a projection of T_2 ($T_1 \lesssim T_2$) if and only if:* $\forall d_1 : T_1 \; \exists d_2 : T_2.d_1 \lesssim d_2$.

As for the value projection relation, the type projection relation is semantics, and states that a type T_1 is a projection of a type T_2 if, for each data instance d_1 conforming to T_1, there exists a data instance d_2 conforming to T_2 such that d_1 is a projection of d_2.

Type projection is quite different from standard subtyping, since it is based on the idea that $T_1 \lesssim T_2$ if T_1 matches a fragment of T_2, while $T_1 < T_2$ implies that T_1 is more specific than T_2.

To use type projection in mapping correctness checking, we must correlate type projection and mapping correctness. To this aim, we can rely on the result type of a query as inferred by our type system, as shown in the following theorem.

Theorem 2 (Completeness of Type Projection). *Given a mapping $m = \{q_k\}_k$ from $\mathcal{V}_i$ to $\mathcal{V}_j$, m is correct if $\forall q_k. \; \Gamma \vdash q_k : T$ and $T \lesssim \mathcal{V}_j$, where Γ is an environment obtained from $\mathcal{V}_i$.*

The previous theorem states that, if one can establish a projection relation between the inferred type and the target schema of a mapping, the correctness of the mapping is proved.

The type projection relation is still not operational, since its definition involves a universal quantification on the data instances of the source schema. To overcome this problem and obtain a practical way of checking type projection, we introduce the notion of *type approximation*. Type approximation weakens types by enriching base and element types with a union with the empty sequence type; this allows one to relate type projection to standard subtyping for unordered types, whose decidability has been proved in [20].

5.1 Type Approximation

Type approximation is based on the idea of weakening types by introducing unions with the empty sequence type.

Definition 8 (Type Approximation). *Given a type U, we indicate with $U^\lhd$ the type obtained by U just by replacing each subexpression U', corresponding to a tree type $l[\_]$ or B, with U'? (that is $(U' \mid ())$). Formally*

$$()^\lhd \triangleq () \qquad T \mid U^\lhd \triangleq T^\lhd \mid U^\lhd \qquad l[T]^\lhd \triangleq l[T^\lhd]?$$
$$B^\lhd \triangleq B? \qquad T, U^\lhd \triangleq T^\lhd, U^\lhd \qquad T*^\lhd \triangleq T^\lhd*$$

It is easy to prove that $T < T^\lhd$. To prove the main results about type approximation, we have to introduce the notion of *contexts*, whose grammar is shown below.

Contexts $C ::= x \mid () \mid C, C \mid l[C] \mid b$

A context is a partially specified forest, where variables indicate arbitrary forests. Variables are always assumed to be unique, and context instantiation is indicated as C_ρ, where ρ is a set of variable assignments $x \mapsto f$. We indicate with $C_{()}$ the forest obtained by C by replacing each variable with the empty sequence.

If we indicate with $f \simeq f'$ the fact that the two forests are equal up to ordering among children and values at leafs, we can state the following lemma.

Lemma 3. *Given two forests f_1 and f_2, the following relation holds:*

$$f_1 \lesssim f_2 \Leftrightarrow \exists C. \exists \rho.\ C_{()} \simeq f_1 \wedge f_2 \simeq C_\rho$$

The following theorem correlates $T^\lhd$ with T.

Theorem 3.
$$T^\lhd \lesssim T$$

Lemma 4. *For each type U:*

1. $\forall f : U^\lhd.\ (f \neq () \Rightarrow \exists C,\ \rho,\ f' : U.\ C_{()} = f \wedge f' = C_\rho)$
2. $\forall f : U, C, \rho.\ (f = C_\rho \Rightarrow C_{()} : U^\lhd)$
3. $\forall C.\ (C_{()} \neq () \wedge C_{()} : U^\lhd \Rightarrow \exists f : U. \exists \rho.\ f = C_\rho)$

The previous lemma serves to prove the following main theorem.

Theorem 4 (Type Projection as Sub-typing).

$$T \lesssim U \Leftrightarrow T < U^\lhd$$

The previous theorem states that type projection between T and U can be checked by weakening U and, then, by checking for the existence of a subtyping relation between T and $U^\lhd$. This theorem proves the decidability of type projection, since decidability of subtyping for a superset of our type language has been proved in [20]. For what concerns the complexity of type projection, we recently proved that, for our type language, type projection can be checked in polynomial type, hence making our maintenance approach more effective.

5.2 Improving Precision of Type Inference

As already observed, inferred types cannot precisely capture query semantics. However, there is some space for gaining more precision, which implies less false-negative in checking mapping correctness. This is typical of every approach based on result analysis, including those of languages of the XDuce family.

As shown in [18][10], by tuning the operator $Split(T)$, we may improve the precision of the type system. Under the assumption $Split(T) = \{T\}$, the presented type system is not precise enough when, for example, there are variables that occur more than once (*non-linear* variables) and with a union type. For example, consider the (artificial) type $X = data[mbl[]+ \mid phn[]+]$, and the sequence query $(x/mbl, x/phn)$. When x has type X, this query yields either a sequence of elements $mbl[]$ or a sequence of elements $phn[]$. Instead, as in XQuery, our type system infers a type $(mbl[]*, phn[]*)$, which also contains sequences with both $mbl[]$ and $phn[]$ elements. If this type is compared with $(mbl[]* \mid phn[]*)$, in order to check whether the query output conforms to this expected type, the checking will fail thus producing a false negative.

We solve these problems by using in the rules a finer $Split()$ function, which produces more precise types. For example, if the input type $X = data[mbl[]+ \mid phn[]+]$ is split in the two types $data[mbl[]+]$ and $data[phn[]+]$, and, then, two separate analysis are performed, we obtain the types $data[mbl[]*]$ and $data[phn[]*]$. Then the query type is the union of these two types, and thus a subtype of the previous expected type, thus avoiding a false negative.

The definition of $Split(T)$ is non-trivial in the presence of recursive types. In [18][10] we propose a solution that works under a mild restrictions over the use of recursion. Here, we propose the same definitions without making any restriction as recursive types have already been excluded.

Definition 9 (*Split(T)*).

$$
\begin{array}{ll}
Split(()) \triangleq \{()\} & Split(T \mid U) \triangleq Split(T) \cup Split(U) \\
Split(B) \triangleq \{B\} & Split(l[T]) \triangleq \{l[A] \mid A \in Split(T)\} \\
Split(U*) \triangleq \{U*\} & Split(T, U) \triangleq \{(A, B) \mid A \in Split(T) \wedge B \in Split(U)\}
\end{array}
$$

Splitting stops when a *-type is met. As shown in [10], this ensures acceptable complexity for a very wide class of cases, while ensuring good precision at the same time, as in schemas most union types are the form $(T \mid U)*$, which are not split.

To have an idea of the precision that we gain by splitting, we have that a query Q without where conditions always evaluates to (), under well-typed substitutions, if and only if its inferred type is (); as shown in [10], this does not hold without splitting. As a second example, the reader can run the rules over Example 1, and realize that the inferred type is quite precise and is a projection of the target type.

To conclude, since we are considering non recursive types, we believe that an alternative typing for $\overline{x}$ dos :: *NodeTest* expressions, based on the abstract execution of the descendant-or-self operator over the type bound to $\overline{x}$, by possibly using splitting, may further improve precision. We leave this issue as future work.

6 Related Work

To the best of our knowledge, the only alternative technique for detecting corrupted mappings in XML p2p systems is the one described in [9]. We have already discussed differences between the present approach and that work. Other works on p2p systems [16] [5] do not address the problem of checking mapping correctness: they always assume mappings to be correct, with a correctness notion very close to our semantic correctness. Starting from correct mappings, [16] proposes a correct and complete query answering algorithm for p2p data integration systems.

Our type system is a variation of the type systems of [10] and [9], obtained by dropping error-checking in favor of a better precision in type inference. In these works we have already outlined advantages of these type systems wrt to the W3C XQuery type system [21].

7 Conclusions and Future Work

This paper presented a novel technique for detecting corrupted mappings in XML p2p data integration systems. This technique can be used in any context where a schema mapping approach is used, and it is based on a semantic notion of mapping correctness, unrelated to the query transformation algorithms being used. This form of correctness works on the ability of a mapping to satisfy the target schema, and it is independent from queries.

To check mapping correctness, we introduced a notion of type projection for XML types. By reducing type projection to standard subtyping among weakened types, it follows that type projection is decidable [20]. We recently proved that type projection can be checked in polynomial time.

We proved that mapping correctness can be reduced to type projection between the inferred result type of the mapping and the target schema, and showed that our approach is *complete*, i.e., all errors will be detected. To decrease false negatives, we augment the precision of type inference through type splitting.

Although this work is not in its infancy, much work remains to do as it forms the basis for a massive future work. In particular, we plan, in the near future, to implement this technique in a centralized, logical p2p system, so to verify its applicability in a background maintenance activity. Finally, we plan to enrich our approach with some form of *self-healing* technique, so to suggest to the user possible corrections for any detected wrong mapping.

References

1. Dabek, F., Brunskill, E., Kaashoek, M.F., Karger, D.R., Morris, R., Stoica, I., Balakrishnan, H.: Building peer-to-peer systems with chord, a distributed lookup service. In: HotOS. (2001) 81–86
2. : (The FreePastry System. www.cs.rice.edu/cs/systems/pastry/freepastry/)
3. Boag, S., Chamberlin, D., Fernandez, M.F., Florescu, D., Robie, J., Siméon, J.: XQuery 1.0: An XML Query Language. Technical report, World Wide Web Consortium (2003) W3C Working Draft.

4. Halevy, A.Y., Ives, Z.G., Mork, P., Tatarinov, I.: Piazza: data management infrastructure for semantic web applications. In: Proceedings of the Twelfth International World Wide Web Conference, WWW2003, Budapest, Hungary, 20-24 May 2003, ACM (2003) 556–567

5. Franconi, E., Kuper, G.M., Lopatenko, A., Zaihrayeu, I.: Queries and updates in the codb peer to peer database system. In: VLDB. (2004) 1277–1280

6. Goasdoué, F., Rousset, M.C.: Answering queries using views: A krdb perspective for the semantic web. ACM Trans. Internet Techn. **4** (2004) 255–288

7. Ullman, J.D.: Principles of Database and Knowledge-Base Systems, Volume I. Computer Science Press (1988)

8. Ullman, J.D.: Principles of Database and Knowledge-Base Systems, Volume II. Computer Science Press (1989)

9. Colazzo, D., Sartiani, C.: Typechecking Queries for Maintaining Schema Mappings in XML P2P Databases. In: Proceedings of the 3th Workshop on Programming Language Technologies for XML (Plan-X), in conjunction with POPL 2005. (2005)

10. Colazzo, D., Ghelli, G., Manghi, P., Sartiani, C.: Types for Path Correctness of XML Queries. In: Proceedings of the 2004 International Conference on Functional Programming (ICFP), Snowbird, Utah, September 19-22, 2004. (2004)

11. Abiteboul, S., Manolescu, I., Preda, N.: Sharing Content in Structured P2P Networks. Technical report, INRIA (2005)

12. Tatarinov, I.: Semantic Data Sharing with a Peer Data Management System. PhD thesis, University of Washington (2004)

13. Tatarinov, I., Halevy, A.Y.: Efficient query reformulation in peer-data management systems. In: SIGMOD Conference. (2004) 539–550

14. Madhavan, J., Halevy, A.Y.: Composing mappings among data sources. In: VLDB. (2003) 572–583

15. Hosoya, H., Pierce, B.C.: XDuce: An XML Processing Language (1999) Preliminary Report.

16. Calvanese, D., Giacomo, G.D., Lenzerini, M., Rosati, R.: Logical foundations of peer-to-peer data integration. In: PODS. (2004) 241–251

17. Marian, A., Siméon, J.: Projecting xml documents. In: VLDB. (2003) 213–224

18. Colazzo, D.: Path Correctness for XML Queries: Characterization and Static Type Checking. PhD thesis, Dipartimento di Informatica, Università di Pisa (2004)

19. Fernandez, M., Siméon, J., Wadler, P.: A Semi-monad for Semi-structured Data. In: ICDT. (2001) 263–300

20. Dal-Zilio, S., Lugiez, D., Meyssonnier, C.: A logic you can count on. In Jones, N.D., Leroy, X., eds.: POPL, ACM (2004) 135–146

21. Draper, D., Fankhauser, P., Fernandez, M., Malhotra, A., Rose, K., Rys, M., Siméon, J., Wadler, P.: XQuery 1.0 and XPath 2.0 Formal Semantics. Technical report, World Wide Web Consortium (2005) W3C Working Draft.

22. Benzaken, V., Castagna, G., Frisch, A.: Cduce: an xml-centric general-purpose language. In: ICFP. (2003) 51–63

Inconsistency Tolerance in P2P Data Integration: An Epistemic Logic Approach

Diego Calvanese[1], Giuseppe De Giacomo[2], Domenico Lembo[2],
Maurizio Lenzerini[2], and Riccardo Rosati[2]

[1] Faculty of Computer Science, Free University of Bolzano/Bozen,
Piazza Domenicani 3, I-39100 Bolzano, Italy
`calvanese@inf.unibz.it`
[2] Dipartimento di Informatica e Sistemistica,
Università di Roma "La Sapienza",
Via Salaria 113, 00198 Roma, Italy
`{degiacomo, lembo, lenzerini, rosati}@dis.uniroma1.it`

Abstract. We study peer-to-peer data integration, where each peer models an
autonomous system that exports data in terms of its own schema, and data in-
teroperation is achieved by means of mappings among the peer schemas, rather
than through a global schema. We propose a multi-modal epistemic semantics
based on the idea that each peer is conceived as a rational agent that exchanges
knowledge/belief with other peers, thus nicely modeling the modular structure of
the system. We then address the issue of dealing with possible inconsistencies,
and distinguish between two types of inconsistencies, called local and P2P, respectively. We define a nonmonotonic extension of our logic that is able to reason
on the beliefs of peers under inconsistency tolerance. Tolerance to local inconsistency essentially means that the presence of inconsistency within one peer does
not affect the consistency of the whole system. Tolerance to P2P inconsistency
means being able to resolve inconsistencies arising from the interaction between
peers. We study query answering and its data complexity in this setting, and we
present an algorithm that is sound and complete with respect to the proposed
semantics, and optimal with respect to worst-case complexity.

1 Introduction

In this paper we study data integration in a peer-to-peer (P2P) architecture. In a P2P data
integration system (P2PDIS), each peer is an autonomous information system providing
part of the overall information available from a distributed environment, and acts both
as a client and as a server. Information integration in these systems does not rely on
a single global view (as in traditional data integration [22]): instead, it is achieved by
establishing mappings between peers, and by exploiting such mappings to collect and
merge data from the various peers when answering user queries.

P2P data integration has been the subject of several investigations in the last years.
Recent papers focused on providing techniques for evolving from basic P2P networks supporting only file exchanges to more complex systems like schema-based
P2P networks, capable of supporting the exchange of structured contents. From papers like [19,4,18,10,16,27] the idea of peer data management emerges: every peer is

G. Bierman and C. Koch (Eds.): DBPL 2005, LNCS 3774, pp. 90–105, 2005.

characterized by a schema that represents the domain of interest from the peer perspective, and is equipped with mappings to other peers [25], each mapping providing a semantic relationship between pairs of peers. Data integration in such systems is typically virtual: data stored in one peer is not replicated in other peers, and when a query is posed to a peer, query processing is done by both looking at local data, and collecting relevant data from other peers according to the mappings. Cycles in the mappings pose challenging problems, and various proposals have been put forward to deal with them. For example, in [10], an epistemic semantics is proposed that weakens the usual first-order semantics of mappings, and allows for both a better modeling of the modular structure of the system, and decidable (even polynomially tractable w.r.t. data complexity) query answering. Some papers look at peer data management under the perspective of exchanging data between peers. Peers are again interconnected by means of mappings, but in this case, the focus is on materializing the data flowing from one peer to another [14,2].

In this paper we are interested in virtual P2P data integration, and thus we do not deal with the issue of materializing exchanged data. In particular, we aim at addressing an important problem that is still unexplored in P2P data integration, namely inconsistency tolerance, i.e., how to deal with inconsistencies in the data stored by the peers.

The problem of dealing with inconsistency has been addressed in several research projects both in the context of a single database, and in the context of traditional data integration. This problem is closely related to the studies in *belief revision and update* [1,15], which deal with the problem of integrating new information with previous knowledge. In the context of databases, the underlying theory takes the form of a database schema, and the revision process focuses on data. Thus, research in this setting often concentrates on specialized algorithmic and complexity results for this case. The general goal is to provide informative answers even when a database that does not satisfy its integrity constraints (see, for example, [3,8]). Most of these papers rely on the notion of repair as introduced in [3]: a repair of a database is a new database that satisfies the constraints in the schema, and minimally differs from the original one.

The above results are not specifically tailored to the case of different consistent sources that are mutually inconsistent, which is the case of interest in data integration. More recently, some papers (see, e.g., [9,6]) have tackled data inconsistency in a data integration setting, where the basic idea is to apply the repairs to data retrieved from the sources, again according to some minimality criteria. To the best of our knowledge, the only paper that deals with inconsistencies in P2P architectures is [5]. That approach is based on the notion of "solution" for a peer P, i.e., an instance for the peer database schema that respects both the mappings and the trust relationships that P has with other peers, and stays as close as possible to the available data in the system. This mechanism characterizes how each peer locally repairs data collected from other peers. On the converse, we provide here a formal semantics to the whole P2PDIS which does not rely on a particular repairing strategy adopted by the peers.

In this paper we follow the approach of [10] and study its extension as follows:

- We want to stress the modularity of P2P architectures, i.e., the fact that each peer is autonomous. To this end, we formalize a P2P data integration system in terms of a multi-modal epistemic logic, namely $K45_n$, where each peer is modeled as a rational agent that exchanges knowledge/belief with other peers. This is in line with the idea of modeling a distributed information system in terms of multi-agent modal logic [13]. Our formalization nicely models the modular structure of the system, without resorting to any assumptions, such as acyclicity, on its topology.

- We want our semantics to be inconsistency tolerant in two ways. First, we want a P2PDIS to be able to "isolate" peers that are locally inconsistent, i.e., that contain inconsistent data. Second, we aim at a system that is tolerant to P2P inconsistency, i.e., is able to repair inconsistent data coming from different peers. In order to deal with both types of tolerance, we introduce a novel nonmonotonic epistemic logic, called $K45_n^A$, which extends $K45_n$ with nonmonotonic modal operators. Within this logic, we represent a P2PDIS in which each locally inconsistent peer is isolated, and each other peer on the one hand, believes its own data, and, on the other hand, maximizes information coming from other peers, but without falling into inconsistency.

- Finally, we aim at designing a distributed query answering algorithm in the line of the one proposed in [10]. Indeed, we present an algorithm that is sound and complete with respect to our $K45_n^A$-formalization of P2PDISs, thus showing that query answering is decidable. More precisely, under reasonable assumptions on the reasoning capabilities of each peer, our algorithm works in coNP data complexity (i.e., the complexity with respect to the size of the data at the peer sources). We also observe that the problem is coNP-hard already for very simple peer theories, thus showing that our technique is optimal with respect to worst-case complexity.

The paper is organized as follows. In Section 2 we introduce the P2PDIS framework. In Section 3 we model the framework in terms of the multi-modal epistemic logic $K45_n$. In Section 4 we present $K45_n^A$, and use it for handling inconsistency. In Section 5 we provide a sound and complete query answering technique, and establish computational complexity of query answering. In Section 6 we conclude the paper.

2 Framework

In our work, we use the framework for peer-to-peer (P2P) data integration presented in [10], which is briefly described in this section.

We refer to a fixed, infinite, denumerable set Γ of constants. Such constants are shared by all peers, and denote the data items managed by the P2PDIS. Moreover, given a relational alphabet A, we denote with $\mathcal{L}_A$ the set of function-free first-order logic (FOL) formulas whose relation symbols are in A and whose constants are in Γ.

A *P2P data integration system* $\mathcal{P} = \{P_1, \ldots, P_n\}$ is constituted by a set of n peers. Each peer $P_i \in \mathcal{P}$ (cf. [19]) is defined as a tuple $P_i = (id, G, S, L, M, \mathcal{L})$, where:

- id is a symbol that identifies the peer P_i within $\mathcal{P}$, called the identifier of P_i.
- G is the *schema* of P_i, which is a finite set of formulas of $\mathcal{L}_{A_G}$ (representing local integrity constraints), where A_G is a relational alphabet (disjoint from the other alphabets in $\mathcal{P}$) called the *alphabet* of P_i. We assume that the language $\mathcal{L}_{A_G}$ of peer P_i includes the special sentence $\perp_i$ that is false in every interpretation for

$\mathcal{L}_{A_G}$. Intuitively, the peer schema provides an intensional view of the information managed by the peer.

- S is the *(local) source schema* of P_i, which is simply a finite relational alphabet (again disjoint from the other alphabets in $\mathcal{P}$), called the *local alphabet* of P_i. Intuitively, the source schema describes the structure of the data sources of the peer (possibly obtained by wrapping physical sources), i.e., the sources where the real data managed by the peer are stored.

- L is a set of *(local) mapping assertions* between G and S. Each local mapping assertion is an expression of the form $cq_S \rightsquigarrow cq_G$, where cq_S and cq_G are two conjunctive queries of the same arity, respectively over the source schema S and over the peer schema G. The local mapping assertions establish the connection between the elements of the source schema and those of the peer schema in P_i. In particular, an assertion of the form $cq_S \rightsquigarrow cq_G$ specifies that all the data satisfying the query cq_S over the sources also satisfy the concept in the peer schema represented by the query cq_G. In the terminology used in data integration, the combination of peer schema, source schema, and local mapping assertions constitutes a GLAV *data integration system* [22] managing a set of sound data sources S defined in terms of a (virtual) global schema G.

- M is a set of *P2P mapping assertions*, which specify the semantic relationships that the peer P_i has with the other peers. Each assertion in M is an expression of the form $cq' \rightsquigarrow cq$, where cq, called the *head* of the assertion, is a conjunctive query over the peer (schema of) P_i, while cq', called the *tail* of the assertion, is a conjunctive query of the same arity as cq over (the schema of) one of the other peers in $\mathcal{P}$. A P2P mapping assertion $cq' \rightsquigarrow cq$ from peer P_j to peer P_i expresses the fact that the P_j-concept represented by cq' is mapped to the P_i-concept represented by cq. From an extensional point of view, the assertion specifies that every tuple that can be retrieved from P_j by issuing query cq' satisfies cq in P_i. Observe that no limitation is imposed on the topology of the whole set of P2P mapping assertions in the system $\mathcal{P}$, and hence, as in [10], the set of all P2P mappings may be cyclic.

- $\mathcal{L}$ is a relational query language specifying the class of queries that the peer P_i can process. We assume that $\mathcal{L}$ is any fragment of FOL that accepts at least conjunctive queries and the sentence $\bot_i$. We say that the queries in $\mathcal{L}$ are those *accepted by* P_i. Notice that this implies that, for each P2P mapping assertion $cq' \rightsquigarrow cq$ from another peer P_j to peer P_i in M, we have that cq' is accepted by P_j.

An *extension* for a P2PDIS $\mathcal{P} = \{P_1, \ldots, P_2\}$ is a set $\mathcal{D} = \{D_1, \ldots, D_n\}$, where each D_i is an extension of the predicates in the local source schema of peer P_i.

A P2PDIS, together with an extension, is intended to be queried by external users. A user enquires the whole system by accessing any peer P of $\mathcal{P}$, and by issuing a *query q* to P. The query q is processed by P if and only if q is expressed over the schema of P and is accepted by P.

Example 1. Let us consider the P2PDIS in Figure 1, in which we have 4 peers P_1, P_2, P_3, and P_4 (in the following, we assume that each peer P_i is identified by i).

The global schema of peer P_1 is formed by a relation schema Person₁(name, livesIn, citizenship), where name is the key (we underline the key

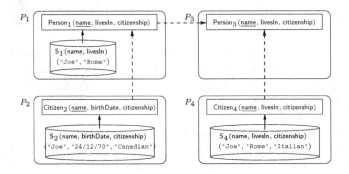

Fig. 1. A P2P system

of a relation). P_1 contains a local source $S_1(\text{name}, \text{livesIn})$, mapped to the global view by the assertion $\{x, y \mid S_1(x, y)\} \rightsquigarrow \{x, y \mid \exists z. \text{Person}_1(x, y, z)\}$. Moreover, it has a P2P mapping assertion $\{x, z \mid \exists y. \text{Citizen}_2(x, y, z)\} \rightsquigarrow \{x, z \mid \exists y. \text{Person}_1(x, y, z)\}$ relating information in peer P_2 to those in peer P_1.

P_2 has $\text{Citizen}_2(\underline{\text{name}}, \text{birthDate}, \text{citizenship})$ as global schema, and a local source $S_2(\text{name}, \text{birthDate}, \text{citizenship})$ mapped to the global schema through the local mapping $\{x, y, z \mid S_2(x, y, z)\} \rightsquigarrow \{x, y, z \mid \text{Citizen}_2(x, y, z)\}$. P_2 has no P2P mappings.

P_3 has $\text{Person}_3(\underline{\text{name}}, \text{livesIn}, \text{citizenship})$ as global schema, contains no local sources, and has a P2P mapping $\{x, y, z \mid \text{Person}_1(x, y, z)\} \rightsquigarrow \{x, y, z \mid \text{Person}_3(x, y, z)\}$ with P_1, and a P2P mapping $\{x, y, z \mid \text{Citizen}_4(x, y, z)\} \rightsquigarrow \{x, y, z \mid \text{Person}_3(x, y, z)\}$ with P_4.

P_4 has $\text{Citizen}_4(\underline{\text{name}}, \text{livesIn}, \text{citizenship})$ as global schema, and a local source $S_4(\text{name}, \text{livesIn}, \text{citizenship})$ mapped to the global schema through the local mapping $\{x, y, z \mid S_4(x, y, z)\} \rightsquigarrow \{x, y, z \mid \text{Citizen}_4(x, y, z)\}$. P_4 has no P2P mappings.

Finally, Figure 1 shows also an extension of the P2P data integration system, which includes $S_1(\text{"Joe"}, \text{"Rome"})$, $S_2(\text{"Joe"}, \text{"24/12/70"}, \text{"Canadian"})$, and $S_4(\text{"Joe"}, \text{"Rome"}, \text{"Italian"})$.

3   Multi-modal Epistemic Formalization

In this section we present a logical formalization of P2PDISs of the kind described above. Although one possible choice for formalizing such systems is classical first order logic, it was argued in [10] that using epistemic logic brings several advantages. However, while [10] resorted to epistemic logic with a single modal operator, here we use a multi-modal epistemic logic, based on the premise that each peer in the system can be seen as a rational agent. Furthermore, we move from the modal logic of knowledge/belief $S5$ to the modal logic $K45$ [11,23]. More precisely, the formalization we provide in this section, is based on $K45_n$, the multi-modal version of $K45$.

The language $\mathcal{L}(K45_n)$ of $K45_n$ is obtained from first-order logic by adding a set $\mathbf{K}_1, \ldots, \mathbf{K}_n$ of modal operators, for the forming rule: if ϕ is a (possibly open) formula, then also $\mathbf{K}_i\phi$ is so, for $1 \leq i \leq n$ for a fixed n. In $K45_n$, each modal operator is used to formalize the epistemic state of a different agent. Informally, the formula $\mathbf{K}_i\phi$ should be read as "ϕ is known to hold by the agent i". In fact, in $K45_n$, we do not have that what is known by an agent must hold in the real world: the agent can have inaccurate knowledge of what is true, i.e., believe something to be true although in reality it is false. Often this kind of knowledge is referred to as belief. On the other hand, $K45_n$ states that the agent has complete information on what it knows, i.e., if agent i knows ϕ then it knows of knowing ϕ, and if agent i does not know ϕ, then it knows that it does not know ϕ. In other words, the following assertions hold for every $K45_n$ formula ϕ:

$$\mathbf{K_i}\phi \supset \mathbf{K_i}(\mathbf{K_i}\phi) \quad \text{known as the axiom schema 4}$$
$$\neg\mathbf{K_i}\phi \supset \mathbf{K_i}(\neg\mathbf{K_i}\phi) \quad \text{known as the axiom schema 5}$$

To define the semantics of $K45_n$, we start from first-order interpretations. In particular, we restrict our attention to first-order interpretations that share a fixed infinite domain Δ. We further assume that for each domain element $d \in \Delta$, we have a unique constant $c_d \in \Gamma$ that denotes exactly d, and, vice versa, that every constant $c_d \in \Gamma$ denotes exactly one domain element $d \in \Delta^1$.

Formulas of $K45_n$ are interpreted over $K45_n$-structures. A $K45_n$-*structure* is a Kripke structure E of the form $(W, \{R_1, \ldots R_n\}, V)$, where: W is a set whose elements are called *possible worlds*; V is a function assigning to each $w \in W$ a first-order interpretation $V(w)$; and each R_i, called the *accessibility relation* for the modality $\mathbf{K_i}$, is a binary relation over W, with the following constraints:

if $(w_1, w_2) \in R_i$ and $(w_2, w_3) \in R_i$ then $(w_1, w_3) \in R_i$, i.e., R_i is transitive
if $(w_1, w_2) \in R_i$ and $(w_1, w_3) \in R_i$ then $(w_2, w_3) \in R_i$, i.e., R_i is euclidean

A $K45_n$-*interpretation* is a pair (E, w), where $E = (W, \{R_1, \ldots R_n\}, V)$ is a $K45_n$-structure, and w is a world in W. A sentence (i.e., a closed formula) ϕ *is true in an interpretation* (E, w) (or, is true on world $w \in W$ in E), written $E, w \models \phi$ iff:[2]

$$\begin{aligned}
E, w &\models P(c_1, \ldots, c_n) &&\text{iff} \quad V(w) \models P(c_1, \ldots, c_n) \\
E, w &\models \phi_1 \wedge \phi_2 &&\text{iff} \quad E, w \models \phi_1 \text{ and } E, w \models \phi_2 \\
E, w &\models \neg\phi &&\text{iff} \quad E, w \not\models \phi \\
E, w &\models \exists x. \psi &&\text{iff} \quad E, w \models \psi_c^x \text{ for some constant } c \\
E, w &\models \mathbf{K_i}\phi &&\text{iff} \quad E, w' \models \phi \text{ for every } w' \text{ such that } (w, w') \in R_i
\end{aligned}$$

We say that a sentence ϕ is *satisfiable* if there exists a $K45_n$-*model* for ϕ, i.e., a $K45_n$-interpretation E, w such that $E, w \models \phi$, *unsatisfiable* otherwise. A *model* for a set Σ of sentences is a model for every sentence in Σ. A sentence ϕ is *logically implied* by a set Σ of sentences, written $\Sigma \models_{K45_n} \phi$, if and only if in every $K45_n$-model E, w of Σ, we have that $E, w \models \phi$.

Notice that, since each accessibility relation of a $K45_n$-structure is transitive and Euclidean, all instances of axiom schemas 4 and 5 are satisfied in every $K45_n$-interpretation, whereas no instance of the axiom schema ($\mathbf{K_i}\phi \supset \phi$) is so.

---

[1] In other words, the constants in Γ act as *standard names* [23].
[2] We have used ψ_c^x to denote the formula obtained from ψ by substituting each free occurrence of the variable x with the constant c.

Due to the characteristics mentioned above, $K45_n$ is well-suited to formalize P2PDISs of the kind presented in Section 2. Let $\mathcal{P} = \{P_1, \ldots, P_n\}$ be a P2PDIS in which each peer P_i has identifier i. For each peer $P_i = (i, G, S, L, M, \mathcal{L})$ we define the theory $\mathcal{T}_K(P_i)$ in $K45_n$ as the union of the following sentences:

- Global schema G of P_i: for each sentence ϕ in G, we have

$$\mathbf{K_i}\phi$$

  Observe that ϕ is a first-order sentence expressed in the alphabet of P_i, which is disjoint from the alphabets of all the other peers in $\mathcal{P}$.
- Local mapping assertions L between G and the local source schema S: for each mapping assertion $\{\mathbf{x} \mid \exists \mathbf{y}.\, body_{cq_S}(\mathbf{x}, \mathbf{y})\} \rightsquigarrow \{\mathbf{x} \mid \exists \mathbf{z}.\, body_{cq_G}(\mathbf{x}, \mathbf{z})\}$ in L, we have

$$\mathbf{K_i}(\forall \mathbf{x}.\, \exists \mathbf{y}.\, body_{cq_S}(\mathbf{x}, \mathbf{y}) \supset \exists \mathbf{z}.\, body_{cq_G}(\mathbf{x}, \mathbf{z}))$$

- P2P mapping assertions M: for each P2P mapping assertion $\{\mathbf{x} \mid \exists \mathbf{y}.\, body_{cq_j}(\mathbf{x}, \mathbf{y})\} \rightsquigarrow \{\mathbf{x} \mid \exists \mathbf{z}.\, body_{cq_i}(\mathbf{x}, \mathbf{z})\}$ between the peer j and the peer i in M, we have

$$\forall \mathbf{x}.\, \mathbf{K_j}(\exists \mathbf{y}.\, body_{cq_j}(\mathbf{x}, \mathbf{y})) \supset \mathbf{K_i}(\exists \mathbf{z}.\, body_{cq_i}(\mathbf{x}, \mathbf{z})) \tag{1}$$

  In words, this sentence specifies the following rule: for each tuple of values $\mathbf{t}$, if peer j knows the sentence $\exists \mathbf{y}.\, body_{cq_j}(\mathbf{t}, \mathbf{y})$, then peer i knows the sentence $\exists \mathbf{z}.\, body_{cq_i}(\mathbf{t}, \mathbf{z})$ holds.

We denote by $\mathcal{T}_K(\mathcal{P})$ the theory corresponding to the P2PDIS $\mathcal{P}$, i.e., $\mathcal{T}_K(\mathcal{P}) = \bigcup_{i=1,\ldots,n} \mathcal{T}_K(P_i)$.

Example 2. We provide now the formalization of the P2PDIS of Example 1. The theory $\mathcal{T}_K(P_1)$ modeling peer P_1 is the conjunction of:

$\mathbf{K_1}(\forall x, y, y', z, z'.\, \mathsf{Person}_1(x, y, z) \wedge \mathsf{Person}_1(x, y', z') \supset y = y' \wedge z = z')$
$\mathbf{K_1}(\forall x, y.\, \mathsf{S}_1(x, y) \supset \exists z.\, \mathsf{Person}_1(x, y, z))$
$\forall x, z.\, \mathbf{K_2}(\exists y.\, \mathsf{Citizen}_2(x, y, z)) \supset \mathbf{K_1}(\exists y.\, \mathsf{Person}_1(x, y, z))$

The theory $\mathcal{T}_K(P_2)$ modeling peer P_2 is the conjunction of:

$\mathbf{K_2}(\forall x, y, y', z, z'.\, \mathsf{Citizen}_2(x, y, z) \wedge \mathsf{Citizen}_2(x, y', z') \supset y = y' \wedge z = z')$
$\mathbf{K_2}(\forall x, y, z.\, \mathsf{S}_2(x, y, z) \supset \mathsf{Citizen}_2(x, y, z))$

The theory $\mathcal{T}_K(P_3)$ modeling peer P_3 is the conjunction of:

$\mathbf{K_3}(\forall x, y, y', z, z'.\, \mathsf{Person}_3(x, y, z) \wedge \mathsf{Person}_3(x, y', z') \supset y = y' \wedge z = z')$
$\forall x, y.\, \mathbf{K_1}(\exists z.\, \mathsf{Person}_1(x, z, y)) \supset \mathbf{K_3}\exists z.\, \mathsf{Person}_3(x, z, y)$
$\forall x, y, z.\, \mathbf{K_4}(\mathsf{Citizen}_4(x, y, z)) \supset \mathbf{K_3}\mathsf{Person}_3(x, y, z)$

The theory $\mathcal{T}_K(P_4)$ modeling peer P_4 is the conjunction of:

$\mathbf{K_4}(\forall x, y, y', z, z'.\, \mathsf{Citizen}_4(x, y, z) \wedge \mathsf{Citizen}_4(x, y', z') \supset y = y' \wedge z = z')$
$\mathbf{K_4}(\forall x, y, z.\, \mathsf{S}_4(x, y, z) \supset \mathsf{Citizen}_4(x, y, z))$

The extension $\mathcal{D} = \{D_1, \ldots, D_n\}$ of a P2PDIS $\mathcal{P}$ is modeled as a sentence constituted by the conjunction of all facts corresponding to the tuples stored in the sources, i.e., $DB(\mathcal{D}) = \bigwedge_{i=1}^{n} DB(D_i)$ where $DB(D_i) = \mathbf{K_i}(\bigwedge_{t \in r^{D_i}} r(t))$.

A client of the P2PDIS interacts with one of the peers, say peer P_i, posing a *query* to it. A query q is an open formula $q(\mathbf{x})$ with free variables $\mathbf{x}$ expressed in the language accepted by the peer P_i (we recall that such a language is a subset of first-order logic). The semantics of a query $q \in \mathcal{L}$ posed to a peer $P_i = (i, G, S, L, M, \mathcal{L})$ of $\mathcal{P}$ with respect to an extension $\mathcal{D}$ is defined as the set of tuples $ANS_{K45_n}(q, i, \mathcal{P}, \mathcal{D}) = \{\mathbf{t} \mid \mathcal{T}_K(\mathcal{P}) \cup DB(\mathcal{D}) \models_{K45_n} \mathbf{K_i} q(\mathbf{t})\}$, where $q(\mathbf{t})$ denotes the sentence obtained from the open formula $q(\mathbf{x})$ by replacing all occurrences of the free variables in $\mathbf{x}$ with the corresponding constants in $\mathbf{t}$.

Interestingly, our current formalization extends the one in [10] in two ways. First, we have moved to multi-modal epistemic logic, so as to model each peer as an autonomous agent. Second, we have moved from *S5* to *K45*, hence dropping the assumption that what is believed by an agent is actually true. These modifications set the stage for the treatment of inconsistencies to be presented next.

4   Inconsistency Tolerance

We now modify our basic framework so as to be able to handle inconsistency. In particular, we want the P2PDIS to be inconsistency-tolerant in the following sense:

1. When a peer is *locally inconsistent*, i.e., data at the sources in P_i contradict, via the local mapping, the peer schema, making the whole peer inconsistent, the P2PDIS should be equivalent to the one obtained by eliminating the peer P_i from the system. In other words, an inconsistent peer should be "isolated" from the other peers: in this way, a local inconsistency does not affect the overall consistency (and meaning) of the system. The choice of isolating locally inconsistent peers is motivated by the modularity of P2PDISs pursued by our approach, in which each peer is considered as a black box. Of course, the study of inconsistency might be also interesting in an alternative setting not focused on modularity. However, this is outside the scope of the present paper.

2. In the presence of *P2P inconsistency*, i.e., when in a peer P_i the data coming from another peer P_j (through a P2P mapping) contradict the local data of P_i (or the data coming to P_i from another peer P_k), the peer P_i should not reach an inconsistent state: rather, it should discard a *minimal* amount of the data retrieved from the other peers in order to preserve consistency.

We now formally state the above notions of local inconsistency and P2P inconsistency. Let $\mathcal{P} = \{P_1, \ldots, P_n\}$ be a P2PDIS and $\mathcal{D} = \{D_1, \ldots, D_n\}$ be an extension $\mathcal{D}$ for $\mathcal{P}$. We say that:

- A peer $P_i \in \mathcal{P}$ is *locally inconsistent wrt* D_i if $\mathcal{T}_K^-(P_i) \cup DB(D_i) \models_{K45_n} \mathbf{K_i} \perp_i$, where $\mathcal{T}_K^-(P_i)$ is obtained from $\mathcal{T}_K(P_i)$ by dropping the sentences formalizing the P2P mappings (otherwise we say that P_i is locally consistent wrt D_i).
- A peer $P_i \in \mathcal{P}$ is *P2P inconsistent wrt* $\mathcal{D}$ if P_i is locally consistent wrt D_i and $\mathcal{T}_K(\mathcal{P}) \cup DB(\mathcal{D}) \models_{K45_n} \mathbf{K_i} \perp_i$.

As we said before, we aim at a formalization that makes our system inconsistency-tolerant. It is immediate to see that no monotonic logic, e.g., $K45_n$, is suited for this purpose. Therefore, we now introduce a nonmonotonic variant of our logic, called $K45_n^A$.

The Nonmonotonic Modal Logic $K45_n^A$. The language $\mathcal{L}(K45_n^A)$ is an extension of $\mathcal{L}(K45_n)$, obtained by adding to the first-order modal language a new set of modal operators, $\mathbf{A_1}, \ldots, \mathbf{A_n}$. The semantics of $\mathcal{L}(K45_n^A)$ sentences is *non-monotonic*, and is formally defined as follows. A $K45_n^A$-structure E is a tuple $(W, \{R_1, \ldots, R_n, R_1^a, \ldots, R_n^a\}, V)$, where W is a set of worlds, each R_i and each R_i^a are transitive and Euclidean binary relations over W, and V is a function mapping worlds to first-order interpretations. Therefore, with respect to $K45_n$-structures, $K45_n^A$-structures have n additional accessibility relations $R_1^a, \ldots, R_n^a$. Such relations account for the additional modal operators $\mathbf{A_1}, \ldots, \mathbf{A_n}$.

The notion of truth of a $K45_n^A$ sentence in a world of a $K45_n^A$-structure is analogous to the notion given in Section 3 for $K45_n$, with the addition of:

$$E, w \models \mathbf{A_i}\phi \quad \text{iff} \quad E, w' \models \phi \text{ for each } w' \text{ such that } (w, w') \in R_i^a$$

So far, the logic $K45_n^A$ does not appear as a significant extension of $K45_n$: indeed, according to the above notion of truth, the new modal operators $\mathbf{A_i}$ are treated just like any $\mathbf{K_i}$ operator in $K45_n$, so there is no apparent reason to distinguish the $\mathbf{A_i}$'s operators from the $\mathbf{K_i}$'s. Actually, the different meaning of the two sets of modal operators in the logic $K45_n^A$, as well as its nonmonotonicity, is due to the following notion of $K45_n^A$-model for a sentence ϕ, which makes use of a preference order over $K45_n^A$-structures.

Let $E = (W, \{R_1, \ldots, R_n, R_1^a, \ldots, R_n^a\}, V)$ and $E' = (W', \{R_1', \ldots, R_n', R_1^a, \ldots, R_n^a\}, V')$ be $K45_n^A$-structures. We say that E' *is preferred to* E if the following conditions hold:

1. $W' \supseteq W$ and $V'(w) = V(w)$ for every $w \in W$,
2. $R_i' \supseteq R_i$, for all $i \in \{1, \ldots, n\}$,
3. there exist $w_1 \in W$, $w_2 \in W'$, $i \in \{1, \ldots, n\}$ such that $(w_1, w_2) \in R_i' - R_i$ and there exists no $w' \in W$ such that $(w_1, w') \in R_i$ and $V(w') = V'(w_2)$.

Intuitively, E' is preferred to E if E' is a structure "larger" than E (conditions 1 and 2) and there exists a world w_1 which is connected in E' (through the relation R_i') to a larger set of possible worlds than in E (condition 3), which means that w_1 in E has "less objective knowledge" than in E' with respect to the modality K_i. For instance, it can be immediately verified that, if E' is preferred to E, then, for each first-order sentence ϕ and for each $w \in W$, if $E', w \models \mathbf{K_i}\phi$ then $E, w \models \mathbf{K_i}\phi$, but not vice-versa.

Let $\phi \in \mathcal{L}(K45_n^A)$, let $E = (W, R_1, \ldots, R_n, R_1^a, \ldots, R_n^a, V)$ be a $K45_n^A$-structure, and let $w \in W$. (E, w) is a $K45_n^A$-*model for* ϕ if the following conditions hold:

1. $E, w \models \phi$;
2. $R_i = R_i^a$ for each $i \in \{1, \ldots, n\}$;
3. there exists no $K45_n^A$-structure $E' = (W', \{R_1', \ldots, R_n', R_1^a, \ldots, R_n^a\}, V')$ such that E' is preferred to E, and $E', w \models \phi$.

The notions of model of a set of sentences and of logical implication are defined in the same way as in the case of $K45_n$.

The above semantics formalizes the idea of selecting $K45_n^A$-structures that satisfy two intuitive principles: (*i*) *knowledge is minimal*, which is realized through the notion of preference between structures; and (*ii*) *assumptions are justified by knowledge*, which is realized by the fact that, for each i, the meaning of the operators $\mathbf{A_i}$ and $\mathbf{K_i}$ is the same, since $R_i = R_i^a$. Such semantic principles of minimal knowledge and justified assumptions are well-known in nonmonotonic reasoning [24,26]. In particular, the logic $K45_n^A$ can be seen as a first-order, multimodal generalization of [24].

Handling Local Inconsistency. To capture tolerance wrt local inconsistency, we need to refine the epistemic formalization of P2P mapping assertions presented in Section 3 as follows: for each P2P mapping assertion of peer i in M, we replace in $\mathcal{T}_K(P_i)$ the sentence (1) with

$$\forall \mathbf{x}.\, \neg \mathbf{A_j} \bot_j \wedge \mathbf{K_j}(\exists \mathbf{y}.\, body_{cq_j}(\mathbf{x}, \mathbf{y})) \supset \mathbf{K_i}(\exists \mathbf{z}.\, body_{cq_i}(\mathbf{x}, \mathbf{z}))$$

It is easy to see that, for a P2PDIS $\mathcal{P}$ without locally inconsistent peers, the new formalization of $\mathcal{P}$ coincides with the formalization in the logic $K45_n$.

On the other hand, the following theorem shows that, with the above change, the P2PDIS is tolerant to local inconsistency, in the sense that it isolates the peers that are locally inconsistent.

Theorem 1. *Let $\mathcal{P}$ be a P2PDIS, let $\mathcal{D}$ be an extension for $\mathcal{P}$, let $P_i \in \mathcal{P}$ be a peer locally inconsistent wrt D_i, and let $\mathcal{P}' = \mathcal{P} - \{P_i\}$. Then, for each query q posed to a peer $P_j \in \mathcal{P}$ different from P_i, we have that $ANS_{K45_n^A}(q, j, \mathcal{P}, \mathcal{D}) = ANS_{K45_n^A}(q, j, \mathcal{P}', \mathcal{D})$.*

Handling Both Local and P2P Inconsistency. We are now ready to formalize, in $K45_n^A$, P2PDISs that are inconsistency-tolerant wrt both local and P2P mappings. Again, the $K45_n^A$ theory representing the P2PDIS $\mathcal{P}$, denoted by $\mathcal{T}_A(\mathcal{P})$, is similar to the theory $\mathcal{T}_K(\mathcal{P})$ defined in Section 3, but with an important difference on how to formalize P2P mapping assertions. In particular, such a formalization is obtained by replacing each sentence of the form (1) with

$$\forall \mathbf{x}.\, \neg \mathbf{A_j} \bot_j \wedge \mathbf{K_j}(\exists \mathbf{y}.\, body_{cq_j}(\mathbf{x}, \mathbf{y})) \wedge \neg \mathbf{A_i}(\neg \exists \mathbf{z}.\, body_{cq_i}(\mathbf{x}, \mathbf{z})) \supset \mathbf{K_i}(\exists \mathbf{z}.\, body_{cq_i}(\mathbf{x}, \mathbf{z}))$$

Informally, the above sentence specifies the following rule: for each tuple of values $\mathbf{t}$, if peer j is consistent and knows the sentence $\exists \mathbf{y}.\, body_{cq_j}(\mathbf{t}, \mathbf{y})$, and the sentence $\exists \mathbf{z}.\, body_{cq_i}(\mathbf{t}, \mathbf{z})$ *is consistent with what peer i knows*, then peer i knows the sentence $\exists \mathbf{z}.\, body_{cq_i}(\mathbf{t}, \mathbf{z})$. In other words, information flows from peer j to peer i through a P2P mapping assertion only if adding such information to peer i does not give rise to a P2P inconsistency in peer i. More precisely, the meaning of the above sentence in $K45_n^A$ is that exactly a *maximal* amount of information (i.e., a maximal set of tuples) consistent with peer i flows from peer j to peer i through the P2P mapping assertion.

The semantics $ANS_{K45_n^A}(q, i, \mathcal{P}, \mathcal{D})$ of a query q posed to a peer P_i of a P2PDIS $\mathcal{P}$ wrt an extension $\mathcal{D}$ is defined as for $K45_n$, except that now we have to take into account the $K45_n^A$ formalization of the $\mathcal{P}$. The following theorem shows that such a formalization is a "conservative extension" of the one based on $K45_n$, in the sense that, if no peer is locally inconsistent, and the data at the sources do not give rise to P2P inconsistencies, then the semantics of queries is the same in the two logics.

Theorem 2. *Let $\mathcal{P}$ be a P2PDIS and let $\mathcal{D}$ be an extension for $\mathcal{P}$ such that each peer in $\mathcal{P}$ is neither locally inconsistent, nor P2P inconsistent wrt $\mathcal{D}$. Then, for each peer $P_i \in \mathcal{P}$ and for each query q posed to P_i, $ANS_{K45_n^A}(q, i, \mathcal{P}, \mathcal{D}) = ANS_{K45_n}(q, i, \mathcal{P}, \mathcal{D})$.*

Moreover, the following theorem shows that the new formalization enjoys one of the basic properties for being tolerant to P2P inconsistency.

Theorem 3. *Let $\mathcal{P}$ be a P2PDIS and let $\mathcal{D}$ be an extension for $\mathcal{P}$. If $P_i \in \mathcal{P}$ is locally consistent wrt D_i, then $\mathcal{T}_A(\mathcal{P}) \cup DB(\mathcal{D}) \not\models_{K45_n^A} \mathbf{K}_i \bot_i$.*

Finally, we remark that the above semantics implies that: (*i*) when inconsistency arises between local data and non-local data in a peer, i.e., when data coming from the peer sources through the local mapping contradicts the data retrieved by a peer through a P2P mapping, then the peer always prefers the local data. Formally, in this case there is one $K45_n^A$-model for the P2PDIS, which represents the situation in which non-local data is discarded; (*ii*) when inconsistency arises between two different pieces of non-local data, i.e., when a piece of data retrieved by a peer through a P2P mapping contradicts another piece of data retrieved through the P2P mappings, then no preference is made between these two pieces of information, in the sense that in this case there are two $K45_n^A$-models for the P2PDIS, each of which represents the situation in which one of the two pieces of data is discarded.

Example 3. Consider the P2PDIS of Example 1. It is easy to see that P_3 gets from P_1 that Person3("Joe", "Rome", "Canadian") and from P_4 that Person3("Joe", "Rome", "Italian"), but since name is a key for Person3 this would give rise to an inconsistency. As a result, we have two $K45_n^A$ models, one in which Person3("Joe", "Rome", "Canadian") holds, and one in which Person3("Joe", "Rome", "Italian") holds, and hence P_3 does not know anymore the citizenship of "Joe". However, P_3 still knows that "Joe" lives in "Rome". In other words, the query $\{x \mid \exists y. \text{Person}_3("Joe", x, y)\}$ returns $\{"Rome"\}$, while the query $\{y \mid \exists x. \text{Person}_3("Joe", x, y)\}$ returns the empty set.

5   Query Processing

In this section we study query answering in a P2P setting. We present a distributed algorithm for answering queries in a P2P system, we prove its termination, soundness and completeness, and then we use it to provide the complexity characterization of the query answering problem. The algorithm extends the one presented in [7] with the capability in handling inconsistency in accordance to the P2P system formalization in the multimodal logic $K45_n^A$.

The Algorithm. The algorithm is based on two main functionalities, called *user query handler* and *peer query handler*, that are described in Figure 2. Each peer must provide such functionalities in order to answer a user query posed to any peer in the P2P system $\mathcal{P}$. Such functionalities are executed over an extension $\mathcal{D}$ of $\mathcal{P}$.

Algorithm P.user-query-handler, with $P = (id, G, S, L, M, \mathcal{L})$
Input: user query $q \in \mathcal{L}$
Output: $ANS_{K45_n^A}(q, id, \mathcal{P}, \mathcal{D})$
begin
  generate a new transaction id T;
  $(DP, r_q) := P.$peer-query-handler(q, T);
  return $Eval(r_q, DP)$;
end

Algorithm P.peer-query-handler
Input: query $q \in \mathcal{L}$, transaction id T
Output: Datalog$^\neg$ program $DP = (DP_I, DP_E)$, query predicate r_q in DP_I
begin
  $(r_q, DP_I) :=$ computePerfectRef$(q, \sigma(P))$;
  $(\perp_{id}, DP'_I) :=$ computePerfectRef$(\perp_{id}, \sigma(P))$;
  $DP_I = DP_I \cup DP'_I$; $DP_E := \emptyset$;
  for each predicate $r \in S \cup AuxAlph(P)$ occurring in DP_I **do**
    if getTransaction$(r, T) = notProcessed$
    then begin
      setTransaction$(r, T, processed)$;
      if $r \in S$ **then** $DP_E := DP_E \cup Ext(r, \mathcal{D})$;
      else if isConsistent$(\pi(r))$
      then begin
        $(DP', r') := \pi(r).$peer-query-handler$(Q(r), T)$;
        $\rho := r(\mathbf{x}) \leftarrow r'(\mathbf{x}), not \perp_{id}$;
        $DP_I := DP_I \cup \rho \cup DP'_I$;
        $DP_E := DP_E \cup DP'_E$;
      end
    end
  return (DP, r_q);
end

Fig. 2. Algorithms user-query-handler and peer-query-handler, executed over an extension $\mathcal{D}$

Each user query q to the peer P is the input of the user query handler of P. Such a module computes the set $ANS_{K45_n^A}(q, \mathcal{P}, \mathcal{D})$ by evaluating a suitable Datalog$^\neg$ program, i.e., a Datalog program enriched with unstratified negation, which is returned by the peer query handler of P. Roughly speaking, the module peer query handler reformulates the query q in terms of a Datalog$^\neg$ program over the data sources of P, and combines rules and facts thus obtained with the programs provided by consistent peers connected to P that the module queries by calling their own peer query handler. A suitable rule (using negation in its body) is also added to the program to make data coming from other peers contribute to answer computation only if they do not generate inconsistency within P (i.e., they do not contradict local data of the peer P or data coming from another peer). Obviously, each queried peer can in turn propagate the computation by invoking the peer query handlers of its neighborhoods. The association of the identifier of a transaction (started by the user query handler) to each peer query handler call ensures termination of the process (even in the presence of cycles among peers).

In the algorithms of Figure 2, DP denotes a Datalog$^\neg$ program constituted by a set of rules DP_I, and a set of facts DP_E. The pair (r_q, DP_I), denotes a Datalog$^\neg$ query, whereas $Eval(r_q, DP)$ indicates the evaluation of the predicate r_q over the stable models of the program DP [28]. Also, starting from $P = (id, G, S, L, M, \mathcal{L})$ we define a simplified peer $\sigma(P) = (id, G, S \cup AuxAlph(P), L \cup L_{AuxAlph(P)}, \emptyset, \mathcal{L})$, where we drop the P2P mapping assertions, and "simulate" their effects by adding the new source symbols $AuxAlph(P)$ (one for each assertion) and the new local mappings $L_{AuxAlph(P)}$ involving them. In particular for a mapping $cq' \rightsquigarrow cq$ from peer P' to P, we introduce a new source relation r with a local mapping $\{x \mid r(x) \rightsquigarrow cq$, and use the notation $Q(r)$ to denote cq' and $\pi(r)$ to denote P' (see also [10] for further details).

The peer query handler makes use of a function computePerfectRef which, taken as input a query q and $\sigma(P)$, returns the *perfect reformulation of q in $\sigma(P)$*, that is a query q_r such that, for each extension D of the source predicates $S \cup AuxAlph(P)$, $q_r^D = \{t \mid \mathcal{T}(\sigma(P)) \cup \mathcal{T}_D \models q(t)\}$, where $\mathcal{T}(\sigma(P))$ is the first-order theory obtained from $\mathcal{T}_K(\sigma(P))$ by dropping the modal operator in front of the assertions constructed from G and $L \cup L_{AuxAlph(P)}$ (see Section 3) and $\mathcal{T}_D$ is used denote the set of facts corresponding to D. In the terminology used in data integration, computePerfectRef computes the query that returns the certain answers to the query q posed to the single peer $\sigma(P)$ wrt a source database D [22].

We assume that each peer P is able to compute the perfect reformulation in $\sigma(P)$ of any query q accepted by P. We also assume that such reformulation can be expressed in Datalog$^\neg$, and call *reformulation capable* each peer that satisfies the above assumptions. Notable cases in which the above assumption holds can be found in the extensive literature on data integration and data exchange (see, e.g., [20,12]).

The use of the functions getTransaction and setTransaction guarantees that a peer query handler never processes the same mapping query twice in the same transaction, whereas isConsistent($\pi(r)$) is used to check if the peer $\pi(r)$ is locally consistent. This function is implemented by asking the query $\bot_j$ to $\pi(r)$, where j is the identifier of $\pi(r)$. Furthermore, $Ext(r, \mathcal{D})$ denotes the set $\{r(t) \mid t \in r^\mathcal{D}\}$, i.e., the extension of r in $\mathcal{D}$. Finally, the rule $\rho := r(\mathbf{x}) \leftarrow r'(\mathbf{x}), not \bot_{id}$ specifies that data coming from the peer $\pi(r)$ contribute to the answer to the query q only if they do not generate any inconsistency in the peer P. Such a mechanism does the job since we include in the program DP_I the rules that define the predicate $\bot_{id}$ by means of the function call computePerfectRef($\bot_{id}, \sigma(P)$).

Termination and Correctness. Termination of the algorithm follows immediately from the fact that, through the use of the transaction states of the procedures getTransaction and setTransaction in P.peer-query-handler, each mapping query associated with a predicate in $AuxAlph(P)$ is processed at most once for each user query. Moreover, the algorithm is sound and complete with respect to the $K45_n^A$ formalization of the P2P system.

Theorem 4. *Let $\mathcal{P}$ be a P2P system, $P = (id, G, S, L, M, \mathcal{L})$ a peer in $\mathcal{P}$, $q \in \mathcal{L}$ a query of arity n over P, and $\mathcal{D}$ an extension for $\mathcal{P}$. Then, the execution of P.user-query-handler(q) over $\mathcal{D}$ terminates, and a n-tuple t of constants in Γ is in the set of returned answers if and only if $t \in ANS_{K45_n^A}(q, id, \mathcal{P}, \mathcal{D})$.*

Complexity. Finally, we characterize the computational complexity of the problem of query answering in our P2P data integration setting, with respect to the size of data stored in the peers of $\mathcal{P}$, i.e., the size of the extension $\mathcal{D}$ for $\mathcal{P}$ (*data complexity*). Notice that computing perfect reformulations through the algorithm computePerfectRef does not depend on the data at the sources, therefore it does not affect data complexity.

Theorem 5. *Let $\mathcal{P}$ be a P2P system where each peer is reformulation capable. Let $P = (id, G, S, L, M, \mathcal{L})$ be a peer in $\mathcal{P}$, $\mathcal{D}$ an extension for $\mathcal{P}$, $q \in \mathcal{L}$ a query of arity n over P, and $\mathbf{t}$ a n-tuple of constants in Γ. The problem of establishing whether $\mathbf{t} \in ANS_{K45_n^A}(q, id, \mathcal{P}, \mathcal{D})$ is in coNP in the size of $\mathcal{D}$ (i.e., in data complexity). Moreover, it is coNP-hard in data complexity even in a setting where only key constraints are allowed in peer schemas.*

Proof (sketch). Membership in coNP follows from Theorem 4 and from the fact that checking whether $\mathbf{t} \in Eval(r_q, DP)$, where DP is a Datalog$^\neg$ program, is coNP-complete in data complexity [17]. The hardness part can be proved by a reduction of the three-colorability problem to our problem in the setting where only key constraints are allowed in peer schemas. The proof follows the line used for establishing coNP-hardness of query answering in the setting of a single inconsistent database in [8]. □

According to the above theorem, query answering in a P2PDIS under the $K45_n^A$ semantics is decidable and our algorithm turns out to be optimal with respect to worst-case data complexity. Notice that assuming that each peer is reformulation capable strips off cases in which query answering is undecidable and guarantees its membership in coNP. Obviously, with respect to [10], a computational complexity blow up in query answering arises, which is the price that we have to pay to deal with inconsistent data.

6 Conclusions

In this paper we have proposed a multi-modal nonmonotonic formalization for P2PDISs which allowed us to properly model the modularity of a P2P system, localize local inconsistency, and handle peers that may provide mutually inconsistent data. We have also provided an algorithm for query processing in our setting that is sound and complete with respect to the multi-modal semantics of the system, and have characterized the computational complexity of the query answering problem. The results reported here can be extended in several directions. First, we can remove the assumption that all peers share a common alphabet of constants by making use of mapping tables [21]. Also, we believe that preferences between peers can be smoothly integrated in our framework, in the line of [5]. We aim also at extending the framework to the case in which each peer in the system has its own strategy for resolving data inconsistency.

Acknowledgements. This research has been partially supported by the projects IN-FOMIX (IST-2001-33570), and TONES (IST-007603) funded by the EU, and by the project HYPER, funded by IBM through a Shared University Research Award Grant. The authors wish to thank Luciano Serafini for precious comments about the paper.

References

1. C. E. Alchourrón, P. Gärdenfors, and D. Makinson. On the logic of theory change: Partial meet contraction and revision functions. *J. of Symbolic Logic*, 50:510–530, 1985.

2. M. Arenas, P. Barcelo, R. Fagin, and L. Libkin. Locally consistent transformations and query answering in data exchange. In *Proc. of PODS 2004*, pages 229–240, 2004.

3. M. Arenas, L. E. Bertossi, and J. Chomicki. Consistent query answers in inconsistent databases. In *Proc. of PODS'99*, pages 68–79, 1999.

4. P. A. Bernstein, F. Giunchiglia, A. Kementsietsidis, J. Mylopoulos, L. Serafini, and I. Za-ihrayeu. Data management for peer-to-peer computing: A vision. In *Proc. of WebDB 2002*, 2002.

5. L. E. Bertossi and L. Bravo. Query answering in peer-to-peer data exchange systems. In *In Proc. of the EDBT Workshop on Peer-to-Peer Computing and Databases (P2P&DB 2004)*, pages 476–485, 2004.

6. L. Bravo and L. Bertossi. Logic programming for consistently querying data integration systems. In *Proc. of IJCAI 2003*, pages 10–15, 2003.

7. A. Calì, D. Calvanese, G. De Giacomo, and M. Lenzerini. Data integration under integrity constraints. *Information Systems*, 29:147–163, 2004.

8. A. Calì, D. Lembo, and R. Rosati. On the decidability and complexity of query answering over inconsistent and incomplete databases. In *Proc. of PODS 2003*, pages 260–271, 2003.

9. A. Calì, D. Lembo, and R. Rosati. Query rewriting and answering under constraints in data integration systems. In *Proc. of IJCAI 2003*, pages 16–21, 2003.

10. D. Calvanese, G. De Giacomo, M. Lenzerini, and R. Rosati. Logical foundations of peer-to-peer data integration. In *Proc. of PODS 2004*, pages 241–251, 2004.

11. B. F. Chellas. *Modal Logic: An introduction.* Cambridge University Press, 1980.

12. O. M. Duschka, M. R. Genesereth, and A. Y. Levy. Recursive query plans for data integration. *J. of Logic Programming*, 43(1):49–73, 2000.

13. R. Fagin, J. Y. Halpern, Y. Moses, and M. Y. Vardi. *Reasoning about Knowledge.* The MIT Press, 1995.

14. R. Fagin, P. G. Kolaitis, and L. Popa. Data exchange: Getting to the core. In *Proc. of PODS 2003*, pages 90–101, 2003.

15. R. Fagin, J. D. Ullman, and M. Y. Vardi. On the semantics of updates in databases. In *Proc. of PODS'83*, pages 352–365, 1983.

16. E. Franconi, G. Kuper, A. Lopatenko, and L. Serafini. A robust logical and computational characterisation of peer-to-peer database systems. In *Proc. of the VLDB International Workshop On Databases, Information Systems and Peer-to-Peer Computing*, 2003.

17. M. Gelfond and V. Lifschitz. The stable model semantics for logic programming. In *Proc. of the 5th Logic Programming Symposium*, pages 1070–1080. The MIT Press, 1988.

18. S. Gribble, A. Halevy, Z. Ives, M. Rodrig, and D. Suciu. What can databases do for peer-to-peer? In *Proc. of WebDB 2001*, 2001.

19. A. Halevy, Z. Ives, D. Suciu, and I. Tatarinov. Schema mediation in peer data management systems. In *Proc. of ICDE 2003*, pages 505–516, 2003.

20. A. Y. Halevy. Answering queries using views: A survey. *VLDB Journal*, 10(4):270–294, 2001.

21. A. Kementsietsidis, M. Arenas, and R. J. Miller. Mapping data in peer-to-peer systems: Semantics and algorithmic issues. In *Proc. of ACM SIGMOD*, pages 325–336, 2003.

22. M. Lenzerini. Data integration: A theoretical perspective. In *Proc. of PODS 2002*, pages 233–246, 2002.

23. H. J. Levesque and G. Lakemeyer. *The Logic of Knowledge Bases*. The MIT Press, 2001.
24. V. Lifschitz. Minimal belief and negation as failure. *Artificial Intelligence*, 70:53–72, 1994.
25. J. Madhavan, P. A. Bernstein, P. Domingos, and A. Y. Halevy. Representing and reasoning about mappings between domain models. In *Proc. of AAAI 2002*, pages 80–86, 2002.
26. R. Rosati. Reasoning about minimal belief and negation as failure. *J. of Artificial Intelligence Research*, 11:277–300, 1999.
27. I. Tatarinov and A. Halevy. Efficient query reformulation in peer data management. In *Proc. of ACM SIGMOD*, 2004.
28. J. D. Ullman. *Principles of Database and Knowledge Base Systems*, volume 1. Computer Science Press, 1988.

XML Data Integration with Identification

Antonella Poggi[1,2] and Serge Abiteboul[1]

[1] INRIA Futurs - Parc Club Orsay-University,
4 rue Jean Monod, F-91893 Orsay Cedex, France
Name.Surname@inria.fr
[2] Dipartimento di Informatica e Sistemistica "Antonio Ruberti",
Università di Roma "La Sapienza" - Via Salaria 113, I-00198 Roma, Italy
surname@dis.uniroma1.it

Abstract. Data integration is the problem of combining data residing at different sources, and providing the user with a virtual view, called global schema, which is independent from the model and the physical origin of the sources. Whereas many data integration systems and theoretical works have been proposed for relational data, not much investigation has been focused yet on XML data integration. Our goal is therefore to address some of its related issues. In particular, we highlight two major issues that emerge in the XML context: (i) the global schema may be characterized by a set of constraints, expressed by means of a DTD and XML integrity constraints, (ii) the concept of *node identity* requires to introduce semantic criteria to identify nodes coming from different sources. We propose a formal framework for XML data integration systems based on an expressive XML global schema, a set of XML data sources and a set of mappings specified by means of a simple tree language. Then, we define an identification function that aims at globally identifying nodes coming from different sources. Finally, we propose algorithms to answer queries under different assumptions for the mappings.

1 Introduction

Data integration is the problem of combining data residing at different sources, and providing the user with a virtual view, called global schema, which is independent from the model and the physical origin of the sources. Users query the global schema, while the system carries out the task of suitably accessing different sources and assembling the data retrieved at each source into the final answer to the query. Whereas many data integration systems [8, 10] and theoretical works [9, 6, 12] have been proposed for relational data, not much investigation has been focused yet on XML data integration. Our goal is therefore to address some of its related issues. In particular, we highlight two major issues that emerge in the XML context: (i) the global schema may be characterized by a set of constraints, expressed by means of a DTD and XML integrity constraints, (ii) the concept of *node identity* requires to introduce semantic criteria to identify nodes coming from different sources. The latter is similar to the well-studied problem of identifying objects in mediators systems [11]. However, it requires some particular solution in the context of XML data integration.

As for relational data, in order to answer a query posed over the global schema, the system needs the specification of the relationship between the sources and the global

G. Bierman and C. Koch (Eds.): DBPL 2005, LNCS 3774, pp. 106–121, 2005.

schema, which is called *mapping*. Different approaches have been proposed to specify mappings. We chose here to focus on the *Local-As-View* (LAV) approach, which consists in characterizing the information content of the sources in terms of the global schema. An important property of mappings concerns the accuracy of the source with respect to the corresponding view. If a source provides only a subset of the data accessible from the global schema throw the corresponding view, then, we say that the mapping is *sound*. Otherwise, if the source provides exactly the corresponding view, we say that the mapping is *exact*. It is well-known that this case is more difficult to deal with. The main contributions of our work are as follows.

- First, we propose a formal framework for XML data integration systems based on (i) a global schema specified by means of a set of (simplified) DTD and a set of *XML integrity constraints* as defined in [5], (ii) a source schema specified by means of DTDs, and (iii) a set of LAV mappings specified by means of *prefix-selection-query language* that is inspired from the query language defined in [1].
- Second, we define an *identification* function, that aims at globally identifying nodes coming from different sources. As already mentioned, the need for this function is motivated by the concept of *node identity*.
- Finally, we address the query answering problem in the XML data integration setting. In particular, given the strong connection with query answering with incomplete information, we propose an approach that is reminiscent of such a context. We provide three algorithms to answer queries under the assumptions of sound, exact and mixed mappings, and study their complexity.

The paper is organized as follows. In Section 2, we illustrate XML data integration and some of its related issues by an example. In Section 3, we present the data model and the query language used in the paper. Then, the formal framework for XML data integration is introduced in Section 4, where we define the identification function. In Section 5, we introduce query answering and propose different algorithms to answer queries under the assumption of sound, exact and mixed mappings. Section 6 concludes the paper with a discussion about future works and XML data integration open issues.

Related Work. The only XML data integration system we are aware of, that takes into account integrity constraints, is the one presented in [3]. The authors propose the grammar AIG to specify the integration of data coming from different relational sources in a document that conforms to a DTD and satisfies a set of integrity constraints. However, in their work (i) mappings follow the *Global-As-View* (GAV) approach which has a more procedural flavor, since it characterizes the information content of the global schema in terms of the sources, (ii) the sources are relational, and (iii) whenever the retrieved data does not satisfy a constraint, the query evaluation is aborted. Closer to our work is the investigation of [2], which concerns XML data exchange. In this setting, the aim is to materialize an instance of a target schema, given an instance of a source schema, where both schemas are specified by means of DTDs. In particular, they address consistency and query answering over the target schema. However, our work considers multiple sources, whereas in data exchange the source is unique. More interestingly, no integrity constraints can be expressed over their target schema and their query language allows only for the extraction of tuples, whereas our query language extracts trees.

2 XML Data Integration by Example

In this section, we illustrate by an example XML data integration.

Suppose that an hospital offers access to information about patients and their treatments. Information is stored in XML documents managed in different offices of the hospital, whereas users (e.g. statisticians), because of privacy and security reasons, have access to a global DTD S_G that has the following form:

S_G :
```
<!ELEMENT hospital (patient+, treatment+)>
<!ELEMENT patient (SSN, name, cure*, bill?)>
<!ELEMENT treatment (trID, procedure?)>
<!ELEMENT procedure (treatment+)>
```

Following a common approach for XML data, we will consider XML documents as unordered trees, with nodes labeled with elements names. The above DTD says that the document contains data about patients and hospital treatments, where a cure is nothing but a treatment id. Moreover, a set of keys and foreign key constraints are specified over the global schema. In particular, we know that two patients cannot have the same social security number SSN, that two treatments cannot have the same number $trID$ and that all the prescribed cures have to appear among the treatments of the hospital. Such constraints correspond respectively to two key constraints and one foreign key constraint. Finally, assume that the sources consist in the following two documents, D_1 and D_2, with the following DTDs. Mappings tell us that D_1 contains patients with a name and a social security number lower than 100000, and D_2 contains patients that paid a bill and were prescribed at least one dangerous cure (we assume that these have numbers smaller than 35).

D_1 :
```
<hospital>
  <patient>
    <name>Parker</name>
    <SSN>55577</SSN>
  </patient>
  <patient>
    <name>Rossi</name>
    <SSN>20903</SSN>
  </patient>
</hospital>
```

S_1 :
```
<!ELEMENT hospital (patient*)>
<!ELEMENT patient (name, SSN)>
```

D_2 :
```
<hospital>
  <patient>
    <SSN>55577</SSN>
  </patient>
</hospital>
```

S_2 :
```
<!ELEMENT hospital (patient*)>
<!ELEMENT patient (SSN)>
```

Suppose now that the user asks for the following queries:

1. Find the name and the SSN for all patients having a name and a SSN, that paid a bill and that were prescribed at least one cure.
2. Does the hospital offer dangerous treatments?

Typically, in data integration systems, the goal is to find the *certain* answers, e.g. the answers that are returned by all data trees that satisfy the global schema and conform to the data at the sources. By adapting data integration terminology [9] to our setting, we call them *legal data trees*. A crucial point here is that legal data trees can be constructed by merging the source trees. We therefore need to identify nodes that should be merged, using the constraints of the global schema. Note, however, that data retrieved may not satisfy these constraints. In particular, there are two kinds of constraints violation. Data may be incomplete, i.e. it may violate constraints by not providing all data required according to the schema. Or, data retrieved may be inconsistent, i.e. it may violate constraints by providing two elements that are "semantically" the same but cannot be merged without violating key constraints. In this paper, we will address the problem of answering queries in the presence of incomplete data, while we will assume that data does not violate key constraints. Coming back to the example, it is easy to see that the sources are consistent. Thus, the global schema constraints specification allows to answer Query 1 by returning the patient with name "Parker" and social security number "55577", since thanks to the key constraint we know that there cannot be two patients with the same SSN. Note that Query 2 can also be answered with certainty. Mappings let us actually infer that the patient named "Parker" was prescribed a dangerous cure. In addition, thanks to the foreign key constraint, we know that every cure that is prescribed to some patient is provided by the hospital.

We conclude the section by highlighting the impact of the assumption of having sound/exact mappings. Suppose that no constraints were expressed over the global schema. Under the exact mapping assumption, by inspecting the data sources, it is possible to conclude that there is only one way to merge data sources and satisfy the schema constraints. Indeed, since every patient has a name and a SSN number, we can deduce that all patients in D_2 with a SSN lower than 100000 belong also to D_1. Therefore the answer to Query 1 would be the same as in the presence of constraints, whereas no answer would be returned to Query 2, since no information is given on that portion of the global schema. On the other hand, under the assumption of sound mappings, since in the absence of constraints there could be two patients with the same SSN, both queries would return empty answers.

3   Data Model and Query Language

In this section we introduce our data model and query language, inspired from [1].

Data Trees and Prefixes. XML documents are represented as labeled unordered trees, called *data trees*. Given an infinite set $\mathcal{N}$ of nodes, a finite set Σ of element names (labels), and a domain $\Gamma = \Gamma' \cup \{0\}$ for the data values, a *(data) tree* T over Σ is a quadruple $T = \langle t, \lambda, \nu \rangle$, where:

 - t is a finite rooted tree (possibly empty) with nodes from $\mathcal{N}$;
 - λ, called the *labeling function*, associates a label in Σ to each node in t; and
 - ν, the *data mapping*, assigns a value in Γ to each node in t.

We call *datanodes* those nodes n of t such that $\nu(n) \neq 0$. Note that 0 is a special data value that represents the empty value.

A *prefix* of $T = \langle t, \lambda, \nu \rangle$ is a data tree $T' = \langle t', \lambda', \nu' \rangle$, written $T' \leq T$, such that there exists a homomorphism h from (all) the nodes of t' to (some of) the nodes of t such that h is recursively defined as follows:

- if n' is the root of t' then $h(n')$ is defined and it is the root of t; we say that h preserves the root;
- for every node n'' that is a child of n' in t', such that $h(n')$ is defined, $h(n'')$ is defined and it is a child of $h(n')$ in t; thus h preserves the parent-child relationships;
- for every node n' in t' such that $h(n')$ is defined, $\lambda(h(n')) = \lambda'(n')$; thus h preserves the labeling;
- for every node n' in t' such that $h(n')$ is defined and $\nu(n') \neq \mathbf{0}$, $\nu(h(n')) = \nu'(n')$; thus h preserves the data mapping if and only if it maps a datanode.

Note that the empty tree, i.e. the tree that does not contain any node, denoted $T_\emptyset$, is a prefix of all data trees. Moreover, if $T' \leq T$ and $T \leq T'$, then we say that T and T' are *isomorphic*, written $T \simeq T'$. Finally, we introduce the *intersection* of two data trees. Given two data trees T_1 and T_2, their intersection, denoted $T' = T_1 \cap T_2$, is such that: (i) $T' \leq T_1, T' \leq T_2$, and (ii) for all T'' not isomorphic to T', if $T'' \leq T_1$ and $T'' \leq T_2$, then $T'' \leq T'$, i.e. T' is the maximal prefix of both T_1 and T_2.

Proposition 1. *The intersection of two data trees is unique up to tree isomorphism.*

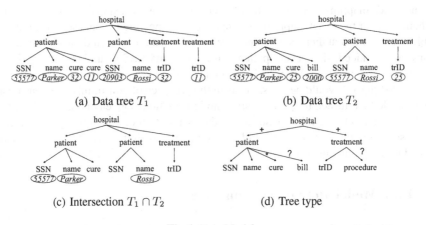

(a) Data tree T_1 (b) Data tree T_2

(c) Intersection $T_1 \cap T_2$ (d) Tree type

Fig. 1. Data Model

Example 1. The data trees T_1 and T_2, resp. in Fig. 1(a) and 1(b), represent data about patients and treatments of an hospital. Note that only data values different from $\mathbf{0}$ are represented and are circled. In Fig. 1(c) we show the intersection $T_1 \cap T_2$. It is easy to verify that it is the maximal prefix of both T_1 and T_2.

Tree Type. We call *tree type* over an alphabet Σ a simplified version of DTDs that can be represented as a triple $\langle \Sigma_\tau, r, \mu \rangle$, where Σ_τ is a set of labels, i.e. $\Sigma_\tau \subseteq \Sigma, r \in \Sigma_\tau$ is a special label denoting the root, and μ associates to each label $a \in \Sigma_\tau$ a *multiplicity atoms* $\mu(a)$ representing the *type* of a, i.e. the set of labels allowed for children of nodes labeled a, together with some multiplicity constraints. More precisely, $\mu(a)$ is an expression $a_1^{\omega_1}...a_k^{\omega_k}$, where a_i are distinct labels in Σ, $\omega_i \in \{*, +, ?, 1\}$, for $i = 1, ...k$.

Given an alphabet Σ, we say that a data tree T over Σ *satisfies* a tree type $S = \langle \Sigma_\tau, r, \mu \rangle$ over Σ, noted $T \models S$, if and only if: (i) the root of T has label r, and (ii) for every node n of T such that $\lambda(n) = a$, if $\mu(a) = a_1^{\omega_1}...a_k^{\omega_k}$, then all the children of n have labels in $\{a_1..a_k\}$ and the number of children labeled a_i is restricted as follows:

- if $\omega_i = 1$, then exactly one child of n is labeled with a_i;
- if $\omega_i = ?$, then at most one child of n is labeled with a_i;
- if $\omega_i = +$, then at least one child of n is labeled with a_i;
- if $\omega_i = *$, then no restrictions are imposed on the children of n labeled with a_i.

Given a tree type, we call *collection* a label a such that there is an occurrence of either a_i^* or a_i^+ in $\mu(a)$, for some $a_i \in \Sigma$. Moreover a_i is called *member of the collection* a.

Unary Keys and Foreign Keys. Given a tree type $S = \langle \Sigma_\tau, r, \mu \rangle$, we recall and adapt to our framework the definition of *(absolute) unary keys and foreign keys* from [5, 4]:

- Keys are assertions of the form: $a.k \rightarrow a$, where $a \in \Sigma_\tau$ and $k^1 \in \mu(a)$. The semantics of keys is the following. Given a tree T satisfying S, $T \models a.k \rightarrow a$ if and only if there does not exist two nodes n, n' of T labeled a such that their respective unique children labeled k have the same data value.
- Foreign keys are assertions of the form: $a.h_a \subseteq b.k_b$, where k_b is a key for b, $a \in \Sigma_\tau$ and $h_a^\omega \in \mu(a)$ for some ω. In this paper, we consider in particular *uniquely localizable foreign keys*, by imposing that b is such that there is a unique label path $r, l_1, .., l_s, b$ from the root to any node labeled b, where for $i = 1, .., s$, l_i is not the member of any collection. The semantics of foreign keys is the following. Given a tree T satisfying S, $T \models a.h_a \subseteq b.k_b$ if and only if for every node n of T labeled h_a that is a child of a node labeled a, there exists a node n' labeled k_b, child of a node p' labeled b, such that n and n' carry the same value (that is a key fo p').

Schema Satisfaction. Given a tree type $S_{\mathcal{G}}$, a set of keys Φ_K and a set of foreign keys Φ_{FK}, we call *schema* a triple $\mathcal{G} = \langle S_{\mathcal{G}}, \Phi_K, \Phi_{FK} \rangle$. Moreover, we say that a tree T *satisfies* the schema $\mathcal{G}$ if and only if $T \models S_{\mathcal{G}}$, $T \models \Phi_K$ and $T \models \Phi_{FK}$.

Example 2. The DTD $S_{\mathcal{G}}$ from Section 2 corresponds to the tree type, represented graphically in Fig. 1(d), where $r = $ hospital and μ can be specified as follows:

```
hospital  →  patient⁺ treatment⁺
patient   →  SSID name cure* bill?
treatment →  trID procedure?
```

Note that *patient* and *treatment* are both elements of the same collection *hospital*. The following sets of constraints express those mentioned in Section 2:

$$\Phi_K : \{\text{patient.SSN} \rightarrow \text{patient};$$
$$\text{treatment.trID} \rightarrow \text{treatment}\}$$
$$\Phi_{FK} : \{\text{patient.cure} \subseteq \text{treatment.trID}\}$$

The tree of Fig. 1(a) satisfies the schema $\mathcal{G} = \langle S_{\mathcal{G}}, \Phi_K, \Phi_{FK} \rangle$, whereas the tree of Fig. 1(b) does not since it contains two patients with the same SSN.

Prefix-Selection Queries. Intuitively, *prefix-selection queries* (shortly referred as *ps-queries*) browse the input tree down to a certain depth starting from the root, by reading nodes with specified element names and possibly with data values satisfying selection conditions. Existential subtree patterns can also be expressed. When evaluated over a data tree T, a boolean ps-query checks for the existence of a certain tree pattern in T. A ps-query that is not boolean returns the minimal tree that is isomorphic to the set of all the nodes involved in the pattern, that are selected by the query.

Formally, a *ps-query q over an alphabet* Σ is a quadruple $\langle t, \lambda, cond, sel \rangle$ where:

- t is a rooted tree;
- λ associates to each node a label in Σ, where sibling nodes have distinct labels.
- *cond* is a partial function that associates to each node in t a condition c that is a boolean formula of the form $p_0 b_0 p_1 b_1 ... p_{m-1} b_{m-1} p_m$, where p_i are predicates to be applied to datanodes values and b_j are boolean operators for $i = 0..m$, $m \geq 0$ and $j = 0..m - 1$; for example, if $\Gamma' = \mathbb{Q}$, then predicates that can be applied to datanodes values have the form $op\ v$, where $op \in \{=, \neq, \leq, \geq, <, >\}$ and $v \in \mathbb{Q}$;
- *sel* is a total function that assigns to each node in t a boolean value such that if $sel(n) = false$ then $sel(n') = false$, for every children n' of n; intuitively, *sel* indicates whether a node is selected by the query, with the constraint that whenever n is not selected, then all the nodes of the subtree rooted at n cannot be selected.

We call *boolean ps-query* a query $q = \langle t, \lambda, cond, sel \rangle$ such that $sel_q(r_q) = false$, where r_q is the root label of t_q.

We next formalize the notion of answer to a ps-query using the auxiliary concepts of valuation and query valuation image. Given a query $q = \langle t_q, \lambda_q, cond_q, sel_q \rangle$ and a data tree $T = \langle t, \lambda, \nu \rangle$, a *valuation* γ *from* q *to* T is a homomorphism from the nodes of t_q to the nodes of t preserving the root, the parent-child relationships, the labeling and such that: for every $n_q \in t_q$, if $cond_q(n_q)$ is defined then $\nu(\gamma(n_q))$ is a datanode, i.e. $\nu(\gamma(n_q)) \neq 0$, and $\nu(\gamma(n_q))$ satisfies $cond_q(n_q)$. The *valuation image I of q posed over* T is the subset of nodes of T that are in the image of some valuation. We call *positive subset P(I) of I* the subset of I such that for every $n \in P(I)$, there exists a valuation γ such that $sel_q(\gamma^{-1}(n)) = true$. Intuitively, $P(I)$ represents the subset of nodes of I that are selected by q.

We now define the semantics of an *answer* to a ps-query q *posed over* T, denoted as $q(T)$. If the valuation image of q posed over T is empty, then $q(T) = false$. Otherwise, $q(T)$ is a data tree such that (i) $q(T)$ is isomorphic to $P(I)$ and (ii) there does not exist a data tree T', not isomorphic to $q(T)$, such that $T' \leq q(T)$ and T' is isomorphic to $P(I)$ (i.e. $q(T)$ is the minimal tree that is isomorphic to $P(I)$). Note that if $P(I)$ is empty, then $q(T)$ is the empty tree, i.e. $q(T) = T_\emptyset$. This case occurs when q is boolean and it returns *true*.

Proposition 2. *Given a ps-query q and a data tree T over* Σ, *the answer q(T) is unique (up to tree isomorphism). Moreover, if q(T)* $\neq$ *false, then q(T) is the minimal prefix of T such that there exists a homomorphism h from P(I) to q(T) preserving parent-child relationships among nodes, labeling and data mapping.*

Example 3. Consider the queries in Fig. 2(a) and 2(c) posed over the tree of Fig. 1(a). They select respectively (i) the name and the SSN of patients having a SSN smaller than 100000, (ii) the SSN of patients that paid a bill and were prescribed at least one

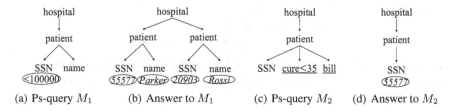

Fig. 2. Querying a data tree

dangerous cure (i.e. a cure with id lower than 35). The answers to the queries are given in Fig. 2(b) and 2(d). Note that we graphically represent an existential subtree pattern in a query by underlying the label of its root.

4   Data Integration Framework

In this section we first formally define a data integration system. Then we start discussing query answering by introducing an *identification function*.

4.1   Formal Definition

An XML data integration system $\mathcal{I}$ can be characterized by a triple $\langle \mathcal{G}, \mathcal{S}, \mathcal{M} \rangle$, where:

– The XML global schema $\mathcal{G} = \langle S_\mathcal{G}, \Phi_K, \Phi_{FK} \rangle$ is expressed in terms of a tree type $S_\mathcal{G} = \langle \Sigma_\tau, r, \mu \rangle$, a set Φ_K of key constraints and a set Φ_{FK} of uniquely localizable foreign keys. We assume that at most one key constraint is expressed for each element (e.g. Φ_K are *primary keys* [5]);
– $\mathcal{S}$ is a set of source schemas $\mathcal{S} = \{S_1, S_2, ..., S_m\}$, where S_i is a tree type, $i = 1, ..., m$; note that dealing with such kind a sources is not restrictive since we can assume that suitable wrappers are available that present the sources in this format;
– $\mathcal{M}$ is the set of (LAV) mappings between $\mathcal{G}$ and $\mathcal{S}$, one for each data source S_i in $\mathcal{S}$; they are expressions of the form: (S_i, M_i, as_i), for $i = 1, ..., m$, where $as_i \in \{sound, exact\}$ and M_i is a ps-query (not boolean) that is *coherent with* S_i, i.e. for every D_i satisfying S_i, there exists T such that $D_i \leq T$ and $M_i(T) \simeq D_i$.

Example 4. Consider the data integration system $\mathcal{I} = \langle \mathcal{G}, \mathcal{S}, \mathcal{M} \rangle$ that corresponds to the one discussed in Section 2. The global schema $\mathcal{G} = \langle S_\mathcal{G}, \Phi_K, \Phi_{FK} \rangle$ is the one of the Example 2. The source schema is $\mathcal{S} = \{S_1, S_2\}$, where S_1, S_2 correspond to the DTDs of Section 2. Finally, the mapping $\mathcal{M}$ is a set of expressions of the form: (S_i, M_i, as_i), for $i = 1, 2$, where M_i's are those of Fig. 2(a) and Fig. 2(c) and $as_i \in \{sound, exact\}$.

Given a set of data sources $\mathcal{D} = \{D_1, ..., D_m\}$ that conform to $\mathcal{S} = \{S_1, ..., S_m\}$ (i.e. $D_i \models S_i$, $i = 1, ..., m$), the semantics of a data integration system consists of all the legal data trees that conform to the schema $\mathcal{G}$ and satisfy the mappings $\mathcal{M}$. More precisely, we have the following:

$$sem(\mathcal{I}, \mathcal{D}) = \{T | T \models S_{\mathcal{G}}, T \models \Phi_K, T \models \Phi_{FK},$$
$$\forall i = 1, ...m, D_i \leq M_i(T) \text{ if } as_i = sound$$
$$D_i \simeq M_i(T) \text{ if } as_i = exact\}$$

According to the above definition, it may happen that no legal data tree exists that belongs to $sem(\mathcal{I}, \mathcal{D})$. In this case, the setting is *inconsistent*. This may happen for the following reasons.

- The global schema specification may be *inconsistent*, i.e. there may not exist any tree that satisfies both $S_{\mathcal{G}}$ and the set of constraints. It was shown in [5], that in the case of a general DTD, the problem is decidable and its complexity is NP-complete.
- A mapping may be *trivially inconsistent*, i.e. for every tree T that satisfies the global schema, $M_i(T) = T_{\emptyset}$. It is possible to check whether a mapping is trivially inconsistent by verifying that, given the global schema $S_{\mathcal{G}} = \langle \Sigma_\tau, r, \mu \rangle$ and a mapping $(S_i, M_i, as_i) \in \mathcal{M}$, with $M_i = \langle t_{q_i}, \lambda_{q_i}, cond_{q_i}, sel_{q_i} \rangle$, we have that for every $n \in t_{q_i}$: (i) if n is the root of t_{q_i}, then $\lambda_{q_i}(n) = r$, (ii) if $\lambda_{q_i}(n) = a$, all children n_i of n have distinct labels among those in $\mu(a)$. This check is clearly polynomial.
- There may be an *empty mapping*, i.e. given a source D_i, there might not exist any data tree T such that $M_i(T) \leq D_i$. This problem is also decidable. A PTIME algorithm would consist in building from M_i the query M_i' that results by ignoring the existential subtree patterns of M_i, and then checking whether $M_i'(D_i) \simeq D_i$.
- Finally, there may occur some inconsistencies among data sources and $\mathcal{G}$. In our example this would happen if two sources contain patients with the same SSN but different names.

In what follows, we will assume to deal with consistent data integration systems (note that decidability of data integration consistency problem is an open problem).

4.2   Query Answering with Identification

The main task of a data integration system is obviously to answer queries. Following the classical approach, we define a *certain answer* to a ps-query q posed over a data integration system $\mathcal{I} = \langle \mathcal{G}, \mathcal{S}, \mathcal{M} \rangle$ w.r.t. to a set of data sources $\mathcal{D}$, as follows:

$$q^{\mathcal{I}, \mathcal{D}} = \bigcap_{T \in sem(\mathcal{I}, \mathcal{D})} q(T)$$

i.e. $q^{\mathcal{I}, \mathcal{D}}$ is the intersection of the answers to q over all legal data trees w.r.t. $\mathcal{I}$.

Theorem 1. *Given a set of sources $\mathcal{D}$, a consistent data integration system $\mathcal{I} = \langle \mathcal{G}, \mathcal{S}, \mathcal{M} \rangle$ and a ps-query q, $q^{\mathcal{I}, \mathcal{D}}$ is the maximal data tree that is a prefix of $q(T)$, for every legal data tree T w.r.t. to $\mathcal{I}$.*

Remark. The certain answer to a query q posed over a data integration system $\mathcal{I}$ w.r.t. to a set of data sources $\mathcal{D}$ is a data tree T such that there may not exist any T' such that $q(T') = T$. This is not surprising since by the previous theorem we have that the certain answer is the maximal *prefix of the answers* to q over all legal data trees, which only means that for every legal data tree T'', T is a prefix of the answer $q(T'')$.

To illustrate identification, let us observe the following. Suppose that no existential tree patterns were expressed in any mapping and that node ids were available that were shared among data sources. Then computing the certain answer would basically consists in merging the data sources, adding nodes to satisfy the constraints, querying the resulting tree and returning the "certain" prefix of the answer. Following this intuition, we possibly extend each data source D_i by a data source $D_i' = \langle t_i', \lambda_i', \nu_i' \rangle$ that is obtained from D_i by adding nodes whose presence can be inferred in every legal data tree from the mapping specification (S_i, M_i, as_i), where $as_i \in \{sound, complete\}$. These nodes correspond to existential tree patterns nodes in M_i. More precisely, for each leaf $n \in D_i = \langle t_i, \lambda_i, \nu_i \rangle$ labeled a_j, we consider the node n_q of t_q such that there exists a valuation γ from t_q to D_i with $\gamma(n_q) = n$ (note that this node exists and is unique since we assumed that M_i is coherent with S_i and mappings are neither trivially inconsistent, nor empty). If m_q is a child of n_q such that $sel_q(m_q) = false$, then we recursively proceed as follows. For every node m_q' in the subtree rooted at m_q, a node m is added in $D_i = \langle t_i, \lambda_i, \nu_i \rangle$ such that we can extend γ by defining $\gamma(m_q') = m$, where:

- m is child of the node n of t_i' such that $\gamma^{-1}(n)$ is defined and it is the parent of m_q';
- $\lambda_i'(m) = \lambda_q(m_q)$;
- if $cond_q(m_q)$ is defined, then $\nu_i'(m) = v_s$ where v_s is a fresh Skolem constant such that $cond_q(m_q)$ is satisfied.

Next, we define the *Identification* function whose aim is to obtain from each extended data source D_i' a new data source, called *identified data source*, whose nodes have global ids that depend on $\mathcal{G}$, such that two nodes have the same global id only if they are merged in every legal data tree. In order to introduce the identification, we start by recursively defining the domain $\mathcal{N}^I$ of global ids:

- $\epsilon \in \mathcal{N}^I$;
- if $\mathbf{n} \in \mathcal{N}^I$, then $\mathbf{n}.a_i[.\gamma_i] \in \mathcal{N}^I$, where $a_i \in \Sigma$ and γ_i is an optional value in $\bar{\Gamma} = \Gamma \cup \mathcal{V}^S$, where $\mathcal{V}^S$ is a set of Skolem constants.

Finally, $Id(D)$ is obtained by recursively associating to each node n in $D_i' = \langle t_i', \lambda_i', \nu_i' \rangle$ a global id $\mathbf{id_n}$ in $\mathcal{N}^I$:

- if n is the root of t_i', then $\mathbf{id_n} = \epsilon$;
- if n labeled a_j is child of a node p labeled a, $\mathbf{id_n} = \mathbf{id_p}.a_j[.\gamma]$ where γ is an optional value appearing if:
  - either there exists $a_j.k \rightarrow a_j \in \Phi_K$; then if n has a child m labeled k, then $\gamma = \nu(m)$, otherwise $\gamma = v_s$ where v_s is a fresh constant in $\mathcal{V}^S$;
  - or $a_j^{\omega_j} \in \mu(a)$, where $\omega_j \in \{+, *\}$; then $\gamma = v_s$, with v_s fresh constant in $\mathcal{V}^S$.

Note that, by an abuse of notation, we denote $Id(D_i)$ the data source obtained by first extending the original data source and then identifying nodes as described. $Id(D_i)$ is such that all its nodes have a global id. If $\mathbf{id_n}$ does not contain any Skolem constant, we say that n is uniquely identified. In the following example, we illustrate identification.

Example 5. Given the data integration system of Example 4 and the source D_1 given in Fig. 2(d), $Id(D_1)$ is represented in Fig. 3, where the labels of nodes added by the

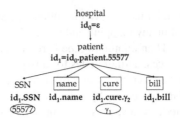

Fig. 3. Identified tree $Id(\mathcal{D})$

identification are boxed, the global ids are marked in bold and γ_i represent Skolem constants in $\mathcal{V}^S$, for $i = 1, 2$. Note that all nodes are uniquely identified, except for the node labeled cure. Moreover, γ_1 represents a data value lower than 35.

By identifying data sources, clearly, two nodes are assigned the same global id only if they are merged in every legal data tree. Moreover, the data sources extension does not modify the sources content that is mapped to every legal data tree. It therefore does not affect certain answers. Indeed, it is straightforward to prove the following theorem.

Theorem 2. *Given a set of data sources $\mathcal{D}$ and a data integration system $\mathcal{I} = \langle \mathcal{G}, \mathcal{S}, \mathcal{M} \rangle$, the following holds:*

$$q^{\mathcal{I},\mathcal{D}} = \bigcap_{T \in sem(\mathcal{I},\mathcal{D})} q(T) = \bigcap_{T \in sem(\mathcal{I},Id(\mathcal{D}))} q(T).$$

From now on, the previous theorem will let us consider $sem(\mathcal{I}, Id(\mathcal{D}))$ rather than $sem(\mathcal{I}, \mathcal{D})$.

5   Query Answering Algorithms

In this section, we provide three algorithms that use identification to answer ps-queries over $\mathcal{I}$, under the assumption of sound, exact and mixed mappings. All proposed algorithms follow an approach that is typical in the presence of incomplete information. This is not surprising since it is well-known [6] that LAV data integration query answering is strongly related to the problem of querying an incomplete database. Indeed, data sources provide only partial information on legal data trees. Thus, our algorithms are all based on the idea of constructing a weak representation system **T** [7], to represent all legal trees (i.e. $sem(\mathbf{T}) = sem(\mathcal{I}, Id(\mathcal{D}))$), such that for each **T** and each ps-query q there exists a representation $\mathbf{q}(\mathbf{T})$ such that $\bigcap\{T | T \in sem(\mathbf{q}(\mathbf{T}))\} = \bigcap\{q(T) | T \in sem(\mathbf{T})\}$. It follows that the complexity is given by (i) the complexity of computing **T**, (ii) the complexity of constructing $\mathbf{q}(\mathbf{T})$, and (iii) the complexity of computing the intersection of answers represented by $\mathbf{q}(\mathbf{T})$.

5.1   Query Answering Under Sound Mappings

Before introducing the algorithm for query answering, we highlight that, as mentioned earlier, it is based on the idea of building a weak representation system **T**. Because of lack of space, instead of introducing formally **T**, we intuitively present it as a special tree with values in $\bar{\Gamma}$. In particular, **T** may have Skolems as data values that are constrained to satisfy conditions similar to those expressed by ps-queries (note that this may happen, for example, when nodes are added in order to satisfy existential subtree patterns in the mappings, or a constraint of the schema). The valuation of a query q over **T** has to be modified accordingly. In particular, $\mathbf{q}(\mathbf{T})$ may contain Skolem constants for data values, since it has to be equivalent to **T** from the point of view of certain answers to q.

Given a query q, a system $\mathcal{I}$ and a set of sources $\mathcal{D} = \{D_1, ..., D_m\}$, our algorithm for query answering under the assumption of sound mappings proceeds as follows.

1. We compute $Id(\mathcal{D})$ $w.r.t.$ to $\mathcal{G}$ and obtain a data tree with global ids and with data values in $\bar{\Gamma}$. However, this tree may contain nodes that are semantically equivalent, i.e. they represent the same node in every legal data tree, but have different node identifiers. In particular, this may happen when $Id(D_i)$ and $Id(D_j)$ contain resp. nodes n_i, n_j labeled a uniquely identified by the same id $\mathbf{id_n}$ and nodes m_i, m_j, labeled b, resp. children of n_i, n_j, that are identified with different global ids, whereas according to $S_{\mathcal{G}}$, nodes labeled a should have at most one child labeled b. To simplify, suppose that they are not datanodes. If at least one among m_i, m_j, say m_i, is not uniquely identified, then the sources are consistent and we say that m_i, m_j can be *unified*, by replacing the global id of n_i with the id of n_j. We then obtain the *retrieved global data tree* $w.r.t.$ to $\mathcal{D}$, denoted $ret(\mathcal{I}, \mathcal{D})$. It is possible to prove that if the setting is consistent, then $ret(\mathcal{I}, \mathcal{D})$ is such that $ret(\mathcal{I}, \mathcal{D}) \leq T$, for every legal data tree T.

2. We compute the representation system $\mathbf{T} = \langle t^*, \lambda^*, \nu^* \rangle$ for all legal data trees, by adding nodes to $ret(\mathcal{I}, \mathcal{D})$ in order to satisfy $\mathcal{G}$. More precisely, we proceed by applying the following rules:

   (a) For each p labeled a, if $a_i^{\omega_i} \in \mu(a)$ where $\omega_i \in \{1, +\}$ and n' has not any child labeled a_i, then we add to **T** the child n of p, with $\lambda^*(n) = a_i$ and $\nu^*(n) = \mathbf{0}$. If $a_i.k \rightarrow a_i \in \Phi_K$ or $\omega_i = +$, then $\mathbf{id_n} = \mathbf{id_p}.a_i.\gamma_s$ where γ_s is a fresh constant from $\mathcal{V}^s$, otherwise $\mathbf{id_n} = \mathbf{id_p}.a_i$.

   (b) For each m_a labeled h_a, child of n_a labeled a, if $a.h_a \subseteq b.k_b \in \Phi_{FK}$, and there is not any node labeled b with key value $\nu(m_a)$, then we add a set of nodes, one node n' for each label l that occurs from the root to the parent of the node labeled b in $S_{\mathcal{G}}$, where $\lambda^*(n') = l$ and $\nu^*(n') = \mathbf{0}$, so that the tree satisfies the global schema. Note that since the foreign key constraints are uniquely localizable, all these nodes are uniquely identified and therefore their global ids depend only on $\mathcal{G}$. Suppose that p is the last node that is added, and that its global id is $\mathbf{id_p}$. Then we add the node n_b child of p, with global id $\mathbf{id_{n_b}} = \mathbf{id_p}.\nu(m_a)$ and such that $\lambda^*(n_b) = b$ and $\nu^*(n_b) = \mathbf{0}$. Moreover, we add the child m_b of n_b, with global id $\mathbf{id_{m_b}} = \mathbf{id_{n_b}}.k_b$ such that $\lambda^*(m_b) = k_b$ and $\nu^*(m_b) = \nu(m_a)$.

Intuitively, this step corresponds to computing the well-known technique of the *Chase* over $ret(\mathcal{I}, \mathcal{D})$. Since the Chase may not stop and lead to an infinite data tree, we proceeds as long as the algorithm adds nodes (that are required by the schema) that have either the form $\mathbf{id_n} = \mathbf{id_p}.a$ or the form $\mathbf{id_n} = \mathbf{id_p}.a.\gamma_s$ where

$a \in \Sigma_{\tau}$, $\gamma_s \in \mathcal{V}^s$ is a Skolem constant and there is not any node with global id $\mathrm{id_n} = \mathrm{id_p.a.}\gamma_s'$ where $\gamma_s' \in \mathcal{V}^s, \gamma_s' \neq \gamma_s$.

3. We compute $\mathbf{q}(\mathbf{T})$ and return its certain prefix $\bar{T} = \langle \bar{t}, \bar{\lambda}, \bar{\nu} \rangle$. Note in particular that for every n in $\mathbf{q}(\mathbf{T})$ such that $\nu^*(n)$ is a Skolem, we set $\bar{\nu}(n) = \mathbf{0}$.

Claim. Given a consistent data integration system, the above algorithm terminates.

Theorem 3. *Given a consistent data integration system $\mathcal{I}$ with sound mappings, a set of sources and a ps-query q, $q^{\mathcal{I},\mathcal{D}} = \bar{T}$, where $\bar{T}$ is computed as above.*

Complexity. Let us discuss the computational complexity of the above algorithm. In particular, we focus on data complexity, which refers to the size of the set of data sources $\mathcal{D}$. It is easy to see that the construction of the data tree $\mathbf{T}$ is polynomial in the size of $\mathcal{D}$. Moreover, the size of $\mathbf{T}$ is polynomial. Then, since the construction of $\mathbf{q}(\mathbf{T})$ is polynomial in the size of $\mathbf{T}$, we have that our algorithm is PTIME.

5.2   Query Answering Under Exact Mappings

Suppose now that mappings are exact. As for the representation of legal data trees, we can use incomplete trees of [1], known to be a strong representation system for ps-queries. However, we have to deal with three major differences *w.r.t.* [1]. The first is that persistent node ids are not available in our setting. As for global ids obtained by first identifying the sources and then computing possible unifications, there still may occur two nodes with different global ids that represent the same node in every legal data tree. Recall the example from the end of Section 2. Let us call n_1, n_2 the two nodes labeled patient belonging to D_1, n_3 the node with the same label belonging to D_2. Without keys, n_1, n_2, n_3 would be assigned different global ids. However, as already discussed, under exact mappings, we can conclude that n_1 and n_3 are the same in every legal tree. Thus, in order to correctly identify source nodes, view definitions should also be taken into account. Of course, this would notably increase the query answering complexity.

Therefore, we introduce the *Visible Keys Restriction (VKR)* for $\mathcal{I}$:

– For every element a, member of a collection of $S_\mathcal{G}$, there exists $a.k \rightarrow a \in \Phi_K$.
– For every view M_i such that $(S_i, M_i, exact) \in \mathcal{M}$, M_i is such that whenever it selects an element with a key, it also selects its key.

This ensures that all nodes can be uniquely identified. Then, by identifying the sources, we reduce our setting to the case of [1] where global ids play the role of persistent ids.

The second major difference *w.r.t.* [1] is the ps-query language. In this paper, we extend ps-queries of [1] in order to make them express existential subtree patterns. It is possible to prove that such an extension maintains all the good properties of ps-queries. In particular, incomplete trees (whose construction is accordingly modified) are still a strong representation system for our query language.

The third major difference *w.r.t.* [1] is the presence of foreign keys. Intuitively, we introduce additional sources that contain the data required to satisfy foreign keys. More precisely, given a foreign key $a.h_a \subseteq b.k_b \in \Phi_{FK}$, for each sequence of labels from the root to nodes labeled h_a in $Id(\mathcal{D})$, we introduce a source D_{m+j} containing all nodes m_a in $Id(\mathcal{D})$ labeled h_a characterized by that sequence of labels, together with their ancestors. Moreover, the source will contain all the nodes from the root to nodes n_b, m_b with respective labels b, k_b, such that for each node m_a there is a node n_b with key value $\nu(m_b) = \nu(m_a)$. Note that, after identification, under the assumption of uniquely localizable foreign keys, all the ancestors of nodes labeled b are uniquely identified.

Under VKR assumption, the algorithm with exact mappings proceeds as follows.

1. We compute $Id(\mathcal{D})$.
2. To guarantee the satisfaction of foreign key constraints, for every $a.h_a \subseteq b.k_b \in \Phi_{FK}$ and for every different sequence of labels from the root to nodes $n \in Id(\mathcal{D})$ labeled a, we build a data source and the corresponding view definition as described above. We call $D_{m+1}, ... D_{m+k}$ the new data sources. Then we add the corresponding exact mappings to $\mathcal{M}$, for every $j = m + 1, ... m + k$.
3. We compute the incomplete tree $\mathbf{T_i}$ s.t. $sem(\mathbf{T_i}) = \{T | M_i(T) \simeq Id(D_i)\}$, for $i = 1, .., m$ and $\mathbf{T_j}$ s.t. $sem(\mathbf{T_j}) = \{T | M_j(T) \simeq Id(D_j)\}$, for $j = m+1, .., m+k$.
4. We compute the incomplete tree $\mathbf{T'}$ such that $sem(\mathbf{T'}) = \bigcap_{i \in \{1,...,m+k\}} sem(\mathbf{T_i})$.
5. In order to take into account the tree type $S_\mathcal{G}$, we compute the incomplete tree $\mathbf{T}$ such that $sem(\mathbf{T}) = sem(\mathbf{T'}) \cap sem(S_\mathcal{G})$.
6. We query the incomplete tree $\mathbf{T}$ and obtain the representation $\mathbf{q(T)}$.

Theorem 4. *Given a consistent* $\mathcal{I} = \langle \mathcal{G}, \mathcal{S}, \mathcal{M} \rangle$, *with* $\mathcal{M}$ *all exact, a set of sources* $\mathcal{D}$ *for* $\mathcal{I}$ *and a ps-query* q, *under the VKR assumption,* $q^{\mathcal{I},\mathcal{D}} = \bigcap \{T | T \in sem(\mathbf{q(T)})\}$.

Complexity. In [1], it was shown that computing $\mathbf{q(T)}$ is PTIME in data complexity. Moreover, checking whether $\bar{T}$ is a certain prefix of $\mathbf{q(T)}$ is PTIME in the size of $q(\mathbf{T})$, itself PTIME. We strongly conjecture that checking whether $\bar{T}$ is the maximal certain prefix is also PTIME. On the other hand, it was also shown in [1] that the problem of deciding whether $\bar{T}$ is a certain prefix of $\mathbf{q(T)}$ is NP-complete in the sequence of ps-queries. We therefore conjecture that checking whether $\bar{T}$ is a certain answer of q over $\mathcal{I}$ is NP-complete in the number of data sources.

5.3   Query Answering Under Mixed Mappings

We now present an algorithm to answer queries under sound and/or exact mappings. Suppose that a different color C_i is associated to each source D_i characterized by a sound mapping. The idea is to reduce the query answering algorithm under mixed mappings to query answering with exact mappings. Suppose that we have a collection of nodes labeled a_i in $S_\mathcal{G}$ and a source D_i provides some sound information about this collection. We can abstractly consider D_i as the source providing exactly the nodes with label a_i and color C_i. This requires to add the information about the color to each node of the collection. Then, under the VKR assumption, we are able to answer queries.

1. We compute the extended tree type $\hat{S}_\mathcal{G} = \langle \hat{\Sigma}_\tau, r, \hat{\mu} \rangle$ by modifying $S_\mathcal{G}$ so that $\hat{\Sigma}_T = \Sigma_T \cup C$, and $\hat{\mu}$ is defined as follows:

$$\forall a \in \hat{\Sigma}, \hat{\mu}(a) = \begin{cases} \mu(a)C^* & \text{if } a \text{ is a member of some collection of } S_\mathcal{G} \\ \mu(a) & \text{otherwise} \end{cases}$$

2. For every sound mapping, we build $\hat{M}_i = \langle \hat{t}_i, \hat{\lambda}_i, \hat{cond}_i, \hat{sel}_i \rangle$ by modifying $M_i = \langle t_i, \lambda_i, cond_i, sel_i \rangle$ so that for every node $n \in t_i$ such that $\hat{\lambda}_i(n) = a$, where a is a member of some collection in $\mathcal{S}_{\mathcal{G}}$, n has a child m labeled C, such that $\hat{cond}_i(m) = " = C_i"$, where C_i is the color of D_i.

3. For every data source D_i with color C_i, characterized by a sound mapping, we build the data source $\hat{D}_i = \langle \hat{t}_i, \hat{\lambda}_i, \hat{\nu}_i \rangle$ by adding to every node $n \in D_i$, labeled with a member of a collection, a child data node m labeled with C such that $\hat{\nu}_i(m) = C_i$.

4. We apply the algorithm described in the previous section and obtain the incomplete tree $\hat{T}$. Then we query it and obtain the representation $\mathbf{q}(\hat{T})$.

Theorem 5. *Given a consistent* $\mathcal{I} = \langle \mathcal{G}, \mathcal{S}, \mathcal{M} \rangle$, *with* $\mathcal{M}$ *mixed, a set of sources* $\mathcal{D}$ *for* $\mathcal{I}$ *and a ps-query* q, *under the VKR assumption,* $q^{\mathcal{I}, \mathcal{D}} = \bigcap \{ T | T \in sem(\mathbf{q}(\hat{T})) \}$.

Complexity. Obviously, the complexity is the same as in the previous case.

6   Discussion and Future Works

We have presented a formal framework for XML data integration, based on an expressive global schema specified by means of a simplified DTD and XML keys and foreign keys. We have shown how to address the issue of identifying nodes coming from different sources. Then, we have proposed query answering algorithms assuming that mappings are sound and/or exact. It turns out that under sound mappings assumption, we are able to answer queries in polynomial time in data complexity. In the exact case, in order to limit the complexity, we have introduced an extra condition, namely the *Visible Key Restriction (VKR)*. We strongly conjecture that, under this assumption, the query answering problem is NP in the number of views. This apparent loss allows to gain very much in terms of expressivity of the representation system that we use to answer queries. In particular, we may ask for *possible answers*. We may also extract a precise description about missing information as shown in [1]. This information may be used to guide our system in finding additional data sources to answer queries. Moreover, we showed how to incorporate information about the data origin. This may be very useful to optimize query answering. In fact, our algorithms are all naive, in that they proceed by first constructing a representation of all legal data trees and then by querying it. The next step is to propose more efficient algorithms that do not need to build such representation but only the portion of interest with respect to the query.

In the future, we plan to follow several other research directions. In particular, we will study more carefully the complexity of query answering in the exact case. Then, we plan to consider more expressive query languages for the specification of the mappings as well as for querying the system. An orthogonal issue would concern data sources inconsistencies. To this aim, repair techniques for XML data would be required.

Acknowledgements. We are very grateful to Maurizio Lenzerini and Diego Calvanese for the helpful discussions that lead to the revision of the first draft, to Ioana Manolescu and Bogdan Cautis for having helped us by carefully reading the paper and giving precious feedbacks, and to Luc Segoufin for many interesting discussions about the topic. Finally we would also like to thank the referees for several very useful comments.

References

1. S. Abiteboul, L. Segoufin, and V. Vianu. Representing and querying xml with incomplete information. In *Proc. of ACM PODS*, 2001.
2. M. Arenas and L. Libkin. Xml data exchange: Consistency and query answering. In *Proc. of ACM PODS*, 2005. To Appear.
3. M. Benedikt, C. Chan, W. Fan, J. Freire, and R. Rastogi. Capturing both Types and Constraints in Data Integration. In *Proc. of ACM SIGMOD*, 2003.
4. P. Buneman, S. Davidson, W. Fan, C. Hara, and W. Tan. Keys for XML. In *Proc. of the Int. WWW Conf.*, pages 201–210, 2001.
5. W. Fan and L. Libkin. On XML Integrity Constraints in the Presence of DTDs. *J. ACM*, 49(3):368–406, 2002.
6. A.Y. Halevy. Answering queries using views: A survey. *Very Large Database J.*, 10(4):270–294, 2001.
7. J. Imielinski and W. Lipski. Incomplete information in relational databases. *JACM*, 31(4), 1984.
8. T. Kirk, A. Y. Levy, Y. Sagiv, and D. Srivastava. The information manifold. In C. Knoblock and A. Levy, editors, *Information Gathering from Heterogeneous, Distributed Environments*, Stanford University, Stanford, California, 1995.
9. M. Lenzerini. Data integration: A theoretical perspective. In *Proc. of ACM PODS*, 2002.
10. C. Li, R. Yerneni, V. Vassalos, H. Garcia-Molina, Y. Papakonstantinou, J. D. Ullman, and M. Valiveti. Capability based mediation in TSIMMIS. In *Proc. of ACM SIGMOD*, 1998.
11. Y. Papakonstantinou, S. Abiteboul, and H. Garcia-Molina. Object fusion in mediator systems. In *Proc. of VLDB*, 1996.
12. Jeffrey D. Ullman. Information integration using logical views. In *Proc. of Intl. Conf. on Database Theory*, 1997.

Satisfiability of XPath Queries with Sibling Axes

Floris Geerts[1] and Wenfei Fan[2]

[1] Hasselt University and University of Edinburgh
[2] University of Edinburgh and Bell Laboratories

Abstract. We study the satisfiability problem for XPath fragments supporting the following-sibling and preceding-sibling axes. Although this problem was recently studied for XPath fragments without sibling axes, little is known about the impact of the sibling axes on the satisfiability analysis. To this end we revisit the satisfiability problem for a variety of XPath fragments with sibling axes, in the presence of DTDs, in the absence of DTDs, and under various restricted DTDs. In these settings we establish complexity bounds ranging from NLOGSPACE to undecidable. Our main conclusion is that in many cases, the presence of sibling axes complicates the satisfiability analysis. Indeed, we show that there are XPath satisfiability problems that are in PTIME and PSPACE in the absence of sibling axes, but that become NP-hard and EXPTIME-hard, respectively, when sibling axes are used instead of the corresponding vertical modalities (e.g., the wildcard and the descendant axis).

1 Introduction

We revisit the *satisfiability problem* for XPath [7] in the presence of DTDs. It is the problem to determine, given an XPath query Q and a DTD D, whether or not there exists an XML document T such that T conforms to D and satisfies Q, i.e., the set $Q(T)$ of nodes of T selected by Q is nonempty.

The prevalent use of XPath highlights the need for the satisfiability analysis of XPath queries. Indeed, XPath has been commonly used in specifying XML constraints (e.g., [6, 9, 27]), queries (e.g., XSLT, XQuery), updates (e.g., [26]), and access control (e.g., [10]). In many applications both XPath expressions and DTDs are present. The static satisfiability analysis of XPath addresses the interaction between XPath and DTDs, and is useful in query optimization, update manipulation and reasoning about XML access control, among other things. An alternative to the static analysis would be a dynamic approach. As an example, consider an access-control policy S defined in terms of a DTD and XPath queries, which is to prevent disclosure of XML documents to unauthorized users by validating that the documents "satisfy" S. One could simply attempt to validate a document with respect to S at run-time. This, however, would not tell us whether repeated failures are due to inconsistency between the XPath queries and the DTD, or problems with the documents.

The satisfiability problem has been studied for a large number of XPath fragments [2, 13, 15, 17], in the presence and in the absence of DTDs. The previous work has mostly focused on XPath queries with only vertical modalities

G. Bierman and C. Koch (Eds.): DBPL 2005, LNCS 3774, pp. 122–137, 2005.

such as *child, parent, descendant* and *ancestor* axes (referred to "$\downarrow, \uparrow, \downarrow^*, \uparrow^*$", respectively). However, XML data is ordered and it is often desirable to access this order using XPath. Indeed, consider an XML document storing items bought by customers over a period of time. The items are grouped under customers and appear according to their date of acquisition. In order to detect customer behavior over time, one needs to be able to pose queries involving order. Therefore, it is common to find XPath queries that need sideways traversal via *horizontal* modalities such as (immediate) *right-sibling* and *left-sibling* axes (denoted by "$\rightarrow, \rightarrow^*, \leftarrow, \leftarrow^*$", respectively). It is natural to ask whether the presence of sibling axes simplifies or complicates the satisfiability analysis. For example, consider a fragment $\mathcal{X}(\downarrow, [\,])$ that supports wildcard ($\downarrow$) and qualifiers ([ ]) and characterizes well-studied tree pattern queries [1, 2, 28, 29]. One would want to know whether the satisfiability analysis becomes easier or harder for $\mathcal{X}(\rightarrow, [\,])$ (resp. $\mathcal{X}(\leftarrow, [\,])$), the horizontal counterpart of $\mathcal{X}(\downarrow, [\,])$ by substituting $\rightarrow$ (resp. $\leftarrow$) for $\downarrow$. The complexity of the satisfiability analysis is not yet known for a variety of XPath fragments with sibling axes.

Related to the satisfiability analysis is the *containment problem*, which is to determine, given two XPath queries Q_1, Q_2 and a DTD D, whether or not for all XML documents T that conform to D, $Q_1(T)$ is contained in $Q_2(T)$. While there has also been a host of work on the containment analysis [8, 17, 19, 22, 29], the previous results cannot answer the questions of the satisfiability analysis. Indeed, as already observed by [2], the lower bounds for the containment analysis are often much higher than its satisfiability counterpart. Worse still, to our knowledge there has not been a full treatment of the containment problem for various fragments with the sibling axes or XPath negation.

Main Results. To this end we investigate the satisfiability problem for a variety of XPath fragments with sibling axes, in the following settings:

- XPath fragments: with or without recursion axis (e.g., $\rightarrow^*, \leftarrow^*, \downarrow^*, \uparrow^*$), qualifiers ([ ]), data-value joins (denoted by =), and negation ($\neg$);
- DTDs: in the presence of DTDs vs. in the absence of DTDs; fixed DTDs vs. arbitrary DTDs; and restricted DTDs with or without DTD recursion, disjunction, and Kleene star in element type definitions.

We establish lower and upper bounds for the satisfiability analysis in these settings, which range from NLOGSPACE to undecidable. We also explore the impact of sibling axes on the analysis. We show that in the absence of XPath qualifiers, the presence of sibling axes does not complicate the satisfiability analysis. In contrast, in the presence of qualifiers, sibling axes make the analysis harder. Indeed, we show the following. (a) The satisfiability problem for $\mathcal{X}(\rightarrow, [\,])$ is NP-hard under fixed, disjunction-free DTDs, whereas it is in PTIME for its vertical counterpart $\mathcal{X}(\downarrow, [\,])$ in the same setting [2]. (b) It is EXPTIME-hard for $\mathcal{X}(\uparrow, \rightarrow, \cup, [\,], \neg)$, a fragment with upward and sibling axes and negation but without recursion; in contrast, it is in PSPACE for the vertical counterpart $\mathcal{X}(\downarrow, \uparrow, \cup, [\,], \neg)$ [2]. (c) Under non-recursive and fixed DTDs and in the absence of DTDs, it is still unknown [2] whether or not the satisfiability problem is decidable for $\mathcal{X}(\downarrow, \downarrow^*, \uparrow, \uparrow^*, \cup, [\ ], \neg, =)$, a fragment with negation, data-value joins and all the vertical axes. In contrast, the problem is undecidable when sibling axes are introduced; indeed, it is undecidable for $\mathcal{X}(\uparrow, \leftarrow, \rightarrow, \rightarrow^*, \cup, [\ ], =, \neg)$ in the same settings.

In addition to the complexity bounds for the satisfiability problems, we also explore the connection between vertical and horizontal axes and the connection between the satisfiability and containment analysis, establishing first lower bound results for the containment analysis of XPath fragments with sibling axes.

These results help us understand the interaction between different XPath axes, as well as their interaction with various DTD constructs. Taken together, these results and the previous work [2, 13, 15, 17] provide a detailed treatment of the satisfiability analysis for a large number of XPath fragments commonly found in practice, in a variety of DTD settings.

Related Work. The satisfiability problem has been studied in [2, 13, 15, 17]. Complexity bounds were provided in [2] for various XPath fragment under a variety of DTDs. However, no sibling axes were considered there. Our results in this paper complement and extend the results of [2]. The main focus of [17] is about extensions of XPath, and it provided EXPTIME (lower and upper) bounds on equivalence for an extension of XPath in the presence of DTDs, which implies an EXPTIME bound for our fragment with all the axes and negation but without data-value joins. We will show in Section 4.3 that the EXPTIME-hardness already holds for a subclass of the fragment without recursion axes. The XPath queries considered in [15] are basically tree patterns with node equality, inequality and limited use of data joins; neither negation nor sibling axes were considered there; furthermore, DTDs were restricted to be non-recursive disjunction-free in [15]. In the absence of DTDs, [13] studied the satisfiability problem for XPath without negation and data-value joins. From the results of [2], we already know that these bounds do not hold in the presence of DTDs. In particular, [13] gave PTIME bounds for XPath fragments with qualifiers, sibling axes, upward axes, and a root test in the absence of DTDs. We show that in the presence of DTDs, the problem is NP-hard, and we give PTIME bounds in the absence of qualifiers, and in the presence of sibling, upward axes and DTDs.

There has also been work on the containment problem for XPath fragments in the absence and in the presence of DTDs [8, 17, 19, 22, 29]. Most of the work (except [22, 17]) only studied fragments without upward axes, sibling axes, data-value joins and negation. The negation defined in [22] is quite different from the general XPath negation operator. See [25] for a recent survey. As shown in [2], the complexity bounds for the containment analysis are typically much higher than its satisfiability counterpart in the absence of negation. In the presence of negation, the connection between the containment analysis and its satisfiability counterpart was explored in [2] and will be further discussed in Section 5.

Other active areas of XPath research include the expressive power of XPath (e.g., [3, 12, 16, 17, 18, 20, 21]) and query rewriting and minimization (e.g., [1, 9, 11, 23, 28]). While XPath satisfiability is not the focus in those areas, the satisfiability analysis is useful for XPath rewriting, minimization and optimization.

Organization. Section 2 reviews DTDs and defines XPath fragments. Section 3 explores the connection between sibling and vertical axes. Section 4 studies the satisfiability problem for XPath fragments with sibling axes, followed by the containment analysis in Section 5. Section 6 summarizes the main results of the paper. All proofs can be found in the full paper.

2 Preliminaries

In this section we first review DTDs [5] and describe the XPath [7] fragments considered in this paper. We then state the satisfiability problem in the presence of DTDs and address its connection with the counterpart in the absence of DTDs.

2.1 DTDs

Without loss of generality, we represent a Document Type Definition (DTD [5]) D as (Ele, Att, P, R, r), where (1) Ele is a finite set of *element types*, ranged over by $A, B, \ldots$; (2) r is a distinguished type in Ele, called the *root type*; (3) P is a function that defines the element types: for each A in Ele, $P(A)$ is a regular expression over Ele; we refer to $A \rightarrow P(A)$ as the *production* of A; (4) Att is a finite set of *attribute names*, ranged over by $a, b, \ldots$; and (5) R defines the attributes: for each A in Ele, $R(A)$ is a subset of Att.

A DTD $D = (Ele, Att, P, R, r)$ is said to be *disjunction-free* if for any element type $A \in Ele$, $P(A)$ does not contain disjunction '$+$'. It is called *no-star* if for any $A \in Ele$, $P(A)$ does not contain the Kleene star '$*$' (this should not be confused with star-free regular expressions). It is *recursive* if the dependency graph of D, which contains an edge (A, B) iff B is in $P(A)$, has a cycle.

An XML document is typically modeled as a (finite) node-labeled tree [5], with nodes additionally annotated with values for attributes. We refer to this as an *XML tree*. An XML tree T *satisfies* (or *conforms to*) a DTD $D = (Ele, Att, P, R, r)$, denoted by $T \models D$, if (1) the root of T is labeled with r; (2) each node n in T is labeled with an Ele type A, called an A *element*; the label of n is denoted by $\mathsf{lab}(n)$; (3) each A element has a list of *children* such that their labels are a word in the regular language defined by $P(A)$; and (4) for each A in Ele and each $a \in R(A)$, each A element n has a unique a *attribute value*, denoted by $n.a$. We call T an *XML tree of D* if $T \models D$.

Example 1. Consider a DTD $D_1 = (Ele, Att, P, R, r)$ defined as

$$Ele = \{r, \ X, \ A, \ B\}.$$
$$P: \quad r \rightarrow X^*, \qquad X \rightarrow (A, B^*)^*$$
$$Att = \emptyset, \quad R(X) = R(T) = R(F) = \emptyset.$$

It is non-recursive and disjunction-free. An XML tree of D_1 is shown at the left in Fig. 1.

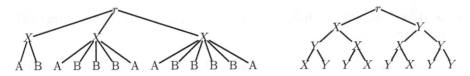

Fig. 1. XML trees of the DTDs D_1 (left) and D_2 (right) given in Example 1

Another DTD $D_2 = (Ele, Att, P, R, r)$ is defined as

$$Ele = \{r,\ X,\ Y\}.$$
$$P: \quad r \to X, Y, \qquad\quad X \to Y, X + \epsilon, \qquad\quad Y \to X, Y + \epsilon$$
$$Att = \emptyset, \quad R(X) = R(T) = R(F) = \emptyset.$$

It is recursive and no-star. An XML tree of D_2 is shown at the right in Fig. 1. ∎

Note that a DTD D may not have any XML tree T such that $T \models D$. This is because some element type A in D is *non-terminating*, i.e., there exists no finite subtree rooted at an A element that satisfies D. Fortunately, one can determine whether this is the case for any element type of D in $O(|D|)$ time, where $|D|$ is the size of D [14]. In the remainder of the paper we will assume that all element types in a DTD are terminating. This does not affect any of our results.

2.2 XPath Fragments

Over an XML tree, an XPath query specifies the selection of nodes in the tree. Assume a (possibly infinite) alphabet Σ of labels. The largest fragment of XPath studied in this paper, denoted by $\mathcal{X}(\downarrow, \downarrow^*, \uparrow, \uparrow^*, \leftarrow, \leftarrow^*, \rightarrow, \rightarrow^*, \cup, [\ ], =, \neg)$, is defined syntactically as follows:

$$p ::= \quad \epsilon \quad | \quad A \quad | \quad \downarrow \quad | \quad \downarrow^* \quad | \quad \uparrow \quad | \quad \uparrow^* \quad | \quad \rightarrow \quad | \quad \rightarrow^*$$
$$| \quad \leftarrow \quad | \quad \leftarrow^* \quad | \quad p/p \quad | \quad p \cup p \quad | \quad p[q],$$

where ϵ and A denote the empty path (the *self-axis*) and a label in Σ (the *child-axis*); '$\downarrow$' and '$\downarrow^*$' stand for the wildcard (*child*) and the *descendant-or-self-axis*, while $\uparrow$ and $\uparrow^*$ denote the *parent-axis* and *ancestor-or-self-axis*, respectively; '$\rightarrow^*$' (resp. '$\leftarrow^*$') is the following-sibling (resp. preceding-sibling) axis, and '$\rightarrow$' (resp. '$\leftarrow$') denotes the immediate right sibling (reps. the immediate left sibling); '$/$' and '$\cup$' stand for concatenation and union, respectively; and finally, q in $p[q]$ is called a *qualifier* and is defined by:

$$q ::= \quad p \quad | \quad \mathrm{lab}() = A \quad | \quad p/@a \text{ op } c \quad | \quad p/@a \text{ op } p'/@b$$
$$| \quad q_1 \wedge q_2 \quad | \quad q_1 \vee q_2 \quad | \quad \neg q,$$

where p is as defined above, A is a label in Σ, op is either '$=$' or '$\neq$' (referred to as *data-value joins*), a, b stand for attributes, c is a constant (string value), and $\wedge, \vee, \neg$ stand for *and* (conjunction), *or* (disjunction) and *not* (negation), respectively.

It is worth mentioning that while XPath [7] does not explicitly define '$\leftarrow, \rightarrow$', these operators are definable in terms of the preceding-sibling and following-sibling axes, together with *position()*, as follows:

$$\leftarrow \; = \; \leftarrow^*[position() = 1], \qquad\qquad \rightarrow \; = \; \rightarrow^*[position() = 1].$$

A query p in $\mathcal{X}(\downarrow, \downarrow^*, \uparrow, \uparrow^*, \leftarrow, \leftarrow^*, \rightarrow, \rightarrow^*, \cup, [\,], =, \neg)$ over an XML tree T is interpreted as a binary predicate on the nodes of T, while a qualifier is interpreted as a unary predicate. More specifically, for any node n in T, T *satisfies* p *at* n iff $T \models \exists n'\, p(n, n')$, where $T \models p(n, n')$ and the associated version for qualifiers, $T \models q(n)$, are defined inductively on the structure of p, q, as follows:

1. if $p = \epsilon$, then $n = n'$;
2. if $p = l$, then n' is a child of n, and is labeled l;
3. if $p = \downarrow$, then n' is a child of n, regardless of its label;
4. if $p = \downarrow^*$, then n' is either n or a descendant of n;
5. if $p = \uparrow$, then n' is the parent of n;
6. if $p = \uparrow^*$, then n' is either n or an ancestor of n;
7. if $p = \rightarrow$, then n' is the immediate right sibling of n.
8. if $p = \rightarrow^*$, then n' is either n or a right sibling of n.
9. if $p = \leftarrow$, then n' is the immediate left sibling of n.
10. if $p = \leftarrow^*$, then n' is either n or a left sibling of n.
11. if $p = p_1/p_2$, then there exists a node v in T such that $T \models p_1(n, v) \wedge p_2(v, n')$;
12. if $p = p_1 \cup p_2$, then $T \models p_1(n, n') \vee p_2(n, n')$;
13. if $p = p_1[q]$, then $T \models p_1(n, n')$ and $T \models q(n')$, where q is a unary predicate of the following cases:
    (a) q is p_2: then $T \models \exists n''\, p_2(n', n'')$;
    (b) q is $lab() = A$: then the label of n' is A;
    (c) q is $p_2/@a$ op 'c': then $T \models \exists n_1\, (p_2(n', n_1) \wedge n_1.a$ op 'c'), where $n_1.a$ denotes the value of the a attribute of n_1; that is, there exists a node n_1 in T such that $T \models p_2(n', n_1)$, n_1 has attribute a and $n_1.a$ op 'c';
    (d) q is $p_2/@a$ op $p_2'/@b$: then T satisfies the existential formula: $T \models \exists n_1\, \exists n_2\, (p_2(n', n_1) \wedge p_2'(n', n_2) \wedge n_1.a$ op $n_2.b)$;
    (e) q is $q_1 \wedge q_2$: then $T \models (q_1(n') \wedge q_2(n'))$;
    (f) q is $q_1 \vee q_2$: then $T \models (q_1(n') \vee q_2(n'))$;
    (g) q is $\neg q'$: then $T \not\models q'(n')$; for instance, if q is $\neg p_2$, then $T \models \forall n''\, \neg p_2(n', n'')$.

Here n is referred to as the *context node*. If $T \models p(n, n')$ then we say that n' is *reachable* from n via p. We use $n[\![p]\!]$ to denote the set of all the nodes reached from n via p, i.e., $n[\![p]\!] = \{n' \mid n' \in T,\ T \models p(n, n')\}$.

We investigate various fragments of $\mathcal{X}(\downarrow, \downarrow^*, \uparrow, \uparrow^*, \leftarrow, \leftarrow^*, \rightarrow, \rightarrow^*, \cup, [\,], =, \neg)$. We denote a fragment $\mathcal{X}$ by listing the operators supported by $\mathcal{X}$: the presence or absence of negation '$\neg$', data-value joins '$=, \neq$', upward traversal '$\uparrow$' ('$\uparrow^*$'), sideways traversal '$\leftarrow$' ('$\leftarrow^*$') and '$\rightarrow$' ('$\rightarrow^*$'), wildcard '$\downarrow$', recursive axis '$\downarrow^*, \uparrow^*$, $\leftarrow^*$', and '$\rightarrow^*$', qualifiers '$[\,]$', and union and disjunction '$\cup$'. The concatenation operator '$/$' is *included in all fragments by default*.

Example 2. Consider the XML tree T of D_2 shown in Fig. 1, and the following XPath queries. (a) Over T, $\downarrow^*[\downarrow/\rightarrow[\text{lab}() = X]]$ is to find all the nodes in T that have child whose right sibling is labeled X. This query is in the fragment $\mathcal{X}(\downarrow, \downarrow^*, \rightarrow, [\,])$. (b) Posed on T, $\downarrow^*[\neg\downarrow^*[X/\rightarrow[\text{lab}() = Y]]]$ is to find all the nodes in T that have no descendant which has children X and Y in this order. This query is in $\mathcal{X}(\downarrow, \downarrow^*, \rightarrow, [\,], \neg)$. (c) Over the XML tree T_1 of D_1 shown in Fig. 1, $\downarrow^*[A/\rightarrow/\rightarrow^*[\text{lab}() = A] \wedge \neg(B/\rightarrow/\rightarrow^*[\text{lab}() = B]/\rightarrow/\rightarrow^*[\text{lab}() = B])]$ is to find all the nodes that have at least two A children but at most three B children. It is in $\mathcal{X}(\downarrow, \downarrow^*, \rightarrow, \rightarrow^*, [\,], \neg)$.

2.3   The Satisfiability Problem

We say that an XML tree T *satisfies* a query p, denoted by $T \models p$, iff $T \models \exists n\, p(r, n)$, where r is the root of T. In other words, $r[\![p]\!] \neq \emptyset$. We focus on the satisfiability of XPath queries applied to the root of T. The complexity results of this paper remain intact for arbitrary context nodes.

We study the satisfiability problem for XPath queries considered together with a DTD. That is the problem to determine whether a given XPath query p and a DTD D are satisfiable by an XML tree. We say that an XML tree T *satisfies p and D*, denoted by $T \models (p, D)$, if $T \models p$ and $T \models D$. If such a T exists, we say that (p, D) is *satisfiable*.

Formally, for a fragment $\mathcal{X}$ of XPath we define the *XPath satisfiability problem* $\mathsf{SAT}(\mathcal{X})$ as follows:

PROBLEM:	$\mathsf{SAT}(\mathcal{X})$
INPUT:	A DTD D, an XPath query p in $\mathcal{X}$.
QUESTION:	Is there an XML document T such that $T \models (p, D)$?

We are also interested in the complexity of the satisfiability analysis in the query size alone. The *satisfiability problem for a fragment $\mathcal{X}$ in the absence of DTDs* is the problem of determining, given any query p in $\mathcal{X}$, whether or not there is an XML tree T such that $T \models p$. As shown in [2], this problem is a *special case* of $\mathsf{SAT}(\mathcal{X})$, when DTDs D are restricted to have a certain syntactic form. Since such DTDs can be computed in low polynomial of the size of the input queries, all the lower bounds for $\mathsf{SAT}(\mathcal{X})$ established in this paper, except Proposition 6, also hold in the absence of DTDs.

3   Horizontal Versus Vertical Traversal

In this section we study the basic properties of XPath fragments with sibling axes, and explore the connection between these fragments and the corresponding fragments without sibling axes.

Increase in Expressive Power. We first show that the sibling axes do add expressive power to fragments without horizontal modalities.

Proposition 1. *The sibling axes are not expressible in* $\mathcal{X}(\downarrow, \downarrow^*, \uparrow, \uparrow^*, \cup, [\,], =, \neg)$, *our largest fragment with only vertical axes.* ∎

Proof. Consider an XPath query $Q = A/\rightarrow$, and two XML trees T_1 and T_2, where T_1 consists of a root with two A children, and T_2 has a root with three A children. Over T_1 and T_2, Q is to find all A children of the root except the very first one. One can verify that Q is not expressible in $\mathcal{X}(\downarrow, \downarrow^*, \uparrow, \uparrow^*, \cup, [\,], =, \neg)$, in which T_1 and T_2 are not distinguishable. Similarly for $\leftarrow, \rightarrow^*$ and $\leftarrow^*$. ∎

We say that an XPath fragment $\mathcal{X}$ has the *finite model property* if for any query p in $\mathcal{X}$, if p is satisfiable by a (possibly infinite) tree, then there exists a finite tree that satisfies p. An XPath fragment $\mathcal{X}$ has the *small model property* if there exists a recursive function f such that for each $p \in \mathcal{X}$, if p is satisfiable, then p has a finite model of size at most $f(|p|)$, where $|p|$ is the size of p.

As another evidence for the increase of expressive power, observe that the fragment $\mathcal{X}(\rightarrow, [\,], \neg)$ does not have the finite model property. Indeed, the query $\epsilon[A \wedge \neg A[\neg\rightarrow[\mathsf{lab}() = A]]]$ does not have the finite model. Thus we have:

Proposition 2. *The satisfiability problem for any fragment that subsumes* $\mathcal{X}(\rightarrow, [\,], \neg)$ *does not have the finite model property, in the presence of DTDs and in the absence of DTDs.* ∎

In contrast, [2] has shown the following: (a) $\mathcal{X}(\downarrow, \uparrow, \cup, [\,], \neg)$ has the small model property in the presence of DTDs and in the absence of DTDs, and (b) $\mathcal{X}(\downarrow, \downarrow^*, \uparrow, \uparrow^*, \cup, [\,], \neg)$ has the small model property over non-recursive DTDs. This shows that the sibling axes may complicate the satisfiability analysis.

DTD Coding. We next show that certain DTDs can be encoded in terms of a qualifier in $\mathcal{X}(\downarrow, \downarrow^*, \rightarrow, [\,], \neg)$. Recall the following from [2]: a *normalized DTD* restricts its productions $A \rightarrow \alpha$ such that α is of the following forms:

$$\alpha \quad ::= \quad \epsilon \quad | \quad B_1, \ldots, B_n \quad | \quad B_1 + \cdots + B_n \quad | \quad B^*$$

where B_i is a type in *Ele*. It was shown there that any DTD can be "normalized" in linear time, and moreover, for any XPath fragment with $\cup$ and $\downarrow$ and without sibling axes, the normalization has no impact on the complexity bounds of its satisfiability analysis. Below we further show that we can actually encode a normalized DTD in terms of XPath qualifiers in $\mathcal{X}(\downarrow, \downarrow^*, \rightarrow, [\,], \neg)$.

Proposition 3. *A normalized DTD D can be expressed as a qualifier q_D in any XPath fragment that subsumes* $\mathcal{X}(\downarrow, \downarrow^*, \rightarrow, [\,], \neg)$. *That is, for any query Q in a fragment that subsumes* $\mathcal{X}(\downarrow, \downarrow^*, \rightarrow, [\,], \neg)$, *$(Q, D)$ is satisfiable iff $\epsilon[q_D]/Q$ is satisfiable in the absence of DTDs.* ∎

Proof. We show that for any A in the set *Ele* of the element types of a normalized DTD, the production $A \rightarrow P(A)$ can expressed as a qualifier Q^A in $\mathcal{X}(\downarrow, \downarrow^*, \rightarrow, [\,], \neg)$, by induction on the structure of $P(A)$. Putting these together, we obtain a single qualifier $q_D = \epsilon[\bigwedge_{A \in Ele} Q^A]$ at the root. ∎

As an immediate result, for any XPath fragment $\mathcal{X}(\downarrow, \downarrow^*, \rightarrow, \rightarrow^*, [\ ], \neg, \ldots)$, its satisfiability analysis in the presence of normalized DTDs is equivalent to its counterpart in the absence of DTDs.

In contrast, below we show that normalized DTDs are not expressible in fragments without sibling axes. Indeed, it was shown in [2] that without sibling axes, the lower bounds for XPath satisfiability analysis in the presence of DTDs typically do not carry over to the counterpart in the absence of DTDs, although the analysis without DTDs is a special case of its counterpart with DTDs.

Proposition 4. *A normalized DTD D cannot be expressed as a qualifier q_D in* $\mathcal{X}(\downarrow, \downarrow^*, \uparrow, \uparrow^*, \cup, [\ ], =, \neg)$. ∎

Proof. One can verify that two different DTDs D_1 and D_2 are not distinguishable by any XPath query in $\mathcal{X}(\downarrow, \downarrow^*, \uparrow, \uparrow^*, \cup, [\ ], =, \neg)$, where D_1 has a single production $r \rightarrow A, A$, and D_2 consists of a single production $r \rightarrow A, A, A$. ∎

Encoding Horizontal Traversal in Terms of Vertical Modalities. Let $\mathcal{X}(\rightarrow, \rightarrow^*, [\ ], \ldots)$ be any class of XPath queries that allows '$\rightarrow, \rightarrow^*$' and qualifiers. Let $\mathcal{X}^*(\downarrow, \uparrow, \cup, [\ ], \ldots)$ be a variation of $\mathcal{X}(\rightarrow, \rightarrow^*, [\ ], \ldots)$ by (a) supporting $\downarrow, \uparrow$, and $\cup$, (b) supporting the general Kleene closure defined by β^*, where β is a simple path $A_1[q_1]/ \ldots /A_k[q_k]$, where A_i is a label and $[q_i]$ is a Boolean combination of simple label testing qualifiers (of the form $\mathsf{lab}() = A$), and (c) discarding any queries with '$\rightarrow, \rightarrow^*$'. Note that $\mathcal{X}^*(\downarrow, \uparrow, \cup, [\ ], \ldots)$ is far more restrictive than the regular XPath fragment introduced and studied in [17].

Proposition 5. *For any class $\mathcal{X}(\rightarrow, \rightarrow^*, [\ ], \ldots)$ of XPath queries, there exists a PTIME computable function N from DTDs to DTDs, and there exists a PTIME computable function f from queries in $\mathcal{X}(\rightarrow, \rightarrow^*, [\ ], \ldots)$ to queries in $\mathcal{X}^*(\downarrow, \uparrow, \cup, [\ ], \ldots)$ such that, for any DTD D and any XPath query $p \in \mathcal{X}(\rightarrow, \rightarrow^*, [\ ], \ldots)$, there exists an XML tree T such that $T \models (p, D)$ iff there exists an XML tree T' such that $T' \models (f(p), N(D))$.* ∎

Proof. The mapping N is based on the canonical binary encoding of instances of the input D, which introduces new labels. Then f can be defined such that it traverses "descendants" and "siblings" by visiting left subtrees and right subtrees in the binary trees, respectively. The query translation requires the use of $\downarrow, \uparrow, \cup, [\ ]$ and simple paths of the form $A_1[q_1]/ \ldots /A_k[q_k]$ as described above. ∎

This tells us that, upon the availability of upper bounds for conditional and regular XPath fragments [17] without siblings, the bounds can carry over to our fragments with sibling axes.

4   Complexity of XPath Satisfiability with Sibling Axes

In this section we study the satisfiability problem for various XPath fragments with sibling axes, and contrast the complexity bounds with their counterparts for the corresponding fragments without sibling axes. To understand the impact of different XPath modalities on the satisfiability analysis, we start with a simple fragment $\mathcal{X}(\downarrow, \downarrow^*, \rightarrow, \rightarrow^*, \cup)$, and then extend the fragment gradually by adding qualifiers, data-value joins, and negation one by one. To study the interaction between XPath modalities and DTD constructs, we also consider the analysis under DTDs restricted to have certain constructs and in the absence of DTDs.

4.1   XPath Fragments Without Qualifiers

Without sibling axes, the absence of qualifiers simplifies the satisfiability analysis [2]. Below we show that it is also the case for XPath fragments with siblings.

Proposition 6. SAT$(\mathcal{X}(\downarrow^*))$ *is NLOGSPACE-hard in the presence of DTDs.* ∎

Proof. This can be verified by LOGSPACE reduction from directed graph connectivity with specified source and target, which is NLOGSPACE-hard [24].   ∎

In the absence of DTDs, all queries in $\mathcal{X}(\downarrow, \downarrow^*, \cup)$ are always satisfiable [2].

Theorem 1. *Both* SAT$(\mathcal{X}(\downarrow, \downarrow^*, \rightarrow, \rightarrow^*, \cup))$ *and* SAT$(\mathcal{X}(\downarrow, \downarrow^*, \leftarrow, \leftarrow^*, \cup))$ *are NLOGSPACE-complete in the presence of DTDs.*

Proof. We provide a NLOGSPACE algorithm for checking the satisfiability of (Q, D) for an input DTD D and query $Q \in \mathcal{X}(\downarrow, \downarrow^*, \rightarrow, \rightarrow^*, \cup)$ (resp. $\leftarrow, \leftarrow^*$). The key idea is to code vertical navigation using a query graph G_Q of Q and horizontal moves using NFAs of the regular expressions in D. This only requires us to store triplets (q, v, A) at each step, where q is a NFA state, v is node in G_Q and A is a label. This only needs LOGSPACE.   ∎

Recall that SAT$(\mathcal{X}(\downarrow, \downarrow^*, \cup))$ is in PTIME [2], which contains NLOGSPACE. Thus Theorem 1 tells us that in the absence of qualifiers, the addition of sibling axes does not complicate the satisfiability analysis. As another evidence:

Theorem 2. SAT$(\mathcal{X}(\rightarrow, \leftarrow))$ *is in PTIME in the presence of DTDs.*   ∎

In contrast, SAT$(\mathcal{X}(\downarrow, \uparrow))$ is NP-hard [2]. The difference between $\mathcal{X}(\downarrow, \uparrow)$ and $\mathcal{X}(\rightarrow, \leftarrow)$ is that while a query in $\mathcal{X}(\downarrow, \uparrow)$ can constrain the subtree of a node by moving downward and upward repeatedly in the subtree, queries in $\mathcal{X}(\rightarrow, \leftarrow)$ are not able to do it: as soon as the navigation moves down in a tree, it cannot move back to the same node. Leveraging this we are able to develop a PTIME algorithm, based on dynamic programming, for deciding the satisfiability of (Q, D) for a given DTD D and query $Q \in \mathcal{X}(\rightarrow, \leftarrow)$.

From these we can see that XPath queries with sibling axes are quite well behaved in the absence of qualifiers.

4.2   Positive XPath Queries with Qualifiers

We now consider *positive* XPath fragments, i.e., fragments supporting qualifiers but not including negation ($\neg$). Positive fragments are contained in positive existential two-variable first-order logic over trees, with binary predicates *child*, *descendant*, and *sibling* [17]. It is known that qualifiers make the satisfiability analysis harder for XPath fragments without siblings [2]. We show that this is also the case when sibling axes are considered instead of vertical modalities.

Theorem 3. *The satisfiability problem for the following fragments is NP-hard:*

1. $\mathsf{SAT}(\mathcal{X}([\,]))$ *under nonrecursive DTDs;*
2. $\mathsf{SAT}(\mathcal{X}(\rightarrow,[\,]))$ *and* $\mathsf{SAT}(\mathcal{X}(\leftarrow,[\,]))$ *under fixed, disjunctive-free and nonrecursive DTDs;*
3. $\mathsf{SAT}(\mathcal{X}(\rightarrow,\cup,[\,]))$ *and* $\mathsf{SAT}(\mathcal{X}(\leftarrow,\cup,[\,]))$ *in the absence of DTDs.*   ∎

Proof. These can be verified by reduction from the 3SAT problem, which is NP-complete (cf. [24]).   ∎

Here by *fixed DTDs* we mean that the input to the satisfiability analysis consists of only a query rather than both a query and a DTD, and the XML trees considered are required to conform to a predefined DTD.

Contrast these with the following results in [2]. (a) $\mathsf{SAT}(\mathcal{X}(\downarrow,[\,]))$ is NP-hard under normalized DTDs. Here we improve that result by showing that $\mathsf{SAT}(\mathcal{X}([\,]))$ is already intractable under (not necessarily normalized) DTDs. (b) While $\mathsf{SAT}(\mathcal{X}(\downarrow,[\,]))$ is NP-complete for arbitrary DTDs, but it is in PTIME when DTDs are restricted to be disjunction-free. In contrast, Theorem 3 shows that it is no longer the case when $\downarrow$ is replaced by $\rightarrow$ or $\leftarrow$. (c) In the absence of DTDs, $\mathsf{SAT}(\mathcal{X}(\downarrow,\cup,[\,]))$ is in PTIME, as opposed to Theorem 3. Thus sibling axes complicate the satisfiability analysis in the presence of qualifiers.

Recall that $\mathsf{SAT}(\mathcal{X}(\downarrow,\downarrow^*,\uparrow,\uparrow^*,\cup,[\,],=))$ is in NP [2]. The result below shows that the addition of the sibling axes does not increase the upper bound.

Theorem 4. $\mathsf{SAT}(\mathcal{X}(\downarrow,\downarrow^*,\uparrow,\uparrow^*,\leftarrow,\leftarrow^*,\rightarrow,\rightarrow^*,\cup,[\,],=))$ *is in NP.*   ∎

Proof. It suffices to show that $\mathsf{SAT}(\mathcal{X}^*(\downarrow,\downarrow^*,\uparrow,\uparrow^*,\cup,[\,],=))$ is in NP by Proposition 5. A NP decision algorithm is then provided for this fragment, by extending the NP algorithm for $\mathsf{SAT}(\mathcal{X}(\downarrow,\downarrow^*,\uparrow,\uparrow^*,\cup,[\,],=))$ developed in [2].   ∎

4.3   XPath Fragments with Negation

In contrast to positive XPath fragments, negation introduces universal quantifiers and complicates the satisfiability analysis without sibling axes [2]. We show that in the presence of sibling axes the situation is also bad, and may be worse.

It is known that $\mathsf{SAT}(\mathcal{X}(\downarrow,[\,],\neg))$ is PSPACE-hard in the presence of DTDs [2]. We show that the lower bound remains intact if we substitute $\rightarrow$ (resp. $\leftarrow$) for $\downarrow$ in the fragment, even when the DTDs are restricted or left out.

Theorem 5. SAT$(\mathcal{X}(\rightarrow, [\;], \neg))$ *and* SAT$(\mathcal{X}(\leftarrow, [\;], \neg))$ *are PSPACE-hard in the following settings: (1) under non-recursive and no-star DTDs; and (2) in the absence of DTDs.*   ∎

Proof. The lower bounds can be proved by reduction from 3QSAT, a well-known PSPACE-complete problem (cf. [24]).   ∎

Theorem 6. SAT$(\mathcal{X}(\downarrow, \uparrow, \leftarrow, \leftarrow^*, \rightarrow, \rightarrow^*, \cup, [\;], \neg))$ *is PSPACE-complete under no-star DTDs.*   ∎

Proof. The upper bound can be verified by reduction to SAT$(\mathcal{X}(\downarrow, [\;], \neg))$, based on a variation of the proof of Proposition 5.   ∎

It is known [17] that SAT$(\mathcal{X}(\downarrow, \downarrow^*, \cup, [\;], \neg))$ is EXPTIME-hard and that SAT$(\mathcal{X}(\downarrow, \downarrow^*, \uparrow, \uparrow^*, \leftarrow, \leftarrow^*, \rightarrow, \rightarrow^*, \cup, [\;], \neg))$ is in EXPTIME. We now show that we already have the EXPTIME hardness in the presence of *neither recursion in XPath nor recursion in DTDs*.

Theorem 7. SAT$(\mathcal{X}(\uparrow, \rightarrow, [\;], \neg))$ *is EXPTIME-hard under fixed, nonrecursive and disjunction-free DTDs.*   ∎

This can be verified by reduction from the two-player game of corridor tiling, which is EXPTIME-complete (cf. [4]). To see why the result holds, observe the following. One can encode a certain recursive DTD D_1 in terms of a "flattened" DTD D_2, and based on this a mapping N can be defined from XML trees of D_1 to XML trees of D_2 via "unnesting"; furthermore, there is a mapping f such that for certain queries Q in $\mathcal{X}(\downarrow, \downarrow^*, \cup, [\;], \neg)$, $f(Q)$ is in $\mathcal{X}(\uparrow, \rightarrow, [\;], \neg)$ and moreover, if Q is satisfiable by an XML tree T of D_1, then $f(Q)$ is satisfiable by $N(T)$. In $N(T)$, the child, parent and right sibling axes suffice to access certain elements that are deep in T. From this it follows that a reduction from the two-player game of corridor tiling to SAT$(\mathcal{X}(\downarrow, \downarrow^*, \cup, [\;], \neg))$ can be coded in terms of a query in $\mathcal{X}(\uparrow, \rightarrow, [\;], \neg)$ and a fixed, nonrecursive DTD as described above. This explains why the EXPTIME lower bounds is robust in the absence of XPath and DTD recursions, and demonstrates the power of sibling axes.

4.4   XPath Fragments with Negation and Data Values

Finally, we investigate the satisfiability analysis for XPath fragments with data-value joins, negation and sibling axes. As observed in [2], the interaction between data-value joins and negation is already intricate in the absence of sibling axes. Indeed, SAT$(\mathcal{X}(\downarrow, \downarrow^*, \uparrow, \uparrow^*, \cup, [\;], =, \neg))$ is undecidable in presence of fixed recursive DTDs [2]. However, it is not yet known whether or not the undecidability result still holds (a) under non-recursive DTDs, (b) under fixed DTDs, and (c) in the absence of DTDs. In contrast, we next show that in the presence of sibling axes but without vertical XPath recursion $\downarrow^*$ and $\uparrow^*$, the problem remains undecidable in all the settings mentioned above.

Theorem 8. SAT($\mathcal{X}(\uparrow, \leftarrow, \rightarrow, \rightarrow^*, \cup, [\,], =, \neg)$) *is undecidable in any of the following setting: (1) under non-recursive, fixed and disjunction-free DTDs; and (2) in the absence of DTDs.* ∎

The undecidability result can be verified by reduction from the halting problem for two-register machines, which is known to be undecidable (see, e.g., [4]). The proof extends the undecidability proof of [2] for SAT($\mathcal{X}(\downarrow, \downarrow^*, \uparrow, \uparrow^*, [\,], =, \neg)$) under fixed recursive DTDs, by "flattening" DTDs in the same way as mentioned above. The proof leverages the following observation: by means of XPath qualifiers with $\rightarrow, \rightarrow^*, \leftarrow$ and $\uparrow$, (a) DTD linear recursion introduced by productions of the form $A \rightarrow A + \epsilon$ can be coded with productions of the form $A \rightarrow B^*$; (b) disjunction in a DTD can also be coded in terms of the use of Kleene star. This allows us to get rid of linear recursion and disjunction required by the undecidability proof of [2], and again shows the expressive power of sibling axes.

5   The Containment Analysis for XPath with Siblings

In this section we present a few lower bounds for the containment analysis of XPath fragments with sibling axes, by exploring the connection between the containment analysis and its satisfiability counterpart, and by using the complexity results for the satisfiability analysis given in the last section.

The *containment problem* for a fragment $\mathcal{X}$ in the presence of DTDs, denoted by CNT($\mathcal{X}$), is the problem to determine, given any queries $Q_1, Q_2 \in \mathcal{X}$ and a DTD D, whether or not for any XML tree T of D, $r[\![Q_1]\!] \subseteq r[\![Q_2]\!]$, where r is the root of T. If this holds then we say that $Q_1 \subseteq Q_2$ *under* D.

It is easy to see that for any fragment $\mathcal{X}$, SAT(X) is reducible to the complement of CNT($\mathcal{X}$). Recall that for a complexity class K, coK stands for $\{\bar{P} \mid P \in \mathsf{K}\}$.

Proposition 7. *[2] For any class $\mathcal{X}$ of XPath queries, if CNT($\mathcal{X}$) is in K for some complexity class K, then SAT($\mathcal{X}$) is in coK. Conversely, if SAT($\mathcal{X}$) is K-hard, then CNT($\mathcal{X}$) is coK-hard.*

From this and Theorems 3, 5, 7 and 8 it immediately follows:

Corollary 1. *For the containment problem,*

1. CNT($\mathcal{X}(\rightarrow, [\,])$) *and* CNT($\mathcal{X}(\leftarrow, [\,])$) *are coNP-hard under fixed, disjunction-free and nonrecursive DTDs;*
2. CNT($\mathcal{X}(\rightarrow, \cup, [\,])$) *and* CNT($\mathcal{X}(\leftarrow, \cup, [\,])$) *are coNP-hard in the absence of DTDs;*
3. CNT($\mathcal{X}(\rightarrow, [\,], \neg)$) *and* CNT($\mathcal{X}(\leftarrow, [\,], \neg)$) *are PSPACE-hard (a) under non-recursive and no-star DTDs, and (b) in the absence of DTDs;*
4. CNT($\mathcal{X}(\uparrow, \rightarrow, [\,], \neg)$) *is EXPTIME-hard under fixed, disjunction-free and nonrecursive DTDs;*
5. CNT($\mathcal{X}(\uparrow, \leftarrow, \rightarrow, \rightarrow^*, \cup, [\,], =, \neg)$) *is undecidable (a) under non-recursive, disjunction-free and fixed DTDs, and (b) in the absence of DTDs.* ∎

These are among the first lower bound results for the containment problem for XPath fragments with sibling axes. Indeed, the only other result that we are aware of is the EXPTIME lower bound given by [17] for $\mathsf{CNT}(\mathcal{X}(\downarrow, \downarrow^*, \cup, [\,], \neg))$. Corollary 1 strengthens that result by showing that $\mathsf{CNT}(\mathcal{X}(\uparrow, \rightarrow, [\,], \neg))$ is already EXPTIME-hard under restricted DTDs.

As observed in [2], the upper bound for $\mathsf{SAT}(\mathcal{X})$ is often much lower than its counterpart for $\mathsf{CNT}(\mathcal{X})$. However, for certain fragments $\mathcal{X}$ without sibling axes, $\mathsf{SAT}(\mathcal{X})$ and $\mathsf{CNT}(\mathcal{X})$ actually coincide. These include the following: (a) the class $\mathcal{X}_{(bl,\ [\,],\neg)}$ of *Boolean queries*, i.e., queries of the form $\epsilon[q]$, in any class $\mathcal{X}(\ldots, [\,], \neg)$ with negation and qualifiers; and (b) any class containing negation and closed under the *inverse operator* that is defined as a simple extension of $\mathsf{inverse}(\downarrow) = \uparrow$, $\mathsf{inverse}(\downarrow^*) = \uparrow^*$, $\mathsf{inverse}(\uparrow) = \downarrow$ and $\mathsf{inverse}(\uparrow^*) = \downarrow^*$.

We next show that this result of [2] carries over to XPath fragments with sibling axes, by extending (a) the class $\mathcal{X}_{(bl,\ [\,],\neg)}$ by including Boolean queries with sibling axes; (b) the definition of $\mathsf{inverse}$ such that $\mathsf{inverse}(\leftarrow) = \rightarrow$, $\mathsf{inverse}(\leftarrow^*) = \rightarrow^*$, $\mathsf{inverse}(\rightarrow) = \leftarrow$, $\mathsf{inverse}(\rightarrow^*) = \leftarrow^*$.

Proposition 8. *For any class $\mathcal{X}_{(bl,\ [\,],\neg)}$ of Boolean queries, $\mathsf{CNT}(\mathcal{X}_{(bl,\ [\,],\neg)})$ is reducible in constant time to the complement of $\mathsf{SAT}(\mathcal{X}_{(bl,\ [\,],\neg)})$. For any class $\mathcal{X}$ with negation and closed under $\mathsf{inverse}$, $\mathsf{CNT}(\mathcal{X})$ is reducible in linear time to the complement of $\mathsf{SAT}(\mathcal{X})$.* ∎

6 Conclusions

We have established complexity bounds for a number of XPath fragments with sibling axes, in the presence of DTDs, in the absence of DTDs, and under various restricted DTDs. The main results of the paper are summarized in Table 1. As immediate corollaries of these results, we have also provided several lower bounds

Table 1. The complexity of $\mathsf{SAT}(\mathcal{X})$ for various fragments $\mathcal{X}$ under different DTDs

NLOGSPACE -comp.	$\mathcal{X}(\downarrow, \downarrow^*, \rightarrow, \rightarrow^*, \cup)$, $\mathcal{X}(\downarrow, \downarrow^*, \leftarrow, \leftarrow^*, \cup)$	any DTDs nonrec. DTDs
PTIME	$\mathcal{X}(\leftarrow, \rightarrow)$	any DTD
NP-hard	$\mathcal{X}([\,])$	nonrec DTDs
NP-hard	$\mathcal{X}(\leftarrow, [\,])$, $\mathcal{X}(\rightarrow, [\,])$	fixed, '+'-free, nonrec DTDs
NP-hard	$\mathcal{X}(\leftarrow, \cup, [\,])$, $\mathcal{X}(\rightarrow, \cup, [\,])$	no DTDs
NP-comp.	$\mathcal{X}(\downarrow, \downarrow^*, \uparrow, \uparrow^*, \leftarrow, \leftarrow^*, \rightarrow, \rightarrow^*, \cup, [\,], =)$	any DTD
PSPACE-hard	$\mathcal{X}(\rightarrow, [\,], \neg)$, $\mathcal{X}(\leftarrow, [\,], \neg)$	nonrec, no-star DTDs no DTDs
PSPACE-comp.	$\mathcal{X}(\downarrow, \uparrow, \leftarrow, \leftarrow^*, \rightarrow, \rightarrow^*, \cup, [\,], \neg)$	no-star DTDs
EXPTIME-hard	$\mathcal{X}(\uparrow, \leftarrow, [\,], \neg)$	fixed, '+'-free, nonrec. DTDs
undecidable	$\mathcal{X}(\uparrow, \leftarrow, \rightarrow, \rightarrow^*, \cup, [\,], \neg, =)$	fixed, '+'-free, nonrec DTDs no DTDs

for the containment problem for XPath queries. Our main conclusion is that while sibling axes do not complicate the satisfiability analysis in the absence of qualifiers, they do make our lives harder in the presence of qualifiers.

To the best of our knowledge, the results of this paper are among the first results for the satisfiability and containment analyses of XPath fragments with sibling axes. They are complementary to the recent study on the satisfiability problem for XPath fragments without sibling axes [2]. They are useful not only for XML query and update optimization, but also for the static analysis of inference control for XML security, among other things.

There is naturally much more to be done. One open problem is to close the complexity gaps. For example, we do not know yet whether $\mathsf{SAT}(\mathcal{X}([\ ]))$ is still intractable under fixed and disjunction-free DTDs, and whether or not $\mathsf{SAT}(\mathcal{X}(\to, [\ ], \neg))$ is in PSPACE under arbitrary DTDs. Another topic for future work is to study the satisfiability problem for XPath in the presence of XML Schema, which typically consists of both a type (a specialized DTD) and a set of XML constraints. This setting was considered in [8] for the containment analysis.

Acknowledgment. The authors would like to thank Frank Neven for giving the proof idea for Theorem 1. Wenfei Fan is supported in part by EPSRC GR/S63205/01, EPSRC GR/T27433/01 and NSFC 60228006. Floris Geerts is postdoctoral researcher of the FWO Vlaanderen and is supported in part by EPSRC GR/S63205/01.

References

1. S. Amer-Yahia, S. Cho, L. Lakshmanan, and D. Srivistava. Minimization of tree pattern queries. In *SIGMOD*, 2001.
2. M. Benedikt, W. Fan, and F. Geerts. XPath satisfiability in the presence of DTDs. In *PODS*, 2005.
3. M. Benedikt, W. Fan, and G. M. Kuper. Structural properties of XPath fragments. In *ICDT*, 2003.
4. E. Börger, E. Grädel, and Y. Gurevich. *The Classical Decision Problem*. Springer, 1997.
5. T. Bray, J. Paoli, and C. M. Sperberg-McQueen. Extensible Markup Language (XML) 1.0. W3C Recommendation, Feb 1998. http://www.w3.org/TR/REC-xml.
6. P. Buneman, S. Davidson, W. Fan, C. Hara, and W. Tan. Keys for XML. *Computer Networks*, 39(5):473–487, 2002.
7. J. Clark and S. DeRose. *XML Path Language (XPath)*. W3C Recommendation, Nov. 1999.
8. A. Deutsch and V. Tannen. Containment for classes of XPath expressions under integrity constraints. In *KRDB*, 2001.
9. A. Deutsch and V. Tannen. Reformulation of XML queries and constraints. In *ICDT*, 2003.
10. W. Fan, C. Chan, and M. Garofalakis. Secure XML querying with security views. In *SIGMOD*, 2004.
11. G. Gottlob, C. Koch, and R. Pichler. Efficient algorithms for processing XPath queries. In *VLDB*, 2002.

12. G. Gottlob, C. Koch, and K. Schulz. Conjunctive queries over trees. In *PODS*, 2004.
13. J. Hidders. Satisfiability of XPath expressions. In *DBPL*, 2003.
14. J. E. Hopcroft and J. D. Ullman. *Introduction to Automata Theory, Languages and Computation (2nd Edition)*. Addison Wesley, 2000.
15. L. Lakshmanan, G. Ramesh, H. Wang, and Z. Zhao. On testing satisfiability of tree pattern queries. In *VLDB*, 2004.
16. L. Libkin. Logics over unranked trees: an overview. In *ICALP*, 2005.
17. M. Marx. XPath with conditional axis relations. In *EDBT*, 2004.
18. M. Marx. First order paths in ordered trees. In *ICDT*, pages 114–128, 2005.
19. G. Miklau and D. Suciu. Containment and equivalence for a fragment of XPath. *JACM*, 51(1):2–45, 2004.
20. M. Murata. Extended path expressions for XML. In *PODS*, 2001.
21. F. Neven and T. Schwentick. Expressive and efficient languages for tree-structured data. In *PODS*, 2000.
22. F. Neven and T. Schwentick. XPath containment in the presence of disjunction, DTDs, and variables. In *ICDT*, 2003.
23. D. Olteanu, H. Meuss, T. Furche, and F. Bry. XPath: Looking forward. In *XMLDM*, 2002.
24. C. H. Papadimitriou. *Computational Complexity*. Addison-Wesley, 1994.
25. T. Schwentick. Xpath query containment. *SIGMOD Rec.*, 33(1):101–109, 2004.
26. G. Sur, J. Hammer, and J. Siméon. An XQuery-based language for processing updates in XML. In *PLAN-X*, 2004.
27. H. Thompson et al. XML Schema. W3C Recommendation, Oct. 2004. `http://www.w3.org/TR/xmlschema1`.
28. P. T. Wood. Minimising simple XPath expressions. In *WebDB*, 2001.
29. P. T. Wood. Containment for XPath fragments under DTD constraints. In *ICDT*, 2003.

XML Subtree Queries: Specification and Composition

Michael Benedikt and Irini Fundulaki

Bell Labs, Lucent Technologies, USA

Abstract. A frequent task encountered in XML processing is to filter an input document to produce a subdocument; that is, a document whose root-to-leaf paths are root-to-leaf paths of the original document and which inherits the tree structure of the original document. These are what we mean by subtree queries, and while they are similar to XPath filters, they cannot be naturally specified either in XPath or in XQuery. Special-purpose subtree query languages provide a natural idiom for specifying this class of queries, but both composition and evaluation are problematic. In this paper we show that for natural fragments of XPath, the resulting subtree query languages are closed under composition. This closure property allows a sequence of subtree queries to be rewritten as a single subtree query, which can then be evaluated either by a subtree-query specific evaluator or via translation to XQuery. We provide a set of composition algorithms for each common XPath fragment and discuss their complexity.

1 Introduction

In many aspects of data and document processing, one requires queries that describe a *subdocument* (*subtree*) of the document on which the queries are evaluated. For instance, a data integration application might describe a view of multiple (virtual) XML documents into a single document by specifying subtrees of the documents of each source to be merged; an access-control view might be imposed on top of this, filtering out part of the resulting integrated document for access control purposes, while an end-user query may ask for yet another subtree of the filtered view. The ultimate result delivered to the end-user is logically the composition of the three queries.

Motivation: Consider a source document D for the XMark [16] schema illustrated in Fig. 1 and suppose that a subscriber to this dataset is only permitted to see the subtree of the original document that includes information about the European region. This view is the result of query Q_1, which evaluates the XPath expression `/site/regions/europe` and closes the result set upwards and downwards. The result of this subtree query on document D is given in Fig. 1 (where the returned nodes are marked in grey).

One group of users in the subscribing company is permitted to see only the data about (i) the items that *are not associated with* a quantity, and (ii) the

G. Bierman and C. Koch (Eds.): DBPL 2005, LNCS 3774, pp. 138–153, 2005.

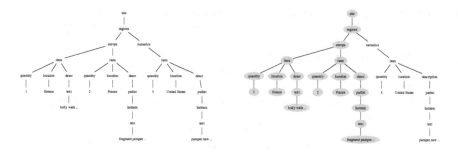

Fig. 1. XMark Document D and the subtree associated with Q_1 for D

locations of items. This subdocument is returned by query Q_2 that takes all nodes above or below the result of XPath expression: `//item[not(quantity)]` | `//item/location`. Finally, an end-user wants to obtain the subtree that contains the items that have either a location or a description. This subdocument is returned by evaluating query Q_3, which takes the result of XPath expression `//item[location | descr]` and closes the result set upwards and downwards.

For this family of queries, XQuery does not give a natural syntax. In fact, XQuery does not, strictly speaking, allow the expression of subtree queries at all, since in an XQuery result fresh node identifiers will always be generated. Fig. 2 shows an XQuery expression that would mimic the subtree query Q_2, matching the intended result up to the renaming of node identifiers. Observe that, even allowing a result that is correct only "up to node identifiers", the translation of XPath expressions used to specify subtree queries to the XQuery representation of these subtree queries is not straightforward: in the presence of union, we need to retain the order of the elements from the original document in the output result, while a naive translation of the subtree query would result in different parts of different components of the union being contiguously ordered in the result. The complexity of the translation escalates for subtree queries based on XPath with negation, upward axes and union.

It is fairly clear that one does not wish to write XQuery representations of subtree queries directly. An obvious solution is to use the XPath expressions themselves as the user syntax. The subtree query language is thus parameterized by a fragment of XPath and converts an XPath nodeset query into a subtree query that "filters" the input document by the XPath expression to return a subdocument.

Subtree queries can be evaluated via conversion on top of an arbitrary XQuery or XSLT processor. However, this "evaluation via translation" is unsatisfactory in terms of query performance. Since subtree queries are analogous to XPath expressions, it is natural that they be evaluated using processing techniques similar to those used for XPath. In a generated XQuery expression as in Fig. 2, however, the subtree nature of the query is hidden and cannot be exploited by the XQuery processor.

The problem is compounded when one composes subtree queries. Suppose one wishes to perform a user query like Q_3 on a chain of views given by queries Q_2

```
for $a in doc('xmark.xml')/site[regions[europe[item[self :: *[not(quantity)] |
                                                self :: *[quantity][location]]]]] return
< site >
   { for $b in $a/regions[europe[item[self :: *[not(quantity)] |
                                     self :: *[quantity][location]]]] return
      < regions >
        {for $cin$b/europe[item[self :: *[not(quantity)]| self :: *[quantity][location]]]return
          < europe >
            { for $d in $c/(child :: *[self : item[not(quantity)]],
                            child :: *[self :: item[quantity][location]]) return
                if ($d[self :: item[not(quantity)]]) then $d else
                if ($d[self :: item[quantity][location]]) then
                < item > { for $e in $d/location return $e } < /item > else 1} }
          < /europe > }
      < /regions > }
< /site >
```

Fig. 2. XQuery representation for Q_2

and Q_1. For efficiency and security reasons, one might wish to send the composed query $Q_3 \circ Q_2 \circ Q_1$ to the source, instead of evaluating the queries within the application or middleware. Following the "XQuery-translation approach" to subtree queries outlined above, one would compose by translating each Q_i to an XQuery expression, use XQuery's composition operator to obtain the composed query, and evaluate with a general-purpose XQuery engine. But now the fact that this composition is actually another subtree query is completely buried. What we require, then, is a composition algorithm that works *directly on the XPath surface syntax of these subtree queries*, generating a new subtree query within the same language. The resulting queries could be evaluated either via a special-purpose evaluator, or via translation to XQuery.

In this work, we deal with composition algorithms for subtree queries based on fragments of XPath 1.0 [6]. We show that for natural fragments of XPath, the resulting subtree query languages are *closed under composition*, and present the associated composition algorithms. In [2] we present experimental evidence that these composition algorithms provide benefits both when the composed queries are evaluated with a special-purpose subtree query engine, and also when they are translated to XQuery and evaluated with an off-the-shelf XQuery processor. Unlike for XQuery, composition algorithms for subtree queries are non-trivial – indeed we will show that for some choices of the XPath fragment, the corresponding subtree query language is not closed under composition at all. This is because our subtree query languages have no explicit composition operator; furthermore, since the XPath fragments we deal with are variable-free, the standard method of composition by means of variable introduction and projection is not available[1]. Our algorithms make heavy use of both the subtree

---

[1] Note that we do not deal with the compositionality of XPath location paths on the same document, but of the corresponding subtree queries.

nature of the queries and the restrictions imposed by the different XPath fragments.

Summarizing, the main contribution of the paper is a set of composition algorithms for each variant of the subtree query language (depending on the XPath fragment), which allow us to compose subtree queries to form new subtree queries in the same language, and also allow the composition of a subtree query with an XPath user query.

Although we study here a particular XPath-based subtree query language, we believe our composition algorithms should be applicable to other contexts in which XPath is used implicitly or explicitly to define subdocuments of documents (e.g. [1, 5]).

Organization: Section 2 presents the framework for subtree queries and the fragments of XPath we will focus on. Section 3 presents the composition algorithms and discusses complexity results. Finally we conclude in Section 4.

Related Work: Subtree queries cannot be expressed faithfully in XQuery, but they can be expressed in various XML update language proposals [17]; indeed, our work can be thought of roughly as giving special-purpose composition and evaluation algorithms for the "delete-only" subset of these languages. We know of no work dealing with the problem of efficiently composing declarative XML updates. Our framework for subtree queries was first introduced in [8]. In [15, 14] a very restricted family of these queries was studied in the context of the Bell Labs GUPster project. [14] presents translation methods for subtree queries (from this restricted family) to XQuery queries and XSLT programs.

Our work on composition stems partially from an earlier study of closure properties of XPath [4]. That work studies closure under *intersection* for XPath using the standard nodeset semantics – the emphasis is on proving/disproving closure not on algorithms or complexity bounds. In this work we deal with composition for the corresponding subtree query languages, and give effective algorithms, upper bounds, and lower bounds. Although composition is quite different from intersection (e.g. composition is not commutative), we believe that the basic ideas here can be used to give effective algorithms and bounds for the intersection problem as well. To our knowledge, composition algorithms for XQuery have been considered only in [7], where an algorithm is given for a much broader fragment of XQuery. It is not presented stand-alone, but in conjunction with query generation in a publishing setting. The algorithm of [7] would not preserve the XPath-based sublanguages we give here. Not only are these sublanguages easier to analyze and optimize than general XQuery, they are also much easier to evaluate – since our subtree queries are based on XPath 1.0, they can be evaluated with linear time combined complexity [9]. Even in the presence of data value comparisons, languages based on XPath 1.0 have low evaluation complexity [10]. The fact that XPath 1.0 is variable-free leads to the low complexity, but also makes the composition problem much more difficult than for XPath 2.0.

2 XPath-Based Subtree Queries

XPath: Subtree queries are based on XPath expressions, which describe the nodes in the input document we wish to retain in the output. XPath expressions are built up from an infinite set of labels (tags, names) Σ. The fragments of XPath[2] studied in this paper are all contained in the fragment denoted by $\mathcal{X}^{\uparrow}_{r,[\,],\neg}$ that is syntactically defined as:

$$p ::= \epsilon \mid \emptyset \mid l \mid * \mid // \mid .. \mid ..^* \mid p/p \mid p\,|\,p \mid p[q]$$

where ϵ, $\emptyset$, l in the production rules above denote the empty path ('.' in XPath), the empty set, and a name in Σ, respectively; '|' and '/' stand for union and concatenation, '*' and '..' for the *child*-axis and *parent*-axis, '//' and '..*' for the *descendant-or-self*-axis and *ancestor-or-self*-axis[3], respectively; and finally, q in $p[q]$ is called a *qualifier* and defined by:

$$q ::= p \mid \text{label} = l \mid q \text{ and } q' \mid \text{not}(q)$$

where p is an $\mathcal{X}^{\uparrow}_{r,[\,],\neg}$ expression and l is a name in Σ. All of the semantics of these expressions are as usual in XPath (see, for example, [18, 6]).

XPath Fragments: We use the following notations for subclasses of the XPath fragment $\mathcal{X}^{\uparrow}_{r,[\,],\neg}$: all the fragments will include the subscript '[ ]', to indicate that the subclass allows qualifiers, where qualifiers always include $q ::= p \mid \text{label} = l$.

Subscript 'r' indicates support for recursion in the fragment (the *descendant-or-self* '//' and *ancestor-or-self* '..*' axes), superscript '$\uparrow$' denotes the support for upward modality (the *parent* '..' and the *ancestor-or-self* '..*' axes in the case of subscript r) while the subscript '$\neg$' indicates that filters allow negation.

Thus the smallest class we consider is $\mathcal{X}_{[\,]}$, which has only the child axis and does not allow negation in filters. The classes $\mathcal{X}_{r,[\,]}$, $\mathcal{X}^{\uparrow}_{[\,]}$, $\mathcal{X}_{[\,],\neg}$ extend this basic fragment with the descendant and the parent axes, and negation in filters, respectively. Above these, we have the fragments $\mathcal{X}_{r,[\,],\neg}$, $\mathcal{X}^{\uparrow}_{r,[\,]}$, and $\mathcal{X}^{\uparrow}_{[\,],\neg}$ which combine two of the three features. The relationship of these fragments is shown in the left diagram of Fig. 3.

In [4] it is shown that $\mathcal{X}_{[\,]}$ and $\mathcal{X}^{\uparrow}_{[\,]}$ return the same node-sets when evaluated on the root of a tree (*root equivalence*, which we will always use here by default). It is also shown there that $\mathcal{X}_{r,[\,]}$ and $\mathcal{X}^{\uparrow}_{r,[\,]}$ are equally expressive. By similar means it can be shown that upward navigation can be removed from $\mathcal{X}^{\uparrow}_{[\,],\neg}$, to obtain an equivalent expression in $\mathcal{X}_{[\,],\neg}$: this is discussed further in Section 3.4. Thus, up to expressive equivalence, the fragments appear in the right diagram in Fig. 3. In the figure, the fragments shown at the same vertex are equally

---

[2] For syntactic convenience we permit nesting of unions in expressions, which is forbidden in XPath 1.0; in XPath 1.0 this would be simulated by rewriting these nested unions as top level ones.

[3] We introduce the notation '..*' for the ancestor-or-self axis here in the absence of an abbreviated syntax for this in XPath 1.0.

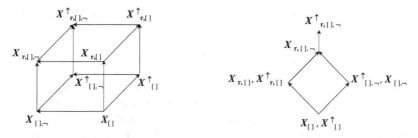

Fig. 3. XPath fragments (left) and their relationship based on their expressive power (right)

expressive. If an arrow connects two fragments F_1 and F_2, then F_1 is strictly less expressive than F_2.

Semantics of Subtree Queries: We present here a framework for *turning XPath queries into subtree queries*. Under the subtree semantics, the result of the evaluation of an XPath expression q on a document D is document $q(D)$ (subdocument of D) obtained as follows:

1. evaluate q using the usual XPath semantics;
2. for each node n obtained from step 1, get its *descendant* and *ancestor* nodes up to the root node of D;
3. finally, construct $q(D)$ by removing all nodes of D that are not in the set of nodes obtained from the previous step.

Note that the resulting document $q(D)$ is a subdocument of D whose root-to-leaf paths are a subset of the set of root-to-leaf paths of D and which inherits the tree structure of D.

Subtree Query Notation: For two subdocuments D_1 and D_2 of D, $D_1 \mid_D D_2$ is the subdocument whose nodes (edges) are the union of the nodes (edges) in D_1 and D_2.

From this point on, when we write an XPath expression in this paper, we will by default consider it as returning a document, using the subtree semantics. The reader can thus think of subtree queries as particularly simple XML queries, with a concise syntax. When we want to make clear whether an XPath expression E is to be considered under the standard XPath semantics we write $\langle E \rangle$, and under the subtree semantics we write $\lfloor E \rfloor$. Similarly, we write $\langle E \rangle(D)$ to denote the result of evaluating E under the XPath semantics and $\lfloor E \rfloor(D)$ to denote the result of evaluating E on document D under the subtree semantics.

3   Composing Subtree Queries

For any XPath fragment F used to define the subtree queries, the *subtree composition problem* for that fragment can be defined as follows: given two expressions

E_1 and E_2 in F, find a single subtree query E' such that for any document D it holds that:

$$\lfloor E' \rfloor(D) = \lfloor E_1 \rfloor(\lfloor E_2 \rfloor(D))$$

From this point on, we refer to expression E_1 as the outer query and E_2 as the inner query (the former is evaluated on the result of the evaluation of the latter), and use $E_1 \circ E_2$ to denote the function satisfying the definition above.

Thus there is a variant of this problem for each XPath fragment; indeed, there are many XPath fragments where no such E' exists for such queries. Closure under composition fails for tree patterns (see below); it also fails for XPath with ancestor and descendant axes, but without qualifiers. Our goal is to give efficient algorithms that solve the composition problems for important fragments of XPath. We begin with a composition algorithm for tree patterns in Section 3.1, extend this to unions of tree patterns in Section 3.2, and to $\mathcal{X}_{r,[\ ],\neg}$ in Section 3.3. In Section 3.4 we show how these techniques extend to fragments in our diagram with upward axes. A related problem is the composition of an XPath query with a subtree query in which the outer query E_1 and the desired E' are both interpreted under XPath semantics. The algorithms presented here discuss the composition of subtree queries. We leave the simple extension to the composition of XPath queries with subtree queries for the full paper.

3.1   Subtree Composition for Tree Patterns

As a step towards a composition algorithm for subtree queries based on XPath without negation, we begin with a composition algorithm for *tree patterns*. The algorithm is based on finding homomorphisms of the outer query into the inner query (as done in query containment algorithms for conjunctive queries).

Tree Patterns: A tree pattern is a tree with labels on nodes and edges. Nodes are labeled by names of Σ. Edges are either *child edges* labeled with $*$, or *descendant edges*, labeled with $//$. There is also a set of *selected nodes* which denote the nodes returned by the pattern. A special case are the *unary tree patterns* (see [4, 3]) that have a single selected node. A general tree pattern Q is evaluated as follows: for each match of one of the patterns in Q, we return any of the nodes labeled as the selected node. Tree patterns return nodesets, and can be translated into XPath queries in $\mathcal{X}_{r,[\ ]}$. Thus we can consider them under the subtree semantics as well. For two patterns P_1 and P_2, we write $\lfloor P_1 \rfloor = \lfloor P_2 \rfloor$ to mean these are equivalent under the subtree semantics.

We now note that *tree patterns are not closed under composition*: if one considers the tree patterns $E_1 = //\texttt{listitem}$ and $E_2 = //\texttt{parlist}$, then it is easy to see that there is no tree pattern E' for which $\lfloor E' \rfloor(D) = \lfloor E_1 \rfloor(\lfloor E_2 \rfloor(D))$. Closure under composition can be obtained by adding top-level union. A *union of tree patterns* is a set of tree patterns, and similarly a union of unary tree patterns is a set of unary tree patterns. Such a query returns the union of the result of its component patterns. In [4] it is shown that unions of tree patterns with descendant edges have exactly the same expressiveness as the XPath fragment $\mathcal{X}_{r,[\,]}$ consisting of expressions built up with descendant and child axes, while the XPath fragment $\mathcal{X}_{[\,]}$ is equivalent to tree patterns with only child edges. Our next goal will be to give a composition algorithm for unions of tree patterns (and hence for $\mathcal{X}_{r,[\,]}$ and $\mathcal{X}_{[\,]}$).

We say that a unary tree pattern is a *path pattern* if all its nodes are linear-ordered by the edge relation of the pattern and where the selected node is not necessarily a leaf node. Path patterns P have the property that for all unary tree patterns Q_1, Q_2, and for any document D:

$$\lfloor P \rfloor (\lfloor Q_1 \mid Q_2 \rfloor(D)) = \lfloor P \rfloor(\lfloor Q_1 \rfloor(D)) \mid_D \lfloor P \rfloor(\lfloor Q_2 \rfloor(D))$$

The equality follows because, according to subtree semantics, for some instance D, if the witness of the selected node of P is in $Q_i(D)$, then so are the witnesses of its ancestors and descendants in P. We will see that this gives a particularly simple algorithm for the composition of a path pattern P with a unary tree pattern Q.

Embeddings: Given a tree pattern Q, an *expansion* of Q is an extension Q' of the pattern with additional nodes, which must be either a) adjacent wildcard nodes as descendants of selected nodes or b) additional wildcard nodes inserted between two nodes, ancestors of selected nodes, that were connected in Q with a descendant edge. We refer to the nodes in $Q' - Q$ as *expansion nodes*.

A *pattern embedding* from a path pattern P to a unary tree pattern Q is a mapping m from all the nodes in P to some expansion Q' of Q, where 1) the range of m includes all the expansion nodes of Q' 2) m preserves child edge relationships from P to Q', maps nodes related by descendant edges in P to transitively related nodes in Q', and maps the root of P to the root of Q' 3) the label of node n in P is consistent with that of $m(n)$ (i.e. either they match, or the label of either n or $m(n)$ is the wildcard) 4) all nodes in the range must be comparable to a selected node (i.e. be either ancestors or descendants of the selected node).

Given m, P and Q, let $m(P, Q)$ be the tree pattern obtained from Q' by adding, for every expansion node k in Q' that is a wildcard such that $m(n) = k$, the label of n. The selected node of $m(P, Q)$ is (a) the selected node in Q, if $m(n)$ is an ancestor of the selected node in Q', or (b) $m(n)$, if $m(n)$ is a child wildcard expansion node in Q'. In the presence of a DTD, we can optimize using *DTD-based pruning*: we can check whether any parent/child or ancestor/descendant edge in $m(P, Q)$ contradicts the dependency graph of the DTD (which can be pre-computed), and discard $m(P, Q)$ from the result if there is such a clash.

Example 1. Consider the unary tree pattern $Q_4 = $ /site/regions//item[quantity] and the path pattern $Q_1 = $ /site/regions/europe given previously (they are both shown as tree patterns in Fig. 4). A double line signifies a descendant edge, a single line a child edge and the selected nodes are starred. To calculate the embedding from Q_1 to Q_4, we expand Q_4 to Q_4' (given in Fig. 4). The dotted lines between the

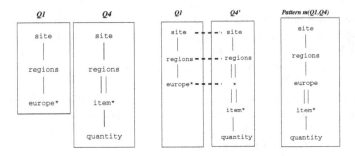

Fig. 4. Path pattern Q_1 and unary tree pattern Q_4 (left), the expansion Q'_4 of Q_4 and the embedding of Q_1 into Q_4 (middle) and the pattern $m(Q_1, Q_4)$ (right)

nodes of Q_1 and Q'_4 show the embedding from Q_1 into Q_4. The pattern $m(Q_1, Q_4)$ obtained from the embedding of the path pattern Q_1 into the unary tree pattern Q_4 is illustrated in Fig. 4.

Lemma 1. *Let P be a path pattern and $Q = \bigcup Q_i$ be a union of unary tree patterns Q_i. For any document D and node n in $\lfloor P \rfloor (\lfloor Q \rfloor (D))$, there is some pattern embedding m from P to Q and node n' returned by $m(P, Q)$, such that n is either an ancestor or descendant of n' in D. In particular $P \circ Q$ is the union of $m(P, Q)$ over all pattern embeddings m.*

In the case where neither P nor Q contain descendant axes there is *at most one* embedding m of P to each Q_i which can be found in time linear in $|P| + |Q_i|$ by proceeding top-down in parallel in P and Q_i, where in Q_i we proceed down the path towards the selected node. We can be more efficient by noting that to find embeddings of P into Q_i, we care only about the query nodes in the path to the selected node of Q_i. Hence we can abstract away the subtrees outside of this path (i.e. the filters associated with the nodes), and leave them as additional annotations on the nodes of Q_i, to be used only after the embedding is found.

The algorithm runs in time bounded by the size of the number of embeddings of the outer query into the inner query. This number is exponential in the worst case (e.g. bounded by $min(2|outer|^{2|inner|}, (2|inner|)^{|outer|})$, since the embeddings are order-preserving). The following result shows that a blow-up is unavoidable:

Proposition 1. *For queries I and O, let $F(I, O)$ denote the minimum size of a tree pattern query expressing the composition $O \circ I$, and let $f(n)$ denote the maximum of $F(I, O)$ over I and O of size at most n. Then $f(n) \in \Omega(2^{\lfloor n/2 \rfloor})$.*

The proof is by considering the composition of outer query $E_1 = //A_1// \ldots //A_n$ and inner query $E_2 = //B_1// \ldots //B_n$ where the A_i and B_j are tags. It is easy to see that a tree pattern contained in $E_1 \circ E_2$ can represent only one interleaving of the B's and A's, hence a composition must include a distinct pattern for each interleaving, and there are more than 2^n of these. Note that if n' is the size of the queries, then $n = n'/2$.

3.2   Subtree Composition for Positive XPath

For P a general unary tree pattern, and $Q = \bigcup Q_i$, one needs to deal with the fact that distinct paths in P may be witnessed in distinct Q_i. Hence we find it convenient to first calculate the possible *fusings* of the inner query and then look at embeddings into these fused patterns. The fusings of the inner queries are represented as tree patterns with multiple selected nodes (recall that these are interpreted semantically in the subtree languages by taking all root-to-leaf paths through any of the selected nodes).

Example 2. Consider the union of tree patterns $q = q_1 \mid q_2$ (inner query) below and the unary tree pattern $p = $/site/regions/europe/item[location]/descr/text.

$$q_1 = /\text{site/regions/europe/item[quantity]/location}$$
$$q_2 = /\text{site/regions/europe/item/descr}$$

One can observe that distinct paths in p are witnessed in distinct q_i's: location sub-elements of item elements are returned by q_1 and descr sub-elements are returned by q_2. The queries obtained by fusing q_1 and q_2 are:

$q_a =$ /site/(regions/europe/item[quantity]/location|regions/europe/item/descr)

$q_b =$ /site/regions/(europe/item[quantity]/location | europe/item/descr)

$q_c =$ /site/regions/europe/(item[quantity]/location | item/descr)

$q_d =$ /site/regions/europe/item[quantity]/(location | descr)

In general, a fusing of tree patterns $P_1 \ldots P_n$ is determined by an equivalence relation E on the underlying nodes in expansions $P'_1 \ldots P'_n$ of the patterns, such that equivalent nodes have consistent labels, every equivalence class contains a node in some P_i, and such that: if for two nodes n and n' it holds that nEn', then the parent of n is E-equivalent to the parent of n'. The corresponding fusing is obtained by identifying equivalent nodes and arranging node and edge labels via the strictest node and edge relation represented in the equivalence class. The selected nodes are the equivalence classes of selected nodes in any P'_i. It can be shown that the conditions above guarantee that the resulting quotient structure is a tree pattern. The fusings between two patterns can be enumerated using a top-down algorithm that finds all matches for the siblings of the root of one tree with descendants of the root in another tree, and then recursively searches for matches of the subtrees of these siblings. This can be extended to multiple patterns by using the equation $Fusings(F_1 \mid F) = \bigcup_{P \in Fusings(F)} Fusings(F_1, P)$. We can trim the number of fusings by restricting to those that correspond to some embedding of root-to-leaf paths from the outer query into nodes of the inner query. Each such embedding generates an equivalence relation on the inner query, by considering which nodes are mapped to by the same element of the outer query.

The last restriction shows that when the outer query is a single tree pattern, the size of the output of the composition algorithm can be bounded by the number of functions taking root-to-leaf paths in the outer query to nodes in an expansion of the inner query. This in turn is bounded by $(2|inner|)^{|outer|}$. In the case that the outer query is a union of tree patterns with multiple components, note that $\lfloor (O_1|O_2) \circ I \rfloor (D) = \lfloor (O_1 \circ I) \rfloor (D) \mid_D \lfloor (O_2 \circ I) \rfloor (D)$, so we can treat each component of the outer query separately. For a union of tree patterns Q, let $br(Q)$ be the number of trees in Q and $l(Q)$ be the maximum size of any tree in Q. The argument above shows that a composition can be produced in time at most $br(O)(2|I|)^{l(O)}$. Again a worst-case exponential lower bound in output size holds (using the same example as in Proposition 1).

From the algorithm above, we can get composition closure for $\mathcal{X}_{[\,]}$ and $\mathcal{X}_{r,[\,]}$, since each XPath query in these fragments can be translated into a union of tree patterns. However, the translation to tree patterns itself requires an exponential blow-up, since our $\mathcal{X}_{[\,]}$ and $\mathcal{X}_{r,[\,]}$ allow the '|' (union) operator to be nested arbitrarily (in contrast to XPath 1.0, where union is permitted only at top-level). One can give modifications of these embedding algorithms that work directly on $\mathcal{X}_{[\,]}$ and $\mathcal{X}_{r,[\,]}$, and give only a single-exponential blow-up; we omit these variations for space reasons and explain only the corresponding bounds. We redefine br and l, and extend them to filters, using $br(E_1 \mid E_2) = br(E_1) + br(E_2)$, $br(E_1/E_2) = max\{E_1, E_2\}$, $l(E_1 \mid E_2) = max\{l(E_1), l(E_2)\}, l(E_1/E_2) = l(E_1) + l(E_2)$. br and l are both preserved in filter steps and are equal to 1 for step expressions. For filters, $\wedge$ and $\vee$ are handled analogously to '|' and '/' above. Then the number of embeddings from $\mathcal{X}_{r,[\,]}$ expression O into $\mathcal{X}_{r,[\,]}$ expression I in this more general sense is again bounded by $br(O)(2|I|)^{l(O)}$, and so this gives a bound on the running time of an embedding-based algorithm for $\mathcal{X}_{[\,]}$ and $\mathcal{X}_{r,[\,]}$ as well.

3.3   Extending to Fragments with Negation

When we turn towards fragments with negation, we again have to deal with the fact that the outer query can interact with different components of the inner query. Consider for example the outer query Q_3 and the inner query Q_2:

$Q_3 = //\texttt{item[location | descr]}$ $Q_2 = //\texttt{item[not(quantity)]} \mid //\texttt{item/location}$

both first presented in Section 1. One can observe that information about item elements requested by the outer query Q_3 can be found in both subqueries of the inner query Q_2. However, in this case we can make use of negation to rewrite the inner query in such a way that different components of a union are "disjoint", and hence that all parts of a match lie in the same component. Once this normalization is done, we will have a straightforward inductive approach, with more succinct output. The fact that the algorithm for fragments with negation is simpler is not surprising, since generally we expect that the addition of more features to the language will make composition easier, while potentially making the composed queries harder to optimize.

Normalization Step: We define first the notion of *strongly disjoint queries* that we will use in the following in order to perform the normalization step.

Two XPath queries q and q' are said to be *strongly disjoint* if for any document D, for any nodes n returned by q and n' returned by q' on D, the root-to-leaf paths to n and n' meet only at the root. An XPath expression E is said to be in *separable normal form* (SNF) if for every subexpression of E of the form $E_1 \mid \ldots \mid E_n$, the E_i are *pairwise strongly disjoint*. Normalization is done by taking a subexpression $E_1 \mid E_2 \mid \ldots \mid E_n$ and breaking up any leading filters into boolean combinations to ensure that the filters are either disjoint or identical, grouping together expressions with the same filter, and recursing on the remaining subexpression. The significance of strong disjointness is the following simple lemma:

Lemma 2. *Suppose E_1 and E_2 are in separable normal form and P, E_1, E_2 are in the fragment $\mathcal{X}_{r,\,[\,],\neg}$. Then, for all documents D it holds that:*

$$\lfloor P \rfloor(\lfloor E_1 \mid E_2 \rfloor(D)) = \lfloor P \rfloor(\lfloor E_1 \rfloor(D)) \mid_D \lfloor P \rfloor(\lfloor E_2 \rfloor(D))$$

Using this we get a simple algorithm for composing any subtree query in the fragment $\mathcal{X}_{r,\,[\,],\neg}$ with any E in separable normal form. The algorithm is shown in Fig. 5, making use of an auxiliary function used for filters.

Example 3. Consider the outer query Q_3 and the inner query Q_2 given previously. When the inner query is translated into separable normal form, we obtain:

$$Q'_2 = //\texttt{item}([\textsf{not}(\texttt{quantity})]/(\epsilon \mid \texttt{location}) \mid [\texttt{quantity}]/\texttt{location})$$

The query resulting from the application of the inductive algorithm, the application of the simplification rules from [4] ($E/\emptyset = \emptyset$, $E \mid \emptyset = E$ and $E \mid E = E$) and the final composed query are shown in Fig. 6.

The example above shows that our algorithms rely on post-processing using some basic simplification rules. Currently we use the rules from [4].

An important feature of the algorithm is that it runs in polynomial time in the size of the queries, under the assumption of normalization (for un-normalized queries, there is a provable exponential blow-up as before). Furthermore, it does not require normalization of the outer query, only the inner one. Another key advantage of this algorithm is that it can be easily extended to deal with data value equality and inequality: we have to add an extra case to handle filters $E_1 = E_2$ or $E_1 \neq E_2$ to the auxiliary function given in Fig. 5, and these are handled by a trivial recursive call. Indeed, one can show that there are subtree queries using data value equality but no negation, whose composition *requires* negation to be expressed.

3.4 Composition for Fragments with Upward Axes

We now discuss how these algorithms extend to the remaining fragments in Fig. 3. For $P, Q \in \mathcal{X}_{[\,]}^{\uparrow}$, one approach is to first apply the algorithms of [4, 13] to remove upward qualifiers, and then proceed as for $\mathcal{X}_{[\,]}$. Similarly, by removing upward axes from $\mathcal{X}_{r,\,[\,]}^{\uparrow}$ and applying the embedding algorithm for $\mathcal{X}_{r,\,[\,]}$, we get

function $\circ_{ind}(O : \mathcal{X}_{r,[\ ],\neg},\ I : \mathcal{X}_{r,[\ ],\neg}$ in SNF)
returns $\mathcal{X}_{r,[\ ],\neg}$ expression
[1] **switch** O
[2]   **case** $O_1|O_2$ **return** $(\circ_{ind}(O_1,I)\ |\ \circ_{ind}(O_2,I))$
[3]   **case** $[F]/O_2$ **return** $([\circ_f(F,I)]/\circ_{ind}(O_2,I))$
[4]   **case** A/O_2
[5]   **switch** I
[6]   **case** $I_1|I_2$ **return** $(\circ_{ind}(O,I_1)\ |\ \circ_{ind}(O,I_2))$
[7]   **case** $[F]/I_2$ **return** $([F]/\circ_{ind}(O,I_2))$
[8]   **case** $\emptyset$ **return** $(\emptyset)$
[9]   **case** ϵ **return** (O)
[10]   **case** A/I_2 **return** $(A/\circ_{ind}(O_2,I_2))$
[11]   **case** $B/I_2,\ B \neq A$ **return** $(\emptyset)$
[12]   **case** $//I_2$ **return** $((A/\circ_{ind}(O_2,//I_2))\ |\ \circ_{ind}(O,I_2))$
[13]   **end switch**
[14]   **case** $//O_2$
[15]   **switch** I
[16]   **case** $I_1|I_2$ **return** $(\circ_{ind}(O,I_1)\ |\ \circ_{ind}(O,I_2))$
[17]   **case** $[F]/I_2$ **return** $([F]/\circ_{ind}(O,I_2))$
[18]   **case** $\emptyset$ **return** $(\emptyset)$
[19]   **case** ϵ **return** (O)
[20]   **case** A/I_2 **return** $(A/\circ_{ind}(O,I_2)\ |\ \circ_{ind}(O_2,I))$
[21]   **case** $//I_2$ **return** $(//(\circ_{ind}(I,O_2)|\circ_{ind}(O,I_2)))$
[22]   **end switch**
[23]   **case** ϵ **return** (I)
[24]   **case** $\emptyset$ **return** $(\emptyset)$
[25] **end switch**
     end

function $\circ_f(F : \mathcal{X}_{r,[\ ],\neg}$ filter, $I : \mathcal{X}_{r,[\ ],\neg}$ query in SNF)
returns $\mathcal{X}_{r,[\ ],\neg}^{\uparrow}$
[1] **switch** F
[2]   **case** $\neg F_1$ **return** $(\neg \circ_f(F_1,I)$
[3]   **case** $F_1\ op\ F_2,\ op \in \{\text{and},|\}$ **return** $(\circ_f(F_1,I)\ op\ \circ_f(F_2,I))$
[4]   **case** E **return** $(\circ_{ind}(E,I))$
[5] **end switch**
     end

Fig. 5. Inductive Algorithm and Inductive Filter Composition

an algorithm for $\mathcal{X}_{r,[\ ]}^{\uparrow}$. For $\mathcal{X}_{[\ ],\neg}^{\uparrow}$, one can also remove upward axes (although this is not stated explicitly in [13,4]). Indeed, a simple inductive algorithm can compute from a $\mathcal{X}_{[\ ],\neg}^{\uparrow}$ query Q a query Q' that is equivalent to Q in every context (not just the root), such that Q' is a union of queries either of the form $[F_0]/../[F_1]/.../../[F_n]/E_n$, where F_i are filters in $\mathcal{X}_{[\ ],\neg}$ and E_i is an expression in $\mathcal{X}_{[\ ],\neg}$, or of the form $[F]/E$. When one restricts to applying Q' at the root, the components of the union of the first form can be eliminated.

We refer to these as "eliminate-first algorithms', since they eliminate upward axes before composing, producing a composed query with no upward axes. Although the upward-axis removal algorithms of [4, 13] themselves require an exponential blow-up, they produce from a query Q a new query Q' without upward axes such that $l(Q') = l(Q)$ and $br(Q') < 2^{br(Q)}$. Combining these bounds with the upper bounds on the number of embeddings, we see that the output of eliminate-first composition algorithms has size bounded by $2^{br(O)}(2 \cdot 2^{|I|})^{l(O)} = 2^{br(O)}2^{(|I|+1)l(O)}$, single-exponential in both inputs.

Result of the inductive algorithm:
$Q_3 \circ Q_2 = //\text{item} [([\text{not(quantity)}]/(\text{descr} \mid \emptyset) \mid [\text{quantity}]/\emptyset) \mid$
$\qquad\qquad\qquad ([\text{not(quantity)}]/(\text{location} \mid \text{location}) \mid [\text{quantity}]/\text{location})]$

Application of the simplification rules:
$Q_3 \circ Q_2 = //\text{item}[[\text{not(quantity)}]/\text{descr} \mid ([\text{not(quantity)}]/\text{location} \mid [\text{quantity}]/\text{location})]$

Composed Query:
$Q_3 \circ Q_2 = //\text{item} [[\text{not(quantity)}]/\text{descr} \mid [\text{not(quantity)}]/\text{location}] \mid$
$\qquad\qquad //\text{item}[\text{quantity}]/\text{location}$

Fig. 6. Queries resulting from the application of the inductive algorithm and the simplification rules

An alternative is to compose queries first, and then (if possible, and if desired) remove upward axes from the result. Somewhat surprisingly, if one simply wants to perform composition for fragments with upward axes, one can do so in polynomial time. We show this for the largest XPath fragment, $\mathcal{X}^{\uparrow}_{r,[\ ],\neg}$, leaving the details for other fragments for the full paper. Note that $\mathcal{X}^{\uparrow}_{r,[\ ],\neg}$ does not eliminate upward axes (consider, for example, the query asking for all location nodes that have only item nodes as ancestors), so only an eliminate-first algorithm is not applicable here. The polynomial time method for composing subtree queries uses a trick from [12]. One can simply take the outer query and "pre-test" each node to see if satisfies the inner query. Officially, for each query Q, let Q^r be the query obtained from changing occurrences of $/R$ to the equivalent $*/[\text{label} = R]$, and then reversing each of the axes in Q that do not occur within a filter. Let IN_Q be the query $Q^r[\text{not}(..)]$. Clearly, the filter $[IN_Q]$ returns true exactly when a node is in the result of the XPath expression Q. If we take Q to be the inner query, and we add the filter $[(//|..^*)[IN_Q]]$ to each step of the outer query, we are checking whether nodes witnessed in the outer query are actually in the result of the inner query. Hence the result is the composition. In the case where the outer query has only downward axes, we need only add these filters to the leaves of the syntax tree. Similar algorithms are available for fragments without negation; for example, in the case of $\mathcal{X}^{\uparrow}_{[\ ]}$, a root test not(..) is unnecessary, since one can test statically whether a path leads back to the root by just "counting steps". For $\mathcal{X}^{\uparrow}_{[\ ]}$ and $\mathcal{X}^{\uparrow}_{r,[\ ]}$ one can combine this PTIME algorithm with upward-axis removal, obtaining a composed query with no upward axes in exponential time.

These last composition algorithms are only useful when significant optimization is in place in the query evaluation engine; the resulting composed query
clearly includes an enormous amount of upward and downward navigation, even
when the initial queries lack upward axes completely. We are still developing
optimization rules for fragments with upward axes and negation; However, to
the extent that special-purpose optimizers are developed for $\mathcal{X}^{\uparrow}_{r,[\ ],\neg}$, composing while staying within this fragment can be helpful. This example also serves
to emphasize that closure under composition becomes easier as the fragment
becomes larger. Taking the algorithms altogether, what we have shown is the
following:

Theorem 1 (Composition Closure). *Let F be any of the XPath fragments
in Fig. 3, or either of the XPath fragment $\mathcal{X}^{\uparrow}_{r,[\ ],\neg}$ $\mathcal{X}_{r,[\ ],\neg}$ extended with data
value equality. Then for any Q and Q' in F there is $Q'' \in F$ such that for every
document D it holds that:*

$$\lfloor Q \rfloor(\lfloor Q' \rfloor(D)) = \lfloor Q'' \rfloor(D)$$

In addition for every such $Q, Q' \in F$ we can get $Q'' \in F$ such that

$$\langle Q \rangle(\lfloor Q' \rfloor(D)) = \langle Q'' \rangle(D)$$

4   Conclusion

In this paper we discussed the specification and composition of subtree queries
for common fragments of XPath. We provided composition algorithms for each
of the resulting subtree languages and showed that these languages are closed
under composition. Despite the complexity of the composition algorithms, experiments in [2] show that we can have important benefits over XQuery trivial
composition (when the composed subtree query is translated into an XQuery
expression and evaluated with an off-the-shelf XQuery evaluator). The composition algorithms presented in this paper are used in the Incognito access control
system being developed at Bell Laboratories. Incognito uses the Vortex rules
engine [11] to resolve user context information and applies the composition algorithms to compose user queries with access control views (all of these being
subtree queries) to compute the authorized user query that will be evaluated
against XML documents.

References

1. S. Abiteboul, A. Bonifati, G. Cobena, I. Manolescu, and T. Milo. Dynamic XML
   Documents with Distribution and Replication. In *SIGMOD*, 2003.
2. B. Alexe, M. Benedikt, and I. Fundulaki. Specification, Composition and Evaluation of XML Subtree Queries. Technical report, Bell Laboratories, 2005. Available
   at http://db.bell-labs.com/user/fundulaki/.
3. S. Amer-Yahia, S. Cho, L. V. Lakshamanan, and D. Srivastava. Minimization of
   Tree Pattern Queries. In *SIGMOD*, 2001.

4. M. Benedikt, W. Fan, and G. Kuper. Structural Properties of XPath Fragments. *Theoretical Computer Science*, 2003.
5. E. Bertino and E. Ferrari. Secure and Selective Dissemination of XML Documents. *TISSEC*, 5(3):290–331, 2002.
6. J. Clark et. al. (eds.). XML Path Language (XPath) 1.0. W3C Recommendation, 1999. http://www.w3c.org/TR/xpath.
7. M. Fernandez, Y. Kadiyska, D. Suciu, A. Morishima, and W.-C. Tan. SilkRoute: A framework for publishing relational data in XML . *TODS*, 27(4):438–493, 2002.
8. I. Fundulaki, G. Giraud, D. Lieuwen, N. Onose, N. Pombourq, and A. Sahuguet. Share your data, keep your secrets. In *SIGMOD*, 2004. (Demonstration Track).
9. G. Gottlob and C. Koch. Monadic Datalog and the Expressive Power of Languages for Web Information Extraction. In *PODS*, 2002.
10. G. Gottlob, C. Koch, and R. Pichler. Efficient Algorithms for Processing XPath Queries. In *VLDB*, 2002.
11. R. Hull, B. Kumar, and D. Lieuwen. Towards Federated Policy Management. In *Int'l Workshop on Policies for Distributed Systems and Networks*, 2003.
12. M. Marx. XPath with conditional axis relations. In *EDBT*, 2004.
13. D. Olteanu, H. Meuss, T. Furche, and F. Bry. XPath: Looking forward. XMDM, 2002.
14. A. Sahuguet and B. Alexe. Sub-document queries over XML with XSquirrel. In *WWW*, 2005.
15. A. Sahuguet, B. Alexe, I. Fundulaki, P. Lalilgand, A. Shikfa, and A. Arnail. User Profile Management in Converged Networks. In *CIDR*, 2005.
16. A. Schmidt, F. Waas, M. Kersten, M. Carey, I. Manolescu, and R. Busse. XMark: a benchmark for XML Data Management. In *VLDB*, 2002.
17. I. Tatarinov, Z. Ives, A.Y. Halevy, and D.S. Weld. Updating XML. In *SIGMOD*, 2001.
18. P. Wadler. Two Semantics for XPath. Technical report, Bell Laboratories, 2000. Technical Memorandum.

On the Expressive Power of XQuery Fragments

Jan Hidders[1], Stefania Marrara[2], Jan Paredaens[1], and Roel Vercammen[1,*]

[1] University of Antwerp, Dept. Math and Computer Science,
Middelheimlaan 1, BE-2020 Antwerp, Belgium
[2] Universitá degli Studi di Milano, Dipartimento di Tecnologie dell'Informazione,
Via Bramante 65, I-26013 Crema (CR), Italy

Abstract. XQuery is known to be a powerful XML query language with many bells and whistles. For many common queries we do not need all the expressive power of XQuery. We investigate the effect of omitting certain features of XQuery on the expressive power of the language. We start from a simple base fragment which can be extended by several optional features being aggregation functions such as count and sum, sequence generation, node construction, position information in for loops, and recursion. In this way we obtain 64 different XQuery fragments which can be divided into 17 different equivalence classes such that two fragments can express the same functions iff they are in the same equivalence class. Moreover, we investigate the relationships between these equivalence classes.

1 Introduction

XQuery [2], the W3C standard query language for XML, is a very powerful query language which is known to be Turing Complete [8]. As the language in its entirety is too powerful and complex for many queries, there is a need to investigate the different properties of frequently used fragments. Most existing theoretical work focuses on XPath, a rather limited subset of XQuery. For example, Benedikt, Fan, and Kuper studied structural properties of XPath fragments [1], the computational complexity of query evaluation for a number of XPath fragments was investigated by Gottlob, Koch, and Pichler in [4], and Marx increased the expressive power of XPath by extending it in order to be first order complete. It was not until recently that similar efforts were made for XQuery: Koch studies the computational complexity of nonrecursive XQuery [9], Vansummeren looks into the well-definedness problem for XQuery fragments [13] and the expressive power of the node construction in XQuery is studied in [10]. In this paper we will investigate the expressive power of XQuery fragments in a similar fashion as was done for the relational algebra [12] and SQL [11]. In order to do this, we establish some interesting properties for these fragments. We start from a small base fragment in which we can express many commonly used features such as some built-in functions, arithmetic, boolean operators, node and

---

* Roel Vercammen is supported by IWT – Institute for the Encouragement of Innovation by Science and Technology Flanders, grant number 31581.

G. Bierman and C. Koch (Eds.): DBPL 2005, LNCS 3774, pp. 154–168, 2005.

value comparisons, path expressions, simple for-loops and XPath set operations. This base fragment can be extended by a number of features that are likely to increase the expressive power such as recursion, aggregate functions, sequence generators, node constructors, and position information. The central question is which features of XQuery are really necessary in these fragments and which ones are only syntactic sugar, simplifying queries that were already expressible without this feature. Our most expressive fragment corresponds to LiXQuery [5], which is conjectured to be as expressive as XQuery.

This paper is organized as follows. Section 2 introduces the syntax and the semantics of the different XQuery fragments that we are going to analyze. In Section 3 we present some expressibility results for these fragments and in Section 4 we show some properties that hold for some of the fragments. These results are combined in Section 5, where we partition the set of fragments into classes of fragments with the same expressive power. Finally, Section 6 outlines the conclusions of our work.

2   XQuery Fragments

This section formally introduces the XQuery fragments for which we study the expressive power in this paper. We will use LiXQuery [5] as a formal foundation, which is a light-weight sublanguage of XQuery, fully downwards compatible with XQuery. The syntax of each of the XQuery fragments is defined in Subsection 2.1. In Subsection 2.2 we briefly describe the semantics of a query.

2.1   Syntax

The syntax of the fragment XQ is shown in Figure 1, by rules [1-19] [1]. This syntax is an abstract syntax [2]. The XQuery fragment XQ contains simple arithmetic, path expressions, "for" clauses (without "at"), the "if" test, "let" variable bindings, the existential semantics for comparison, typeswitches and some built-in functions. Adding non-recursive function definitions to XQ would clearly not augment the expressive power of XQ. We use 6 attributes for fragments: C, S, at, ctr, to and R (cf. Figure 2 for the syntax of the attributed fragments). The fragment XQ^R denotes XQ augmented with (recursive) functions definitions, XQ_C is XQ plus the "count" function, XQ_S denotes the inclusion of the "sum" function, XQ_{at} includes the "at" clause in a for expression, XQ^{ctr} indicates the inclusion of the node constructors, and finally the XQ^{to} denotes the sequence generator "to". The fragment XQ can be attributed by a set of these attributes. In this way, we obtain 64 fragments of XQuery. The aim of this paper is to investigate and to compare the expressive power of these fragments. With XQ^* we denote the fragment $XQ_{C,S,at}^{R,to,ctr}$ expressed by rules [1-26]. Following auxiliary definitions will be used throughout the paper:

---

[1] Note that expressions which are not allowed in a fragment definition must be considered as not occurring in the right hand side of a production rule. As an example *FunCall* and *Count* do not occur in rule [2] for XQ.

[2] It assumes that extra brackets and precedence rules are added for disambiguation.

Definition 1. *The language* $\mathbf{L}(XF)$ *of an XQuery fragment* XF *is the (infinite) set of all expressions that can be generated by the grammar rules for this fragment with* $\langle Query \rangle$ *as start symbol. The set* Φ *is the set of all 64 XQuery fragments defined in Figure 2.*

Similar to LiXQuery, we ignore static typing and do not consider namespaces[3], comments, processing instructions, and entities. There are some features left out from LiXQuery in the definition of XQ^*, such as the union, the filter expression, the functions "position()" and "last()", and the parent step (".."), but they can easily been simulated in XQ^* (see the details in [6]). From these considerations, we can claim that XQ^* has the same expressive power as LiXQuery.

2.2 Semantics

We will now introduce the semantics of our XQuery fragments which is the same as that of LiXQuery and downwards compatible with the XQuery Formal Semantics[3].

Expressions are evaluated against an *XML store* which contains XML fragments created as intermediate results, and all the web documents[4]. First we need some definitions of sets for the formal specification of the LiXQuery semantics. The set $\mathcal{A}$ is the set of all atomic values, $\mathcal{V}$ is the set of all nodes, $\mathcal{S} \subseteq \mathcal{A}$ is the set of all strings, and $\mathcal{N} \subseteq \mathcal{S}$ is the set of strings that may be used as tag names.

Definition 2. *An* **XML Store** *is a 6-tuple* $St = (V, E, <, \nu, \sigma, \delta)$ *where* $V = V^d \cup V^e \cup V^a \cup V^t$ *is a finite countable set of nodes* $(V \subseteq \mathcal{V})$ *consisting of the pairwise disjoint sets of document nodes* V^d, *element nodes* V^e, *attribute nodes* V^a, *and text nodes* V^t; (V, E) *is a forest (with nodes* V *and directed edges* E); *if* $(m, n) \in E$ *then we say that* n *is a child of* m; $<$ *is the sibling order for the trees in* (V, E); $\nu : V^e \cup V^a \to \mathcal{N}$ *labels the element and attribute nodes with their node name;* $\sigma : V^a \cup V^t \to \mathcal{S}$ *labels attribute and text nodes with their string value;* $\delta : \mathcal{S} \to V^d$ *is a partial function that associates with a URI or a file name, a document node. It is called the document function. This function represents all the URIs of the Web and all the names of the files, together with the documents they contain. We suppose that all the documents are in the store.*

Moreover, for each store, each document node is the root of a tree and contains exactly one child, which is an element node; attribute nodes and text nodes do not have any children; in the $<$-*order attribute children precede the element and text children; two sibling text nodes are separated by at least one non-text sibling node; for all text nodes* n_t *of* V^t *holds* $\sigma(n_t) \neq$ *""; all attribute children of a common node have a different name.*

The set ST *is the set of all (valid) XML Stores.*

---

[3] In types and built-in functions, such as "xs:integer", the "xs:" part indicates a namespace. Although we do not handle namespaces we use them here to be compatible with XQuery.

[4] This assumption models correctly the formal semantics since each time a "doc" function is called for the same document, the same document node is returned.

[1]	$\langle Query \rangle$	$\rightarrow$ $(\langle FunDecl \rangle$ ";" $)^*\langle Expr \rangle$
[2]	$\langle Expr \rangle$	$\rightarrow$ $\langle Var \rangle$ | $\langle BuiltIn \rangle$ | $\langle IfExpr \rangle$ | $\langle ForExpr \rangle$ | $\langle LetExpr \rangle$ | $\langle Concat \rangle$ | $\langle AndOr \rangle$ | $\langle ValCmp \rangle$ | $\langle NodeCmp \rangle$ | $\langle AddExpr \rangle$ | $\langle MultExpr \rangle$ | $\langle Step \rangle$ | $\langle Path \rangle$ | $\langle Literal \rangle$ | $\langle EmpSeq \rangle$ | $\langle Constr \rangle$ | $\langle TypeSw \rangle$ | $\langle FunCall \rangle$ | $\langle Count \rangle$ | $\langle Sum \rangle$
[3]	$\langle Var \rangle$	$\rightarrow$ "\$"$\langle Name \rangle$
[4]	$\langle Literal \rangle$	$\rightarrow$ $\langle String \rangle$ | $\langle Integer \rangle$
[5]	$\langle EmpSeq \rangle$	$\rightarrow$ "()"
[6]	$\langle BuiltIn \rangle$	$\rightarrow$ "doc("$\langle Expr \rangle$")" | "name("$\langle Expr \rangle$")" | "string("$\langle Expr \rangle$")" | "xs:integer("$\langle Expr \rangle$")" | "root("$\langle Expr \rangle$")" | "concat("$\langle Expr \rangle$, $\langle Expr \rangle$")" | "true()" | "false()" | "not("$\langle Expr \rangle$")" | "distinct-values(" $\langle Expr \rangle$ ")"
[7]	$\langle IfExpr \rangle$	$\rightarrow$ "if " "("$\langle Expr \rangle$")" "then"$\langle Expr \rangle$ "else"$\langle Expr \rangle$
[8]	$\langle ForExpr \rangle$	$\rightarrow$ "for"$\langle Var \rangle(\langle AtExpr \rangle))?$ "in"$\langle Expr \rangle$ "return"$\langle Expr \rangle$
[9]	$\langle LetExpr \rangle$	$\rightarrow$ "let"$\langle Var \rangle$":="$\langle Expr \rangle$ "return"$\langle Expr \rangle$
[10]	$\langle Concat \rangle$	$\rightarrow$ $\langle Expr \rangle$","$\langle Expr \rangle$
[11]	$\langle AndOr \rangle$	$\rightarrow$ $\langle Expr \rangle$("and" | "or")$\langle Expr \rangle$
[12]	$\langle ValCmp \rangle$	$\rightarrow$ $\langle Expr \rangle$("=" | "<")$\langle Expr \rangle$
[13]	$\langle NodeCmp \rangle$	$\rightarrow$ $\langle Expr \rangle$("is" | "<<") $\langle Expr \rangle$
[14]	$\langle AddExpr \rangle$	$\rightarrow$ $\langle Expr \rangle$ ("+" | "-") $\langle Expr \rangle$
[15]	$\langle MultExpr \rangle$	$\rightarrow$ $\langle Expr \rangle$ ("*" | "idiv") $\langle Expr \rangle$
[16]	$\langle Step \rangle$	$\rightarrow$ "." | $\langle Name \rangle$ | "@"$\langle Name \rangle$ | "*" | "@*" | "text()"
[17]	$\langle Path \rangle$	$\rightarrow$ $\langle Expr \rangle$("/" | "//")$\langle Expr \rangle$
[18]	$\langle TypeSw \rangle$	$\rightarrow$ "typeswitch " "("$\langle Expr \rangle$")" ("case" $\langle Type \rangle$ "return"$\langle Expr \rangle$)$^+$ "default" "return"$\langle Expr \rangle$
[19]	$\langle Type \rangle$	$\rightarrow$ "xs:boolean" | "xs:integer" | "xs:string" | "element()" | "attribute()" | "text()" | "document-node()"
[20]	$\langle Count \rangle$	$\rightarrow$ "count(" $\langle Expr \rangle$ ")"
[21]	$\langle Sum \rangle$	$\rightarrow$ "sum(" $\langle Expr \rangle$ ")"
[22]	$\langle AtExpr \rangle$	$\rightarrow$ "at" $\langle Var \rangle$
[23]	$\langle SeqGen \rangle$	$\rightarrow$ $\langle Expr \rangle$ "to" $\langle Expr \rangle$
[24]	$\langle FunCall \rangle$	$\rightarrow$ $\langle Name \rangle$"("($\langle Expr \rangle$(","$\langle Expr \rangle$)*)?")"
[25]	$\langle FunDecl \rangle$	$\rightarrow$ "declare" "function" $\langle Name \rangle$ "(" ($\langle Var \rangle$ ("," $\langle Var \rangle$)*)? ")" "{" $\langle Expr \rangle$ "}"
[26]	$\langle Constr \rangle$	$\rightarrow$ "element" "{"$\langle Expr \rangle$"}" "{"$\langle Expr \rangle$"}" | "attribute" "{"$\langle Expr \rangle$"}" "{"$\langle Expr \rangle$"}" | "text" "{"$\langle Expr \rangle$"}" | "document" "{"$\langle Expr \rangle$"}"

Fig. 1. Syntax for XQ^* queries and expressions

$$XQ \; [1\text{-}19]$$
$$C \quad + \; [20]$$
$$S \quad + \; [21]$$
$$at \quad + \; [22]$$
$$to \quad + \; [23]$$
$$R \quad + \; [24\text{-}25]$$
$$ctr \quad + \; [26]$$

Fig. 2. Definition of XQuery fragments

We now give an example to illustrate this definition. In both this example and the rest of the paper, we will use the function ξ, which maps a sequence of items and a store to its serialization, as defined in [7].

Example 1. Let $St = (V, E, <, \nu, \sigma, \delta)$ be an XML store that is shown in Figure 3.

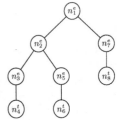

- The set of nodes V consists of $V^e = \{n_1^e, n_2^e, n_3^e, n_5^e,$ $n_7^e\}$, $V^t = \{n_4^t, n_6^t, n_8^t\}$, $V^d = V^a = \emptyset$.
- The set of edges is $E = \{(n_1^e, n_2^e), (n_1^e, n_7^e), (n_2^e, n_3^e),$ $(n_2^e, n_5^e), (n_3^e, n_4^t), (n_5^e, n_6^t), (n_7^e, n_8^t)\}$.
- The order relation $<$ is defined by $n_2^e < n_7^e, n_3^e < n_5^e$.
- Furthermore $\nu(n_1^e) =$"a", $\nu(n_2^e) = \nu(n_7^e) =$"b", $\nu(n_3^e) = \nu(n_5^e) =$"c", and $\sigma(n_4^t) = $ "t1", $\sigma(n_6^t) = $ "t2", $\sigma(n_8^t) = $ "t3" [5].

Fig. 3. XML tree of Example 1

In this example $\xi(n_1^e, St) = $ "`<a><b><c>t1</c><c>t2</c></b><b>t3</b></a>`" is the serialization of the node n_1^e.

For the evaluation of queries we do not only need an XML store, but also an environment, which contains information about functions, variable bindings, the context sequence, and the context item. This environment is defined as follows:

Definition 3 (Environment). *An* environment *of an XML store St is a 4-tuple $En = (\mathbf{a}, \mathbf{b}, \mathbf{v}, \mathbf{x})$ where $\mathbf{a} : \mathcal{N} \to \mathcal{N}^*$ is a partial function that maps a function name to its formal arguments (it is used in rule [1,24,25]); $\mathbf{b} : \mathcal{N} \to \mathbf{L}(XQ^*)$ maps a function name to the body of the function (it is also used in rules [1,24,25]); $\mathbf{v} : \mathcal{N} \to (\mathcal{V} \cup \mathcal{A})^*$ maps variable names to their values; $\mathbf{x}$ which is undefined or an item of St and indicates the context item (it is used in rule [16,17]).*

Let $XF \in \Phi$ be an XQuery fragment. The set of XF-environments($EN[XF]$) is the set of all environments for which it holds that $\forall f \in \mathbf{rng}(\mathbf{b}) : f \in \mathbf{L}(XF)$.

If En is an environment, n a name, and y an item then we let $En[\mathbf{v}(n) \mapsto y]$ denote the environment that is equal to En except that the function $\mathbf{v}$ maps n to y. We write $St, En \vdash e \Rightarrow (St', v)$ to denote that the evaluation of expression e against the XML store St and environment En of St may result in the new XML store St' and a result sequence v, where v can only contain nodes of St' and atomic values. The semantics of XQ^* expressions is defined by means of reasoning rules, following the notation detailed in [5].

We define the expressive power of an XQuery fragment as the set of *XQuery functions* that can be expressed in this fragment. XQuery functions are defined as partial multivalued functions that map a store and a variable assignment over that store to a new store and a result sequence over this result store. We assume that the result store does not contain nodes that are no longer reachable, since such nodes can be safely garbage collected. More precisely, the garbage collection is defined as follows:

---

[5] We do not mention here the documents on the Web and on files.

Definition 4 (Garbage Collection). *Garbage Collection (Γ_s) maps a store St and a sequence s to a new store St' by removing all trees from St for which the root node is not in* **rng**(δ) *and for which no node of the tree is in s.*

We now define the notion of XQuery function as follows:

Definition 5 (XQuery Function). *The XQuery function corresponding to an expression e is* $\{((St, \mathbf{v}), (\Gamma_v(St'), v)) \mid St, (\phi, \phi, \mathbf{v}, \bot) \vdash e \Rightarrow (St', v)\}$. *An element of this set is called an* evaluation pair. *If two expressions e_1 and e_2 have the same corresponding XQuery functions then they are said to be equivalent, denoted as $e_1 \sim e_2$.*

This measure of expressive power can be justified by the XQuery Processing Model[3]. There it is possible to set variables in an initial environment. Moreover, the serialization of the result sequence is optional and an XQuery query can be embedded into another processing environment.

3   Expressibility Results

Adding extra features to XQuery fragments does not always extend the set of XQuery functions expressible in the fragment. In this section we will show how to simulate certain features in fragments that, syntactically, do not include this feature.

Lemma 1. *The "count" operator can be expressed in XQ_{at}.*

Proof. It is clear that "$\max(e_1)$" and "$\texttt{empty}(e_1)$" can be expressed in XQ. Hence the following expression is equivalent to "$\texttt{count}(e_1)$":

```
let $v := max(for $i at $pos in e₁ return $pos)
return
   if (empty($v)) then 0 else $v
```

Lemma 2. *The "count" operator can be expressed in XQ_S.*

Proof. Following XQ_S expression is equivalent to "$\texttt{count}(e_1)$":

```
sum(for $i in e₁ return 1)
```

Lemma 3. *The "to" operator can be expressed in XQ^R.*

Proof. We can define a recursive function "to" such that "e_1 to e_2" is equivalent to "$\texttt{to}(e_1, e_2)$" as follows:

```
declare function to($i ,$j) {
   if ($j < $i) then () else (to($i, $j - 1), $j)
};
```

Lemma 4. *The "sum" operator can be expressed in XQ_C^{to}.*

Proof. Following XQ_C^{to} expression is equivalent to "sum(e_1)":

```
count(
    for $i in e₁ return
        for $j in (1 to $i) return 1)
```

Lemma 5. *The "count" operator can be expressed in* $XQ^{ctr,R}$.

Proof. We can define a recursive function "count-nodes" such that "count(e_1)" is equivalent to following $XQ^{ctr,R}$ expression:

```
count-nodes(
    for $e in e₁ return element {"e"} {()}
)
```

This expression generates as many new nodes as there are items in the input e_1 and then applies a newly defined function "count-nodes" to this sequence, which counts the number of distinct nodes in a sequence. This can be done by decreasing the input sequence of the function call to "count-nodes" by exactly one node in each recursion step, which is possible since all items in the input sequence of "count-nodes" have a different node identity and hence we can remove each step the first node (in document order) of the newly created nodes. Note that, since the count operator returns only atomic values, none of the newly created nodes that were used to count the number of items in the sequence is reachable after applying garbage collection.

Lemma 6. *The "at" clause in a for expression can be expressed in* XQ_C^{ctr}.

Proof. The proof is based on the idea that it is possible to transform sequence order into document order by creating new nodes as children of a common parent such that the new nodes will contain all information of each item in the sequence and they are in the same order as the items in the original sequence. It can be shown that we can in XQ_C^{ctr} express the (non-recursive) functions "pos" and "atpos", which respectively give the position of a node in a document-ordered sequence and returns a node at a certain position in such sequence. If we can define XQ_C^{ctr} functions "encode" and "decode" (to make sure that we do not lose any information in creating a new node for an item in the result sequence of the "in" clause) then the following XQ_C^{ctr} expression is equivalent to the $XQ_{C,at}^{ctr}$ expression "for $x at $pos in e₁ return e₂" (where e_1 and e_2 are XQ_C^{ctr} expressions):

```
let $seq    := e₁ return
let $newseq := encode($seq) return
for $x in $newseq
return (
    let $pos := pos($x, $newseq) return
    let $x   := decode($x, $seq)
    return e₂ )
```

Since the result sequence of e_1, seq, is used both in the "in" clause of the for expression and as actual parameter for the "decode" function, we have to assign this result to a new variable, otherwise by simple substitution a node construction that is done in e_1 would be evaluated more than once. Furthermore the expression e_2 is guaranteed to have the right values for the variables "x" and "pos" iff the function "decode" behaves as desired. We assume that e_2 does not use variables "seq" and "$newseq$", since they are used in the simulation[6].

We now take a closer look at how to define the functions "decode" and "encode". The function "encode" needs to create a new sequence in which we simulate all items by creating a new node for each item. By adding these nodes as children of a newly constructed element (named "newseq") we ensure that the original sequence order is reflected in the document order for the newly constructed sequence. Atomic values are simulated by putting their value as text node in an element which denotes the type of atomic value. Encoding nodes cannot be done by making a copy of them, since this would discard all information we have about the node identity. Therefore we store for a node all information we need to retrieve the node later using the function "decode". We do this by storing the root of the node and the position where the node is located in the descendant-or-self list of its root node. We assume that we can define the (non-recursive) XQ_C^{ctr} functions "pos" (which we already assumed earlier in this proof), and "atpos" (to find the nth node in a sequence of nodes ordered by document order).

Note that none of the previous functions used recursion. Hence we do not actually need functions since we could inline the function definitions in the expressions. Hence the simulation of the "at" clause can be written in XQ_C^{ctr}. Furthermore there is no newly created node in the result sequence of the simulation, so all newly created nodes are garbage collected and hence "at" can be expressed in XQ_C^{ctr}.

4 Properties of the Fragments

The previous section provided some expressibility results. In this section we prove that certain fragments do not have certain properties, hence they have different degrees of expressive power. For most of the lemmas we do not have enough space here to present the complete proofs. We refer the reader for these proofs to our technical report [6].

The first two properties just claim that there are fragments in which it is not possible to distinguish between sequences with the same set or bag representation. To formalize this notion we define set-equivalence and bag-equivalence between evironments and between sequences. In this definition **Set** (**Bag**) maps a sequence to the set (bag) of its items.

---

[6] This issue can of course easily be solved by choosing two unused variables to replace these variables.

Definition 6. *Consider a store St and two environments $En = (\mathbf{a}, \mathbf{b}, \mathbf{v}, \mathbf{x})$ and $En' = (\mathbf{a}', \mathbf{b}', \mathbf{v}', \mathbf{x}')$ over the store St. We call En and En' set-equivalent iff it holds that $\mathbf{a} = \mathbf{a}'$, $\mathbf{b} = \mathbf{b}'$, $dom(\mathbf{v}) = dom(\mathbf{v}')$ and $\forall s \in dom(\mathbf{v}) : \mathbf{Set}(\mathbf{v}(s)) = \mathbf{Set}(\mathbf{v}'(s))$, and finally $\mathbf{x} = \mathbf{x}'$.*

The environments En and En' are called bag-equivalent *iff they are set-equivalent and it holds that $\forall s \in dom(\mathbf{v})$:$\mathbf{Bag}(\mathbf{v}(s)) = \mathbf{Bag}(\mathbf{v}'(s))$*

Lemma 7. *Let St be a store, $En, En' \in EN[XQ^R]$ two set-equivalent XQ^R environments, and e an expression in XQ^R. If the result of e is defined for both En and En', then for each sequence r and r' for which it holds that $St, En \vdash e \Rightarrow (St, r)$ and $St, En' \vdash e \Rightarrow (St, r')^7$, it also holds that $\mathbf{Set}(r) = \mathbf{Set}(r')$.*

Proof. (Sketch). This lemma can be proven by induction on the query syntax tree in which each node corresponds to a construct of rules [3–18, 24] in Figure 1.

Lemma 8. *The fragment XQ_C does not have the property of Lemma 7.*

Proof. If we consider an environment $En \in EN[XQ^R]$, then $En_1 = En[\mathbf{v}("seq") \mapsto \langle 1, 1 \rangle]$ and $En_2 = En[\mathbf{v}("seq") \mapsto \langle 1 \rangle]$ are two set-equivalent XQ^R environments. The expression "`count($seq)`" returns $\langle 2 \rangle$ in the evaluation against En_1 and $\langle 1 \rangle$ against En_2.

Lemma 9. *Let St be a store, $En, En' \in EN[XQ_C^R]$ two bag-equivalent XQ_C^R environments and e be an expression in XQ_C^R. If the result of e is defined for both En and En', then for each sequence r and r' for which it holds that $St, En \vdash e \Rightarrow (St, r)$ and $St, En' \vdash e \Rightarrow (St, r')$, it also holds that $\mathbf{Bag}(r) = \mathbf{Bag}(r')$.*

Proof. For all XQ^R expressions we can show similar to the proof of Lemma 7 that evaluations against bag-equivalent environments result in bag-equivalent result sequences.

Lemma 10. *The fragment XQ_{at} does not have the property of Lemma 9.*

Proof. If we consider an environment $En \in EN[XQ_C^R]$, then $En_1 = En[\mathbf{v}("seq") \mapsto \langle 1, 2 \rangle]$ and $En_2 = En[\mathbf{v}("seq") \mapsto \langle 2, 1 \rangle]$ are two bag-equivalent XQ_C^R environments, but the evaluation of the expression

```
for $i at $pos in $seq
return if ($pos=1) then $i else ()
```

returns $\langle 1 \rangle$ when evaluated against environment En_1 and $\langle 2 \rangle$ when evaluated against En_2.

The maximum size of the output for all queries in certain XQuery fragments can be identified as being bounded by a class of functions w.r.t. the input size. For proving the inexpressibility results related to the output size, we introduce following notions for the maximal input and output size for both sequences and items:

---

[7] Since e does not contain node constructors in its subexpressions, it is easy to see that all subexpressions are evaluated against the same store St and that the result store of all these subexpressions will also be St.

Definition 7 (Auxiliary Notations). *Let $St = (V, E, <, \nu, \sigma, \delta)$ be a store, $En = (\mathbf{a}, \mathbf{b}, \mathbf{v}, \mathbf{x})$ an environment over St and s a sequence over St. The set of atomic values in a sequence s is defined as $A_s = \mathbf{Set}(s) \cap \mathcal{A}$, the set of atomic values in a store St is $A^{St} = (\mathbf{rng}(\nu) \cup \mathbf{rng}(\sigma)) \cap \mathcal{A}$, while the set of atomic values in the environment En is $A^{En} = \bigcup_{s \in \mathbf{rng}(\mathbf{v})} A_s$.*

The size Δ_{St}^{forest} is the size of the forest in St, i.e., $\Delta_{St}^{forest} = |V|$ and Δ_{St}^{tree} is the size of the largest tree of the forest in St, i.e., $\Delta_{St}^{tree} = \max(\bigcup_{n_1 \in V} \{c | c = |\{n_2 | (n_1, n_2) \in E^*\}|\})$.[8]

The function **size** *maps an atomic value to the number of cells needed to represent this item on the tape of a Turing Machine.*

Definition 8 (Largest Sequence/Item Sizes). *Consider the evaluation pair $((St, En), (St'', v))$ of a query e, where $St = (V, E, <, \nu, \sigma, \delta)$, $En = (\mathbf{a}, \mathbf{b}, \mathbf{v}, \mathbf{x})$, and $\Gamma(St'', \{v\}) = St' = (V', E', <', \nu', \sigma', \delta')$. The largest input sequence size is defined as $d_I^s = \max(\{|s| \, | \, s \in \mathbf{rng}(\mathbf{v})\} \cup \{\Delta_{St}^{tree}\})$. The largest input item size is $d_I^i = \max(\{\mathbf{size}(a) | a \in (A^{St} \cup A^{En})\} \cup \{\lceil \log(\Delta_{St}^{forest} + 1) \rceil\})$. The largest output sequence size is $d_O^s = \max(\{|v|, \Delta_{St'}^{tree})$. Finally, the largest output item size is $d_O^i = \max(\{\mathbf{size}(a) | a \in (A^{St'} \cup A_v)\} \cup \{\lceil \log(\Delta_{St'}^{forest} + 1) \rceil\})$.*

In the definition of the largest sequence sizes we include the size of the largest tree in the store, since one can generate such a sequence by using the descendant-or-self axis. Note that in the definition of the largest item sizes the first set of the union contains all sizes needed to represent the atomic values that occur in the store (or environment) and the second set contains only one value which indicates how much space we need to represent a pointer to a node in the store. Furthermore, we consider in the definition the maximal size for the entire store (including the entire web). This is a theoretical simplification, but it does not have an influence on the input/output size results: if we have to show that the result of a certain evaluation has an upper bound $f(n)$ where n is the input size, then we have to show that this upper bound holds for all input stores and hence also for the "minimal input store", i.e., the store that only contains these input nodes that are actually accessed during the evaluation. Furthermore, the inclusion of the nodes of the output store in the output size is allowed for two reasons. The first reason is that all upper bound functions that we use in our lemmas are at least linear functions and the input nodes that occur in the output store just add a linear factor to the upper bound function. The second reason is that the nodes of the output store that do not occur in the input store have to be reachable by nodes in the result sequence since for each fragment applied garbage collection.

The following inexpressibility results use the observation that the maximum item and/or sequence output size can be bounded by a certain class of functions in terms of the input size.

Lemma 11. *For each evaluation $St, En \vdash e \Rightarrow (St', v)$ where $e \in \mathbf{L}(XQ^{ctr,to})$ and $En \in EN[XQ^{ctr,to}]$ it holds that $d_O^i \leq p(d_I^i)$ for some polynomial p.*

---

[8] E^* denotes the reflexive and transitive closure of E.

Proof. (Sketch) For each polynomial p that has $\mathbb{N}$ or $\mathbb{N}^2$ as its domain there always exists an increasing polynomial p' such that p' is an upper bound for p. Therefore we assume all functions that are used as an upper bound in this and following proofs to be increasing functions. We then prove the lemma by induction on the size of the abstract syntax tree of the query q. In this tree the nodes correspond to the $\langle Expr \rangle$ non-terminal of the $XQ^{ctr,to}$ grammar and as a consequence each node corresponds to a construct of rules $[3-18, 23, 26]$ in Figure 1, so we prove the induction step for each of these rules.

Lemma 12. *The fragment XQ_C does not have the property of Lemma 11.*

Proof. If we consider the empty store St_0, the environment $En = (\{\}, \{\}, \{("\$input", \langle 1, \ldots, 1 \rangle)\}, \bot)$, and the expression $e = "\texttt{count(\$input)}"$ where the length of the sequence bound to variable $\$input$ equals k, then the evaluation $St_0, En \vdash e \Rightarrow (St', v)$ has largest input item size $d_I^i = 1$ and output item size $d_O^i = \lceil \log(k+1) \rceil$.

Lemma 13. *For each evaluation $St, En \vdash e \Rightarrow (St', v)$ where $e \in \mathbf{L}(XQ_{at,S}^{ctr})$ and $En \in EN[XQ_{at,S}^{ctr}]$ it holds that $d_O^s \leq p_1(d_I^s)$ and $d_O^i \leq p_2(\log(d_I^s), d_I^i)$ for some polynomials p_1 and p_2.*

Proof. (Sketch) This lemma can be proven by induction on the size of the abstract syntax tree of the query q. In this syntax tree the nodes correspond to the $\langle Expr \rangle$ non-terminal of the $XQ_{at,S}^{ctr}$ grammar and as a consequence each node corresponds to a construct of rules $[3-18, 21, 26]$ in Figure 1.

Lemma 14. *The fragment XQ^{to} does not have the property of Lemma 13.*

Proof. If we consider the empty store St_0, the environment $En = (\{\}, \{\}, \{("\$input", \langle k \rangle)\}, \bot)$, and the expression $e = "\texttt{1 to \$input}"$, then the evaluation $St_0, En \vdash e \Rightarrow (St', v)$ has maximal input sequence size $d_I^s = O(\log(k))$ and maximal output sequence size $d_O^s = O(k \log(k))$.

Lemma 15. *For each evaluation $St, En \vdash e \Rightarrow (St', v)$ where $e \in \mathbf{L}(XQ_{at}^{ctr,to})$ and $En \in EN[XQ_{at}^{ctr,to}]$ it holds that $d_O^s \leq p_1(d_I^s, 2^{d_I^i})$ and $d_O^i \leq p_2(\log(d_I^s), d_I^i)$ for some polynomials p_1 and p_2.*

Proof. (Sketch) Similar to the proof of Lemma 13 this lemma can be proven by induction on the query syntax tree. We already know that for all XQ_{at}^{ctr} expressions there is a polynomial relation between the largest input sequence/item sizes and the largest output sequence/item sizes. Furtermore, the "to" expression can construct a sequence of size, at worst, $O(2^{d_I^i})$ with values that need at most $O(d_I^i)$ space. As a consequence is can easily be seen that all $XQ_{at}^{ctr,to}$ expressions have output sizes within the bounds specified by this lemma when evaluated against an $XQ_{at}^{ctr,to}$ environment.

Lemma 16. *The fragment XQ^R does not have the property of Lemma 15.*

Proof. (Sketch) Clearly there are expressions in XQ^R that do not have this property. Indeed, there are expressions that can be simulated in the fragment, such as the power function, that can potentially have largest input item size $d_I^i = \lceil \log(k+1) \rceil$, largest input sequence size $d_I^s = 1$ and largest output sequence size $O(k^k)$.

Finally, we show that the number of possible output values is polynomially bounded by the largest input sequence size and the size of the set of possbile atomic values in the input store and environment.

Definition 9 (Possible Results). *Consider an expression e, a (finite) alphabet $\Sigma \subset A$ and a number S. The set Res of possible results for evaluations of e constrained by Σ and S is defined as the set of all pairs (St', v) for which it holds that there exists an evaluation $St, En \vdash e \Rightarrow (St', v)$ (with En in the same fragment as e) such that for this evaluation $d_I^s \leq S$ and $A^{St} \cup A^{En} \subseteq \Sigma$.*

In other words, given an expression e, an alphabet Σ and a number S, the set *Res* contains all possible outputs of the evaluations of e restricted to Σ and S. We will now show that the number of (different) atomic values in this set is polynomially bounded by S and the size of Σ.

Lemma 17. *Consider a (finite) alphabet $\Sigma \subset A$ and a number S. If $N = |\Sigma|$ then for each XQ_{at}^{ctr} expression e it holds that if Res is the set of possible results for evaluations of e constrained by Σ and S, then the number of atomic values in the possible outputs is polynomially bounded as follows:*
$$\left| \bigcup_{(St', v) \in Res} (A^{St'} \cup A_v) \right| \leq p(N, S) \text{ for some polynomial } p$$

Proof. This lemma can be proven by induction on the query syntax tree where each expression corresponds to the $\langle Expr \rangle$ non-terminal of the XQ_{at} grammar and as a consequence each node corresponds to a construct of rules $[3 - 18, 22]$ of Figure 1.

Lemma 18. *The fragment $XQ_{at,S}$ does not have the property of Lemma 17.*

Proof. Consider the alphabet $\Sigma = \{1, 2, 4, \ldots, 2^{n-1}\}$ and $S = n$. Since "$x" can contain any combination of elements of Σ, the result of the sum can be any number between 1 and $2^n - 1$. However, there exists no polynomial p such that for each n it holds that $2^n - 1 \leq p(n, n)$. Hence we know that we cannot express the sum in XQ_{at}.

5   Expressive Power of the Fragments

As we have shown in the two previous sections, some LiXQuery features can be simulated in some fragments that do not contain them and some can not. We will now study the relationships between all 64 fragments in terms of expressive power. In order to be able to compare fragments, we first have to define what "equivalent" and "more expressive" means for XQuery fragments.

Definition 10 (Equivalent Fragments). *Recall that Φ is the set of 64 XQuery fragments as defined in Figure 2. Consider two XQuery fragments XF_1, XF_2 $\in \Phi$.*

- $XF_1 \succeq XF_2 \iff \forall e_1 \in \mathbf{L}(XF_1) : \exists e_2 \in \mathbf{L}(XF_2) : e_1 \sim e_2$
  (XF_1 can simulate XF_2)
- $XF_1 \equiv XF_2 \iff ((XF_1 \succeq XF_2) \wedge (XF_2 \succeq XF_1))$
  (XF_1 is equivalent to XF_2)
- $XF_1 \succ XF_2 \iff ((XF_1 \succeq XF_2) \wedge (XF_1 \not\equiv XF_2))$
  (XF_1 is more expressive than XF_2)

In this definition, the relation $\succeq$ is a partial order on Φ, and $\equiv$ is an equivalence relation on Φ. We use these relations to investigate the relationships between all XQuery fragments defined in Section 2. We show that the equivalence relation $\equiv$ partitions Φ (containing 64 fragments) into 17 equivalence classes. In Figure 4 we show these 17 equivalence classes and their relationships. Each node of the graph represents an equivalence class, i.e., a class of XQuery fragments with the same expressive power. The white and grey nodes represent classes with and without node construction, respectively. Each edge is directed from a more expressive class C_1 to a less expressive one C_2 and points out that each fragment in C_1 is

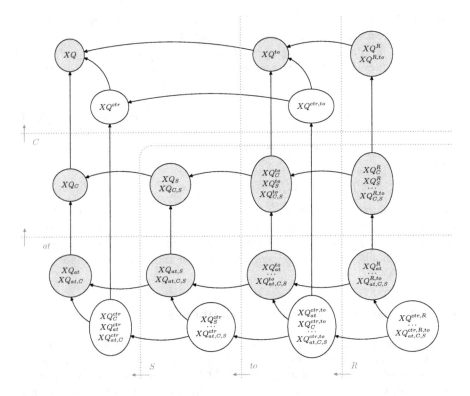

Fig. 4. Equivalence classes of XQuery fragments

more expressive than all fragments of C_2 (i.e., $\forall X F_1 \in C_1, X F_2 \in C_2 : X F_1 \succ X F_2$).

Theorem 1. *For the graph in Figure 4 and for all fragments $X F_1, X F_2 \in \Phi$ it holds that*

- *$X F_1 \equiv X F_2 \iff X F_1$ and $X F_2$ are within the same node*
- *$X F_1 \succ X F_2 \iff$ there is a directed path from the node containing $X F_1$ to the node containing $X F_2$*

Proof. (Sketch) Informally, the dotted borders in Figure 4 divide the set of fragments (Φ) in two parts: one in which the attribute that labels the border can be expressed and one in which this attribute cannot be expressed. The arrows that cross the borders all go in one direction, i.e., from the set of fragments where you can express a certain construct to the the set where you cannot express it. We call the set of fragments that can simulate the construct the right-hand side of the border and the other set the left-hand side of the border. The correctness of the dotted borders can be proven by showing that you can express something in the least expressive fragment of the right-hand side that you cannot express in the most expressive fragment of the left-hand side. In order to prove this, we need the lemmas of Section 3 and 4. All previous results can now be combined to complete the proof:

- If $X F_1$ and $X F_2$ are in the same node then it follows that they are equivalent: This can easily be shown by the lemmas from Section 3.
- If $X F_1$ and $X F_2$ are equivalent then they occur in the same node: Suppose that $X F_1$ and $X F_2$ are not in the same node. There are two possibilities: if one of the two fragments contains a node constructor (suppose $X F_1$) and the other ($X F_2$) does not then you obviously cannot simulate the node construction in $X F_2$. Else it follows from the figure that they are seperated by a dotted border and hence we know that there is something in one fragment that you cannot express in the other fragment, so $X F_1 \not\equiv X F_2$.
- If there is a directed path from the node containing $X F_1$ to the node containing $X F_2$ then we know that $X F_1 \succeq X F_2$ and since $X F_1$ and $X F_2$ appear in a different node they are not equivalent, so $X F_1 \succ X F_2$: This follows from the fact that there is a fragment $X F_1'$ equivalent to $X F_1$ and $X F_2'$ equivalent to $X F_2$ such that $\mathbf{L}(X F_2') \subseteq \mathbf{L}(X F_1')$.
- If $X F_1 \succ X F_2$ then there is a directed path from the node containing $X F_1$ to the node containing $X F_2$: Suppose that $X F_1 \succ X F_2$ and there is no directed path from $X F_1$ to $X F_2$. Then either there is a directed path from $X F_2$ to $X F_1$ such that $X F_2 \succ X F_1$ and hence $X F_1 \not\succ X F_2$ or there is no directed path at all between the nodes of both fragments. In this case we know by inspecting Figure 4 that there are (at least) two borders seperating the nodes of both fragments where for the first border $X F_1$ is in the more expressive set of fragments and for the second border $X F_2$ is in the more expressive set of fragments. Hence $X F_1$ and $X F_2$ are incomparable so $X F_1 \not\succ X F_2$.

6 Conclusion

We investigated the expressive power of XQuery fragments in order to outline which features really add expressive power and which ones simplify queries already expressible. The main results of this paper outline that, using six attributes (count, sum, to, at, ctr and recursion), we can define 64 XQuery fragments, which can be divided into 17 equivalence classes, i.e., classes including fragments with the same expressive power. We proved the 17 equivalence classes are really different and own a different degree of expressive power.

References

1. M. Benedikt, W. Fan, and G. M. Kuper. Structural properties of XPath fragments. In *ICDT 2003*, pages 79–95, 2003.
2. S. Boag, D. Chamberlin, M. Fernández, D. Florescu, J. Robie, and J. Siméon. XQuery 1.0: An XML query language. W3C Working Draft, 2005. Available at http://www.w3.org/TR/xquery/.
3. D. Draper, P. Frankhauser, M. Fernández, A. Malhotra, K. Rose, M. Rys, J. Siméon, and P. Wadler. XQuery 1.0 and XPath 2.0 formal semantics. W3C Working Draft, 2005. Available at http://www.w3.org/TR/xquery-semantics/.
4. G. Gottlob, C. Koch, and R. Pichler. The complexity of XPath query evaluation. In *PODS 2003*, pages 179–190, 2003.
5. J. Hidders, J. Paredaens, R. Vercammen, and S. Demeyer. A light but formal introduction to XQuery. In *XSym 2004*, pages 5–20, 2004.
6. J. Hidders, J. Paredaens, R. Vercammen, and S. Marrara. Expressive power of recursion and aggregates in XQuery. Technical Report TR2005-05, University of Antwerp, 2005. Available at http://www.adrem.ua.ac.be/pub/TR2005-05.pdf.
7. M. Kay, N. Walsh, and H. Zongaro. XSLT 2.0 and XQuery 1.0 serialization. W3C Working Draft, 2005. Available at http://www.w3.org/TR/xslt-xquery-serialization.
8. S. Kepser. A simple proof of the Turing-completeness of XSLT and XQuery. In T. Usdin, editor, *Extreme Markup Languages 2004*. IDEAlliance, 2004. Available at http://www.mulberrytech.com/Extreme/Proceedings/html/2004/Kepser01/EML2004Kepser01.html
9. C. Koch. On the complexity of nonrecursive XQuery and functional query languages on complex values. In *PODS 2005*, pages 84–97, 2005.
10. W. Le Page, J. Hidders, P. Michiels, J. Paredaens, and R. Vercammen. On the expressive power of node construction in XQuery. In *WebDB 2005*, pages 85–90, 2005. Available at http://webdb2005.uhasselt.be/webdb05_eproceedings.pdf.
11. L. Libkin. Expressive power of SQL. *Theoretical Computer Science*, 296(3):379–404, 2003.
12. J. Paredaens. On the expressive power of the relational algebra. *Information Processing Letters*, 7(2):107–111, 1978.
13. S. Vansummeren. Deciding well-definedness of XQuery fragments. In *PODS 2005*, pages 37–48, 2005.

A Type Safe DOM API

Peter Thiemann

Universität Freiburg
http://www.informatik.uni-freiburg.de/~thiemann

Abstract. DOM (Document Object Model) is the W3C recommendation for an API for manipulating XML documents. The API is stated in terms of a language neutral IDL with normative bindings given for Java and ECMAScript. The type system underlying the DOM API is a simple object-based one which relies entirely on interfaces and interface extension. However, this simplicity is deceiving because the DOM architects implicitly impose a large number of constraints which are only stated informally. The long list of exceptions that some DOM methods may raise witnesses these constraints.

The present work defines a refinement of Java's type system which makes most of these constraints accessible and thus checkable to the compiler. Technically, we graft a polymorphic annotation system on top of the host language's types and propagate the annotations using ideas borrowed from affine type systems. We provide a type soundness proof with respect to an operational semantics of a Java core language.

1 Introduction

DOM is the standard API for traversing and manipulating XML documents[10]. It has implementations (bindings) for a number of object-based languages, like Java, C++, ECMAScript, just to name a few. In particular, its ECMAScript binding is widely used in the context of client-side Web scripting, where all changes of the visual appearance of a Web page are effected by DOM methods. The same combination (ECMAScript+DOM) also provides animated graphical content via the scalable vector graphics (SVG[1]) standard.

Problems with DOM. Although DOM consists solely of a collection of interfaces and the standard explicitly states that no particular implementation is implied, it is clear that its designers had a particular memory model in mind. This memory model consists mainly of objects that implement the so-called **Node** interface and other interfaces derived from it, like **Document**, **Element**, **Attr**, **Text**, and so on. The methods and fields of these interfaces imply that the manipulated nodes maintain various references among them. To understand these references first requires a look at the big picture.

The representation of a document is essentially a tree of nodes, where the tree structure is supported with an ordered list of references from parent node to child node. The root of this tree is a **Document** node which may contain at most one node representing the document type and at most one reference to the node representing the root element of the XML document (and two other items

G. Bierman and C. Koch (Eds.): DBPL 2005, LNCS 3774, pp. 169–183, 2005.
© Springer-Verlag Berlin Heidelberg 2005

which we ignore for brevity). Since the document type attached to a `Document` node may have an impact on the treatment of element and attribute nodes, the creation of each node takes place in the context of a document node, the node maintains a reference to its document node, and the operations refuse to mix up nodes from different documents. However, nodes may exist without being connected to a root element to enable the construction of document fragments. The `parentNode` field of the `Node` interface, an up-reference in the document tree, indicates whether a node is disconnected. Further references point to the previous and the next sibling of the node in the context of its parent node.

The network of references enables non-recursive traversals of the tree but the presence of *e.g.* the `parentNode` implies that child nodes (and attribute nodes, which are slightly different) may not be shared among multiple parents. This restriction turns out to be fairly subtle because some operations (*e.g.*, `appendChild`) tacitly reparent a node. This behavior can lead to surprising results for the unwary programmer[1]. It's not quite understandable why the DOM architects have opted against a cheap dynamic check for the presence of a parent when they are insisting on a much more expensive check for the absence of loops in the node structure: `appendChild` may raise a `HIERARCHY_REQUEST_ERR`, which is "raised [...] if the node to append is one of this node's ancestors or this node itself [...]". In addition, the omission of the childhood check is inconsistent with the operations that deal with attributes: *e.g.*, `setAttributeNode` raises an `INUSE_ATTRIBUTE_ERR` if the attribute node is already attached to an element.

Last but not least, although operations like `appendChild` accept an arbitrary `Node` argument as the child node to add, not all combinations of parent and child are accepted and invalid combinations give rise to a `HIERARCHY_REQUEST_ERR`. The standard defines the valid combinations in Section 1.1.1.

Overview. DOM imposes a number of non-obvious and non-trivial invariants which are not captured by the types in the interfaces. These invariants make DOM hard to use for programmers and incur a cost for checking the invariants at runtime. The present work demonstrates in Sec.2 what a strongly typed DOM API that **guarantees the invariants statically** could look like by working through a series of examples. Sec.3 defines the language DOMJAVA and formalizes its type system which supports all features demonstrated in the examples. Thus a DOMJAVA compiler can track these DOM invariants statically and reject ill-behaved programs right away. Sec.4 and 5 complete the formal underpinnings of DOMJAVA by defining an operational semantics and providing a type soundness proof. Sec.6 discusses some related work and Sec.7 concludes.

2   Towards a Typed DOM API

This section examines a sequence of code examples that illustrate the hidden assumptions of the DOM interfaces. To show that types can capture runtime errors

---

[1] In fact, the JDOM API (see `http://www.jdom.org`) has a separate operation to detach nodes from the parents and only allows attaching orphaned nodes to a new parent.

from both DOM and JDOM, the paper considers a slightly modified DOM which disallows implicit reparenting of child nodes. To simplify the formal development we only consider a representative selection of DOM run-time errors.

2.1 Attribute Ownership

The first example deals with ownership of attributes.

```
void highlight (Document doc, Element el1, Element el2) {
  Attr attr = doc.createAttribute ("class");
  attr.value = "highlight";
  el1.setAttributeNode (attr);
  el2.setAttributeNode (attr);    // runtime error
}
```

The operation `highlight` attempts to attach a single attribute node to two element nodes, `el1` and `el2`. It relies on two DOM operations:

`Attr createAttribute (String)` which belongs to the `Document` interface and `Attr setAttributeNode (Attr)` which belongs to the `Element` interface. It returns the replaced attribute if the `Element` had a like-named attribute before.

Running the code gives rise to an `INUSE_ATTRIBUTE_ERR` exception. Our proposed type system detects this problem statically if the initial type assumptions contain the following

$$\forall \delta, \kappa. \quad (\text{N}\langle \text{Attr}, \delta, \text{O}, \text{R}\rangle) \ [\text{N}\langle \text{Document}, \delta, \kappa, \text{R}\rangle] \ \texttt{createAttribute(String name)}$$
$$\forall \delta, \kappa, \phi. \ (\text{N}\langle \text{Attr}, \delta, \text{O}, \text{R}\rangle) \ [\text{N}\langle \text{Element}, \delta, \kappa, \phi\rangle] \ \texttt{setAttributeNode(N}\langle \text{Attr}, \delta, \text{O}, \text{R}\rangle)$$

There are three differences compared to the above Java signatures of the two methods. First, all DOM types are subsumed in a single N type with special annotations that convey information about the actual type (like `Attr`, `Element`, and `Document`), their use, and their kinship, second, the method signatures are universally quantified over annotations, and third, the type explicitly mentions the receiver object in square brackets to be able to reason about its annotated type. Stripping these three extensions leaves exactly the original Java signatures of the methods.

The DOM type $\text{N}\langle di, d, k, f\rangle$ consists of a DOM interface name di, a document identifier d (a variable δ in the example), a kinship status k (variable κ in the example), and a father information f (also present as variable ϕ). The kinship status may be either orphaned (O) or parented (P), and the father information may either indicate that no father is available (R)[2] or it may refer to an explicit father (F(f)). Here, O, P, and R are type constants of suitable kind and F is a type constructor.

---

[2] The R comes from the document root object which has no father node, but attributes do not have father nodes, either.

The important point about the kinship annotation is that the "orphaned" status is an *affine property*. It means that the property may be discarded but not be duplicated. In effect, whenever there is more than one reference to an object in scope, then at *most one* may have the "orphaned" status.

In the example, the `createAttribute` creates a new `Attr` object in status "orphaned". However, this object is used twice in the local scope. Hence, only one of the invocations of `setAttributeNode` can be well typed because the other will receive the `Attr` object in status "parented".

Our type system enforces this restriction by having each operation declare the state in which it expects its operands ("orphaned" in this case). Whenever a variable has more than one uses, the type system splits its annotations so that the first use gets exactly what it expects (if that is possible) and the remaining uses have to split the leftover annotation among them. In the example, `attr` starts off with type $N\langle Attr, \delta, O, R\rangle$. The method invocation on `el1` expects `attr` in this type and changes the type of `attr` for the rest of the program to $N\langle Attr, \delta, P, R\rangle$ (because O splits into O and P). Now the method invocation on `el2` fails to type check because it expects an argument in O state but gets one in P state: P splits only into P and P.

To make the example well-typed, the `Attr` object must be cloned before it is handed to the second invocation of `setAttributeNode`, using the operation `Node.cloneNode` of the following type

$$\forall \delta, \kappa, \phi, \phi', \gamma. \ (N\langle \gamma, \delta, O, \phi'\rangle) \ [N\langle \gamma, \delta, \kappa, \phi\rangle] \ \texttt{cloneNode(Bool deep)}$$

```
el1.setAttributeNode (attr);
el2.setAttributeNode (attr.cloneNode(false));    // accepted
```

The type of `cloneNode` goes beyond the offerings of Java. It relies on bounded polymorphism to restrict the actual type of the receiver to the interface `Node` while retaining the actual type of the object for the result type. A design closer to Java would require a cast operation that retains the type annotations.

The inferred signature of the `highlight` operation reflects that the two elements must belong to the same document δ:

$$\forall \delta, \kappa, \kappa_1, \kappa_2, \phi_1, \phi_2. \ \texttt{highlight}(\ N\langle Document, \delta, \kappa, R\rangle \ \texttt{doc},$$
$$N\langle Element, \delta, \kappa_1, \phi_1\rangle \ \texttt{el1}, N\langle Element, \delta, \kappa_2, \phi_2\rangle \ \texttt{el2})$$

This typing relies on the fact that all operations that create a new document have a *generative type*, that is, each invocation of such an operation has a result type different from all other invocations. Generative types are introduced by a binder $\nu\delta$ abstracting over the document identity δ. The ν binder behaves similar to an existential but provides the stronger guarantee that every two abstracted identities are different. Here is the type of the operation for creating a document, for illustration:

$$\forall \phi.\nu\delta. \ (N\langle Document, \delta, O, R\rangle) \ [DOMImplementation]$$
$$\texttt{createDocument}(\texttt{String}, \texttt{String}, N\langle DocumentType, \delta, O, \phi\rangle)$$

2.2   Parent-Child Relations

This subsection concerns the enforcement of the parent-child relationship and the avoidance of cyclic references in the document structure. The key operation considered attaches a node as the last child to another node and returns the new child node as its result.

$$\forall \delta, \kappa, \phi, \gamma_p, \gamma_c. \ (\gamma_p, \gamma_c) \in \textsc{ParentChild} \Rightarrow$$
$$(\text{N}\langle \gamma_c, \delta, \text{P}, \text{F}(\phi) \rangle) \ [\text{N}\langle \gamma_p, \delta, \kappa, \phi \rangle] \ \texttt{appendChild}(\text{N}\langle \gamma_c, \delta, \text{O}, \text{F}(\phi) \rangle)$$

The `appendChild` operation relies on a binary predicate $\textsc{ParentChild}$ that characterizes the possible parent-child relationships: a parent of type γ_p only accepts a child of type γ_c if $(\gamma_p, \gamma_c) \in \textsc{ParentChild}$. The DOM specification defines this relation in Section 1.1.1.

Now, let's try to append an element `el` to itself to create a cyclic reference. The $\textsc{ParentChild}$ relation does not stop us from doing so because (`Element`, `Element`) $\in \textsc{ParentChild}$. However, the construction of a type for `el` runs into a problem. When used as the receiver of the operation, the type must have the form $\text{N}\langle \texttt{Element}, \delta, \kappa, \phi \rangle$, for some δ, κ, and ϕ. As the argument of the operation, however, the type must be $\text{N}\langle \texttt{Element}, \delta, \text{O}, \text{F}(\phi) \rangle$. These two demands are contradictory because there is no (finite) instantiation for ϕ such that $\phi = \text{F}(\phi)$. Hence, the type checker rejects the term `el.appendChild (el)`.

2.3   The Rest of the Story

So far we have covered direct uses of the DOM API. However, any user-defined object may carry DOM nodes in its fields and the methods of the object may refer to these DOM nodes. Thus, a method invocation may change the receiver's type annotation which in turn may make certain methods impossible to call.

In the following code, an object of class `A` contains a DOM attribute in a field and there is a method that attaches the attribute to an element.

```
class A {
  Attr anAttr;
  A (Document d, String name, String value) {
    anAttr = d.createAttribute (name);
    anAttr.value = value;
  }
  void attach (Element el) {
    el.setAttributeNode (anAttr);
  }
}
```

As it stands, the method `attach` should be called at most once on every object of class `A` and the attribute contained in the field should belong to the same document as the element passed to `attach`. Here is a failing attempt to make the signature of `attach` reflect these restrictions

$$\forall \delta, \kappa, \phi. \ \texttt{void} \ [\text{A}] \ \texttt{attach}(\text{N}\langle \texttt{Element}, \delta, \kappa, \phi \rangle \ \texttt{el})$$

This type signature cannot enforce the desired restrictions because the type A is not sufficiently informative. The solution is to augment the type A with information about the fields that contain DOM-relevant types analogous to a record type. As it turns out, the record type is only necessary for reading the field because it may change over time. For class A the (initial) type boils down to $A \{anAttr : N\langle Attr, \delta, O, R\rangle\}$ yielding the following signature

$$\forall \delta, \kappa, \phi. \text{ void } [A \{anAttr : N\langle Attr, \delta, O, R\rangle\}] \text{ attach}(N\langle Element, \delta, \kappa, \phi\rangle \text{ el})$$

Why does this type prevent a program from invoking **attach** twice in a row? Again, the affine treatment of the O annotation causes the type $A \{anAttr : N\langle Attr, \delta, O, R\rangle\}$ to split into one reference with the same type and another with P in place of the O annotation. The definition of environment splitting below will make this notion precise.

Types are now permitted to be recursive as long as the recursion crosses at least one record boundary. Recursive instantiations of the fatherhood variables, ϕ, remain verboten.

3   The Language DOMJava

DOMJAVA is a variant of CLASSICJAVA[6] specialized to tracking properties of the DOM API. To simplify the exposition (and following other work on Java's foundations [6, 9]) it concentrates on classes and the expression language while omitting control structures in favor of recursive method calls. It also omits inheritance in favor of interfaces because interfaces seem to be of prime importance in DOM programming and a further simplification of the formal model ensues.

DOMJAVA infers extra type annotations for a type correct CLASSICJAVA program (without inheritance). The definition of DOMJAVA's syntax in Fig. 1 indicates these inferred annotations as well as nonterminals that solely generate annotations by underlining. There are five main additions.

- Class types are enriched with a record of field types.
- The type of a DOM object $N\langle di, d, k, f\rangle$ has annotations that determine the target interface, di, the document, d, that the object belongs to, the kinship status, k, of the object (parented P or orphaned O), and, f, the degree of kinship.
- The type of a method includes the type of the receiver object. This way, method types can refer to the annotation of the receiver's type.
- The type of a method may be universally quantified over the DOM type annotations and over class names (in case of a method in an interface). In addition, a method may introduce new document identities by using the binding notation $\nu\delta^*$ and its type may include a variety of constraints.
- Constraints can be equalities on kinship indicators k, conditional depending on such an equality, and predicates Q on class names (including subtyping, interface implementation, and the PARENTCHILD relationship).

$$
\begin{array}{lll}
P & ::= & defn^*\ e \\
defn & ::= & \textbf{class}\ cl\ \{\ field^*\ meth^*\ \}\ |\ \textbf{interface}\ i\ \textbf{extends}\ i^*\ \{\ field^*\ meth^*\ \} \\
field & ::= & t\ fd \\
cl & ::= & \text{a class name} \\
\\
fd & ::= & \text{a field name} \\
md & ::= & \text{a method name} \\
di & ::= & \gamma\ |\ \text{a DOM interface name} \\
d & ::= & \delta\ |\ \text{a document identifier} \\
k & ::= & \kappa\ |\ \text{P}\ |\ \text{O} \\
f & ::= & \phi\ |\ \text{R}\ |\ \text{F}(f)\ |\ f + f \\
t & ::= & cl\ \{\ field^*\ \}\ |\ \text{N}\langle di, d, k, f \rangle \\
meth & ::= & pre\ methsig\ \{\ body\ \} \\
methsig & ::= & t\ [t]\ md\ ((t\ var)^*) \\
pre & ::= & \nu\delta^*.\forall\delta^*\ \kappa^*\ \phi^*\ \gamma^*.C \Rightarrow \\
C & ::= & k = k\ |\ k = k \Rightarrow C\ |\ Q\ di^*\ |\ C \wedge C\ |\ \textsc{True} \\
Q & ::= & \text{a predicate name} \\
body & ::= & e\ |\ \textbf{abstract} \\
e & ::= & \textbf{new}\ cl\ |\ var\ |\ \textbf{null}\ |\ e.fd\ |\ e.fd = e\ |\ e.md(e^*)\ |\ \textbf{let}\ var = e\ \textbf{in}\ e \\
A & ::= & \emptyset\ |\ A, var : t \\
\end{array}
$$

Fig. 1. Syntax of DOMJAVA

Four judgments (defined in Fig.2) govern the typing of DOMJAVA.

- $\vdash P$ a well-formed program
- $P \vdash_d defn$ a well-formed class or interface definition
- $P, C, \Delta, A \vdash_e e : t$ an expression e that has type t in the context of program P, constraints C, document identities Δ, and type assumptions A
- $P, C, \Delta, t \vdash_m methsig\ \{\ e\ \}$ checks a method body for consistency with its signature $methsig$.

Further judgments cover the extraction of method signatures from the program text (Fig.3), splitting of environments and types (Fig.4), and subtyping (Fig.5).

We will not repeat the explanation of the parts of the formal system that come from CLASSICJAVA (for example, the definitions of all the premises of the $\vdash P$ rule, which are mostly intuitively clear) and refer the reader to the respective literature [6].

Instead, we concentrate on the novel aspects. The first of these aspects is the affine typing for kinship indicator (P or O) of the DOM objects. An orphaned DOM object can be used once in orphaned mode (in an operation that assigns it a parent) and many times in parented mode. Enforcing this restriction requires *splitting judgments* for environments and types: The judgment $C \vdash A \prec A_1; A_2$ splits environment A into environments A_1 and A_2 so that each type annotation in A is split appropriately. Each typing rule with more than one antecedent applies splitting judgments to distribute the environments to the antecedents. The core rule (Fig.4) splits an O type into an O type and a P type, whereas a

Expressions

$$\frac{\textbf{class } cl \ \{ \ \textit{field}^* \ \textit{meth}^* \ \} \in P}{P,C,\emptyset,A \vdash_e \textbf{new } cl : cl \ \{ \ \textit{field}^* \ \}}$$

$$\frac{A(\textit{var}) = t}{P,C,\emptyset,A \vdash_e \textit{var} : t}$$

$$P,C,\emptyset,A \vdash_e \textbf{null} : t$$

$$\frac{P,C,\Delta,A \vdash_e e : cl \ \{ \dots t \ \textit{fd} \dots \}}{P,C,\Delta,A \vdash_e e.\textit{fd} : t}$$

$$\frac{\begin{array}{c} \textbf{class } cl \ \{ \ \textit{field}^* \ \textit{meth}^* \ \} \in P \quad t' \ \textit{fd} \in \textit{field}^* \\ P,C,\Delta_1,A_1 \vdash_e e : cl \ \{\textit{field}^*\} \quad P,C,\Delta_2,A_2 \vdash_e e' : t' \\ C \vdash A \prec A_1; A_2 \quad \vdash \Delta \prec \Delta_1; \Delta_2 \end{array}}{P,C,\Delta,A \vdash_e e.\textit{fd} = e' : t'}$$

$$\frac{\begin{array}{c} C \vdash A \prec A_0; A_1' \quad C \vdash A_1' \prec A_1; A_2' \quad \dots \quad C \vdash A_{p-1}' \prec A_{p-1}; A_p \\ \vdash \Delta \prec \Delta_0; \Delta_1' \quad \dots \quad \Delta_p' \prec \Delta_p; {\delta'}^* \\ P,C,\Delta_0,A_0 \vdash_e e_0 : t_0' \quad (\forall j) \ P,C,\Delta_j,A_j \vdash_e e_j : t_j' \\ t_0', md \leadsto_P \nu {\delta'}^* \forall \delta^* \ \kappa^* \ \phi^* \ \gamma^*.C' \Rightarrow t \ [t_0] \ md \ (t_1 \ \textit{var}_1 \dots t_n \ \textit{var}_n) \\ S = [\delta^* \mapsto d^*, \kappa^* \mapsto k^*, \phi^* \mapsto f^*, \gamma^* \mapsto cl^*] \quad t_j' = S(t_j) \quad t_0' = S(t_0) \quad C \Vdash S(C') \end{array}}{P,C,\Delta,A \vdash_e e_0.md(e_1,\dots,e_p) : S(t)}$$

$$\frac{\begin{array}{c} C \vdash A \prec A_1; A_2 \quad \vdash \Delta \prec \Delta_1; \Delta_2 \\ P,C,\Delta_1,A_1 \vdash_e e_1 : t_1 \\ P,C,\Delta_2,A_2, \textit{var} : t_1 \vdash_e e_2 : t_2 \end{array}}{P,C,\Delta,A \vdash_e \textbf{let } \textit{var} = e_1 \textbf{ in } e_2 : t_2}$$

$$\frac{P,C,\Delta,A \vdash_e e : t_1 \quad C \Vdash t_1 \leq t_2}{P,C,\Delta,A \vdash_e e : t_2}$$

Methods, definitions, and programs

$$\frac{P,C,\Delta, [\textbf{this} : t_0, \textit{var}_1 : t_1, \dots, \textit{var}_n : t_n] \vdash_e e : t}{P,C,\Delta,t_0 \vdash_m t \ [t_0] \ md \ (t_1 \ \textit{var}_1 \dots t_n \ \textit{var}_n) \ \{ \ e \ \}}$$

$$\frac{\begin{array}{c} (\forall j) \ P,C_j,\Delta_j, cl \ \{\textit{field}^*\} \vdash_m \textit{methsig}_j \ \{ \ \textit{body}_j \ \} \\ (\forall j) \ \textit{meth}_j = \nu {\delta'}_j^* \forall \delta_j^* \ \kappa_j^* \ \phi_j^* \ \gamma_j^*.C_j \Rightarrow \textit{methsig}_j \ \{ \ \textit{body}_j \ \} \\ \delta_j^* \ \kappa_j^* \ \phi_j^* \ \gamma_j^* = \textit{fv}(C_j \Rightarrow \textit{methsig}_j) \setminus \Delta_j \quad {\delta'}_j^* = \textit{fv}(C_j \Rightarrow \textit{methsig}_j) \cap \Delta_j \\ \textit{meth}^* = \textit{meth}_1 \dots \textit{meth}_m \end{array}}{P \vdash_d \textbf{class } cl \ \{ \ \textit{field}^* \ \textit{meth}^* \ \}}$$

$$\frac{\begin{array}{c} \textit{field}^* = \varepsilon \quad \textit{meth}^* = \textit{meth}_1 \dots \textit{meth}_m \\ (\forall j) \ \textit{meth}_j = \textit{pre}_j \ \textit{methsig}_j \ \{ \ \textbf{abstract} \ \} \end{array}}{P \vdash_d \textbf{interface } di \textbf{ extends } di^* \ \{ \ \textit{field}^* \ \textit{meth}^* \ \}}$$

$$\frac{\begin{array}{c} \textsc{ClassesOnce}(P) \quad \textsc{MethodsOncePerClass}(P) \quad \textsc{FieldOncePerClass}(P) \\ \textsc{InterfacesOnce}(P) \quad \textsc{InterfacesAbstract}(P) \quad \textsc{MethodOncePerInterface}(P) \\ \textsc{CompleteInterface}(P) \quad \textsc{WellFoundedInterfaces}(P) \quad \textsc{ClassFieldsOK}(P) \\ \textsc{ClassMethodsOK}(P) \quad \textsc{InterfaceMethodsOK}(P) \\ P = \textit{defn}_1 \dots \textit{defn}_m \ e \quad (\forall j) \ P \vdash_d \textit{defn}_j \quad P,C,\Delta,\emptyset \vdash_e e : t \end{array}}{\vdash P}$$

Fig. 2. Typing rules

$$\textbf{class } cl \ \{ \ field^* \ meth^* \ \} \in P$$

$$\frac{meth^* \ni (\nu\delta'^*)(\forall\delta^* \ \kappa^* \ \phi^* \ \gamma^*)C \Rightarrow \ t \ [t_0] \ md \ ((t \ var)^*) \ \{ \ e' \ \}}{cl \ \{\cdots\}, md \leadsto_P \nu\delta'^*\forall\delta^* \ \kappa^* \ \phi^* \ \gamma^*.C \Rightarrow t \ [t_0] \ md \ ((t \ var)^*)}$$

$$\textbf{interface } di \textbf{ extends } di^* \ \{ \ field^* \ meth^* \ \} \in P$$

$$\frac{meth^* \ni (\nu\delta'^*)\forall\delta^* \ \kappa^* \ \phi^* \ \gamma^*.C \Rightarrow t \ [t_0] \ md \ ((t \ var)^*) \ \{ \ \textbf{abstract} \ \}}{\mathrm{N}\langle di, d, k, f\rangle, md \leadsto_P \nu\delta'^*\forall\delta^* \ \kappa^* \ \phi^* \ \gamma^*.C \Rightarrow t \ [t_0] \ md \ ((t \ var)^*)}$$

$$\textbf{interface } di \textbf{ extends } di' \ di^* \ \{ \ field^* \ meth^* \ \} \in P \quad md \notin meth^*$$

$$\frac{\mathrm{N}\langle di', d, k, f\rangle, md \leadsto_P pre \ methsig}{\mathrm{N}\langle di, d, k, f\rangle, md \leadsto_P pre \ methsig}$$

Fig. 3. Auxiliary judgments

$$\vdash \Delta \prec \Delta; \emptyset \qquad \frac{\vdash \Delta'' \prec \Delta; \Delta' \quad \delta' \notin \Delta''}{\vdash \Delta'', \delta' \prec \Delta; \Delta', \delta'}$$

$$C \vdash \emptyset \prec \emptyset; \emptyset \qquad \frac{C \vdash A \prec A_1; A_2 \quad C \vdash t \prec t_1; t_2}{C \vdash A, x : t \prec A_1, x : t_1; A_2, x : t_2}$$

$$\frac{C \Vdash (k_1 = \mathrm{O} \Rightarrow k = \mathrm{O} \wedge k_2 = \mathrm{P}) \wedge (k_2 = \mathrm{O} \Rightarrow k = \mathrm{O} \wedge k_1 = \mathrm{P})}{C \Vdash (k = \mathrm{P} \Leftrightarrow k_1 = \mathrm{P} \wedge k_2 = \mathrm{P})}{C \vdash \mathrm{N}\langle di, d, k, f\rangle \prec \mathrm{N}\langle di, d, k_1, f\rangle; \mathrm{N}\langle di, d, k_2, f\rangle}$$

$$\frac{(\forall j) \ C \vdash t_j \prec t_j^1; t_j^2}{C \vdash cl \ \{\ldots fd_j : t_j \ldots\} \prec cl \ \{\ldots fd_j : t_j^1 \ldots\}; cl \ \{\ldots fd_j : t_j^2 \ldots\}}$$

Fig. 4. Environment splitting rules

$$C \Vdash X \leq X \qquad C \wedge A \leq B \Vdash A \leq B \qquad C \Vdash \mathrm{O} \leq k$$

$$\frac{C \Vdash f_1 \leq f_2}{C \Vdash \mathrm{F}(f_1) \leq \mathrm{F}(f_2)} \qquad \frac{C \Vdash f \leq f_1}{C \Vdash f \leq f_1 + f_2} \qquad \frac{C \Vdash f_1 \leq f \quad C \Vdash f_2 \leq f}{C \Vdash f_1 + f_2 \leq f}$$

$$\frac{C \Vdash di_1 \leq di_2 \quad d_1 = d_2 \quad C \Vdash k_1 \leq k_2 \quad C \Vdash f_1 \leq f_2}{C \Vdash \mathrm{N}\langle di_1, d_1, k_1, f_1\rangle \leq \mathrm{N}\langle di_2, d_2, k_2, f_2\rangle}$$

$$\frac{C \Vdash cl \leq cl' \quad (\forall j) \ C \Vdash t_j \leq t'_j}{C \Vdash cl \ \{fd_j : t_j\} \leq cl' \ \{fd'_j : t'_j\}}$$

Fig. 5. Subtyping rules for judgment $C \Vdash A \leq B$

P type is just duplicated. The remaining rules propagate this behavior to class types and type environments.

The second aspect is subtyping. The relation between O and P is one source because every O-typed object can be used as P-typed. Interface extension is another source of subtyping, which is also present in CLASSICJAVA. The final source is the degree of kinship f. The kinship degree of a node is either R indicating the document root node, $\mathrm{F}(f')$ indicating that it has a parent of degree f', or $f' + f''$ indicating that there is a choice of different parents resulting in degrees f' or f''. Essentially, the kinship degree indicates a set of paths to the document root node with + being the union operator. The union operator induces subtyping in the usual way. Note that covariant subtyping is sufficient because the assignment operation always uses the *declared* type annotations of an object's field, not the current type annotations.

The third aspect is tracking the identity of document nodes. The system assumes that a program only manipulates a finite number of documents. The limitation is that one program expression cannot be the source for multiple document identities. The Δ component is a list of document identities which is assembled from the leaves of the expression. The join judgment for Δ (in Fig.4) ensures that a document identity occurs at most once in a type derivation.

4   Semantics

Following the lead of CLASSICJAVA, we define a small-step operational semantics for DOMJAVA. The definition in Fig.6 employs evaluation contexts [4].

Hence, the semantics is specified by a transition relation on configurations, where a configuration is a pair of an expression and a state. The relation is indexed by the program P to run. As in CLASSICJAVA, values are either **null** or store locations. A valid store location points to the description $(cl, \mathcal{F})$ of an object consisting of the object's class name cl (or its interface name if it is a DOM object) and a field map $\mathcal{F}$ which maps field names to values.

Evaluation contexts and evaluation steps are slightly simplified with respect to CLASSICJAVA in that they do not cater for inheritance. They specify a left-to-right call-by-value evaluation strategy and initialize fields of new objects to **null**. The rule for method invocation replaces the invocation with the method body after substituting the parameter values for the formal parameters.

The rules for the DOM operations are novel. They only define the behavior up to the modifications in the `ownerDocument` and `parentNode` fields and leave the rest unspecified. For example, `createAttribute(v)` creates a new attribute node with v determining the attribute name. The node is attached to the document that created it and it does not have a parent[3]. The call $\ell_1.\texttt{setAttributeNode}(\ell_2)$ attaches the attribute node ℓ_2 to the element node ℓ_1 unless the attribute is already bound to a different element. In addition, both nodes must have the same `ownerDocument`[4].

5   Type Soundness

The construction of the type soundness proof proceeds in the standard way [15]. First, the typing for expressions must be extended to a typing of configurations.

$$\frac{P, C, \Delta, A \vdash_e e : t \quad \Delta, A \vdash_s \sigma}{P, C, \Delta, A \vdash_c e, \sigma : t}$$

---

[3] For simplicity, we pretend that attributes use the `parentNode` field to indicate their owning element. In fact, they use a separate `ownerElement` field.

[4] The real specification returns the previous attribute node for the same name if such a node exists.

$$\begin{aligned}
\longrightarrow_P &\in \textit{Transition} &= \mathcal{P}(\textit{Exp} \times \textit{Store}) \\
\sigma &\in \textit{Store} &= \textit{Loc} \rightarrow (\textit{ClassName} \times \textit{FieldMap}) \\
\mathcal{F} &\in \textit{FieldMap} &= \textit{FieldName} \rightarrow \textit{Value} \\
v &\in \textit{Value} &= \{\textbf{null}\} \cup \textit{Loc} \\
e &\in \textit{Exp} &\text{set of expressions} \\
cl &\in \textit{ClassName} &\text{set of class names} \\
fd &\in \textit{FieldName} &\text{set of field names} \\
\ell &\in \textit{Loc} &\text{set of locations; infinite subset of the expression variables} \\
& & \text{which is never used in source programs}
\end{aligned}$$

Evaluation contexts

$$E ::= [\,] \mid E.fd \mid E.fd = e \mid v.fd = E \mid E.md(e^*) \mid v.md(v^* E e^*) \mid \textbf{let } var = E \textbf{ in } e$$

Evaluation steps

$$E[\textbf{new } cl], \sigma \longrightarrow_P E[\ell], \sigma[\ell \mapsto (cl, \mathcal{F})]$$
$$\ell \notin dom(\sigma), \mathcal{F} = [fd_1 \mapsto \textbf{null}, \ldots, fd_m \mapsto \textbf{null}], \textbf{class } cl \{ \textit{field}^* \ \textit{meth}^* \} \in P,$$
$$\textit{field}^* = t_1 \ fd_1 \ldots t_m \ fd_m$$
$$E[\ell.fd], \sigma \longrightarrow_P E[v], \sigma$$
$$\ell \in dom(\sigma), \sigma(\ell) = (cl, \mathcal{F}), fd \in dom(\mathcal{F}), v = \mathcal{F}(fd)$$
$$E[\ell.fd = v], \sigma \longrightarrow_P E[v], \sigma[\ell \mapsto (cl, \mathcal{F}[fd \mapsto v])]$$
$$\ell \in dom(\sigma), \sigma(\ell) = (cl, \mathcal{F}), fd \in dom(\mathcal{F})$$
$$E[\ell.md(v_1, \ldots, v_m)], \sigma \longrightarrow_P E[e[var_1 \mapsto v_1, \ldots, var_m \mapsto v_m]], \sigma$$
$$\ell \in dom(\sigma), \ell \mapsto (cl, \mathcal{F}), \textbf{class } cl \{ \textit{field}^* \ \textit{meth}^* \} \in P,$$
$$\textbf{pre } t \ [t_0] \ md \ (t_1 \ var_1 \ldots t_m \ var_m) \{ e \} \in \textit{meth}^*$$
$$E[\textbf{let } var = v \textbf{ in } e], \sigma \longrightarrow_P E[e[var \mapsto v]], \sigma$$

Evaluation of selected DOM operations (only the essential aspects)

$$E[\ell.\texttt{createAttribute}(v)], \sigma \longrightarrow_P E[\ell'], \sigma[\ell' \mapsto (\textbf{Attr}, \mathcal{F}')]$$
$$\sigma(\ell) = (\textbf{Document}, \mathcal{F}), \ell' \notin dom(\sigma), \mathcal{F}' = [\texttt{ownerDocument} \mapsto \ell, \texttt{parentNode} \mapsto \textbf{null}, \ldots]$$
$$E[\ell_1.\texttt{setAttributeNode}(\ell_2)], \sigma \longrightarrow_P E[\textbf{null}], \sigma[\ell_1 \mapsto (\textbf{Element}, \mathcal{F}_1'), \ell_2 \mapsto (\textbf{Attr}, \mathcal{F}_2')]$$
$$\sigma(\ell_1) = (\textbf{Element}, \mathcal{F}_1), \sigma(\ell_2) = (\textbf{Attr}, \mathcal{F}_2), \mathcal{F}_2(\texttt{parentNode}) = \textbf{null},$$
$$\mathcal{F}_1(\texttt{ownerDocument}) = \mathcal{F}_2(\texttt{ownerDocument}), \mathcal{F}_1' = \mathcal{F}_1[\texttt{attributes} \mapsto \ldots],$$
$$\mathcal{F}_2' = \mathcal{F}_2[\texttt{parentNode} \mapsto \ell_1]$$
$$E[\ell.\texttt{cloneNode}(v)], \sigma \longrightarrow_P E[\ell'], \sigma[\ell' \mapsto (di, \mathcal{F}')]$$
$$\ell' \notin dom(\sigma), \sigma(\ell) = (di, \mathcal{F}), \mathcal{F}' = \mathcal{F}[\texttt{parentNode} = \textbf{null}]$$
$$E[\ell.\texttt{createDocument}(v_1, v_2, v_3)], \sigma \longrightarrow_P E[\ell'], \sigma[\ell' \mapsto (\textbf{Document}, \mathcal{F})]$$
$$\ell' \notin dom(\sigma), \mathcal{F} = [\texttt{ownerDocument} = \textbf{null}, \texttt{parentNode} = \textbf{null}, \ldots]$$
$$E[\ell_1.\texttt{appendChild}(\ell_2)], \sigma \longrightarrow_P E[\ell_2], \sigma[\ell_1 \mapsto (dip, \mathcal{F}_1'), \ell_2 \mapsto (dic, \mathcal{F}_2')]$$
$$\sigma(\ell_1) = (dip, \mathcal{F}_1), \sigma(\ell_2) = (dic, \mathcal{F}_2), \mathcal{F}_2(\texttt{parentNode}) = \textbf{null},$$
$$(dip, dic) \in \textsc{ParentChild}, \sigma \not\models \ell_1 \preceq \ell_2, \mathcal{F}_1(\texttt{ownerDocument}) = \mathcal{F}_2(\texttt{ownerDocument}),$$
$$\mathcal{F}_1' = \mathcal{F}_1[\texttt{children} \mapsto \ldots], \mathcal{F}_2' = \mathcal{F}_2[\texttt{parentNode} \mapsto \ell_1]$$

Definition of the descendant relation $\sigma \models \ell_1 \preceq \ell_2$: in store σ, ℓ_1 is a descendant of ℓ_2

$$\sigma \models \ell \preceq \ell \qquad \frac{\sigma(\ell_0) = (di, \mathcal{F}_0) \quad \mathcal{F}_0(\texttt{parentNode}) = \ell_1 \quad \sigma \models \ell_1 \preceq \ell_2}{\sigma \models \ell_0 \preceq \ell_2}$$

Fig. 6. Transition relation

This rule says that a configuration is well-typed at type t if it consists of an expression that is well-typed at type t and a consistent store. A store is consistent with respect to document pointers Δ and a type environment A (see judgment $\Delta, A \vdash_s \sigma$ in Fig.7) if the type markers for documents are unique (judgment $\Delta, A \vdash_u$) and if each store location contains an object of the type indicated by A. The latter is checked with the judgments $\Delta, A, \sigma \vdash_l \ell : t$ (for locations) and $\Delta, A, \sigma \vdash_v v : t$ (for values). The value judgment trivially accepts the **null** pointer for any type. Otherwise it checks the location and its expected type against the assumption in A and then checks the location's contents against its type with $\Delta, A, \sigma \vdash_l \ell : t$. For an object of a user-defined class, the class map $\mathcal{F}$ must be defined on the field names mentioned in the type, the field values must be **null** or defined references in the store, and they must have the types indicated in the augmented class type (as in CLASSICJAVA[6]).

The novel part is the consistency rule for an object with a DOM interface type $N\langle di, d, k, f \rangle$. These objects must have references to a `parentNode` and an `ownerDocument` both of which have to be consistent with what the type says about them. Consistency means that the `ownerDocument` must be a document object with a suitable annotation (it must be a root object and it must not have its `parentNode` set). The `parentNode` can be any `Node` object with the same `ownerDocument`. If the f annotation in the object's type indicates a root object ($f = R$) then it must not have an owner (a requirement for `Document` objects). If the k annotation indicates an orphaned node ($k = O$) then there must not be a parent. In addition, the f annotation must be consistent with the path from the current node to the document root as indicated by the judgment $\sigma \vdash_f f \sim \ell$.

The definition of the latter judgment proceeds upwards along the `parentNode` pointers. Intuitively, f characterizes the path from the current node to the root node of the document. If $f = R$ then the location must match a `Document` object, if $f = F(f')$ then any node matches provided that its `parentNode` matches f'. If $f = f_1 + f_2$, then the current node has to match f_1 or f_2. If there is no path to the root, yet, then the **null** pointer thus encountered matches any path.

Lemma 1 (Type Preservation). *Suppose that $\vdash P$ and $P, C, \Delta, A \vdash_c e, \sigma : t$ with $fv(e) \subseteq Loc$ and $e, \sigma \longrightarrow_P e', \sigma'$.*
Then there are some Δ', A' such that $P, C, \Delta', A' \vdash_c e', \sigma'$ and $fv(e') \subseteq Loc$.

The progress lemma states that an expression is either a value, reduces, or attempts to dereference a **null** pointer. In particular, it is not possible that one of the DOM operations gets stuck because its preconditions are not fulfilled.

Lemma 2 (Progress). *Suppose that $\vdash P$ and $P, C, \Delta, A \vdash_c e, \sigma : t$ with $fv(e) \subseteq Loc$ and C satisfied.*
Then exactly one of the following alternatives applies.

- *e is a value,*
- *$e, \sigma \longrightarrow_P e', \sigma'$,*
- *$e = E[\textbf{null}.fd]$*

$$\frac{dom(\sigma) \subseteq dom(A) \quad (\forall \ell \in dom(\sigma)) \ \Delta, A, \sigma \vdash_l \ell : A(\ell) \quad \Delta, A \vdash_u}{\Delta, A \vdash_s \sigma}$$

$$\Delta, \emptyset \vdash_u \qquad \frac{\Delta, A \vdash_u \quad \delta \notin \Delta}{(\Delta, \delta), A[\ell \mapsto \texttt{N}\langle \texttt{Document}, \delta, k, f \rangle] \vdash_u} \qquad \frac{\Delta, A \vdash_u \quad t \neq \texttt{Document} \dots}{\Delta, A[var \mapsto t] \vdash_u}$$

$$\Delta, A, \sigma \vdash_v \textbf{null} : t \qquad \frac{A(\ell) = t \quad \Delta, A, \sigma \vdash_l \ell : t}{\Delta, A, \sigma \vdash_v \ell : t}$$

$$\frac{\sigma(\ell) = (cl, \mathcal{F}) \quad dom(\mathcal{F}) = \{fd_1, \dots, fd_m\} \quad ran(\mathcal{F}) \subseteq \{\textbf{null}\} \cup dom(\sigma)}{(\forall j) \ \Delta, A, \sigma \vdash_v \mathcal{F}(fd_j) : t_j}{\Delta, A, \sigma \vdash_l \ell : cl \ \{t_1 \ fd_1 \dots t_m \ fd_m\}}$$

$$\frac{\begin{array}{c} \sigma(\ell) = (di', \mathcal{F}) \quad di' \leq di \\ dom(\mathcal{F}) \supseteq \{\texttt{parentNode}, \texttt{ownerDocument}\} \quad ran(\mathcal{F}) \subseteq \{\textbf{null}\} \cup dom(\sigma) \\ \Delta, A, \sigma \vdash_v \mathcal{F}(\texttt{ownerDocument}) : \texttt{N}\langle \texttt{Document}, \delta, \texttt{O}, \texttt{R} \rangle \\ \Delta, A, \sigma \vdash_v \mathcal{F}(\texttt{parentNode}) : \texttt{N}\langle \texttt{Node}, \delta, k', f' \rangle \\ f = \texttt{R} \Leftrightarrow \mathcal{F}(\texttt{ownerDocument}) = \textbf{null} \\ k = \texttt{O} \Rightarrow \mathcal{F}(\texttt{parentNode}) = \textbf{null} \\ \delta \notin \Delta \quad \sigma \vdash_f f \sim \ell \end{array}}{\Delta, A, \sigma \vdash_l \ell : \texttt{N}\langle di, d, k, f \rangle}$$

$$\sigma \vdash_f f \sim \textbf{null} \qquad \frac{\sigma \vdash_f f_1 \sim \ell}{\sigma \vdash_f f_1 + f_2 \sim \ell} \qquad \frac{\sigma \vdash_f f_2 \sim \ell}{\sigma \vdash_f f_1 + f_2 \sim \ell}$$

$$\frac{\sigma(l) = (\texttt{Document}, \mathcal{F})}{\sigma \vdash_f \texttt{R} \sim \ell} \qquad \frac{\sigma(l) = (di, \mathcal{F}) \quad \sigma \vdash_f f \sim \mathcal{F}(\texttt{parentNode})}{\sigma \vdash_f \texttt{F}(f) \sim \ell}$$

Fig. 7. Typing for stores and locations

- $e = E[\textbf{null}.fd = v]$
- $e = E[\textbf{null}.md(v_1, \dots, v_m)]$.

Type preservation and progress combine to type soundness result as usual.

Theorem 1 (Type Soundness). *Suppose that* $P, C, \Delta, \emptyset \vdash e, \emptyset : t$. *Then there are three possible outcomes.*

- *For each* e', σ' *such that* $e, \emptyset \longrightarrow_P^* e', \sigma'$ *there is some* $e', \sigma' \longrightarrow_P e'', \sigma''$.
- *There exists a value* v *such that* $e, \emptyset \longrightarrow_P^* v, \sigma'$.
- $e, \emptyset \longrightarrow_P^* e', \sigma'$ *such that either* $e' = E[\textbf{null}.fd]$, $e' = E[\textbf{null}.fd = v]$, *or* $e' = E[\textbf{null}.md(v_1, \dots, v_m)]$.

6   Related Work

DOMJAVA draws on three areas, Java semantics, type-based program analysis, and linear types. Each of these areas has extensive literature and space does not permit more than a cursory glance at each of them.

Java Semantics. The first models for Java semantics were built to investigate Java's type soundness[3]. Later models were built to provide formal grounds for extensions of Java with generics (Featherweight Java [9]) or with mixins

(CLASSICJAVA[6]). A further contender is Middleweight Java [2] which attempts to stay more faithful to Java's original syntax.

DOMJAVA is inspired by CLASSICJAVA for two reasons. First, unlike Featherweight Java, CLASSICJAVA models object mutation, which is essential because the DOM standard makes extensive use of it. Second, CLASSICJAVA is a simpler framework than Middleweight Java because the latter is geared to provide a formal basis for region analysis of the full Java language through a type and effect system [8]. This additional complexity would distract from the core issues of this work.

Type-Based Program Analysis. The PPA textbook [12] gives a very good overview of different program analysis techniques and type-based ones in particular. One main technique is analysis via a type and effect system. This technique has a long history primarily in the area of functional programming [11] and has recently gained interest in the object-oriented programming community [8, 13]. The latter work [13] analyzes Java programs using method signatures that also include the type of the receiver object and that also quantify over type annotations. However, DOMJAVA does not have an effect system, but a type system with some affine annotations.

Resource and Shape Analysis. Substructural type systems can model resource usage as indicated by Walker's overview article [14]. Linear types have recently gained interest in program analysis of systems code (*e.g.*, [5]) because they are well suited to tracking state changes. Similar notions are used in shape analysis (*e.g.*, [7]).

7   Conclusion

The paper provides a first step towards providing a DOM API with strong guarantees. It mainly lays out the tools required, but leaves a lot to be done.

To obtain a simpler system, DOMJAVA omits some runtime errors of the DOM API which could be handled with similar methods. The remaining errors are either too hard to track with sufficient precision or too vaguely specified.

There are several objectives for further work. We already extended the system to cover inheritance in an attempt to create a general type annotation framework for Java. The most important part of our ongoing work is the development of a type inference algorithm for DOMJAVA and an implementation of a prototype. This task is nontrivial because the algorithm must find a finite representation for recursive object types—which requires some approximation—and ideally it should handle polymorphic recursion in terms of the annotations. Covering generics would be a worthwhile extension as well as an improved treatment of containers.

Acknowledgment. The reviewers have provided a wealth of interesting suggestions. Unfortunately, time and space constraints did not permit addressing all of them in this revision.

References

1. Scalable vector graphics (SVG) 1.1 specification. http://www.w3.org/TR/SVG11/, January 2003.
2. Gavin M. Bierman, Matthew J. Parkinson, and Andrew M. Pitts. An imperative core calculus for Java and Java with effects. Technical Report 563, University of Cambridge Computer Laboratory, April 2003.
3. Sophia Drossopoulou and Susan Eisenbach. Java is type safe—probably. In Mehmet Aksit and Satoshi Matsuoka, editors, *ECOOP'97—Object-Oriented Programming, 11th European Conference*, number 1241 in Lecture Notes in Computer Science, pages 389–418, Jyväskylä, Finland, June 1997. Springer-Verlag.
4. Matthias Felleisen and Robert Hieb. The revised report on the syntactic theories of sequential control and state. *Theoretical Computer Science*, 10(2):235–271, 1992.
5. Cormac Flanagan, Stephen Freund, and Shaz Qadeer. Exploiting purity for atomicity. *IEEE Transactions on Software Engineering*, 31(4), April 2005.
6. Matthew Flatt, Shriram Krishnamurthi, and Matthias Felleisen. A programmer's reduction semantics for classes and mixins. In *Formal Syntax and Semantics of Java*, number 1523 in Lecture Notes in Computer Science, pages 241–269. Springer-Verlag, 1999.
7. Rakesh Ghiya and Laurie J. Hendren. Is it a tree, a DAG, or a cyclic graph? a shape analysis for heap-directed pointers in C. In *Proceedings of the 1996 ACM SIGPLAN Symposium on Principles of Programming Languages*, pages 1–15, St. Petersburg, FL, USA, January 1996. ACM Press.
8. Aaron Greenhouse and John Boyland. An object-oriented effects system. In Rachid Guerraoui, editor, *ECOOP '99 — Object-Oriented Programming 13th European Conference, Lisbon Portugal*, number 1628 in Lecture Notes in Computer Science, pages 205–229, New York, NY, June 1999. Springer-Verlag.
9. Atsushi Igarashi, Benjamin C. Pierce, and Philip Wadler. Featherweight Java: a minimal core calculus for Java and GJ. *ACM Transactions on Programming Languages and Systems*, 23(3):396–450, May 2001.
10. Philippe Le Hégaret, Ray Whitmer, and Lauren Wood. W3C document object model. http://www.w3.org/DOM/, August 2003.
11. John M. Lucassen and David K. Gifford. Polymorphic effect systems. In *Proc. 15th Annual ACM Symposium on Principles of Programming Languages*, pages 47–57, San Diego, California, January 1988. ACM Press.
12. Flemming Nielson, Hanne Riis Nielson, and Chris Hankin. *Principles of Program Analysis*. Springer Verlag, 1999.
13. Christian Skalka. Trace effects and object orientation. In *Proceedings of the ACM Conference on Principles and Practice of Declarative Programming*, Lisbon, Portugal, July 2005.
14. David Walker. Substructural type systems. In Benjamin C. Pierce, editor, *Advanced Topics in Types and Programming Languages*, chapter 1. MIT Press, 2005.
15. Andrew Wright and Matthias Felleisen. A syntactic approach to type soundness. *Information and Computation*, 115(1):38–94, 1994.

Type-Based Optimization for Regular Patterns

Michael Y. Levin[1] and Benjamin C. Pierce[2]

[1] Microsoft Center for Software Excellence
[2] University of Pennsylvania

Abstract. Pattern matching mechanisms based on regular expressions feature in a number of recent languages for processing XML. The flexibility of these mechanisms demands novel approaches to the familiar problems of pattern-match compilation—how to minimize the number of tests performed during pattern matching while keeping the size of the output code small.

We describe semantic compilation methods in which we use the *schema* of the value flowing into a pattern matching expression to generate efficient target code. We start by discussing a pragmatic algorithm used currently in the compiler of XTATIC and report some preliminary performance results. For a more fundamental analysis, we define an optimality criterion of "no useless tests" and show that it is not satisfied by XTATIC's algorithm. We constructively demonstrate that the problem of generating optimal pattern matching code is decidable for finite (non-recursive) patterns.

1 Introduction

A number of recent designs descended from the XDUCE language of Hosoya, Pierce, and Vouillon [12, 11] have showed how to use document format specification languages such DTD, XML Schema, and Relax NG both *statically* for type-checking XML processing code and *dynamically* for evaluation of XML structures. At the core of these languages is the notion of *regular patterns*, a powerful and convenient mechanism for dynamic inspection of XML values.

A significant challenge in compiling languages with regular patterns is understanding how to translate regular pattern matching expressions into a low-level target language efficiently and compactly. One powerful class of techniques that can help achieve this goal relies on using static type information to generate optimized pattern matching code. The work described here aims to integrate type-based optimization techniques with the high-performance, but type-insensitive, compilation methods described in our previous paper [13]. The ideas developed in this paper are used in the compiler for XTATIC—an object-oriented language with regular types and regular pattern matching [7].

Consider the regular pattern `Any,a[]`, which matches sequences composed of an arbitrary prefix (matching `Any`) followed by an a-tagged element with empty contents (matching `a[]`.) This pattern can be compiled to some low-level iteration construct such as a loop or a recursive procedure that skips all of its elements until the last and then checks whether the tag of the last element is a and its contents is empty. This will correctly implement the behavior of the

G. Bierman and C. Koch (Eds.): DBPL 2005, LNCS 3774, pp. 184–198, 2005.

given pattern for any input value. However, suppose we know that the input values always belong to the type a[],(a[]|b[]); i.e., they are two-element sequences whose first element is tagged by a and has empty contents and whose second element is tagged by either a or b and also has empty contents. Knowing this, we can implement the original pattern more efficiently. First, there is no longer any need for an iteration construct, since the input sequence is known to contain exactly two elements: we can simply skip the first element and examine the second. Furthermore, it is unnecessary to check whether the contents of the second element is empty, since this is prescribed by the input type.

Our contributions are as follows:

- In Sections 3 and 4, we present the efficient type-based compilation algorithm used in our implementation of XTATIC and some preliminary measurements that demonstrate the algorithm's effectiveness (compared with XTATIC's previous, type-insensitive compilation method).
- In Section 5, we introduce and justify an optimality criterion that lets us formally compare the efficiency of pattern matching code in target language programs. In Section 6, we demonstrate that optimal compilation is possible, in principle, for matching problems with non-recursive patterns, by presenting a refinement of XTATIC's algorithm that produces optimal target code for this case. We also briefly discuss its generalization to the case with recursive patterns. (The refined algorithm is too inefficient for use in a real compiler; finding a lower bound on the complexity of optimal compilation is left as future work.)

Section 7 discusses related work, in particular the *non-uniform automata* [4] used in Frisch's implementation of CDUCE [1].

2   Background

A *value* is either the empty sequence () or a non-empty sequence of elements, $a_1[v_1] \ldots a_k[v_k]$, each consisting of a label and a nested child value. In the rest of the paper, it will be convenient to view values as binary trees. The empty sequence value () corresponds to the empty binary tree ϵ. A non-empty sequence value $a[v_1],v_2$ corresponds to the labeled binary tree $a(t_1,t_2)$ whose root label and left and right subtrees correspond to the label of the first element, the child value of the first element, and the rest of the sequence respectively.

We use environments mapping variables to values. We write $E[v_1/x, v_2/y]$ to denote an environment mapping x to v_1 and y to v_2 and agreeing with E on all other variables and $E\backslash y$ to denote an environment which is undefined on y and otherwise equal to E.

An *annotated value* can be of the form ϵ_* or $a_*(v_1,v_2)$ where v_1 and v_2 are annotated subvalues, l is an element label, and $* \in \{+,-\}$. We say that a value is annotated *consistently*, if for every node of the form $a_-(v_1,v_2)$, both v_1 and v_2 have all their nodes annotated by $-$. A value is *fully traversed* if all its nodes are annotated by $+$. (The intuition is that $+$ labels mark nodes that are examined while evaluating some pattern match.) The *erasure* of an annotated value v written $|v|$ is an ordinary value of the same structure with all the annotations eliminated.

Let v_1 and v_2 be consistently annotated values. We say that v_1 is *less traversed* than v_2, written $v_1 \leq v_2$, if $|v_1| = |v_2|$ and, for any node in v_1 labeled by $+$, the corresponding node in v_2 is also labeled by $+$. We say that v_1 is *strictly less traversed* than v_2, written $v_1 < v_2$, if $v_1 \leq v_2$ and $v_1 \neq v_2$.

An *annotated value environment* is a mapping from variable names to annotated values. An environment is *fully traversed* if its range contains only fully traversed values. The erasure operation on annotated value environments $|E|$ producing an ordinary environment is defined pointwise. The $<$ and $\leq$ relations on annotated values are extended point-wise to annotated environments.

Regular patterns are described by the following grammar:

$$ p ::= () \mid a[p] \mid p_1, p_2 \mid p_1 | p_2 \mid p* \mid Any \mid X $$

These denote the empty sequence pattern, a labeled element pattern, sequential composition, union, repetition, wild-card, and a pattern variable. Pattern variables are introduced by top-level, mutually recursive declarations of the form *def* $X = p$. Top-level declarations induce a function *def* that maps variables to the associated patterns (e.g. the above declaration implies *def*$(X) = p$.)

In this paper, we use the term *regular types* synonymously with *regular patterns*. In a full-blown source language, regular patterns may also contain variables used to extract fragments of the input value. Here, for simplicity, we omit patterns with variable binding and identify regular types and regular patterns.

The source language used in our examples has primitives for building values, function calls, and `match` expressions. A `match` expression consists of an input expression and a list of clauses, each consisting of a pattern and a corresponding right-hand-side expression. The input expression evaluates to a value that is then matched against each of the patterns in turn; the first clause with a matching pattern is selected, and its right hand side is evaluated. The type checker ensures that the clauses of a `match` expression are exhaustive; i.e., at least one of the patterns in the list of clauses is guaranteed to match the input value.

To illustrate how pattern matching is compiled, we employ a target language all of whose constructs except the pattern matching ones are identical to the corresponding constructs of the source language. Pattern matching is realized by a `case` construct which has the same form as the `match` construct of the source language except that patterns can only be of two kinds: (), matching the empty sequence, and `a[x],y`, matching a sequence starting with an element tagged by `a` and binding the contents of the first element to x and the sequence of the remaining elements to y. If the tag of the first element need not be examined during the rest of pattern matching, it can be replaced by ˜; if the contents of a variable need not be examined, it may be replaced by the wild card _.

Matching automata [13] are a formal model of target language code that gives us a convenient framework for reasoning about the properties of pattern match translations. The function of a matching automaton is to accept a given annotated value and output an integer result depending on its shape. Matching automata are heavily used in the accompanying technical report [14], where we give full details of our constructions. However, since there is not enough space here to discuss matching automata in detail, we prefer to elide them completely, instead using expressions in the target language (which are isomorphic to matching automata in a certain "normalized" form that is the target of the compilation process).

3   XTATIC Pattern Compiler

This section presents an efficient type-based compilation algorithm that is used in the current XTATIC compiler. The goal of the compiler is to construct a target language program that implements pattern matching in a given match expression.

The algorithm manipulates a data structure that is a generalization of sets of patterns. In it, patterns are arranged into a matrix whose rows and columns are associated with results and variables respectively. More formally, a *configuration* consists of a tuple of distinct variables $<x_1,\ldots,x_n>$ and a set of tuples $\{(p_{11}, \ldots, p_{1n}, j_1), \ldots, (p_{m1}, \ldots, p_{mn}, j_m)\}$ each associating a collection of patterns to a result. A configuration can be depicted as follows:

x_1	$\cdots$	x_n	
p_{11}	$\cdots$	p_{1n}	j_1
	$\cdots$		
p_{m1}	$\cdots$	p_{mn}	j_m

The algorithm starts with an *initial configuration* containing the patterns of the match expression intersected with the input type. From this point on, the input type is not taken into account. Figures 1(c) and 1(f) are examples of initial configurations for the source programs shown in (a) and (b).

A configuration describes the work that must still be done before the outcome of pattern matching can be determined. The variables contain subtrees that have yet to be examined. Pattern matching will succeed with the result given at the end of some row if all of the row's patterns match the subtrees stored in the corresponding variables.

When faced with a configuration, the compiler has a choice of which subtree (i.e., which column) to examine next. We use the following heuristic. Let P be a set of patterns. A partition of P into a number of subsets is *disjoint* if for any two patterns $p_1, p_2 \in P$, if $p_1 \cap p_2 \neq \emptyset$, then both p_1 and p_2 are in the same subset. We say that the *branching factor* of a column is the number of subsets in the largest disjoint partition of the column's patterns. The maximal branching factor heuristic then tells us to select the column with the largest branching factor. The motivation behind this heuristic is to arrive at single-result configurations as fast as possible. Such configurations need no further pattern matching, since the result has already been determined.

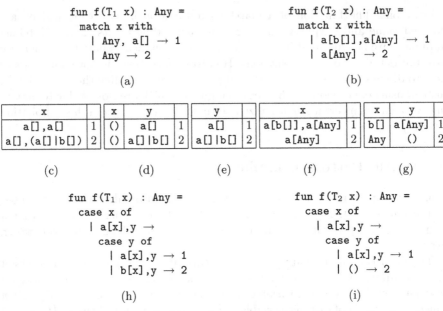

```
fun f(T₁ x) : Any =          fun f(T₂ x) : Any =
  match x with                  match x with
    | Any, a[] → 1                | a[b[]],a[Any] → 1
    | Any → 2                     | a[Any] → 2

        (a)                          (b)
```

x			x	y		y		x		x	y	
a[],a[]	1		()	a[]	1	a[]	1	a[b[]],a[Any]	1	b[]	a[Any]	1
a[],(a[]|b[])	2		()	a[]|b[]	2	a[]|b[]	2	a[Any]	2	Any	()	2

(c)   (d)   (e)   (f)   (g)

```
fun f(T₁ x) : Any =          fun f(T₂ x) : Any =
  case x of                    case x of
    | a[x],y →                   | a[x],y →
      case y of                    case y of
        | a[x],y → 1                 | a[x],y → 1
        | b[x],y → 2                 | () → 2

        (h)                          (i)
```

Fig. 1. Two source programs (a, b); configurations used in code generation (c - g); and the obtained target programs (h, i). Input types are: T_1 = a[],(a[]\|b[]) and T_2 = (a[b[]],a[Any]) | a[Any].

There are several simplification techniques for configurations. We have mentioned one already: a single-result configuration need not be expanded any further. Another involves removing a column all of whose patterns are equivalent. Because of exhaustiveness, the corresponding subtree necessarily matches all of the column's patterns, and, therefore, no run-time tests are needed.

Figure 1 shows two examples. In the first one, the initial configuration (c) contains patterns matching non-empty a-labeled trees. From this configuration, the compiler generates the pattern a[x],y of the outer case and proceeds to the next configuration (d). The first column of this configuration is then eliminated by the simplification technique described above. The resulting configuration (e) is used to generated the clauses of the inner case. In the second example, we get to employ the maximal branching heuristic for configuration (g). The branching factor of its first column is one, since its patterns are overlapping; the branching factor of the second column, on the other hand, is two. Hence, the inner case in Figure 1(i) examines y rather than x.

For some examples the heuristic approach falls short of optimality (both informally and in the precise sense defined in Section 5). Consider this configuration:

x	y	z	
a[]	a[]	a[]|b[]	1
a[]|b[]	b[]	a[]|b[]	2
a[]|b[]	a[]|b[]	b[]	3

As we will see in Section 6, it is more beneficial to examine the y and z columns before examining the x column. The heuristic method defined above, however, considers all three columns equal, since they all have a branching factor of 1. So, the heuristic algorithm can potentially generate a suboptimal target code.

Our experience shows that the maximal branching factor heuristic results in high-quality target code for most source programs.

4   Performance Experiments

To give a sense of the impact of type-based optimization, we compare the performance of three XTATIC programs with and without type-based optimization. The first, addrbook, is a small 60 line application that filters an address book and converts the result into a phone book format. The default input for this program is a 31Kb file containing 1,000 address records. We iterate the processing part of the program 10 times to obtain stable results. The second program, cwn, converts raw XML newsgroup data into a formatted HTML presentation. The source program contains 400 lines of code; the default input is a 7.7Kb file with seven newsgroup articles. This program is also iterated 10 times. The third program, bibtex, is a 700 line program that reads a bibtex file formatted as XML, filters and sorts its contents, and outputs the result as an HTML page. The default input for bibtex is a 560Kb file with approximately 1,500 bibtex entries. This processing step of this program is run only once.

Note that XTATIC's compiler is quite efficient even when its type-based optimization is turned off. It employs a variety of other optimizations that go a long way toward producing efficient code. In fact, a previous version of XTATIC's compiler that did not have type-based optimization compared favorably with several other XML processing languages [6].

Figure 2 displays our measurements. Table (a) lists sizes of the output programs in terms of the number of nodes in their ASTs. Table (b) contains running times of the programs for the default input as well as duplicated inputs whose sizes are factors 2, 3, 4, and 5 of the default input's size. Both size and running time measurements are listed for the case when the program was compiled without ("no tb") and with ("tb") type-based optimization as described above.

addrbook		cwn		bibtex	
no tb	tb	no tb	tb	no tb	tb
710	569	19200	17600	35300	26800

	addrbook		cwn		bibtex	
	no tb	tb	no tb	tb	no tb	tb
$n = 1$	13	12	300	290	3100	900
$n = 2$	17	16	420	390	4000	1900
$n = 3$	23	21	660	510	4900	2900
$n = 4$	31	28	640	590	11500	4000
$n = 5$	39	35	770	690	27400	20300

(a)   (b)

Fig. 2. Size (a) and speed in ms (b) of three source programs with and without type-based optimization; n is a size factor w.r.t. the default input size

Overall, these examples illustrate a steady benefit of type-based optimization. It gives us a 10% to 25% improvement in the size of the target program and a similar—or in case of bibtex even more dramatic—improvement in the running time. Let us take a closer look at these examples individually.

The addrbook program demonstrates a modest improvement in size and speed when compiled with type-based optimization. Just using simple configuration optimizations, the XTATIC compiler generates a fairly efficient output code for this program. The only benefit of type-based analysis in this example is the ability to infer extra information about the first sub-element of every input record and use it to skip it without checking. This is precisely what accounts for the better measurements when addrbook is compiled with type-based optimization.

In the case of cwn, type-based optimization matters less. The only difference of any significance occurs in a function that performs a character-for-character traversal of its input in order to locate a particular substring. Either a match is found in the beginning of the input or the first character is skipped and the same process is repeated from the next character. Since the input type to this function is pcdata—a sequence of character-labeled elements without attributes—there is no need to check for the absence of attributes in every element.

The bibtex program gives us the most revealing example of the benefits of type-based optimization. Most of the improvement arises from a function do_xml that examines the current entry in a bibtex document and determines its type. There are fourteen kinds of bibtex entries each described by a complex regular type; do_xml contains a dispatch function that branches to different subtasks depending on the kind of the current entry or falls through if none is matched.

Because of this default fall-through case in the match expression, a naive compilation strategy that does not take the input type into account results in a *huge* target program that meticulously checks whether the structure of the current element *completely* matches one of the bibtex entry types. Using the input type information, however, the compiler realizes that, since only valid entry elements can be given as arguments to do_xml, and since each entry type has a distinct outer label, checking that outer label is sufficient to determine the type of the entry.

5   Optimality Criterion

We now turn to a formal discussion of what it means for one target program (or matching automaton) to be better than another one.

Ideally, we would like to perform the minimal number of tests for any input value. Figure 3 demonstrates that this is not always possible. The source program shown in Figure 3(a) contains a match expression with three clauses. The clause patterns match sequences starting from a-labeled elements. To determine the outcome, the pattern matcher can first investigate the contents of the first element—as in Figure 3(b)—or else look at the rest of the sequence—as in Figure 3(c). In the former case, two tests are required to determine results 1 and 2, but only one test to determine result 3. In the latter case, it takes two tests to

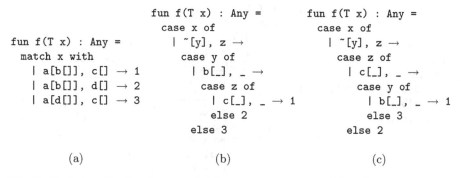

```
                        fun f(T x) : Any =      fun f(T x) : Any =
                          case x of               case x of
fun f(T x) : Any =         | ~[y], z →             | ~[y], z →
  match x with               case y of               case z of
    | a[b[]], c[]  → 1          | b[_], _ →             | c[_], _ →
    | a[b[]], d[]  → 2            case z of               case y of
    | a[d[]], c[]  → 3              | c[_], _ → 1           | b[_], _ → 1
                                   else 2                  else 3
                                 else 3                  else 2

       (a)                        (b)                      (c)
```

Fig. 3. Perfect optimality is unreachable: a source program (a) with input type T = a[b[]],c[] | a[b[]],d[] | a[d[]],c[]; a target program that is fast for the third case (b); a target program that is fast for the second case (c)

determine outcomes 1 and 3 and one to determine result 2. It is not possible for any target language pattern matcher to be as fast as the first program for the input matching the third clause and as fast as the second program for the input matching the second clause.

Consequently, we must settle for near-optimality and, for any pattern matching task, try to build a matcher that is not clearly bested by any other but may not be necessarily *the* best one.

Definition 1. Target program M_1 is said to be *more efficient* than target program M_2 if, for any annotated input value v_1 accepted by M_2, there exists a less traversed annotated value v_2 accepted by M_1 with the same result. We say that M_1 is *strictly more efficient* than M_2 if it is more efficient and there exists an annotated value that is accepted by M_1 but not M_2.

Consider the example in Figure 4. It shows a source program and two possible translations into the target language. The target program in Figure 4(b) is suboptimal. It tests the right subtree of the input value, and, regardless of the result, inspects the left subtree as well. The program in Figure 4(c) is better—it never inspects the right subtree. This program is more efficient than the suboptimal one since, for any annotated value accepted by the latter, the former accepts a less traversed value producing the same result. It is *strictly* more efficient since, for example, $a_+(b_-(\epsilon_-, \epsilon_-), c_+(\epsilon_-, \epsilon_-))$ is accepted by it but not by the suboptimal program.

Note that the proposed measure of optimality does not precisely reflect the amount of work performed by a target program. Consider Figure 5, which shows a source program and two ways of compiling it to the target language. Target program (b) starts by inspecting the right subtree of the input; if it finds a c leaf, it can select the first `match` clause; otherwise, it checks whether the root of left subtree is labeled by b, and selects the first or the second clause depending on that. Target program (c) checks only the left subtree: if its root is b-labeled, it selects the first clause; otherwise the second. The latter program performs

```
                          fun f(T x) : Any =
                            case x of
                            | ~[y],z →              fun f(T x) : Any =
                              case z of               case x of
fun f(T x) : Any =            | b[_],_ →              | ~[y],_ →
  match x with                  case y of               case y of
  | a[a[]], b[]|c[] → 1          | a[_],_ → 1            | a[_],_ → 1
  | a[b[]], c[]    → 2          | c[_],_ → 3            | b[_],_ → 2
  | a[c[]], b[]    → 3        | c[_],_ →               | c[_],_ → 3
                                case y of
                                | a[_],_ → 1
                                | b[_],_ → 2

        (a)                       (b)                     (c)
```

Fig. 4. An illustration of optimality criterion: a source program (a) with input type
T = (a[a[]], b[]|c[]) | a[b[]],c[] | a[c[]],b[]; a suboptimal target program
(b); an optimal target program (c)

```
                          fun f(T x) : Any =
                            case x of
                            | ~[y],z →              fun f(T x) : Any =
fun f(T x) : Any =            case z of               case x of
  match x with               | ~[w],_ →              | ~[y],_ →
  | a[b[Any],Any],             case w of               case y of
    a[Any] → 1                   | c[_],_ → 1            | b[_],_ → 1
  | a[Any],a[b[d[]]]          else                    else 2
     → 2                        case y of
                                 | b[_],_ → 1
                               else 2

        (a)                       (b)                     (c)
```

Fig. 5. Optimality criterion limitation: a source program (a); with input type T =
(a[b[]], a[b[c[]]]) | (a[Any], a[b[d[]]]); an optimal target program (b); a *better* optimal target program (c)

fewer than or the same number of node tests as the former for any input. It is *not*, however, any more efficient according to our definition since, for the values matching a[Any], a[b[c[]]], program (b) completely skips the left subtree, while program (c) inspects its root node.

A more precise measure of optimality would involve counting the number of node tests performed by a target program regardless of where in the input value they occur. According to such a measure, program (c) of Figure 5 would be more efficient than program (b). It is difficult, however, to reason about this kind of a measure. For instance, performing various boolean operations such as intersection and difference on regular patterns does not shed any light on how many node tests may be necessary to match a value against them. We leave investigation of this kind of optimality measures for future work.

6   Optimal Compilation for Finite Patterns

We now show how the algorithm described in Section 3 can be made optimal for non-recursive patterns by describing a better method of selecting the expansion column. Consider the following configuration with two columns and three results.

y	z	
a[Any]	Any	1
Any	Any,c[]	2
c[],Any	Any	3

Would it be better to test the contents of y or z? Testing y is sufficient to determine the outcome: depending on whether its root node is labeled by a, b, or c, the answer is 1, 2, or 3 respectively. We say that the first column determines all three results. The second column determines only result 2: if the root node of the value stored in z is labeled by c, we can conclude 2; if it is labeled by b, however, we cannot determine the result without testing the contents of y.

It would seem that testing y first would result in more efficient pattern matching, but, in fact, neither column is preferable as far as the optimality measure proposed above is concerned. The reason that expanding on the first column does not lead to a more efficient target program than expanding on the second is that the latter target program can output 2 without considering the contents of y at all. We say that neither column is a *better distinguisher* than the other.

If, however, the first row pattern in the second column were changed from b[] to b[]|c[], then the second column would not determine any result and, in that case, testing y first would be more efficient. The first column in this case would be a better distinguisher than the second column. (Figure 4 shows the two target programs that correspond to choosing y or z for the initial inspection.)

Sometimes, no single column determines any result. Consider the following configuration.

y	z	
a[]	a[]	1
a[]|b[]	b[]	2
b[]	a[]|b[]	3

It is not possible to arrive at the result by testing the contents of either column alone. Of course, testing the contents of both y and z is sufficient to find the answer. In this case, it does not matter which column is tested first. So, as in the previous example, neither column is a better distinguisher than the other.

The following example shows that even when no column alone determines any result, it is still possible for some column to be better than another. Consider this configuration.

$$C = \begin{array}{|c|c|c|c|}
\hline
\mathbf{x} & \mathbf{y} & \mathbf{z} & \\
\hline
\texttt{a[]} & \texttt{a[]} & \texttt{a[]|b[]} & 1 \\
\hline
\texttt{a[]|b[]} & \texttt{b[]} & \texttt{a[]|b[]} & 2 \\
\hline
\texttt{a[]|b[]} & \texttt{a[]|b[]} & \texttt{b[]} & 3 \\
\hline
\end{array}$$

As in the previous example, testing any of the three columns alone is not sufficient to determine any result. Unlike the previous example, however, it *does* matter which variable we test first. In particular, it can be shown that testing $\mathbf{z}$ or $\mathbf{y}$ first is more beneficial than testing $\mathbf{x}$ first. (See the accompanying technical report [14].)

For this configuration, we say that both $\mathbf{y}$ and $\mathbf{z}$ are *better distinguishers* than $\mathbf{x}$. We would like to have a formal criterion that allows us to determine whether one column is a better distinguisher than another. Furthermore, we would like this criterion to be semantic so that we can find an optimally distinguishing column without generating and comparing all possible target programs that can arise from the current configuration.

We will satisfy the above concerns as follows. First, we will introduce *decision trees*, which have the same semantics as target programs but are higher level. We will define what it means for one decision tree to be strictly more efficient than another. Then, after establishing a correspondence between decision trees and configurations, we will derive the notion of an optimal expansion column.

Definition 2. A *decision tree* is a tree whose nodes $\bigvee$ are labeled by variables, whose edges are labeled by regular types, and whose leaves are sets of integer results. A path from the root to a leaf may not contain duplicate variables. We say that an environment E is *accepted* by a decision tree t with result j, written $E \in t \Rightarrow j$, if there exists a path $x_1 \xrightarrow{p_1} x_2 \xrightarrow{p_2} \ldots x_k \xrightarrow{p_k} J$ from the root to a leaf, where $x_1 \ldots x_k$ are the variables labeling nodes of the path starting from the root, $p_1 \ldots p_k$ are the regular types labeling the edges of the path, and J is the leaf result set, such that $j \in J$ and $E(x_i) \in p_i$ for all $i \in \{1 \ldots k\}$.

One decision tree is strictly more efficient than another if it accepts any environment by testing a subset of the variables that must be tested by the other decision tree to accept the same environment.

Definition 3. A decision tree t_1 is *strictly more efficient* than an equivalent decision tree t_2 if, for any path $x_1 \xrightarrow{p_1} x_2 \xrightarrow{p_2} \ldots x_k \xrightarrow{p_k} J$ in t_2, there exists a path $y_1 \xrightarrow{q_1} y_2 \xrightarrow{q_2} \ldots y_m \xrightarrow{q_m} J$ in t_1 such that, for any $i \in \{1 \ldots m\}$, there exists $j \in \{1 \ldots k\}$ with $y_i = x_j$ and $q_i = p_j$, and, furthermore, there exists a t_2 path for which the corresponding t_1 path is strictly shorter.

A configuration can give rise to a finite number of decision trees. To help identify the set of all decision trees corresponding to a configuration, we first introduce an auxiliary notion of a partition of a set of regular types.

Definition 4. Let T be an input regular type and $S = \{p_1 \ldots p_m\}$ a set of regular types such that T is a subtype of $p_1 \cup \ldots \cup p_m$. A *partition* of S is a set of mutually disjoint regular types $\{t_1 \ldots t_k\}$ such that $T \cap (p_1 \cup \ldots \cup p_m)$ is a subtype of $t_1 \cup \ldots \cup t_k$ and, for any $i \in \{1 \ldots k\}$ and $j \in \{1 \ldots m\}$, if $t_i \cap p_j$ is non-empty, then t_i is a subtype of p_j.

The idea is to use the elements of a partition to indicate which of the original patterns match a given input value. For example, $\{a[], b[]\}$ is a partition for the input type $T = a[] \mid b[]$ and the collection of patterns $S = \{a[], b[], a[] \mid b[]\}$. If a value v is in $a[]$, then it is in the first and third but not in the second patterns of S; if v is in $b[]$, then it is in the second and third but not in the first patterns of S.

A partition of S with respect to T can be obtained by taking all the non-empty types of the form $T \cap p_1' \cap \ldots \cap p_m'$ where each p_i' is either p_i or $T \backslash p_i$. We say that this is the *minimal partition* of S with respect to T.

Definition 5. A decision tree t is said to *correspond* to a configuration C if two conditions hold: 1) edges from a node x are labeled by regular types each of which is a union of some types from the minimal partition of C's column corresponding to x; and 2) t and C are semantically equivalent.

Given a configuration C, it is possible—albeit very time consuming—to generate all decision trees that satisfy the first condition. It is then easy to check whether any such decision tree is semantically equivalent to C. Combining these two steps, we can obtain an algorithm that produces all of C's decision trees.

Definition 6. Let C be a configuration and c one of C's columns associated with variable x. This column is said to be an *optimal distinguisher* if there exists a decision tree corresponding to C whose root is labeled by x such that there does not exist a strictly more efficient decision tree corresponding to C.

Figure 6 shows a configuration discussed earlier and two optimal decision trees corresponding to it. The columns associated with z and y are both optimal distinguishers for this configuration.

Since the compilation algorithm introduced above can be viewed as an instantiation of the type-insensitive algorithm presented in our previous paper [13]—here the method of selecting expansion columns is specified while there it was left unspecified—the same correctness and termination arguments can be carried over for the algorithm of this paper. Additionally, we can show that the column selection principle introduced above ensures generation of optimal matching automata.

Lemma 1. Let C be a configuration over finite regular types. Let M be a target program generated from C according to the above algorithm. Then there is no target program that is equivalent to C and strictly more efficient than M.

A corollary of this lemma is a *monotonicity* property that states that for any matching problem, given a more specific input type, our compilation algorithm generates a target program that is not worse than the one it generates for the same matching problem with a less specific input type.

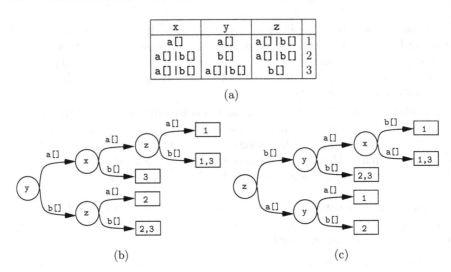

Fig. 6. A configuration (a) and two optimal corresponding decision trees (b) and (c)

The algorithm described here works only for finite patterns; for recursive patterns, it can go into an infinite loop, since expansion may not necessarily yield "smaller" configurations as compilation progresses. The full version [14] describes how to generalize the algorithm to the case with recursive patterns. To do this, we must address several issues: first, we demonstrate that using the input type is beneficial for reducing the number of function calls in the generated program; second, we point out that deciding when exactly to generate function calls can make a substantial difference in the efficiency of the resulting target program. We conclude with an observation that it is impossible to achieve optimality, as it is defined here, in the presence of recursive patterns.

7   Related Work

Frisch was the first to publish a description of a type-based optimization approach for a language with regular pattern matching [4]. His algorithm is based on a special kind of tree automata called *non-uniform automata*. Like matching automata, non-uniform automata incorporate the notion of "results" of pattern matching (i.e., a match yields a value, not just success or failure). Also, like matching automata, non-uniform automata support sequential traversal of subtrees. This makes it possible to construct a deterministic non-uniform automaton for any regular language. Unlike matching automata, non-uniform automata impose a left to right traversal of the input value. Whereas it is possible for a matching automaton to scan a fragment of the left subtree, continue on with a fragment of the right, come back to the left and so on, a non-uniform automaton must traverse the left subtree fully before moving on to the right subtree.

Frisch proposes an algorithm that uses type propagation. His algorithm differs from the tree automaton simplification algorithm in that it must traverse several patterns simultaneously (whereas the latter handles one pattern at a time) and generate result sets that will be used in the transitions of the constructed automaton. Frisch's algorithm does not always achieve optimality. In particular, it generates an automaton that tries to learn as much information from the left subtree as possible, even if this information will not be needed in further pattern matching.

In his dissertation [5], Frisch presents a more flexible form of non-uniform automata that allow arbitrary, rather than strictly left-to-right, order of traversal. There is no formal discussion of optimality however.

Outside of the XDUCE family, a lot of work has been done in the area of XPATH query optimization. Several subsets of XPATH have been considered. Wood describes a polynomial algorithm for finding a unique minimal XPATH query that is equivalent to the given query [15]. The minimization problem is solved for the set of all documents regardless of their schema. When the schema is taken into account, the problem is coNP-hard. Flesca, Furfaro, and Masciari consider a wider subset of XPATH and show that the minimization problem for it is also coNP-hard [2]. They then identify an subset of their subset for which an ad-hoc polynomial minimization is possible.

Genevès and Vion-Dury describe a logic-based XPATH optimization framework [8] in which a collection of rewrite rules is used to transform a query in a subset of XPATH into a more efficient, but not necessarily optimal, form.

Optimizing full XPATH has also been investigated. Gottlob, Koch, and Pichler observe that many XPATH evaluation engines are exponential in the worst case. They propose an algorithm that works for full XPATH and that is guaranteed to process queries in polynomial time and space. Furthermore, they define a useful subset of XPATH for which processing time and space are reduced to quadratic and linear respectively [9, 10]. Fokoue [3] describes a type-based optimization technique for XPATH queries. The idea is to evaluate a given query on the schema of the input value obtaining as a result some valuable information that can be used to simplify the query.

At this point, we hesitate to draw deeper analogies between the above XPATH-related work and our type-based optimization algorithm since the nature of XPATH pattern matching is quite different from that of regular pattern matching.

Acknowledgements

We thank Alain Frisch, Haruo Hosoya, and DBPL reviewers for conversations and comments that resulted in numerous improvements to this work.

References

1. V. Benzaken, G. Castagna, and A. Frisch. CDuce: An XML-centric general-purpose language. In *ACM SIGPLAN International Conference on Functional Programming (ICFP), Uppsala, Sweden*, pages 51–63, 2003.
2. S. Flesca, F. Furfaro, and E. Masciari. On the minimization of xpath queries. In *VLDB*, pages 153–164, 2003.

3. A. Fokoue. Improving the performance of XPath query engines on large collections of XML data, 2002.

4. A. Frisch. Regular tree language recognition with static information. In *Workshop on Programming Language Technologies for XML (PLAN-X)*, Jan. 2004.

5. A. Frisch. *Théorie, conception et réalisation d'un langage adapté á XML*. PhD thesis, Ecole Normale Supérieure, Paris, Paris, France, 2004.

6. V. Gapeyev, M. Y. Levin, B. C. Pierce, and A. Schmitt. XML goes native: Runtime representations for Xtatic. In *14th International Conference on Compiler Construction*, Apr. 2005.

7. V. Gapeyev, M. Y. Levin, B. C. Pierce, and A. Schmitt. The Xtatic experience. In *Workshop on Programming Language Technologies for XML (PLAN-X)*, Jan. 2005. University of Pennsylvania Technical Report MS-CIS-04-24, Oct 2004.

8. P. Genevès and J.-Y. Vion-Dury. Logic-based XPath optimization. In *International ACM Symposium on Document Engineering*, 2004.

9. G. Gottlob, C. Koch, and R. Pichler. Efficient algorithms for processing xpath queries. In *VLDB*, pages 95–106, 2002.

10. G. Gottlob, C. Koch, and R. Pichler. XPath query evaluation: Improving time and space efficiency, 2003.

11. H. Hosoya and B. C. Pierce. XDuce: A statically typed XML processing language. *ACM Transactions on Internet Technology*, 3(2):117–148, May 2003.

12. H. Hosoya, J. Vouillon, and B. C. Pierce. Regular expression types for XML. *ACM Transactions on Programming Languages and Systems (TOPLAS)*, 27(1):46–90, Jan. 2005. Preliminary version in ICFP 2000.

13. M. Y. Levin. Compiling regular patterns. In *ACM SIGPLAN International Conference on Functional Programming (ICFP), Uppsala, Sweden*, 2003.

14. M. Y. Levin and B. C. Pierce. Type-based optimization for regular patterns. Technical Report MS-CIS-05-13, University of Pennsylvania, June 2005.

15. P. T. Wood. Minimising simple xpath expressions. In *WebDB*, pages 13–18, 2001.

Efficient Memory Representation of XML Documents

Giorgio Busatto[1], Markus Lohrey[2], and Sebastian Maneth[3],*

[1] Department für Informatik, Universität Oldenburg, Germany
`giorgio.busatto@informatik.uni-oldenburg.de`
[2] FMI, Universität Stuttgart, Germany
`lohrey@informatik.uni-stuttgart.de`
[3] Faculté I & C, EPFL, Switzerland
`sebastian.maneth@epfl.ch`

Abstract. Implementations that load XML documents and give access to them via, e.g., the DOM, suffer from huge memory demands: the space needed to load an XML document is usually many times larger than the size of the document. A considerable amount of memory is needed to store the tree structure of the XML document. Here a technique is presented that allows to represent the tree structure of an XML document in an efficient way. The representation exploits the high regularity in XML documents by "compressing" their tree structure; the latter means to detect and remove repetitions of tree patterns. The functionality of basic tree operations, like traversal along edges, is preserved in the compressed representation. This allows to directly execute queries (and in particular, bulk operations) without prior decompression. For certain tasks like validation against an XML type or checking equality of documents, the representation allows for provably more efficient algorithms than those running on conventional representations.

1 Introduction

There are many scenarios in which trees are processed by computer programs. Often it is useful to keep a representation of the tree in main memory in order to retain fast access. If the trees to be stored are very large, then it is important to use a memory efficient representation. A recent, most prominent example of large trees are XML documents which are sequential representations of ordered (unranked) trees, and an example application which requires to materialize (part of) the document in main memory is the evaluation of XML queries. The latter is typically done using one of the existing XML data models, e.g., the DOM. Benchmarks show that a DOM representation in main memory is 4–5 times larger than the original XML file. This can be understood as follows: a node of the form `<a/>` needs 4 bytes in XML; but as a tree node it needs at least 16 bytes: a name pointer, plus three node pointers to the parent, the first child, and the next sibling (see, e.g., Chapter 8 of [20]). There are some improvements leading to more compact representations, e.g., Galax [9] uses only 3–4 times more main memory than the size of the file. Another, more memory efficient data model for XML is that of a binary tree. As shown in [21], the known XML query languages can be readily evaluated on the binary tree model.

---

* Present address: National ICT Australia Ltd `sebastian.maneth@nicta.com.au`

G. Bierman and C. Koch (Eds.): DBPL 2005, LNCS 3774, pp. 199–216, 2005.
© Springer-Verlag Berlin Heidelberg 2005

In this paper, we concentrate on the problem of representing binary trees in a space efficient way, so that the functionality of the basic tree operations (such as the traversal along edges) are preserved. Instead of compression, this is often called "data optimization" [14]. Our technique is a generalization of the well-known sharing of common subtrees. The latter means to determine during a bottom-up phase, using a hash table, whether the current subtree has occurred already, and if so to represent it by a pointer to its previous occurrence. In this way the minimal unique DAG (directed acyclic graph) of the tree is obtained in amortized linear time. For common XML documents the minimal DAG is about 1/10 of the size of the original tree [3]. Our representation is based on sharing of common subgraphs of a tree. The resulting sizes are 1/2–1/3 of the size of the minimal DAG. To our knowledge, this is the most efficient pointer-based tree representation that is currently available. At the same time, the complexity of querying, e.g. using XQuery, stays the same as for DAGs [18]. We therefore believe that our representation is better suited for in-memory storage of XML documents, than DAG-based representations.

Of course, an XML document consists of more things than just tree nodes: a node may have attributes, and a leaf may have character data. Both type of values we keep in string buffers. When traversing the XML tree, we keep information on how many nodes before (in document order) the current one (i) have attributes and (ii) how many have character data. These numbers determine for a node the correct indices into the attribute and data value buffers, respectively. With this in mind, it is straightforward to implement a DOM proxy for our representations. Note that attribute and character values can be stored more space efficiently using standard techniques [1]. The XML file compression tool XMill [17] separates data values into containers and compresses them individually using standard methods. The result is stored together with the tree structure. It is likely that compressing the tree structure by the technique presented here will further improve XMill's compression ratios.

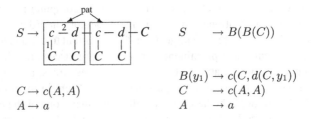

$$S \rightarrow B(B(C))$$

$$B(y_1) \rightarrow c(C, d(C, y_1))$$
$$C \rightarrow c(A, A)$$
$$A \rightarrow a$$

$$C \rightarrow c(A, A)$$
$$A \rightarrow a$$

Fig. 1. Regular and cf tree grammars generating $\{t\}$

We now describe our representation in more detail. Consider the tree $c(c(a, a), c(a, a))$, or, in XML `<c><c><a/><a/></c><c><a/><a/></c></c>`. It consists of seven nodes and six edges. The minimal DAG for this tree has three nodes u, v, w and four edges ('first-child' and 'second-child' edges from u to v and from v to w). The minimal DAG can also be seen as the minimal regular tree grammar that generates the tree [19]: the shared nodes correspond to nonterminals of the grammar. For example, the above DAG is generated by the regular tree grammar with productions $S \rightarrow c(V, V)$,

$V \to c(W, W)$, and $W \to a$. A generalization of sharing of subtrees is the sharing of arbitrary patterns, i.e., connected subgraphs of a tree. In a graph model it leads to the well-known notion of sharing graphs which are graphs with special "begin-sharing" and "end-sharing" edges, called fan-ins and fan-outs [15]. Since fan-in/out pairs can be nested, this structure allows to represent a tree in double-exponentially smaller size. In contrast, a DAG is at most exponentially smaller than the tree it represents. A sharing graph can be seen as a context-free (cf) tree grammar [19]. In a cf tree grammar nonterminals can appear inside of an intermediate tree (as opposed to at the leaves in the regular case); formal parameters $y_1, y_2, \ldots$ are used in productions in order to indicate where to glue the subtrees of the nonterminal which is being replaced. Finding the smallest sharing graph for a given tree is equivalent to finding the smallest cf tree grammar that generates the tree. Unfortunately, the latter problem is NP-hard: already finding the smallest cf (string) grammar for a given string is NP-complete [16]. The first main result of this paper is a linear time algorithm that finds a small cf tree grammar for a given tree. On common XML documents the algorithm performs well, obtaining grammars that are 1.5-2 times smaller than the minimal DAGs. As an example, consider the tree $t = c(c(a, a), d(c(a, a), c(c(a, a), d(c(a, a), c(a, a)))))$ which has 18 edges. The minimal DAG, written as tree grammar, can be seen on the left of Fig. 1. It is the initial input to our algorithm "BPLEX" which tries to transform the grammar into a smaller cf tree grammar. It does so by going bottom-up through the right-hand sides of productions, looking for multiple (non-overlapping) occurrences of patterns. In our example, the tree pattern pat (consisting of two nodes labeled c and d and their left children labeled C) appears twice in the right-hand side of the first production. A pattern p in a tree can conveniently be represented by a tree t_p with formal parameters $y_1, \ldots, y_r$ at leaves: simply add to t_p all children of nodes of p (and the edges), and label the jth such node (in preorder) by y_j. Thus, $t_{\text{pat}} = c(C, d(C, y_1))$. This tree becomes the right-hand side of a new nonterminal B and the right-hand side of the first production becomes $B(B(C))$. The resulting minimal cf tree grammar is shown on the right of Fig. 1.

The BPLEX algorithm is presented in Section 3. In Section 4 we discuss the application of BPLEX to XML documents and present experimental results. In Section 6 we study two problems for our tree grammars G that are important for XML documents: (1) to validate against an XML type and (2) to test equivalence. In fact, we consider both of these problems for so called "straight-line" (for short, SL) context-free tree grammars, which are grammars that are guaranteed to generate at most one tree; the "straight-line" notion is well-known from string grammars (see, e.g., [25, 26]). Since BPLEX generates "SLT grammars" of a more restricted form (additionally: linear in the parameters) we also consider problems (1) and (2) for this restricted case. It is shown that for an XML type T, represented by a (deterministic) bottom-up tree automaton, we can test whether or not the tree represented by G has type T in time $O(a^m \times |G|)$, where m is the maximal number of parameters of the nonterminals of G and a is the size of the automaton. Running a tree automaton is similar to evaluating a query; in [3] it was shown that a 'Core XPath query' Q can be evaluated on an XML document represented by its minimal DAG D in time $O(2^{|Q|} \times |D|)$. Next it is proved that testing the equivalence of two SL cf tree grammars can be done in polynomial space w.r.t. the sum of sizes of the two grammars, and, if the grammars are linear ("SLT") then even in polynomial time w.r.t. their sizes.

2 Preliminaries

For $k \in \mathbb{N}$, the set $\{1, \ldots, k\}$ is denoted by $[k]$. A finite set Σ together with a mapping rank : $\Sigma \to \mathbb{N}$ is called a *ranked alphabet*. The set of all (ordered, rooted, ranked) *trees* over Σ is denoted by T_Σ. For a set A, $T_\Sigma(A)$ is the set of all trees over $\Sigma \cup A$, where all elements of A have rank 0. We fix a set of parameters $Y = \{y_1, y_2, \ldots\}$ and, for $k \geq 0$, $Y_k = \{y_1, \ldots, y_k\}$. For a ranked tree t, $V(t)$ denotes its set of nodes and $E(t)$ its set of edges. Each node in $V(t)$ can be represented by a sequence u of integers describing the path from the root of t to the desired node (Dewey notation), the node itself is denoted by t_u; for example, 1.1.1 denotes the left-most leaf of the tree t from the Introduction (labeled a). The label at node u is denoted $t[u]$ and the subtree rooted at u is denoted t/u. For symbols $a_1, \ldots, a_n$ of rank zero and trees $t_1, \ldots, t_n$, $[a_1 \leftarrow t_1, \ldots, a_n \leftarrow t_n]$ denotes the substitution of replacing each leaf labeled a_i by the tree t_i, $1 \leq i \leq n$.

Context-free (cf) tree grammars are a natural generalization of cf grammars to trees (see, e.g., Section 15 in [13]). A cf tree grammar G consists of ranked alphabets N and Σ of nonterminal and terminal symbols, respectively, of a start symbol (of rank zero), and of a finite set of productions of the form $A(y_1, \ldots, y_k) \to t$. The right-hand side t of a production of the nonterminal A is a tree over nonterminal and terminal symbols and over the parameters in Y_k which may appear at leaves, where k is the rank of A, i.e., $t \in T_{N \cup \Sigma}(Y_k)$. Sentential forms are trees s, s' in $T_{N \cup \Sigma}$ and $s \Rightarrow_G s'$ if s' is obtained from s by replacing a subtree $A(s_1, \ldots, s_k)$ by the tree $t[y_1 \leftarrow s_1, \ldots, y_k \leftarrow s_k]$ where t is the right-hand side of an A-production. Thus, the parameters are used to indicate where to glue the subtrees of a nonterminal, when applying a production to it. The language generated by G is $\{s \in T_\Sigma \mid S \Rightarrow_G^* s\}$. Note that a parameter can cause copying (if it appears more than once in a rhs) or deletion (if it does not appear). For example, the cf tree grammar with productions $S \to A(a)$, $A(y_1) \to A(c(y_1, y_1))$, $A(y_1) \to y_1$ generates the language of all full binary trees over the binary symbol c and the constant symbol a.

A cf tree grammar is *regular* if all nonterminals have rank 0. It is *straight-line* (for short, SL) if each nonterminal A has exactly one production (with right-hand side denoted rhs(A)) and the nonterminals can be ordered as $A_1, \ldots, A_n$ in such a way that rhs(A_i) has no occurrences of A_j for $j \leq i$ (such an order is called "SL order"). Thus, an SL cf tree grammar can be defined by a tuple (N, Σ, rhs) where N is ordered and rhs is a mapping from N to right-hand sides. A cf tree grammar is *linear* if for every production $A(y_1, \ldots, y_k) \to t$, each parameter y_i occurs at most once in t.

In the sequel we use *SLT grammar* to stand for "SL linear cf tree grammar".

3 The BPLEX Algorithm

Grammar-based tree compression means to find a small grammar that generates a given tree. The size of such a grammar can be considerably smaller than the size of the tree, depending on the grammar formalism chosen. For example, finding the smallest regular tree grammar that generates a given tree t can be done in (amortized) linear time, and the resulting grammar is isomorphic to the minimal DAG of the tree. The minimal regular tree grammar G_t is also straight-line (any grammar that generates exactly one element can be turned into an SL grammar). The initial input to our compression algorithm BPLEX is the grammar G_t: BPLEX takes an arbitrary SL regular tree grammar as input and outputs a (smaller) SLT grammar. As mentioned in the Introduction, moving from regular to cf tree grammars corresponds to generalizing the sharing of common subtrees to the sharing of arbitrary tree patterns (connected subgraphs of a tree).

The basic idea of the algorithm is to find tree patterns that appear more than once in the input grammar (in a non-overlapping way), and to replace them by new nonterminals that generate the corresponding patterns. We call this technique *multiplexing* because multiple occurrences of the replaced patterns are represented only once in the output. The order in which the algorithm scans the nodes in the right-hand sides of the input grammar corresponds to scanning the generated tree bottom up; for this reason, the algorithm is called BPLEX (for *bottom-up multiplexing*).

BPLEX (see Fig. 2) takes as input an SL regular tree grammar G and three parameters specifying (1) the maximum number K_N of nodes and productions that are examined when computing patterns matching at a given node, (2) the maximum size K_S of a new pattern, and (3) the maximum rank K_R of a new pattern. If $A_1, \ldots, A_l$ are the nonterminals of G (in SL order) and G is an SLT grammar containing these nonterminals, then $<_G^l$ indicates the ordering over all nodes of $\mathrm{rhs}_G(A_1), \ldots, \mathrm{rhs}_G(A_l)$ obtained by scanning $\mathrm{rhs}_G(A_l)$ through $\mathrm{rhs}_G(A_1)$, each in postorder, and z is the current position

```
procedure BPLEX(G: grammar, K_N: int, K_S: int, K_R: int): grammar
begin
        A_l := last symbol in the SL ordering of G
        z := leftmost leaf of rhs_G(A_l)
        while true do
                repM := RepM(G, z, K_N)
                newM := NewM(G, z, K_N, K_S, K_R)
                if newM ≠ ∅ or repM ≠ ∅ then
                        m := max(newM, repM)
                        if m ∈ repM then
                                G := G[m ← A], with rhs_G(A) = p_m
                        else
                                k := rank(p_m)
                                A := fresh(G, k)
                                G := add(G, A(y_1, ..., y_k) → p_m)
                                G := G[m, c_m ← A]
                        fi
                elseif ∃w ∈ V_G^l : z <_G^l w then z := next(<_G^l, z)
                else break
                fi
        od
        return G
end BPLEX
```

Fig. 2. The BPLEX algorithm

with respect to this ordering. At each step, BPLEX computes a set of *repeated matches* by comparing the patterns occurring at z with the right-hand sides of the last K_N productions of G with index greater than l, and a set of *new matches* by finding pairs of non-overlapping occurrences of patterns at z and at the K_N most recently visited nodes (thus exploiting the well-known idea of a sliding window that appears e.g. in many implementations of the LZ77 compression scheme, cf. the discussion in Section 7). If at least one match is found, BPLEX performs the sharing that provides the highest size reduction for the grammar, it moves to the next node otherwise. If there is no next node, then it returns the current SLT grammar.

We now examine the algorithm in detail. We describe the progress of the computation through a sequence of configurations $(G_1, z_1), \ldots, (G_h, z_h)$ where, for each $i \in [h]$, G_i is an SLT grammar generating the uncompressed tree, and z_i is an *address* (see below) denoting the node that is examined during the i-th iteration (the *current* node). $G_1 = G$ is the input to the algorithm; G_h is the output. For $i \in [h]$, grammar G_i has nonterminals $A_1, \ldots, A_{l_i}$, with $l_1 = l$ and, for $i > 1$, either $l_i = l_{i-1}$ or $l_i = l_{i-1} + 1$ and $A_{l_i} = \text{fresh}(G_{i-1}, k)$ for some $k > 0$. By $\text{fresh}(G, k)$ we denote a nonterminal of rank k that does not occur in G. Given $i \in [h]$ and a grammar G_i, scanning the nodes of $\text{rhs}_{G_i}(A_l)$ through $\text{rhs}_{G_i}(A_1)$ in postorder induces a total order $<^l_{G_i}$ on the set of nodes $V^l_{G_i} = \bigcup_{j \in [l]} V(\text{rhs}_{G_i}(A_j))$. For $i \in [h]$ and $j \in [l]$, a node in $V(\text{rhs}_{G_i}(A_j))$ is denoted by the address $z = (j, u)$, where u is the path to that node in the tree $\text{rhs}_{G_i}(A_j)$. If z is a node in $V^l_{G_i}$ that is not the root of $\text{rhs}_{G_i}(A_1)$, then $\text{next}(<^l_{G_i}, z)$ is the node following z in the order $<^l_{G_i}$. The starting address z_1 is the left-most leaf of $\text{rhs}_{G_1}(A_l)$ and the final address $z_h = (1, \varepsilon)$ is the root of $\text{rhs}_{G_h}(A_1)$.

A tree pattern can be described by a tree with parameters at leaves (parameters denote connected subtrees that are not part of the pattern). Formally, a *(tree) pattern p (of rank k)* is a tree in which each $y \in Y_k$ occurs exactly once. Given a tree t and a node u of t, the pattern p *matches* t in u if there are trees $t_1, \ldots, t_k$ and a pattern p' isomorphic to p such that $t/u = p'\Theta$ where Θ is the substitution $[y_1 \leftarrow t_1, \ldots, y_k \leftarrow t_k]$. The pair (p', Θ) is called a *match* of p (in t) at u. Given a match m, p_m denotes the corresponding pattern. Two matches (p', Θ'), (p'', Θ''), are *overlapping* if p' and p'' have at least one common node. Two matches $m' = (p', [y_1 \leftarrow t'_1, \ldots, y_k \leftarrow t'_k])$, $m'' = (p'', [y_1 \leftarrow t''_1, \ldots, y_k \leftarrow t''_k])$ of the same pattern p are *maximal* if, for all $i \in [k]$, $t'_i[\varepsilon] \neq t''_i[\varepsilon]$ (intuitively: there is no possibility to extend m', m'' to matches of some larger common pattern). Given a grammar G with nonterminals $A_1, \ldots, A_h$ and $j \in [h]$, a pattern p *matches G in $z = (j, u)$* if p matches $\text{rhs}_G(A_j)$ in u; if $m = (p', \Theta)$ is the match of p in $z = (j, u)$, then z is the address of m in G.

The replacement of patterns is defined as follows. Let G be an SLT grammar, p a pattern of rank k with a corresponding production $A(y_1, \ldots, y_k) \to p$ in G, and $m = (p', [y_1 \leftarrow t_1, \ldots, y_k \leftarrow t_k])$ a match of p in the right-hand side of some other production of G. The match m is replaced by A by replacing the subtree rooted at the root of p' and with the tree $A(t_1, \ldots, t_k)$. The resulting grammar is denoted by $G[m \leftarrow A]$. Similarly, for two non-overlapping matches m_1, m_2 of p in G, $G[m_1, m_2 \leftarrow A]$ is the grammar obtained from G by replacing each match m_1 and m_2 by A.

We now discuss how the size of an SLT grammar changes when occurrences of a tree pattern are replaced by a nonterminal that generates the pattern. The *size of a tree* (without parameters) is its *number of edges*. Since the SLT grammars that are generated by BPLEX have the property that all k parameters of a nonterminal appear exactly once in the right-hand side of its rule, and in the order $y_1, y_2, \ldots, y_k$, we do not need to explicitly represent the parameters as nodes of the tree. Hence, we do not count the edges to parameters; thus in general, for a tree t, size(t) is defined as $|E(t)| - |E_y(t)|$ where $E_y(t)$ are the edges to parameters in t. For a tree grammar G, size(G) is the sum of sizes of the right-hand sides of the productions of G. Clearly, size$(G) -$ size$(G[m \leftarrow A])$ $=$ size(p) and size$(G) -$ size$(G[m_1, m_2 \leftarrow A]) = 2 \times$ size(p). If prod is not in G already then the size of the grammar add(G, prod) obtained by adding prod to G is size$(G) +$ size$(\text{rhs}(\text{prod}))$.

Let us turn our attention to the computation of pattern sets. At stage i, BPLEX computes the set RepM(G_i, z_i, K_N) of all matches in z_i of patterns that are isomorphic to some right-hand side rhs$_{G_i}(A_j)$ for $l < j \leq l_i, l_i - j < K_N$. This computation considers at most K_N productions of index greater than l. Note that one can check whether $p = \text{rhs}_{G_i}(A_j)$ matches G_i in z_i in at most size$(p) \leq K_S$ steps by comparing the two trees top-down and binding parameters of p to descendants of z_i. The total cost of computing RepM(G_i, z_i, K_N) is bounded by $K_N \times K_S$ because (see below) a production with index $j > l$ has size at most K_S.

BPLEX also computes the set NewM$(G_i, z_i, K_N, K_S, K_R)$ of all matches in z_i such that, for each $m \in$ NewM$(G_i, z_i, K_N, K_S, K_R)$, we have

- there exists a (non-overlapping) *companion match* c_m of the same pattern in some node w among the last K_N nodes preceding z_i in the order $<^l_{G_i}$;
- $0 <$ size$(p_m) \leq K_S$ and, if size$(p_m) < K_S$, then either (1) m and c_m are maximal, or (2) m and c_m can only be extended to larger matches that overlap;
- the rank of p_m is at most K_R.

The set NewM$(G_i, z_i, K_N, K_S, K_R)$ can be computed by comparing top-down the tree rooted at z_i with trees rooted at nodes preceding z_i. Since the computation stops whenever it encounters a pattern that is larger than K_S, the cost of computing NewM$(G_i, z_i,$ $K_N, K_S, K_R)$ is bounded by $K_N \times K_S$.

BPLEX chooses a match $m \in$ RepM$(G_i, z_i, K_N) \cup$ NewM$(G_i, z_i, K_N, K_S, K_R)$ with maximal size, denoted by max$(\text{repM}, \text{newM})$. If $m \in$ RepM(G_i, z_i, K_N), then the match is replaced by the right-hand side of the corresponding production. If $m \in$ NewM$(G_i, z_i, K_N, K_S, K_R)$, BPLEX adds a production $A \rightarrow p_m$ to the grammar, with $A =$ fresh$(G_i, \text{rank}(p_m))$, and replaces the matches m, c_m by A. In both cases, the size of the grammar is reduced by size(p_m). If no matches are found, BPLEX tries to move the address z_i to the next node with respect to the order $<^l_{G_i}$. The linearity of BPLEX derives from the fact that, for an input grammar G, the loop cannot be executed more than $2 \times |G|$ times (each run through the loop either moves the address forward or reduces the size of the grammar), and from the fact that the sets RepM(G_i, z_i, K_N) and NewM$(G_i, z_i, K_N, K_S, K_R)$ can be computed in constant time. Note that each nonterminal in the output grammar has rank at most K_R (see also Section 6). Finally, note that the indices of nonterminals in the generated grammars do not reflect the SL order; in the examples we have renamed nonterminals to indicate an SL order.

We now illustrate the computation of BPLEX on the regular tree grammar on the left of Fig. 1. BPLEX does not perform any sharing in the third and second production;

$$S \quad \rightarrow E(E(C)) \qquad C \rightarrow c(A, A)$$
$$E(y_1) \rightarrow c(C, D(y_1)) \qquad A \rightarrow a$$
$$D(y_1) \rightarrow d(C, y_1)$$

Fig. 3. Cf tree grammar generating $\{c(c(a, a), d(c(a, a), c(c(a, a), d(c(a, a), c(a, a)))))\}$

it then scans the first production. When the highest d is encountered (address $(1, 2)$) a match m of pattern $d(C, y_1)$ is found, together with a companion c_m matching in $(1, 2.2.2)$. This has size 1 and is chosen for replacement. The new nonterminal D of rank 1 is added to the grammar together with production $D(y_1)$ $\rightarrow d(C, y_1)$, and the two matches are replaced so that the first production becomes $S \rightarrow c(C, D(c(C, D(C))))$. The new pattern $\mathrm{rhs}(D)$ does not match the new grammar in $z = (1, 2)$ and no pairs of new matches are found either. Therefore z is changed to the root of the S production ($z = (1, \varepsilon)$). Here, the right-hand side of D does not match, while the maximal pattern $c(C, D(y_1))$ matches in $(1, \varepsilon)$ and in $(1, 2.1)$. Therefore a new nonterminal E of rank 1 is added together with the production $E(y_1) \rightarrow c(C, D(y_1))$, and the matches are replaced by E, producing the output grammar shown in Fig. 3. Both this grammar and the cf tree grammar on the right of Fig. 1 have size 7. Note that BPLEX has not detected pattern $p = c(C, d(C, y_1))$ appearing in Fig. 1, because the smaller pattern $d(C, y_1)$ is replaced before p has been scanned completely.

4   XML Compression Using BPLEX

In this section we explain how BPLEX can be used to generate a small representation of the tree structure of an XML document. This tree structure can be conveniently modeled as unranked or binary tree. While BPLEX performs (almost) equally well in both models, this is *not* the case for the minimal DAG.

An XML document is a sequential representation of a nested list structure. As mentioned in the Introduction, there are different data models for XML, which vary in their sizes. For example, DOM trees contain bidirectional pointers between a node and its children, its parent node, and its direct left and right sibling; the resulting size is approximately 4-5 times more than the size of the original XML document. Another data model are (ordered) unranked trees which are like DOM trees, but without pointers between siblings. As an example, consider the following XML document skeleton (i.e., without data values).

```
<agenda>
    <person><name/><street/></person>      ⎫
    ...                                      ⎬ 5 times
    <person><name/><street/></person>      ⎭
</agenda>
```

An (ordered) unranked tree representation of this XML document consists of a root node labeled agenda which has associated with it an array of five pointers, each to a node labeled person which in turn has an array of two pointers to nodes labeled name and street, respectively. For each pointer to a child node we can additionally also keep the inverse pointer from the child to its parent node. This doubles the number of pointers in the representation. Our investigations are independent of this choice: we always count in number of edges (these numbers have to be multiplied by the implementation cost of an edge, which possibly involves the cost of two pointers). The size of the unranked tree representation of the above XML document is 15 edges.

$$\text{agenda}^1$$
$$|$$

agenda[1]				

person $-$ person $-$ person $-$ person $-$ person^1

name^2 name^2 name^2 name^2 name^2

street^0 street^0 street^0 street^0 street^0

Fig. 4. Binary tree representation of an unranked tree

The BPLEX algorithm works on (ranked) trees; it is well-known that every unranked tree can be turned into a binary ranked tree without changing the number of edges: delete all edges to non-first children, and add a (second child) edge from any node to its next sibling. Note that a leaf (resp. the last sibling) in the unranked tree has no left (resp. no right) child edge in the binary tree representation; this is denoted by the superscript 2 (resp. 1), and by 0 for a last sibling leaf. In Fig. 4 the binary representation of the unranked tree for the XML document above is shown (with second child edges of person-nodes drawn horizontally). As before, we first turn a (ranked) tree into its minimal DAG, represented as a regular tree grammar, and then apply BPLEX to the grammar. In our example, the corresponding regular tree grammar has the three productions $S \rightarrow \text{agenda}^1(\text{person}(A, \text{person}(A, \text{person}(A, \text{person}(A, \text{person}^1(A))))))$, $A \rightarrow \text{name}^2(B)$, $B \rightarrow \text{street}^0$ and its size is 11. Consider the S-production of this grammar. Its right-hand side contains four occurrences of the pattern $p = \text{person}(A, y_1)$. Thus, given a production $C(y_1) \rightarrow \text{person}(A, y_1)$, each of the occurrences can be replaced by the nonterminal C. However, there is one further occurrence of a similar pattern $p' = \text{person}^1(A)$, which can be obtained by removing the parameter y_1 from the pattern p. Note that, since A is a first child in p, removing y_1 changes person into person^1. In general, we allow a nonterminal K of rank m to appear with any rank $0 \leq r \leq m$ in the right-hand sides of productions, provided it is indicated which parameters are to be deleted; in the implementation, missing parameters are marked by a special "empty tree marker". With this "overloading" semantics of productions in mind, BPLEX turns the above regular tree grammar into:

$$
\begin{aligned}
S &\rightarrow \text{agenda}^1(C(D(D))) & A &\rightarrow \text{name}^2(B) \\
D(y_1) &\rightarrow C(C(y_1)) & B &\rightarrow \text{street}^0 \\
C(y_1) &\rightarrow \text{person}(A, y_1)
\end{aligned}
$$

In this grammar, the D-production generates copies along a path of the binary tree. Repeated applications of such copying productions cause exponential size increase. In this way, the size of the input grammar can, in certain cases, be reduced exponentially. Consider our example, but now with 10000 person entries (thus, a binary tree with

30000 edges). The corresponding minimal regular tree grammar G_{10000} has size 20001 while BPLEX outputs the following grammar of size 20:

$$
\begin{aligned}
S &\rightarrow \text{agenda}^1(A_8(A_5(A_4(A_3(A_1(A_1)))))) \\
A_1(y_1) &\rightarrow A_2(A_2(y_1)) \\
A_2(y_1) &\rightarrow A_3(A_3(y_1)) \\
&\ \ \vdots \\
A_{12}(y_1) &\rightarrow A_{13}(A_{13}(y_1)) \\
A_{13}(y_1) &\rightarrow \text{person}(A_{14}, y_1) \\
A_{14} &\rightarrow \text{name}^2(A_{15}) \\
A_{15} &\rightarrow \text{street}^0
\end{aligned}
$$

In this grammar, the symbol A_{13} generates the tree $\text{person}(\text{name}(\text{street}, y_1))$. More generally, for $j = 1, \ldots, 13$, A_j generates a chain with 2^{13-j} occurrences of this pattern and one parameter y_1 at the end of the chain. It is easy to see that S generates the correct tree with 10000 person entries.

Unranked DAGs with Multiplicities. Before presenting experimental results with BPLEX, we discuss its relation to another tree compression method that has been applied to XML. Recall that we applied BPLEX to the minimal regular tree grammar of a binary tree representation of an unranked tree. An unranked tree has itself a unique minimal DAG (minimal regular tree grammar) which can be obtained in the same way as for ranked trees. However, the size of the minimal DAG of an unranked tree can be different from the one of the minimal DAG of its binary representation! In most cases the minimal unranked DAG is smaller than the binary one. The reason is that chains of second child edges in the binary tree become sibling subtrees in the unranked tree. To see this, consider the binary tree in Fig 4. Clearly, its minimal DAG has only one copy of the subtree $\text{name}^2(\text{street})$ and hence has only 11 edges. On the other hand, the minimal DAG of the corresponding unranked tree has only one copy of the subtree $\text{person}(\text{name}, \text{street})$ and therefore has only 7 edges. As an example of a binary tree with a minimal DAG that is smaller than the one of the corresponding unranked tree, consider the unranked tree $t_u = u(p(x, b, c, b, c), p(y, b, c, b, c), p(z, b, c, b, c))$. Its minimal unranked DAG has 18 edges, but the minimal binary DAG has only 12, because only one copy of the subtree $b^2(c^2(b^2(c^0)))$ appears.

In fact, the size of the minimal DAG representation can even be further reduced by using "multiplicity" counters for consecutive equal subtrees [3]. Then the DAG for the unranked tree of the agenda-example can be represented using only 3 edges, or equivalently, by an (unranked) regular tree grammar with multiplicity counters and productions

$$A \rightarrow \text{agenda}([5]P), \quad P \rightarrow \text{person}(\text{name}, \text{street}).$$

Of course, multiplicity counters take up space, but following Koch et al. this space is neglected (similar to the fact that we do not count edges to parameters in cf tree grammars, see Section 3). Thus, BPLEX produces the grammar dsiplayed on the previous page, which is smaller (size 6) than the minimal DAG of the unranked tree (size 7), but such a minimal DAG has a smaller representation (size 3) when multiplicity counters are added. From now on, we call this DAG representation for an unranked tree its mDAG (minimal DAG with multiplicities). Such representation can easily be turned into a regular tree grammar with the *same size* that generates the binary representation of the original unranked tree. This grammar also contains multiplicity counters at nodes, which are expanded to chains of nodes. We implemented a version of BPLEX which works on such grammars (and does not change the multiplicity counters). As it turns out, only in a few cases we obtained small improvements over BPLEX on the binary regular tree grammar corresponding to the minimal DAG. Thus, the advantage of counters is compensated for, by the ability of BPLEX to exponentially compress chains of nodes. On a few files, the minimal binary DAG was even smaller than the mDAG, due to similar chains as in the tree t_u of above; cf. in Tab. 1 the two catalog files and the file NCBI_gene.chr1.

5 Experimental Results

We implemented BPLEX in C using gcc and the Expat XML parsing library (see http://expat.sourceforge.net/). See http://bplex.sourceforge.net/ for a preliminary version of BPLEX. Our experiments were done on a Pentium 3Ghz running Linux. We tested BPLEX on three different sets of XML documents. The first one contains documents used in [3]: SwissProt (protein data), DBLP (a bibliographic database), Treebank (a linguistic database), and 1998statistics (baseball statistics). The second set contains XML documents generated by XBench [29], and the third contains documents from the Japanese Single Nucleotide Polymorphism database (see http://snp.ims.u-tokyo.ac.jp).

Table 1 shows for each document the size of its tree structure (in number of edges) together with the sizes in three different representations. The minimal unranked DAG (with multiplicities) is consistently smaller than the minimal binary DAG. The smallest sizes are generated by BPLEX, ranging between 0.1% and 21% of the original tree structure; they were obtained by running BPLEX with large input parameters (window

Table 1. BPLEX in highest compression mode. All sizes are in number of edges.

input file	size of tree in #edges	min. binary DAG size		min. unranked mDAG size		BPLEX output size	
SwissProt (457,4 MB)	10,903,568	1,437,445	13.2%	1,100,648	10.1%	311,328	2.9%
DBLP (103.6 MB)	2,611,931	533,183	20.4%	222,754	8.5%	115,902	4.4%
Treebank (55.8 MB)	2,447,727	1,454,494	59.4%	1,301,688	53.2%	519,542	21.2%
1998statistics (657 KB)	28,306	2,403	8.5%	726	2.6%	410	1.4%
catalog-02 (104M)	2,240,231	52,392	2.3%	32,267	1.4%	26,774	1.2%
catalog-01 (11M)	225,194	6,990	3.1%	8,503	2.8%	3,817	1.7%
dictionary-02 (104M)	2,731,764	681,130	24.9%	441,322	16.2%	160,329	5.9%
dictionary-01 (11M)	277,072	77,554	28.0%	46,993	17.0%	20,150	7.3%
JST_snp.chr1 (36M)	655,946	40,663	6.2%	25,047	2.3%	12,858	1.8%
JST_gene.chr1 (11M)	216,401	14,606	6.7%	5,658	2.6%	4,000	1.8%
NCBI_snp.chr1 (190M)	3,642,225	809,394	22.2%	15	<0.1%	59	<0.1%
NCBI_gene.chr1 (24M)	360,350	14,356	4.0%	11,767	3.3%	7,160	2.0%
medline_0378 (123M)	2,790,421	629,853	22.6%	695,505	24.9%	132,733	4.8%

size 30.000, maximal pattern size 20, maximal rank 10). Only late we were informed by the authors of [3] that their DAG compression does not perform well on the medical bibliographies of medline; note, this is the only example in the table for which a binary DAG is slightly smaller than the mDAG. As seen in the last entry of the table, BPLEX performs surprisingly well on medline.

We also implemented a version of BPLEX that runs on unranked trees, instead of binary trees. The results are not shown in the table, because, roughly, they are the same as BPLEX on binary encodings. This means that tree compression by BPLEX is *not* sensible to un-/rankedness of the input. This is interesting, because, as shown in the previous section, this is *not* true for tree compression by DAGs.

Claim. BPLEX is unsensible to unrankedness/bin.-encoding of input.

Performance. Recall from Fig. 2 the three parameters of BPLEX: the window size K_N, the maximal rank K_R of a pattern, and the maximal size K_S of a pattern. Our experiments show that the algorithm performs well with small values of K_R and K_S and that values above 5 and 10 respectively do not increase compression anymore. The main factor for good compression is the window size. BPLEX achieves best compression with a window size of > 100; values above $20,000$ do not change compression. Our current implementation runs slow on large window sizes, requiring several hours to obtain the results shown in Tab. 1. This is mainly due to the way in which matches of patterns are found and recorded; the part of the program should be improved in the future. Interestingly, even with a small window size, BPLEX already compresses considerably better than binary DAGs and unranked mDAGs. If we use $K_N = K_R = K_S = 3$ then all our examples compress in less than one minute; compression rates are SwissProt 4.1%, Treebank 34%, and dictionary-01 12%. It remains to test on a real machine the impact of our compression wrt the total memory consumption for an XML document in main memory.

6 Algorithms on SLT Grammars

SLT grammars are well suited to efficiently represent XML documents. Consider now a grammar in memory which represents a large XML document. How can we process the XML tree, without decompressing the grammar? Any read access like, e.g., reading the label of the root node, or moving along an edge from one node to another, can be realized on the grammar representation with an additional per-step overhead of at most the size h of the grammar [19]. Additionally, a stack of height at most h must be maintained at all times. Thus, the price to be payed for having a small representation that can be accessed without decompression, is a slow down for each read operation. For some special applications, however, it is possible to eliminate the slow-down, or to even achieve speed ups. In this section we investigate such applications.

XML Type Validation. The first application we consider is XML type validation: an XML document represented by an SL cf tree grammar should be validated against an XML type. There are several formalisms for describing XML types, with varying expressiveness, e.g., DTDs, XML Schema, or RELAX NG. All of these can conveniently be modeled by the regular tree languages [23], a classical concept well known from formal language theory [13]. Our first result states that XML type checking can be done in time linear in the size of the grammar G, if the maximal number of parameters m is fixed. The involved constant depends on the size of the XML type definition, and on the maximal number m of parameters of the nonterminals in G; in fact, m appears as an exponent. In BPLEX, m is controlled by the input parameter K_R. Practical experiments show that small values of m already achieve competitive compression ratios; in fact, we observed that for all the files shown in Tab. 1 taking K_R bigger than 10 does not improve the compression anymore. It can therefore be assumed that m is very small with respect to the size of G. As formal model for regular tree languages we use (deterministic bottom-up finite) tree automata. Such an automaton can be defined by a tuple $A = (Q, \Sigma, \{\delta_\sigma\}_{\sigma \in \Sigma}, F)$ where Q is a finite set of states, Σ is a ranked alphabet, $\delta_\sigma : Q^k \to Q$ for $\sigma \in \Sigma$ of rank k, and $F \subseteq Q$ is a set of final states. The transition function δ of A is extended to trees over Σ in the usual way: $\delta(\sigma(t_1, \ldots, t_k)) = \delta_\sigma(\delta(t_1), \ldots, \delta(t_k))$ for $\sigma \in \Sigma$ of rank k and $t_1, \ldots, t_k \in T_\Sigma$. The language accepted by A is $\{s \in T_\Sigma \mid \delta(s) \in F\}$.

Theorem 1. *Given an SL cf tree grammar G and a tree automaton B it can be checked whether $L(G) \cap L(B) = \varnothing$ in worst case time $O(s^m \times |G|)$, where s is the number of states of B and m is the maximal number of parameters of nonterminals of G.*

The proof of Theorem 1 can be found in the Appendix. Note that in [18] it is shown already that the problem of Theorem 1 is PSPACE-complete. The intention of the proof above was to present a more efficient algorithm. Note further that in order to use Theorem 1 in the context of XML types, the corresponding type definition has to first be transformed into a (deterministic bottom-up finite) tree automaton. If the type is given as DTD or as XML Schema, then the transformation into a deterministic tree automaton can be done in time linear in the size of the representation; the reason is that these formalisms are deterministic: there is only one rule per nonterminal, and the regular expressions which are used in right-hand sides are also deterministic (which implies that the corresponding Glushkov automaton is deterministic and can be constructed in time linear in the size of the expression). Hence, the algorithm of the proof of Theorem 1 is highly practical for DTDs and XML Schemas. For RELAX NG (which employs full regular tree languages) it might be less practical, because the size of the corresponding deterministic tree automaton can be exponential in the size of the representation r. However, if the SL cf tree grammar is linear (=SLT, which it is, if it was produced by BPLEX), then Theorem 1 can be extended to the case that the automaton B is nondeterministic: the Ψ_A are now functions from Q^k to 2^Q, where k is the rank of A; they are computed by checking for every state p and states $p_1, \ldots, p_k$ of B whether there is a run on $\text{rhs}(A_n)[y_1 \leftarrow p_1, \ldots, y_k \leftarrow p_k]$ arriving in p. Thus the problem can be solved in time $O(s^{m+1} \times |G|)$.

Equality Test. Consider two SL cf tree grammars G_1 and G_2. Is it possible to test whether both G_1 and G_2 generate the same tree t, without fully uncompressing the grammars, i.e., without deriving the tree t? More precisely, we are interested in the time complexity of testing equivalence of G_1 and G_2.

In the string case, i.e., if G_1, G_2 are SL cf string grammars, then the problem can be solved in polynomial time with respect to the sum of the sizes of G_1 and G_2 [25]. The proof relies on the fact that, for an SL cf string grammar G (in Chomsky nf) of size n, the length of the string derivable from a nonterminal of G is $\leq 2^n$, and therefore can be stored in n bits. Since basic operations (comparing, addition, subtraction, multiplication, etc.) on such numbers work in polynomial time with respect to n, we can compute in polynomial time the length of the word generated by any nonterminal of G. Since in the tree case this property does *not* hold anymore (because the size of t generated by an SL cf tree grammar of size n can be 2^{2^n}) it looks unlikely that the equivalence problem can also be solved by an algorithm running in polynomial time. In fact, we do not know whether such an algorithm exists. The following theorem shows that the problem can be solved using polynomial space, and hence in exponential time. On the other hand, if the grammars G_1, G_2 are linear, then they can be transformed into SL cf string grammars generating a depth-first left-to-right traversal of the corresponding tree; then, the result of [25] can be used to show that in this case testing equivalence can be done in polynomial time. The proof of Theorem 2 can be found in the Appendix.

Theorem 2. *Testing equivalence of two SL cf tree grammars G_1 and G_2 can be done in* PSPACE, *and in polynomial time if G_1 and G_2 are linear.*

7   Related Work

There are succinct pointer-less representations of trees, see, e.g., [14]. In this way, an n-node tree can be represented by $2n + o(n)$ bits, while allowing $O(1)$ time for most read operations on a tree [12]. In the context of XML, pointer-less tree representations can, e.g., be found in XPRESS [22]: label paths in an XML document are encoded by real number intervals following an arithmetic encoding; this allows to run path queries directly on the compressed instance. This method is typically applied directly to XML documents on the file system. While XPRESS has smaller query evaluation times than other systems working on compressed XML files (like, e.g., XGrind [28]), it is unclear how well it compares to other approaches (like ours) when documents are loaded into memory. It is also possible to use strings to represent XML trees in memory [30]; their experiments show that this offers good compression, while still being able to query efficiently the representation. XQueC uses a queriable XML representation that is based on compression of data values [1]. An advanced implementation which basically uses DAG sharing together with compression of data values is presented in [8]; their results are convincing, which strengthens belief in our approach, because replacing DAG sharing by SLT grammars should immediately improve their system.

Consider now the problem of finding the smallest cf string grammar for a given string. This problem is NP-complete and various approximation algorithms have been studied [16]. In particular, the size of the smallest cf grammar is lower bounded by the size of the smallest LZ77 representation of the string (when the size of the sliding window is unbounded) [4, 27]. The question arises whether a similar result holds in the tree case. But for trees it is unclear how an efficient LZ77 representation would look like. The problem is how to specify tree prefixes that have appeared before [7]. In [27] a technique to decrease the size of an SL cf grammar is presented; the idea is to change the grammar in such a way that its derivation trees become balanced trees, in the sense of AVL trees. This technique gives good compression ratios, when applied to an SL cf grammar obtained from the minimal LZ77 representation of the string. Even though there is no obvious way to extend LZ77 to trees, it might be possible to apply the technique of [27] to SL cf tree grammars. Another variation of Lempel-Ziv compression, known as LZ78, can more readily be extended to trees. For LZ78 on strings, new patterns are composed by adding a letter to already existing patterns. A pattern is specified as a pair (i, a) where i is the index of a previous pattern and a is a letter; the case $i = 0$ represents the one-letter pattern a. In this scheme the string $abbbaabbabbb$ is compressed to $(0, a)(0, b)(2, b)(1, a)(3, a)(3, b)$. Thus, the pair $(2, b)$ is the concatenation bb of b (the second pattern) and b, and similarly $(3, a)$ represents bba. The LZ78 encoding has a natural interpretation as an SL cf string grammar (see e.g. [16]). LZ78 can be extended to trees by using a dictionary of tree patterns where, during a top-down scan of the input tree, new patterns are obtained from existing ones by appending subpatterns at parameter positions; in the simplest case, only a one-node subpattern is appended. Such a technique is presented in [5]; other variations, each using a different method for extending the patterns, are presented in [6]. In [5] no experimental results are provided. In [6] the proposed algorithms are applied to term compression, and the best performance is a size reduction to about 50% of the original. It remains to be investigated how these techniques perform on XML documents.

In [10] it was shown that evaluation of Core XPath queries on DAGs is PSPACE complete. Recently we have shown that this result can be extended to linear SL cf tree grammars; this means that, while achieving better compression than DAGs by using BPLEX, the complexity of evaluating a Core XPath still remains the same for outputs of BPLEX as it is for DAGs.

8 Conclusions and Future Work

1A linear time algorithm was presented that transforms a given tree into a small SLT grammar. The algorithm can be used to "compress" the tree structure of an XML document into a highly efficient memory representation. The representation preserves the basic tree operations and can be accessed via DOM (using an appropriate proxy). On average, the size of a compressed instance is one half of the size of the minimal unique DAG of the tree, which in turn is about 1/10 of the size of the original tree [3]. Some problems can, under certain conditions, even be solved more efficiently on the compressed instances than on conventional tree presentations; in particular we considered (1) validation against XML types and (2) testing equality of documents. In [18] we considered XQuery evaluation. It remains to implement these ideas and test how well they behave on practical queries. To further increase memory efficiency, our representation could be combined with a (mild) compression of data values (e.g., similar to the one of [1]). It is also possible to directly keep results of queries in compressed format; this idea has been considered for DAG compression and a fragment of XQuery [2]. It also has been considered for compression by SLT grammars, and macro tree transducers as query formalism [19]. It is not difficult to change BPLEX to take arbitrary SL cf tree grammars as input; in this way it might be possible to achieve further compression by running BPLEX on its on output.

Several recent programming languages allow to process XML documents via pattern matching constructs. Such constructs are compiled into automata which carry out the matching in the document. It seems straightforward to extend this compilation to automata which directly work on SLT grammars. In this way an efficient XML query evaluator is obtained because XQueries and XSLTs can be translated to pattern matching statements. In this context, other optimization might become important (e.g. lazy sequences [11]).

We would like to test how our technique can be used for XML file compression. Maybe the performance of existing compressors, like XMill, can be further improved by using BPLEX for the compression of tree structure.

References

1. A. Arion, A. Bonifati, G. Costa, S. D'Aguanno, I. Manolescu, and A. Pugliese. XQueC: Pushing queries to compressed XML data. In *Proc. VLDB*, pages 1065–1068, 2003.
2. P. Buneman, B. Choi, W. Fan, R. Hutchison, R. Mann, and S. Viglas. Vectorizing and querying large XML repositories. To appear in *Proc. ICDE*, 2005.
3. P. Buneman, M. Grohe, and C. Koch. Path queries on compressed XML. In *Proc. VLDB*, pages 141–152, 2003.
4. M. Charikar et.al. Approximating the smallest grammar: Kolmogorov complexity in natural models. In *Proc. STOC'02*, pages 792–801. ACM Press, 2002.
5. S. Chen and J. H. Reif. Efficient lossless compression of trees and graphs. In *Proc. DCC'96*, page 428. IEEE Computer Society Press, 1996.
6. J. R. Cheney. First-order term compression: techniques and applications. Master's thesis, Carnegie Mellon University, August 1998.
7. J. R. Cheney. Personal communication. 2004.
8. J. Cheng and W. Ng. XQzip: Querying compressed xml using structural indexing. In *Proc. EDBT*, pages 219–236, 2004.
9. M. F. Fernandez, J. Siméon, B. Choi, A. Marian, and G. Sur. Implementing xquery 1.0: The galax experience. In *Proc. VLDB*, pages 1077–1080, 2003.
10. M. Frick, M. Grohe, and C. Koch. Query evaluation on compressed trees (extended abstract). In *Proc. LICS*, pages 188–197. IEEE, 2003.
11. V. Gapeyev, M. Y. Levin, B. C. Pierce, and A. Schmitt. XML goes native: Run-time representations for Xtatic. To appear in *Proc. CC.*, 2005.
12. R. F. Geary, R. Raman, and V. Raman. Succinct ordinal trees with level-ancestor queries. In *Proc. SODA*, pages 1–10, 2004.
13. F. Gécseg and M. Steinby. Tree languages. In *Handbook of Formal Languages, Volume 3*, chapter 1. Springer-Verlag, 1997.
14. J. Katajainen and E. Mäkinen. Tree compression and optimization with applications. *Intern. J. of Foundations of Comput. Sci.*, 1:425–447, 1990.
15. J. Lamping. An algorithm for optimal lambda calculus reductions. In *Proc. POPL'1990*, pages 16–30. ACM Press, 1990.
16. E. Lehman and A. Shelat. Approximation algorithms for grammar-based compression. In *Proc. SODA*, pages 205–212. SIAM Press, 2002.
17. H. Liefke and D. Suciu. XMill: An efficient compressor for XML data. In W. Chen et. al., editor, *Proc. SIGMOD*, pages 153–164. ACM, 2000.
18. M. Lohrey and S. Maneth. Tree automata on compressed trees. Submitted manuscript, 2005.
19. S. Maneth and G. Busatto. Tree transducers and tree compressions. In *Proc. FOSSACS'04*, volume 2987 of *LNCS*, pages 363–377. Springer-Verlag, 2004.

20. D. Megginson. *Imperfect XML: Rants, Raves, Tips, and Tricks ... from an Insider*. Addison-Wesley, 2004.
21. T. Milo, D. Suciu, and V. Vianu. Typechecking for XML transformers. *J. Comp. Syst. Sci.*, 66:66–97, 2003.
22. J. Min, M. Park, and C. Chung. XPRESS: A queriable compression for XML data. In *Proc. SIGMOD*, pages 122–133. ACM Press, 2003.
23. M. Murata, D. Lee, and M. Mani. Taxonomy of XML schema languages using formal language theory. In *Proc. Extreme Markup Languages*, 2000.
24. Christos H. Papadimitriou. *Computational Complexity*. Addison-Wesley, New York, 1994.
25. W. Plandowski. Testing equivalence of morphisms on context-free languages. In *Proc. ESA'94*, volume 855 of *LNCS*, pages 460–470. Springer-Verlag, 1994.
26. W. Rytter. Algorithms on compressed strings and arrays. In *Proc. SOFSEM 1999*, volume 1725 of *LNCS*, pages 48–65. Springer-Verlag, 1999.
27. W. Rytter. Application of Lempel-Ziv factorization to the approximation of grammar-based compression. *Theoret. Comput. Sci.*, 302:211–222, 2002.
28. P. M. Tolani and J. R. Hartisa. XGRIND: A query-friendly XML compressor. In *Proc. ICDE 2002*, pages 225–234. IEEE Computer Society, 2002.
29. B. B. Yao, M. T. Özsu, and N. Khandelwal. XBench benchmark and performance testing of XML DBMSs. In *Proc. ECDE 2004*, pages 621–633. IEEE Computer Society, 2004.
30. N. Zhang, V. Kacholia, and M. T. Özsu. A succinct physical storage scheme for efficient evaluation of path queries in XML. In *Proc. ICDE*, pages 54–65, 2004.

Appendix

Proof of Theorem 1. Let $G = (N, \Sigma, \text{rhs})$ with $N = \{A_1, \ldots, A_n\}$ and $B = (Q, \Sigma, \delta, F)$. We assume that G is reduced, i.e., each nonterminal is used in a (successful) derivation of G. We now run the tree automaton B on the right-hand sides of G. If we do this bottom-up, starting with the right-hand side $\text{rhs}(A_n)$, then for the parameters in $\text{rhs}(A_n)$ we have to try all possibilities of states, obtaining a finite function Ψ_{A_n} from Q^k to Q, where k is the rank of A_n. This function is now used as transition for A_n, when running B on right-hand sides $\text{rhs}(A_m)$ with $m < n$. In this way, for each nonterminal of rank k, $|Q|^k$ many values of Ψ are computed. Hence, in total at most $s^m \times |G|$ computations steps are needed.

This number can be greatly decreased by going *top-down* in a 'lazy' manner through G, starting with $\text{rhs}(A_1)$. Note though, that the price for the improvement is the necessity to maintain recursive calls. Consider the run of B on $\text{rhs}(A_1)$. If B arrives at a nonterminal A_i $(i > 1)$ of rank k, in states $q_1, \ldots, q_k$, then we issue a recursive call to compute $\Psi_{A_i}(q_1, \ldots, q_l)$. Such a call means to substitute q_j for y_j, $1 \leq j \leq k$ in $\text{rhs}(A_i)$ and then to run B on this tree. During the run further recursive calls may be generated. Clearly, in the worst case again at most $s^m \times |G|$ computations are needed. On average, however, the top-down procedure is far more efficient than the above bottom-up algorithm. □

Proof of Theorem 2. Let $G_1 = (\{A_1, \ldots, A_m\}, \Sigma, \text{rhs}_1)$ and $G_2 = (\{B_1, \ldots, B_n\}, \Sigma, \text{rhs}_2)$ be SL cf tree grammars. By Savitch's Theorem (see, e.g., [24]) and the complement closure of PSPACE, it suffices to give a nondeterministic algorithm that tests *in*equivalence. Roughly speaking, the algorithm guesses corresponding paths in the

DAGS d_1 and d_2, generated by G_1 and G_2 respectively, and accepts if the labels of the corresponding nodes are different. The DAG d_i (for $i = 1, 2$) is obtained from G_i by identifying all nodes in a right-hand side that are labeled with the same parameter. The key issue is now that a node in d_i can be represented in polynomial space w.r.t. the size of G_i. This representation is discussed in the end of [19]. It consists of a sequence $(i_1, u_1), (i_2, u_2) \ldots, (i_p, u_p)$ where $i_1 = 1$, $i_1 < \cdots < i_p$ are indices in $\{1, \ldots, m\}$, and for $1 \leq \nu < p$, u_ν is a node in $\mathrm{rhs}_1(A_{i_\nu})$ with label $A_{i_{\nu+1}}$; moreover $\mathrm{rhs}_1(A_{i_p})[u_p] \in \Sigma$. The first pair $(1, u_1)$ denotes that we start a derivation of G_1 with the right-hand side of A_1 and node u_1 marked; the next pair (i_2, u_2) means u_1 is labeled A_{i_2} and that we apply its production with u_2 marked, etc. Since u_p is terminal, the sequence represents a derivation of a node of d_1. Given such a sequence h representing a node u of d_1 it is straightforward to construct a sequence h' representing the i-th child ui of u in d_1 [19]. Note that any such sequence has length $< n$. The algorithm starts with two empty sequences. It then generates the sequences h_1, h_2 representing the root nodes of d_1, d_2, respectively. If their labels are different we accept. Otherwise, we guess a child number i and move down to the i-th child, resulting in h_1', h_2'. If the corresponding labels are different we accept, etc. If there is no child number (we are at a leaf) we reject.

Now let G_1, G_2 be linear. This means that for any nonterminal A of G_1, G_2, of rank k, the tree $A(y_1, \ldots, y_k)$ derives to a tree t over $\Sigma \cup Y_k$ in which y_j occurs at most once, $1 \leq j \leq k$. In fact, it is straightforward to change the grammars in such a way that (1) every y_j occurs exactly once in t and (2) the order of the parameters in t (going depth-first left-to-right) is $y_1, \ldots, y_k$. The idea is now to construct cf string grammars H_1, H_2 which generate depth-first left-to-right traversals of t_1 and t_2, respectively. Let $i \in \{1, 2\}$. For every nonterminal X of G_i of rank $k > 0$ let $X_{0,1}, X_{1,2}, \ldots, X_{k-1,k}, X_{k,0}$ be new nonterminals of H_i, and for every $\sigma \in \Sigma$ of rank $k > 0$ let $\sigma_{0,1}, \sigma_{1,2}, \ldots, \sigma_{k-1,k}, \sigma_{k,0}$ be new terminals of H_i. Nonterminals and terminals of rank zero are taken over to H_i. The right-hand side of the nonterminal $A_{0,1}$ is the traversal starting at the root of the right-hand side of A (indicated by the index 0) up to the first parameter y_1 in the right-hand side of A (indicated by the parameter 1); The right-hand side of $A_{\nu,\nu+1}$ is the traversal starting at the parameter y_ν in the right-hand side of A up to the parameter $y_{\nu+1}$. Similarly, a terminal symbol $g_{2,3}$ means that g was entered coming from its second child and was exited by moving to its third child. It should be clear how to construct the productions of H_i. As an example, consider the tree grammar production $A(y_1, y_2, y_3) \rightarrow B(g(y_1, a, b), h(B(y_2, y_3)))$ and the nonterminal $A_{1,2}$ of the constructed string grammar; its production is $A_{1,2} \rightarrow g_{1,2}\, a\, g_{2,3}\, b\, g_{3,0}\, B_{1,2}\, h_{0,1}\, B_{0,1}$. Clearly, $t_1 = t_2$ if and only if the string w_1 generated by H_1 equals w_2 (gen. by H_2). Moreover, H_1, H_2 are SL cf string grammars of polynomial size w.r.t. G_1, G_2, respectively. By the result of [25], testing $w_1 = w_2$ can be done in polynomial time w.r.t. the sizes of H_1, H_2.   □

N-Ary Queries by Tree Automata

Joachim Niehren, Laurent Planque, Jean-Marc Talbot, and Sophie Tison

INRIA Futurs, LIFL, Lille, France
www.grappa.univ-lille3.fr/mostrare

Abstract. We investigate n-ary node selection queries in trees by successful runs of tree automata. We show that run-based n-ary queries capture MSO, contribute algorithms for enumerating answers of n-ary queries, and study the complexity of the problem. We investigate the subclass of run-based n-ary queries by unambiguous tree automata.

Keywords: XML, databases, information extraction, logic, automata, types, pattern.

1 Introduction

Node selection is the most widespread database querying problem in the context of XML. Beside other applications, node selection is basic to XML transformation languages (Query, XSLT, XDuce, CDuce, tree transducer, etc [13, 7, 15]) and of interest for Web information extraction (Lixto, Squirrel, etc [1, 12, 5]).

Monadic node selection queries in trees define sets of nodes, while *n-ary node selection queries* define sets of n-tuples of nodes. Binary queries, for instance, can be used to select all pairs of products and prices in XML or HTML documents created from the database of some company. Monadic queries have attracted most attention so far, in particular those specified in the W3C standard *XPath* that is used by XQuery and XSLT, or similar path based query languages [17]. *Monadic Datalog* yields attractive alternatives for expressing monadic queries, in particular for visual Web information extraction [11]. More general n-ary queries have been promoted by XML programming languages with pattern matching such as XDuce and CDuce [13, 7]. Their *patterns* or *types* with n capture variables specify n-ary node selection queries in trees.

Monadic second-order logic (MSO) is the classical language for defining regular node selection queries in trees [21]. Every formula of MSO with n free node variables specifies an n-ary query. MSO is highly expressive, succinct, and robust under many wishful operations. Its usage, however, remains limited due to its high combined complexity in query answering. *Tree automata* provide an equally expressive alternative, according to Thatcher and Wright's 1968 theorem [21]. They avoid the algorithmic complexity of MSO at the cost of lower succinctness. N-ary queries are seen as languages of trees whose nodes are annotated by bit vectors of length n, which may be recognizable by tree automata or not.

In this paper, we investigate the more recent approach of defining n-ary queries by *successful runs of tree automata* [2, 13, 18, 10, 19]. Successful runs annotate all nodes of a tree by states. Given a *selection set* of n-tuples of states, a successful run selects

G. Bierman and C. Koch (Eds.): DBPL 2005, LNCS 3774, pp. 217–231, 2005.

all those n-tuples of nodes that it annotates in the selection set. We study the two cases of ranked and unranked trees. In the unranked case, essentially the same representation formalism has been proposed previously by Berlea and Seidl [2], called n-ary queries by *forest grammars*. In the ranked case, run-based n-ary queries have been proposed by Hosoya and Pierce [13] in terms of *pattern automata*.

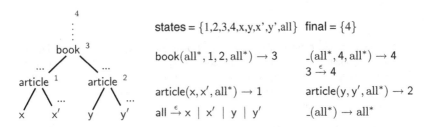

states = {1,2,3,4,x,y,x',y',all} final = {4}

book(all*, 1, 2, all*) → 3   _(all*, 4, all*) → 4
                                  3 $\xrightarrow{\epsilon}$ 4

article(x, x', all*) → 1   article(y, y', all*) → 2

all $\xrightarrow{\epsilon}$ x | x' | y | y'   _(all*) → all*

Fig. 1. Pattern as tree automata; matches correspond to successful runs

N-ary queries by tree pattern are most closely related to run-based queries by tree automata [13]. This is illustrated by the example in Fig. 1. The nodes of the tree pattern on the left become states of the automaton on the right. The root node of the pattern becomes the unique final state. The only selecting n-tuple of automaton states is the n-tuple of capture variables of the pattern. The rules of the automaton express the semantics of the pattern. They can be inferred compositionally. Matches of the pattern correspond to successful runs of the automaton.

In this paper, we prove the folk theorem that run-based n-ary queries capture MSO, to our knowledge for the first time. We then present a deterministic algorithm that can enumerate all answers of an n-ary query by an automaton A with selection set $S \subseteq$ states$(A)^n$ in time $O(|S| * |A| * |t|^n)$. The combined complexity of run-based n-ary queries is thus in deterministic polynomial time for fixed tuple size n. We also prove that this is not the case if we do not bound the tuple size n.

We then investigate the querying power of *unambiguous tree automata*. Unambiguity limits the amount of nondeterminism to at most one successful run per tree, which is more permissive than imposing bottom-up or top-down determinism. Monadic queries by unambiguous tree automata are of particular interest for query induction [5]. They are known to capture the class of monadic MSO-definable queries (since they are the IBAGs of [18]) in contrast to deterministic tree automata.

For the n-ary case, however, we prove that run-based queries by unambiguous automata are strictly less expressive than MSO. They capture only finite unions of Cartesian closed regular queries. This is the class of n-ary queries that can be defined by disjunctions of conjunctions of MSO formulas with one free variable each. We can compute representations of all query answers in time $O(n * |S| * |A| * |t|)$. Emptiness is thereby decidable in polynomial time even for unbounded tuple size n. Finally, we show that it is decidable whether an MSO defined query belongs to that restricted class. We reduce this problem to testing the boundedness of the degree of ambiguity of tree automata [20].

2   MSO Definable and Regular Queries

We develop our theory of *n-ary queries for binary trees* which will be sufficient to deal with unranked trees (see Section 6). This section starts with Thatcher and Wright's theorem [21], slightly reformulated in terms of querying rather than recognition.

Let Σ be a finite signature of binary function symbols f and constants a. A *binary tree* $t \in T_\Sigma$ is a ground term over Σ. A *node* π of a tree t is a word in $\{1, 2\}^*$ that is the relative address of some subtree starting from the root. We write nodes(t) for the set of nodes of t. The empty word ϵ is the root of t. We write $\pi \cdot \pi'$ for the concatenation of the words π and π'. The node $\pi \cdot 1$ of a tree t is the *first child* of the node π in t, while $\pi \cdot 2$ is its *second child*. A node is a *leaf* if it has no child, otherwise it is an *inner node*. We will freely identify trees t over Σ with *labeling functions* of type $t : \text{nodes}(t) \to \Sigma$, such that for all $a, f \in \Sigma, t_1, t_2 \in T_\Sigma$, and $i \cdot \pi \in \{1, 2\}^*$ (where i is the word 1 or 2):

$$a(\epsilon) = a, \qquad f(t_1, t_2)(\epsilon) = f, \qquad f(t_1, t_2)(i \cdot \pi) = t_i(\pi) \quad \text{if } \pi \in \text{nodes}(t_i)$$

Definition 1. *Let* $n \in \mathbb{N}$. *An n-ary query in binary trees over* Σ *is a function* q *that maps trees* $t \in T_\Sigma$ *to sets of n-tuples of nodes, such that* $\forall t \in T_\Sigma : q(t) \subseteq \text{nodes}(t)^n$.

Simple examples for monadic queries in binary trees over Σ are the functions leaf and root that map trees t to the sets of their leaves resp. to the singleton $\{\epsilon\}$. The binary query first_child relates nodes π to their first child $\pi \cdot 1$ if it exists, while the query next_sibl relates first children $\pi \cdot 1$ to their next sibling to the right $\pi \cdot 2$. As another example, we can query for all pairs (π, π') in trees t such that the subtrees of t on below of π and π' are equal in structure. This last query can indeed be expressed by RAG's [18] but cannot be defined in MSO.

In MSO, binary trees $t \in T_\Sigma$ are seen as *logical structures*, whose domain is the set nodes(t). Its signature consists of the binary relation symbols first_child and next_sibl and the monadic relation symbols label$_c$ for all $c \in \Sigma$. These symbols are interpreted by the corresponding node relations of t.

$$\begin{aligned} \text{first\_child}^t &= \{(\pi, \pi \cdot 1) \mid \pi \cdot 1 \in \text{nodes}(t)\} & \text{label}_c^t &= \{\pi \mid t(\pi) = c\} \\ \text{next\_sibl}^t &= \{(\pi \cdot 1, \pi \cdot 2) \mid \pi \cdot 1 \in \text{nodes}(t)\} \end{aligned}$$

Let x, y, z range over an infinite set of first-order variables and p over an infinite set of monadic second-order variables. Formulas ϕ of MSO have the following abstract syntax, where $c \in \Sigma$:

$$\phi ::= p(x) \mid \text{first\_child}(x, y) \mid \text{next\_sibl}(x, y) \mid \text{label}_c(x) \mid \neg\phi \mid \phi_1 \wedge \phi_2 \mid \forall x.\phi \mid \forall p.\phi$$

A variable assignment α into a tree t maps first-order variables to nodes of t and second-order variables to sets of nodes of t. We define the validity of formulas ϕ in trees t under variable assignments α in the usual Tarskian manner, and write $t, \alpha \models \phi$ in this case. Formulas ϕ with n free first-order variables $x_1, ..., x_n$ define n-ary queries, which satisfy for all $t \in T_\Sigma$:

$$q_{\phi(x_1,...,x_n)}(t) = \{(\alpha(x_1), ..., \alpha(x_n)) \mid t, \alpha \models \phi\}$$

Definition 2. *An n-ary query is* MSO definable *if it is equal to some* $q_{\phi(x_1,...,x_n)}$.

An equivalent way of defining n-ary queries in MSO is by formulas ϕ with n free second-order variables $p_1, ..., p_n$. For all $t \in T_\Sigma$ let:

$$q_{\phi(p_1,...,p_n)}(t) = \bigcup_{t,\alpha \models \phi} \alpha(p_1) \times ... \times \alpha(p_n)$$

Lemma 1. *An n-ary query is* MSO definable iff *it is equal to some* $q_{\phi(p_1,...,p_n)}$.

A *tree automaton* A for binary trees [9] over signature Σ consists of two finite sets final$(A) \subseteq$ states(A) and a set rules(A) with elements of the form $a \rightarrow p$ or $f(p_1, p_2) \rightarrow p$ where $f \in \Sigma$ is a binary function symbol, $a \in \Sigma$ a constant, and $p, p_1, p_2 \in$ states(A).

A *run* r of a tree automaton A on a tree t is a mapping $r :$ nodes$(t) \rightarrow$ states(A) that associates states to nodes of t according to the rules of A. Equivalently, we can see runs as trees labeled in states(A) such that nodes$(r) =$ nodes(t). A run is *successful* if it labels the root of the tree by a final state, *i.e.* if $r(\epsilon) \in$ final(A). We write runs$_A(t)$ for the set of all runs of A on t and succ_runs$_A(t)$ for the subset of successful runs. A tree t is *accepted* by a tree automaton A if it permits a successful run by A. The *tree language* $L(A)$ recognized by an automaton A is the set of trees t accepted by A. A tree language is *regular* if it is recognized by some tree automaton.

Queries can be viewed as tree languages. This perspective is close to that of Thatcher and Wright, who view models t, α of MSO formulas as trees t annotated by bit vectors encoding α. Sets of models become languages of annotated trees.

Let $\mathbb{B} = \{0, 1\}$ be the set of Booleans. A Boolean tree β is a binary tree whose nodes are labeled by Booleans (here, Booleans serve both as binary function symbols and as constants). As an auxilary notion for formalising compositions of trees with their annotations, we define products of functions with the same domain. The product of m functions $g_i : C \rightarrow D_i$ is the function $g_1 * ... * g_m : C \rightarrow D_1 \times ... \times D_m$ such that

$$(g_1 * ... * g_m)(c) = (g_1(c), ..., g_m(c)) \qquad \text{for all } c \in C$$

Considering trees as functions, the product $t_1 * ... * t_m$ of m trees with the same domain (but possibly different signatures) is the tree whose labeling function is the product of labeling functions of $t_1, ..., t_n$. A language L of annotated trees over $\Sigma \times \mathbb{B}^n$ corresponds to the following n-ary query:

$$q_L(t) = \{(\pi_1, ..., \pi_n) \mid \exists \beta_1, ..., \beta_n, \ t*\beta_1*...*\beta_n \in L, \ \beta_1(\pi_1) = ... = \beta_n(\pi_n) = 1\}$$

Such languages identify queries uniquely, but conversely, the same query may be represented by many different languages.

Definition 3. *An n-ary query in trees over Σ is* regular iff *it is equal to $q_{L(A)}$ for some tree automaton A over $\Sigma \times \mathbb{B}^n$.*

Theorem 1. *([21]). An n-ary query in trees is* MSO definable iff *it is* regular.

MSO formulas $\phi(p_1, \ldots, p_n)$ define languages of trees over $\Sigma \times \mathbb{B}^n$ representing the query $q_{\phi(p_1,\ldots,p_n)}$. Different formulas may define different languages for the same query. Which formula or language to choose to define n-ary queries will turn out to be crucial for what follows.

Given sets $S' \subseteq S$, we define a characteristic function $c_{S'} : S \rightarrow \mathbb{B}$ so that $c_{S'}(s) \leftrightarrow s \in S'$ for all $s \in S$. Every subset $P \subseteq \mathsf{nodes}(t)$ defines a characteristic function c_P that we identified with the Boolean trees whose labeling function is c_P. This tree has the same nodes as t. Formulas $\phi(p_1, \ldots, p_n)$ define a language of annotated trees over the signature $\Sigma \times \mathbb{B}^n$: $L_{\phi(p_1,\ldots,p_n)} = \{t * c_{\alpha(p_1)} * \ldots * c_{\alpha(p_n)} \mid t, \alpha \models \phi(p_1, \ldots, p_n)\}$.

Lemma 2. *An MSO-formula and the language of annotated trees encoding its models define the same query:* $q_{\phi(p_1,\ldots,p_n)} = q_{L_{\phi(p_1,\ldots,p_n)}}$.

Similarly, we can define $L_{\phi(x_1,\ldots,x_n)}$ by considering all first-order variables x_i as singleton valued second-order variables. We call trees $t * \beta_1 * \ldots * \beta_n \in L_{\phi(x_1,\ldots,x_n)}$ *canonical*, since each of them identifies precisely one tuple of $q_{\phi(x_1,\ldots,x_n)}(t)$, i.e., all sets $\beta_i^{-1}(1)$ are singletons for $1 \leq i \leq n$.

3   Run-Based Queries

Boolean annotations of trees are not necessary to define queries by trees automata. Alternatively, one can use successful runs of tree automata to annotate trees by states, and then select from these state annotations. The idea is that automata states are properties of nodes, which can be verified for nodes by successful runs.

An *existential run-based* n-ary query $q_{A,S}^{\exists}$ in binary trees over Σ is given by a tree automaton A over Σ and a set $S \subseteq \mathsf{states}(A)^n$ of so called *selection tuples*. It selects all those tuples of nodes $(\pi_1, \ldots, \pi_n)$ in a tree t that are assigned to a selection tuple by some successful run of A on t:

$$q_{A,S}^{\exists}(t) = \{(\pi_1, \ldots, \pi_n) \mid \exists r \in \mathsf{succ\_runs}_A(t), (r(\pi_1), \ldots, r(\pi_n)) \in S\}$$

Existential run-based n-ary queries were proposed by Neven and Van den Bussche [18] in the framework of attribute grammars (these can be seen as tree automata whose states are vectors of attribute values). Their BAG's correspond to our monadic case, while their RAG's are more expressive than our n-ary case. Existential run-based n-ary queries in binary trees (with a first match semantics) were proposed by Hosoya and Pierce [13][1]. Seidl and Berlea [2] define run-based n-ary queries for unranked trees (by forest grammars), and present an query answering algorithm for the binary case.

It is known from [18] that monadic existential run-based queries capture the class of monadic MSO definable queries. The analogous result for n-ary existential run-based queries might be expected. It holds indeed as we will prove in Theorem 2.

An example is given in Fig. 2. We consider the binary query that selects pairs of a-leave and next-sibling b-leaves, over the signature $\Sigma = \{f, a, b\}$. We define this query by the automaton A_2 with $\mathsf{states}(A_2) = \{1, 2, *, y\}$ that will produce successful runs

---

[1] They use successful runs implicitly when defining the semantics of their pattern automata. Node selection is defined by pattern variables that are kept distinct from automata states.

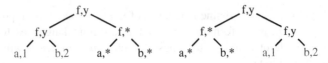

Fig. 2. Selecting pairs of a-leaves and next-sibling b-leaves: $q^{\exists}_{A_2,\{(\mathbf{a},\mathbf{b})\}}$

of the form of Figure 2. The query is represented by $q^{\exists}_{A_2,\{(1,2)\}}$. The automaton A_2 will assign state 1 to selected a-leaves and state 2 to the corresponding next-sibling b-leaves. The final state y will be assigned to all common ancestors of the selected pair of leaves: $\mathrm{final}(A_2) = \{y\}$. State $*$ can be assigned to all other nodes. Every successful run of the automaton A_2 will select a single pair of nodes. The following rules verify these properties:

$$a \to 1 \qquad b \to 2 \qquad f(*,*) \to * \qquad f(1,2) \to y$$
$$a \to * \qquad b \to * \qquad f(y,*) \to y \qquad f(*,y) \to y$$

This example illustrates the trick: different selected tuples are selected in different runs so that their components cannot be mixed up.

Theorem 2. *Existential run-based n-ary queries capture precisely the class of MSO-definable n-ary queries.*

Sketch of proof. On the one hand, we can easily describe successful runs of tree automata in MSO. Existential run-based queries are thus definable in MSO. Let us prove now that every regular query is equal to some existential run-based query. Let $q_{L(A)}$ be a regular n-ary query for some tree automaton A over $\Sigma \times \mathbb{B}^n$. We compute an automaton $\mathrm{proj}(A)$ over Σ by projecting Booleans from the labels into states. Let states $(\mathrm{proj}(A)) = \mathrm{states}(A) \times \mathbb{B}^n$, $\mathrm{final}(\mathrm{proj}(A)) = \mathrm{final}(A) \times \mathbb{B}^n$. The rules of $\mathrm{proj}(A)$ are generated by the following schema for all $a, f \in \Sigma$, $p_1, p_2, p \in \mathrm{states}(A)$ and $b, b_i, b_i^1, b_i^2 \in \mathbb{B}$ where $1 \le i \le n$:

$$\frac{(a, b_1, ..., b_n) \to p \in \mathrm{rules}(A)}{a \to (p, b_1, ..., b_n) \in \mathrm{rules}(\mathrm{proj}(A))}$$

$$\frac{(f, b_1, ..., b_n)(p_1, p_2) \to q \in \mathrm{rules}(A)}{f((p_1, b_1^1, ...b_1^n), (p_2, b_2^1, ..., b_2^n)) \to (p, b_1, ..., b_n) \in \mathrm{rules}(\mathrm{proj}(A))}$$

We define the selection set $S \subseteq \mathrm{states}(\mathrm{proj}(A))^n$ by $S = Q_1 \times ... \times Q_n$ such that for all $1 \le i \le n$: $Q_i = \{(q, b_1, ..., b_n) \in \mathrm{states}(\mathrm{proj}(A)) \mid b_i = 1\}$. It remains to prove that $q_{L(A)} = q^{\exists}_{\mathrm{proj}(A),S}$. This follows from that for any term $t * \beta_1 * ... * \beta_n$ over $\Sigma \times \mathbb{B}^n$: $\mathrm{runs}_{\mathrm{proj}(A)}(t) = \{r * \beta_1 * ... * \beta_n \mid r \in \mathrm{runs}_A(t * \beta_1 * ... * \beta_n)\}$ and $\mathrm{succ\_runs}_{\mathrm{proj}(A)}(t) = \{r * \beta_1 * ... * \beta_n \mid r \in \mathrm{succ\_runs}_A(t * \beta_1 * ... * \beta_n)\}$.

Universal run-based n-ary queries quantify universally rather than existentially over successful runs. Universal n-ary queries were first introduced by Neven and Van den Bussche [18] in the framework of attribute grammars (universal BAGs and RAGs). In the monadic case, they are used by Frick, Grohe, and Koch [10].

$$q^{\forall}_{A,S}(t) = \{(\pi_1, ..., \pi_n) \mid \forall r \in \mathrm{succ\_runs}_A(t), (r(\pi_1), ..., r(\pi_n)) \in S\}$$

Theorem 3. *Existential and universal queries have the same expressiveness.*

This theorem has been proved for the monadic case [18] on basis of the two phase querying answering algorithm, which fails for the n-ary case. As we show here, the theorem generalizes to the n-ary case nevertheless.

Proof. We define the complement q^c of a query q such that for all trees $t \in T_\Sigma$, $q^c(t) = \text{nodes}(t)^n \setminus q(t)$. Existential queries are regular and thus MSO-definable, so their complements are MSO-definable, thus regular, and thus definable by existential run-based queries, too (Theorems 1 and 2). Furthermore, the definitions of existential and universal queries are dual modulo complementation, i.e., for every tree automaton A with selection tuples $S \subseteq \text{states}(A)^n$, $q^\forall_{A,S} = (q^\exists_{A,\text{states}(A)^n \setminus S})^c$.

As complements of existential queries are existential, it follows that universal queries are existential too. Vice versa, let q be an existential query. So q^c is equal to $q^\exists_{A,S}$ for some A, S. Hence, $q = q^\forall_{A,\text{states}(A)^n \setminus S}$, i.e., q can be represented by a universal query.

4   Query Answering

We consider the problems of enumerating all solutions or up to k solutions of run-based queries in a given tree t.

Proposition 1. *We can compute an existential run-based n-ary query $q^\exists_{A,S}(t)$ in deterministic time $O(|S| * |A| * |t|^n)$ and hence in polynomial time for fixed n.*

Proof. The naive algorithm were to guess an n-tuple of nodes and test it for membership to $q^\exists_{A,S}(t)$. By a deterministic algorithm this requires time $O(|S| * |A| * |t|^{n+1})$, so we need less naive algorithm. The idea of our algorithm is to guess a selection tuple $(p_1, \ldots, p_n) \in S$ and a tuple $(\pi_1, \ldots, \pi_{n-1}) \in \text{nodes}(t)^{n-1}$ and to compute the last remaining node by answering a monadic query depending on the previous choices. Let $t^{p_1,\ldots,p_{n-1}}_{\pi_1,\ldots,\pi_{n-1}}$ be the tree over $\Sigma \cup (\Sigma \times \text{states}(A))$ obtained from t by annotating the node labels of π_i by p_i for all $1 \leq i \leq n-1$.

Let $B(A)$ be the tree automaton with signature $\Sigma \cup (\Sigma \times \text{states}(A))$ that operates like A except that maps all annotated nodes to their annotation. We define $\text{states}(B(A))$ as $\text{states}(A)$, $\text{final}(B(A))$ as $\text{final}(A)$ and $\text{rules}(B(A))$ by:

$$\text{rules}(B(A)) = \text{rules}(A) \cup \{(a,p) \to p \mid a \to p \in \text{rules}(A)\}$$
$$\cup \{(f,p)(p_1,p_2) \to p \mid f(p_1,p_2) \to p \in \text{rules}(A)\}$$

We can now compute $q^\exists_{A,S}(t)$ on basis of the following representation:

$$q^\exists_{A,S}(t) = \{(\pi_1, \ldots, \pi_{n-1}, \pi) \mid (p_1, \ldots, p_n) \in S, \ \pi \in q^\exists_{B(A),\{p_n\}}(t^{p_1,\ldots,p_{n-1}}_{\pi_1,\ldots,\pi_{n-1}})\}$$

We have to answer $|S| * |t|^{n-1}$ monadic queries of the form $q^\exists_{B(A),\{p_n\}}(t^{p_1,\ldots,p_{n-1}}_{\pi_1,\ldots,\pi_{n-1}})$ each of which requires linear time $O(|B(A)| * |t|)$. Note that the size of $|B(A)|$ is $2|A|$. Thus, the overall deterministic time complexity is $O(|S| * |A| * |t|^n)$.

The duality of existential and universal queries $q_{A,S}^{\forall} = (q_{A,\text{states}(A)^n \setminus S}^{\exists})^c$ yields an analogous polynomial time complexity bound for answering universal n-ary queries $q_{A,S}^{\forall}(t)$ with fixed tuple size n by $O((|\text{states}(A)|^n - |S|) * |A| * |t|^n)$.

Proposition 2. *The emptiness problem of n-ary queries $q_{A,S}^{\exists}(t) = \emptyset$ is NP-complete for unbounded n, i.e., if n belongs to the input of the problem, as well as the automaton A, the selection set $S \subseteq \text{states}(A)$, and the tree t.*

Proof. The problem is clearly in NP: it suffices to guess a labeling of t by states of A and a selection tuple s from S; one can then check in $O(|A| * |t|)$ whether this labeling is a successful run and that each component of s labels at least one node in this run. Now, we give a polynomial reduction of CNF satisfiability into our problem. The idea is to associate with a given CNF formula ϕ a word w (which can be viewed as a unary tree) over the alphabet $\{\mathsf{x}, \mathsf{a}, \mathsf{n}, \mathsf{p}\}$ of the form $\mathsf{x} l_{11} l_{12}...l_{1n}...\mathsf{x} l_{k1} l_{k2}...l_{kn}$, where n is the number of clauses of ϕ and k the number of Boolean variables. A part $\mathsf{x} l_{i1}...l_{in}$ means that the i-th variable appears positively in the j-th clause if $l_{ij} = \mathsf{p}$, negatively if $l_{ij} = \mathsf{n}$ and does not appear if $l_{ij} = \mathsf{a}$. Then, we give the following rules for an automaton A with states $\{0,1\} \cup \{s_i^b, u_i^b \mid b \in \{0,1\}, 1 \le i \le n\}$:

$$
\begin{array}{llll}
\mathsf{x} \to 0 & \mathsf{x} \to 1 & \mathsf{x}(\_) \to 0 & \mathsf{x}(\_) \to 1 \\
\mathsf{a}(b) \to u_1^b & \mathsf{a}(s_j^b) \to u_{j+1}^b & \mathsf{a}(u_j^b) \to u_{j+1}^b & \\
\mathsf{n}(0) \to s_1^0 & \mathsf{n}(s_j^0) \to s_{j+1}^0 & \mathsf{n}(u_j^0) \to s_{j+1}^0 & \\
\mathsf{n}(1) \to u_1^1 & \mathsf{n}(s_j^1) \to u_{j+1}^1 & \mathsf{n}(u_j^1) \to u_{j+1}^1 & \\
\mathsf{p}(0) \to u_1^0 & \mathsf{p}(s_j^0) \to u_{j+1}^0 & \mathsf{p}(u_j^0) \to u_{j+1}^0 & \\
\mathsf{p}(1) \to s_1^1 & \mathsf{p}(s_j^1) \to s_{j+1}^1 & \mathsf{p}(u_j^1) \to s_{j+1}^1 &
\end{array}
$$

where "$\_$" denotes any state, $b \in \{0,1\}$ and $1 \le j \le n$. We accept all runs. Then the selection set is defined as $S_1 \times ... \times S_n$, with $S_i = \{s_i^b \mid 0 \le b \le 1\}$. As the size of the word is $(n+1) * k$ and the size of the automaton is in $O(n)$, the reduction is polynomial. There is a correspondence between runs of the automaton on w and truth assignments, and a run will be selecting iff the corresponding assignment satisfies all the clauses. The idea is to assign true (1) or false (0) value to a variable (represented by the x symbol) and to select all following clauses satisfied by the assignment. For example, if we consider $\psi = (x_1 \vee \neg x_2) \wedge (x_1 \vee x_3) \wedge x_2$, then $\mathsf{x}\,\mathsf{p}\,\mathsf{p}\,\mathsf{a}\,\mathsf{x}\,\mathsf{n}\,\mathsf{a}\,\mathsf{p}\,\mathsf{x}\,\mathsf{a}\,\mathsf{p}\,\mathsf{a}$ is its encoding, and $1\ s_1^1\ s_2^1\ u_3^1\ 1\ u_1^1\ u_2^1\ s_3^1\ 1\ u_1^1\ s_2^1\ u_3^1$ is a run selecting some n-tuples. So, ψ is satisfiable if and only if $q_{A,S}^{\exists}(w) \ne \emptyset$.

5   Queries by Unambiguous Tree Automata

We next study run-based n-ary queries by unambiguous tree automata. This is a subclass of tree automata with a restricted amount of nondeterminism.

A tree automaton A is *(bottom-up) deterministic* if no two of its rules have the same left hand sides. It is *unambiguous* if no tree permits more than one successful run by the automaton. Deterministic tree automata are clearly unambiguous, while unambiguous automata may be nondeterministic; they have multiple runs on the same tree of which at most one is successful.

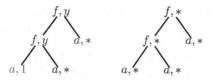

Fig. 3. Selecting left most leaves: $q^{\exists}_{A_3,\{1\}}$. Only the left run of A_3 is successful.

Definition 4. *We call an n-ary query* unambiguous *(resp.* deterministic*) if it has the form* $q^{\exists}_{A,S}$ *for some unambiguous (resp. deterministic) tree automaton A.*

Nondeterministic tree automata can recognize all regular language, but they an not define all MSO-definable queries in run-based fashion. A simple counter example is the monadic query that selects the left-most leaf in binary trees over $\Sigma = \{f,a\}$. It can be defined in run-based fashion as $q^{\exists}_{A_3}, \{1\}$ by automaton A_3 which licences the runs in Fig. 3. Successful runs of A_3 label left most leaves by 1 and all others by $*$. They map ancestors of left most leaves to y and all other inner nodes to $*$. The final states are y and 1. This is done by the following states and rules:

$$\begin{array}{llll} \mathsf{states}(A_3) = \{1,*,y\} & a \to 1 & f(1,*) \to y & f(y,*) \to y \\ \mathsf{final}(A_3) = \{1,y\} & a \to * & f(*,*) \to * & \end{array}$$

Automaton A_3 is not bottom-up deterministic, but unambiguous. Nondeterminism is needed in order to distinguish left most leaves from all others. When processing bottom-up, the automaton has to inspect the context, in order to decide whether a leaf is left-most. So it needs to guess this property for all leaves and then verify the correctness of the guesses later on. Correctness is proved by successful runs.

Proposition 3. *([18, 3]) All monadic MSO-definable queries are unambiguous.*

Proof. We present a sketch of a proof based on Thatcher and Wright's theorem plus projection. Let $\phi(x)$ be MSO formula with one free variable x, which defines a monadic query in binary trees over Σ. We can express the same query by the following MSO formula with one free set variable p:

$$\mathsf{greatest}_\phi(p) = \forall x.p(x) \leftrightarrow \phi(x)$$

This formula requires to collect all possible values for x satisfying ϕ in p, so that p denotes the greatest of set containing nodes selected by $\phi(x)$. By Thatcher and Wright's Theorem 1 there exists a bottom-up deterministic tree automaton A that recognizes the tree language $L_{\mathsf{greatest}_\phi(p)}$, which contains all $\Sigma \times \mathbb{B}$ trees encoding models of $\mathsf{greatest}_\phi(p)$. The projection automaton $\mathsf{proj}(A)$ of A to Σ is unambiguous. To see this, note that the language of A is functional: for every Σ-tree t there exists at most one Boolean tree β such that $t \times \beta \in L(A)$. This holds since the value of β is determined by the result of the query by $\phi(x)$ on t. By determinism of A there is at most one successful run $r \in \mathsf{succ\_runs}_A(t \times \beta)$. Hence, there is at most one successful run $r \times \beta \in \mathsf{succ\_runs}_{\mathsf{proj}(A)}(t)$. Furthermore $q_{L(A)} = q_{\mathsf{proj}(A),\mathsf{states}(A) \times \{1\}}$.

Proposition 4. *Every deterministic monadic MSO defined query can be transformed effectively into a run-based query* $q^\exists_{B,S}$ *by a deterministic automaton B.*

Proof. We proceed as in the proof of Proposition 3. Let A be a deterministic automaton recognizing $L_{\text{greatest}_\phi(p)}$ and $\text{proj}(A)$ is Σ-projection. We know that $\text{proj}(A)$ is unambiguous and that it can express the query by $\phi(x)$. Furthermore, it can be checked that this automaton is deterministic after deleting unproductive states iff the query is deterministic.

5.1   Efficiency and Expressiveness

We call an n-ary query *Cartesian closed* if it is a Cartesian product of monadic queries. If A is unambiguous then we can represent n-ary queries $q^\exists_{A,S}$ as a finite unions of Cartesian closed queries:

$$q^\exists_{A,S} = \bigcup_{(p_1,\ldots,p_n)\in S} q^\exists_{A,\{p_1\}} \times \ldots \times q^\exists_{A,\{p_n\}}$$

This holds, since all components of a tuple will be selected in the same successful run. We can use this representation of the answer set to enumerate answers of unambiguous queries on demand.

Proposition 5. *The emptyness probem* $q^\exists_{A,S}(t) = \emptyset$ *can be solved in time* $O(n * |S| * |A| * |t|)$.

Proof. We compute the above representation of $q^\exists_{A,S}(t)$. For all $(p_1,\ldots,p_n) \in S$ we compute $q^\exists_{A,\{p_i\}}$ and check whether at least one of them is empty. We thus have to compute $O(n * |S|)$ answers to monadic queries each of them in time $O(|A| * |t|)$. Alltogether this requires time $O(n * |S| * |A| * |t|)$.

We can thus decide the emptyness of unambiguous n-ary queries in polynomial time even for unbounded n. This is in contrast to more general run-based n-ary queries by tree automata (Proposition 2).

Theorem 4. *Unambiguous n-ary queries capture the class of finite unions of Cartesian closed regular n-ary queries.*

Proof. We have already seen one direction. Next note that Cartesian closed regular queries are unambiguous. Indeed regular monadic queries are unambiguous by Proposition 3 and Cartesian products of unambiguous queries are clearly unambiguous too. It remains to prove that finite unions of unambiguous queries are unambiguous. Let $q = \cup^k_{j=1} q^\exists_{A_i,S_i}$ be such a union. Let us first assume that all A_i are strictly unambiguous in that they permit precisely one successful run per tree. We then define an unambiguous automaton A as the product of the A_i's such that $\text{final}(A) = \text{final}(A_1) \times \ldots \times \text{final}(A_k)$. Let $\text{proj}_i(p)$ be the $i-$th component of a state p of A. We let the selection set S to be the set of all tuples $(p_1,\ldots,p_n) \in \text{states}(A)^n$ for which there exists $i \in \{1,\ldots,k\}$ such that $(\text{proj}_i(p_1),\ldots,\text{proj}_i(p_n)) \in S_i$. Thus, $q = q^\exists_{A,S}$.

Finally, note that any unambiguous tree automata A_i can be made strictly unambiguous: let $\bar{A}_i$ be the deterministic automaton accepting the trees not accepted by A_i; assuming A_i and $\bar{A}_i$ have disjoint sets of states, we define A_i' as $A_i \cup \bar{A}_i$. This automaton A_i' is strictly unambiguous and moreover, $q_{A_i',S_i}^{\exists} = q_{A_i,S_i}^{\exists}$.

Proposition 6. *A query is unambiguous iff it can be expressed by a Boolean combination (disjunction, conjunction and negation) of monadic MSO formulas.*

Proof. Using that regular and MSO-definable monadic queries coincide, by Theorem 4, an unambiguous n-ary query can be represented as a finite disjunction of formulas of the form $\phi_1(x_1) \wedge \ldots \wedge \phi_n(x_n)$, the ϕ_i's being monadic MSO formulas. Conversely, any Boolean combination of monadic MSO formulas can be turned into a finite disjunction of conjunction of monadic MSO formulas, and thus be represented as a finite union of Cartesian products of monadic regular queries.

5.2 Faithful MSO Formulas

Unambiguity of a query will rely on existence of a faithful formula defining it, where faithful formulae are defined by:

Definition 5. *Let ϕ be a MSO formula with n free second-order variables $p_1, ..., p_n$.*

- *ϕ is k−faithful if $\sup_{t \in T_\Sigma} |\{(\alpha(p_1), ..., \alpha(p_n)) \mid t, \alpha \models \phi\}| \leq k$.*
- *ϕ is faithful if it is k−faithful for some k.*

Proposition 7. *ϕ is faithful iff it is equivalent to a finite disjunction of 1−faithful formulae.*

Proof. More precisely, we prove that ϕ is k−faithful iff it is a finite disjunction of k 1−faithful formulae. A finite disjunction of k 1−faithful formulae is clearly k−faithful. Conversely let ϕ be a k−faithful formula. First, let us recall that the lexicographic ordering over n−uples is MSO definable by $lex(x_1, ...x_n, y_1, ..., y_n) =_{def} \bigvee_{k=1}^n (\bigwedge_{i=1}^{k-1} x_i = y_i \wedge x_k < y_k)$

Now, let us define a total ordering on n−uples of sets of nodes by

$$le(p_1, ..., p_n, q_1, ...q_n) =_{def} \bigwedge_{i=1}^n p_i = q_i \vee \exists x_1, ..., x_n \bigwedge_{i=1}^n p_i(x_i) \wedge \bigvee_{i=1}^n \neg q_i(x_i) \wedge \forall y_1, ..., y_n \, lex(y_1, ...y_n, x_1, ..., x_n) \rightarrow \bigwedge_{i=1}^n [p_i(y_i) \leftrightarrow \bigwedge_{i=1}^n q_i(y_i)].$$

Last, we define a family of 1−faithful formulae ϕ_i, $1 \leq i \leq k$ by:

$$\phi_i(p_1, ..., p_n) =_{def} \phi(p_1, ..., p_n) \wedge \bigwedge_{j=1}^{i-1} \neg \phi_j(p_1, ..., p_n) \wedge \forall q_1, ..., q_n (\phi(q_1, ..., q_n) \wedge (\bigwedge_{j=1}^{i-1} \neg \phi_j(q_1, ..., q_n)) \rightarrow le(p_1, ..., p_n, q_1, ...q_n))$$

It is easy to check that the ϕ_i are 1−faithful and, as ϕ is k−faithful, ϕ is equivalent to $\bigvee_{i=1}^k \phi_i$.

Proposition 8. *A regular n-ary query is*

1. *Cartesian closed iff it can be defined by some 1−faithful formula.*
2. *unambiguous iff it can be defined by some faithful formula.*

Proof. Let q a regular Cartesian closed query defined by ϕ. Let us define $\phi_i(x)$ by $\exists x_1, ..., x_{i-1}, x_{i+1}, ..., x_n, \phi(x_1, ..., x_{i-1}, x, x_{i+1}, ..., x_n)$. Then q can be defined by the 1−faithful formula $\forall x \wedge_{i=1}^{n} (p_i(x) \leftrightarrow \phi_i(x))$

Conversely, if q is defined by a 1−faithful formula, q is clearly Cartesian closed.

The rest of the proposition is then directly obtained by Proposition 7 and Theorem 4. Furthermore, as proofs of Proposition 7 and Theorem 4 are effective, given a query q defined by a formula ϕ and knowing that ϕ is faithful, we can effectively construct (A, S) computing the query q, with A unambiguous.

5.3 Deciding Unambiguity of Queries

We show in this section that one can decide whether a regular n-ary query is unambiguous, or equivalently by Theorem 4 whether the query is a finite union of Cartesian closed regular queries. Note that this property is close to independence of variables in constraint databases [14, 8]; however here we consider an infinite collection of finite tree structures, instead of one fixed structure.

Note that deciding whether a regular query is Cartesian closed is straightforward as it can be defined in MSO. Similarly by using construction of Proposition 7, we can decide k−faithfulness of a MSO formula, for a given k. However, deciding whether a regular query is a finite union of Cartesian closed regular queries requires more sophisticated techniques. First, given a query q, we construct a formula which is faithful iff q is unambiguous. Second, we prove how to decide faithfulness of a formula.

Let q a query defined by the (MSO) formula $\phi_q(x_1, \ldots, x_n)$. We will define $\phi_q^{\max}$, a MSO formula defining q with good compactness properties: it will be faithful as soon as q can be defined by a faithful formula. Roughly speaking, given a tree t, t, α will model $\phi_q^{\max}$ iff it is correct ($\alpha(p_1) * \ldots * \alpha(p_n)$ is included in $q(t)$) and maximal (no node can be added to one $\alpha(p_i)$ while keeping correct). $\phi_q^{\max}(p_1, \ldots, p_n)$ will be the following formula:

$$\forall x_1 \ldots \forall x_n (\wedge_i p_i(x_i)) \rightarrow \phi_q(x_1, \ldots, x_n)$$
$$\wedge_i \forall x_i \neg p_i(x_i) \rightarrow \exists x_1 \ldots \exists x_{i-1} \exists x_{i+1} \ldots \exists x_n \wedge_{j \neq i} p_j(x_j) \wedge \neg\phi_q(x_1, \ldots, x_n)$$

Lemma 3. *A query q is a finite union of Cartesian closed queries iff $\phi_q^{\max}$ is faithful.*

Proof. By Proposition 8 we just have to prove that if the query q is a finite union of Cartesian closed queries, then $\phi_q^{\max}$ is faithful. Let q be a finite union of Cartesian closed queries. There exists some natural number k s.t. $q = \cup_{j=1}^{k} q_j^1 \times \ldots \times q_j^n$, each q_j^i being a monadic query.

Let t be a tree from T_Σ. For each $1 \leq i \leq n$, we define $\equiv_i$, an equivalence relation on nodes(t) by $\pi \equiv_i \pi'$ if for all $(\pi_1, ..., \pi_{i-1}, \pi_{i+1}, ..., \pi_n)$, $(\pi_1, ..., \pi_{i-1}, \pi, \pi_{i+1}, ..., \pi_n)$ belongs to $q(t)$ iff $(\pi_1, ..., \pi_{i-1}, \pi', \pi_{i+1}, ..., \pi_n)$ belongs to $q(t)$. This just means that π and π' are, in some sense, interchangeable in i-th position w.r.t. q. Then, let π

and π' be two nodes. If for each $1 \leq j \leq k$, π belongs to $q_j^i(t)$ iff π' belongs to $q_j^i(t)$, then $\pi \equiv_i \pi'$. This implies that $\equiv_i$ is of finite index bounded by 2^k.

Now let t and α such that $t, \alpha \models \phi_q^{\mathsf{max}}$. Let π be one node selected in the i-th position, i.e. belonging to $\alpha(p_i)$. Then, by maximality of ϕ_q^{max}, if $\pi \equiv_i \pi'$ then π' belongs also to $\alpha(p_i)$. This implies that $\alpha(p_i)$ is a union of equivalence classes for $\equiv_i$. So, the cardinality of the set $\{(\alpha(p_1), ..., \alpha(p_n)) \mid t, \alpha \models \phi_q^{\mathsf{max}}\}$ is upper-bounded by $2^{n.2^k}$.

Let us note that if ϕ_q^{max} is faithful as soon there is a faithful formula defining q, it is non necessarily the "most faithful" one or the "less redundant" one. Indeed let us suppose that q is defined by $\vee_{i=1}^2 r_i(x_1) \wedge s_i(x_2)$ for some r_i, s_i. q is clearly $2-$faithful whereas in ϕ_q^{max}, valuation associated with $(\wedge r_i, \vee s_i)$ or $(\vee r_i, \wedge s_i)$ would be added.

Now, let q be a regular query (given by a tree automaton or a formula): first we construct ϕ_q^{max} and A a deterministic automaton recognizing the tree language over $\Sigma \times \mathbb{B}^n$ $L_{\phi_q^{\mathsf{max}}(p_1,...,p_n)}$. Then, we compute an automaton $\mathsf{proj}(A)$ as in Theorem 2. Clearly the number of accepting runs on t in $\mathsf{proj}(A)$ is the cardinal of $\{(\alpha(p_1), ..., \alpha(p_n)) \mid t, \alpha \models \phi_q^{\mathsf{max}}\}$.

A tree automaton A is said k-ambiguous if for any tree $t \in T_\Sigma$, there exists at most k accepting runs for t in A. The degree of ambiguity of an automaton A is bounded if A is k-ambiguous for some natural number k.

So, by what precedes, q is unambiguous iff the degree of ambiguity of $\mathsf{proj}(A)$ is bounded, which can be decided.

Theorem 5 (Seidl [20]). *Whether the degree of ambiguity of a tree automaton is bounded is decidable. Furthermore its degree of ambiguity can be computed.*

As all contructions are effective, it provides a procedure for deciding ambiguity of q. Furthermore, this gives a way to compute an unambiguous automaton computing q. Indeed, by proposition 8, as soon as we know that ϕ_q^{max} is faithful, we can compute, from an automaton or a formula defining q, (B, S) with B an unambiguous automaton s.t. $q = \mathsf{q}_{B,S}^\exists$.

Theorem 6. *Ambiguity of a query q is decidable. Furthermore, when q is unambiguous, (B, S) with B an unambiguous automaton s.t. $q = \mathsf{q}_{B,S}^\exists$ can effectively be constructed.*

Note that the construction of (B, S) could also be done by eliminating directly ambiguity from $\mathsf{proj}(A)$ defined above. Indeed, let B be an automaton whose ambiguity degree is at most k. We can build an automaton B_k simulating B on trees which have at least k accepting runs in B (by making the product of k copies of B and checking the k runs are different); as the degree of B is k, B_k will be unambiguous. Then, you can build an unambiguous automaton B_{k-1} simulating B on trees which have exactly $k-1$ accepting runs in B, by a similar construction and checking that the tree is not accepted by B_k. By iterating the construction, you can build $(B_i, S_i)_{i=1}^k$, with B_i unambiguous automata simulating B on trees which have exactly i accepting runs in B: q is the union of the corresponding queries and by using effective closure under union, you can then build an unambiguous automaton for q.

6   Querying Unranked Trees

Our results carry over to automata for unranked trees, in particular to the unranked tree automata (UTAs) of Brüggemann, Klein, and Wood [4], where horizontal tree languages are represented by finite word automata.

An unranked tree is built from a set of constants $a, b \in \Sigma$ by the abstract syntax $t ::= a(t_1, \ldots, t_n)$ where $n \geq 0$. A *UTA* H over Σ consists of a set $\mathsf{states}(H)$, a set $\mathsf{final}(H) \subseteq \mathsf{states}(H)$, and a set $\mathsf{rules}(H)$ of rules of the form $a(A) \to p$ where A is finite word automaton with alphabet $\mathsf{states}(H)$ and $p \in \mathsf{states}(H)$. Runs of UTAs H on unranked trees t are functions $r : \mathsf{nodes}(t) \to \mathsf{states}(H)$ defined as

$$\frac{t = a(t_1, \ldots, t_n) \qquad \forall 1 \leq i \leq n : r_i \in \mathsf{runs}_H(t_i)}{a(A) \to p \in \mathsf{rules}(H) \qquad r_1(\epsilon) \ldots r_n(\epsilon) \in L(A)}{p(r_1, \ldots, r_n) \in \mathsf{runs}_H(t)}$$

Queries for the class of unranked trees over Σ are defined as before. The notion of unambiguity (that is the existence of at most one run for a tree) carries over literally to UTAs (in contrast to bottom-up determinism [16]). The same holds for the notions of run-based queries by UTAs.

Theorem 7. *Existential and universal n-ary queries by runs of unranked tree automata capture MSO over unranked trees (comprising the* next_sibl-*relation). Run-based queries by unambiguous UTAs capture the class of finite unions of Cartesian closed queries. This property is decidable.*

We only give a sketch of the proof. The main idea is to convert queries by UTAs into queries by stepwise tree automata [6] for which all results apply. Stepwise tree automata over an unranked signature Σ are tree automata for binary trees with constants in Σ and a single binary function symbol @. Stepwise tree automata can be understood as tree automata that operate on Currified binary encodings of unranked trees. The Currification of $a(b, c(d, e, f), g)$ for instance is the binary tree $a@b@(c@d@e@f)@g$.

Stepwise tree automata were proved to have two nice properties that yield a simple proof of the theorem. 1) N-ary queries by UTAs can be translated to n-ary queries by stepwise automata in linear time, and conversely in polynomial time. The back and forth translations preserve unambiguity. 2) All presented results on run-based n-ary queries for binary trees apply to stepwise tree automata.

Acknowledgements. Thanks to the anonymous referees for the reference to L. Libkin's work [14] and acknowledge discussions with F. Neven, W. Martens, and T. Schwentick.

References

1. R. Baumgartner, S. Flesca, and G. Gottlob. Visual web information extraction with lixto. In *28th International Conference on Very Large Data Bases*, pages 119–128, 2001.
2. A. Berlea and H. Seidl. Binary queries for document trees. *Nordic Journal of Computing*, 11(1):41–71, 2004.

3. R. Bloem and J. Engelfriet. A comparison of tree transductions defined by monadic second order logic and by attribute grammars. *Journal of Comput. and Syst. Sci.*, 61(1):1–50, 2000.

4. A. Bruggemann-Klein, D. Wood, and M. Murata. Regular tree and regular hedge languages over unranked alphabets: Version 1, Apr. 07 2001.

5. J. Carme, A. Lemay, and J. Niehren. Learning node selecting tree transducer from completely annotated examples. In *7th International Colloquium on Grammatical Inference*, volume 3264 of *Lecture Notes in Artificial Intelligence*, pages 91–102. Springer Verlag, 2004.

6. J. Carme, J. Niehren, and M. Tommasi. Querying unranked trees with stepwise tree automata. In *19th International Conference on Rewriting Techniques and Applications*, volume 3091 of *Lecture Notes in Computer Science*, pages 105 – 118. Springer Verlag, 2004.

7. G. Castagna. Patterns and types for querying XML. In *10th International Symposium on Database Programming Languages*, Lecture Notes in Computer Science. Springer Verlag, Aug. 2005.

8. J. Chomicki, D. Q. Goldin, and G. M. Kuper. Variable independence and aggregation closure. In *ACM Conference on Principle of Databases*, pages 40–48, 1996.

9. H. Comon, M. Dauchet, R. Gilleron, F. Jacquemard, D. Lugiez, S. Tison, and M. Tommasi. Tree automata techniques and applications. Available on: http://www.grappa.univ-lille3.fr/tata, 1997.

10. M. Frick, M. Grohe, and C. Koch. Query evaluation on compressed trees. In *18th IEEE Symposium on Logic in Computer Science*, pages 188–197, 2003.

11. G. Gottlob and C. Koch. Monadic queries over tree-structured data. In *Proceedings of the 17th LICS*, Lecture Notes in Computer Science, pages 189–202, Copenhagen, 2002.

12. G. Gottlob, C. Koch, R. Baumgartner, M. Herzog, and S. Flesca. The Lixto data extraction project - back and forth between theory and practice. In *ACM Symposium on Principles of Database Systems*. ACM-Press, 2004.

13. H. Hosoya and B. Pierce. Regular expression pattern matching for xml. *Journal of Functional Programming*, 6(13):961–1004, 2003.

14. L. Libkin. Variable independence for first-order definable constraints. *ACM Transactions on Computational Logics*, 4(4):431–451, 2003.

15. S. Maneth, A. Berlea, T. Perst, and H. Seidl. Xml type checking with macro tree transducers. In *24th ACM Symposium on Principles of Database Systems*, pages 283–294, New York, NY, USA, 2005. ACM-Press.

16. W. Martens and J. Niehren. Minimizing tree automata for unranked trees. In *10th International Symposium on Database Programming Languages*, Lecture Notes in Computer Science. Springer Verlag, Aug. 2005.

17. M. Marx. Conditional XPath, the first order complete XPath dialect. In *Proceedings of the symposium on Principles of database systems*, pages 13–22, 2004.

18. F. Neven and J. V. D. Bussche. Expressiveness of structured document query languages based on attribute grammars. *Journal of the ACM*, 49(1):56–100, 2002.

19. F. Neven and T. Schwentick. Query automata over finite trees. *Theoretical Computer Science*, 275(1-2):633–674, 2002.

20. H. Seidl. On the finite degree of ambiguity of finite tree automata. *Acta Informatica*, 26(6):527–542, 1989.

21. J. W. Thatcher and J. B. Wright. Generalized finite automata with an application to a decision problem of second-order logic. *Mathematical System Theory*, 2:57–82, 1968.

Minimizing Tree Automata for Unranked Trees

[Extended Abstract]

Wim Martens[1,*] and Joachim Niehren[2]

[1] Hasselt University and Transnational University of Limburg,
Agoralaan, gebouw D, B-3590 Diepenbeek, Belgium
wim.martens@uhasselt.be
[2] INRIA Futurs, LIFL, Mostrare project, Lille, France
http://www.grappa.univ-lille3.fr/mostrare

Abstract. Automata for unranked trees form a foundation for XML schemas, querying and pattern languages. We study the problem of efficiently minimizing such automata. We start with the unranked tree automata (UTAs) that are standard in database theory, assuming bottom-up determinism and that horizontal recursion is represented by deterministic finite automata. We show that minimal UTAs in that class are not unique and that minimization is NP-hard. We then study more recent automata classes that do allow for polynomial time minimization. Among those, we show that bottom-up deterministic stepwise tree automata yield the most succinct representations.

1 Introduction

Finite automata for unranked trees constitute the theoretical basis for XML schema languages [16] and are used in numerous areas of XML-related research, such as path and pattern languages [17, 22] and XML querying [7, 18]. Research on automata minimization therefore contributes to each of those fields.

In the context of XML schema languages, minimized schemas would improve the running time on document validation, or on static tests involving the schemas, such as typechecking of XML transformations [13, 26]. Minimal *deterministic* automata for unranked tree languages play a prominent role in recent approaches to query induction for Web information extraction [3]. The objective is to identify a tree automaton for a previously unknown target language from given examples. Standard algorithms from grammatical inference [1, 8, 19] such as RPNI always induce minimal deterministic automata. The smaller this automaton is, the easier it can be inferred.

In this work we focus on the minimization of *automata for unranked tree languages*, which is a fundamental problem to automata theory and recently attracted some attention [6, 21]. The question is particularly relevant for classes of *deterministic automata*, since minimization can be done both efficiently and leads to unique canonical representatives of regular languages, as is well-known

---

* Corresponding author

G. Bierman and C. Koch (Eds.): DBPL 2005, LNCS 3774, pp. 232–246, 2005.

for string languages and ranked tree languages. It is also well-known that minimal non-deterministic automata are neither unique, nor efficiently computable [9, 11].

The investigation of efficient minimization of deterministic automata for un-ranked trees language started quite recently [6, 21]. The deterministic devices considered there, however, differ from the standard deterministic automata in database theory – the bottom-up deterministic unranked tree automata (UTAs) of Brüggemann-Klein, Murata, and Wood [2]. In this paper, we investigate effi-cient (i.e. PTIME) minimization starting from such UTAs.

The transition relation of UTAs uses regular string languages over the states of the automaton to express horizontal recursion. However, it is not specified how these regular string languages should be represented. In practice, this is usually done by finite automata or regular expressions. If we allow for non-deterministic finite automata in bottom-up deterministic UTAs, then minimization becomes PSPACE-hard. As we are interested in *efficient* minimization, we restrict the finite subautomata in UTAs to be deterministic too. These DFAs impose *left-to-right determinstism* in addition to bottom-up determinism.

In the first part of the paper, we will prove two surprising results for these bottom-up and left-to-right deterministic UTAs. We present a counterexample for the uniqueness of minimal UTAs that represent a given regular language. We then prove that minimization becomes NP-complete and thus unfeasible. Both results are in strong contrast to what is known for bottom-up deterministic automata in the ranked case. Our NP-hardness proof refines the proof techniques from [9, 11], showing NP-hardness of minimization for classes of finite automata with limited amount of non-determinism.

In the second part of the paper, we compare the sizes of minimal automata for known automata classes that allow for efficient minimization. We show that bottom-up deterministic *stepwise tree automata* [4] yield the most succinct rep-resentations, both compared to the bottom-up deterministic *parallel UTAs* of [6, 21], as well as with respect to bottom-up deterministic automata over the standard *first-child next-sibling encoding* of regular tree languages (up to in-version). The difference in representation size is quadratic in the first case and exponential in the second case.

Finally we discuss a small minimization result for top-down deterministic tree automata. This notion of top-down determinism is very similar to the notion defined in [6] as it has exactly the same expressive power – but the question of minimizing these automata was not treated.

2   Preliminaries

In this section we provide the necessary background on strings, trees and tree automata.

2.1   Strings

For a finite set S, its *size* $|S|$ is its number of elements. By $\mathbb{N}$ we denote the set of natural numbers. We fix a finite alphabet Σ. When $a \in \Sigma$ we also say that

a is a Σ-*symbol*. A *string* $w = a_1 \cdots a_n$ is a finite sequence of Σ-symbols. We denote the empty string by ε.

We assume familiarity with nondeterministic finite automata (NFAs), deterministic finite automata (DFAs), unambiguous finite automata (UFAs) and regular expressions (REs). Given a fininte automaton or a regular expression A, we sometimes freely identify A with the language $L(A)$ it defines. The *size* of a finite automaton or regular expression is the size of its state set, or its number of symbols respectively. Let $\mathcal{C}$ be a class of representations of regular string languages (that is, NFAs, DFAs, UFAs, or REs). Then the *minimization problem* for $\mathcal{C}$ is defined as follows: Given an $A \in \mathcal{C}$ and an integer m, does there exist an $A' \in \mathcal{C}$ such that A and A' accept the same language and the size of A' is lesser than or equal to m. The *containment* and *equivalence problems* for $\mathcal{C}$ ask, given $A, B \in \mathcal{C}$ whether $L(A) \subseteq L(B)$ or $L(A) = L(B)$ respectively. We recall the following results from formal language theory:

Theorem 1 ([9, 24, 25]).

(1) Containment and equivalence of NFAs and REs is PSPACE-*complete;*
(2) Containment and equivalence of UTAs and DFAs is in PTIME;
(3) Minimizing NFAs and REs is PSPACE-*complete;*
(4) Minimizing UFAs is NP-*complete;*
(5) Minimizing DFAs is in PTIME.

2.2   Unranked Trees

The set of unranked Σ-trees, denoted by $\mathcal{T}$, is the smallest set of strings over Σ and the parenthesis symbols ')' and '(' such that for each $a \in \Sigma$ and $w \in \mathcal{T}^*$, $a(w)$ is in $\mathcal{T}$. So, a tree is either ε (empty) or is of the form $a(t_1 \cdots t_n)$ where each t_i is a tree. The latter denotes the tree where the subtrees $t_1, \ldots, t_n$ are attached to the root labeled a. We write a rather than $a()$. Note that there is no a priori bound on the number of children of a node in a Σ-tree; such trees are therefore *unranked*. In the following, whenever we say tree, we always mean Σ-tree. A *tree language* is a set of trees.

For every tree $t \in \mathcal{T}$, the *set of nodes of* t, denoted by $\mathrm{Dom}(t)$, is the subset of $\mathbb{N}^*$ defined as follows: (i) if $t = \varepsilon$, then $\mathrm{Dom}(t) = \emptyset$; and (ii) if $t = a(t_1 \cdots t_n)$ where each $t_i \in \mathcal{T}$, then $\mathrm{Dom}(t) = \{\varepsilon\} \cup \bigcup_{i=1}^{n}\{iu \mid u \in \mathrm{Dom}(t_i)\}$. For every $u \in \mathrm{Dom}(t)$, we denote by $\mathrm{lab}^t(u)$ the label of u in t.

2.3   Unranked Tree Automata

Definition 2 ([2]). An *unranked tree automaton (UTA)* is a tuple $B = (Q, \Sigma, \delta, F)$, where Q is a finite set of states, $F \subseteq Q$ is the set of final states, and δ is a function $\delta : Q \times \Sigma \to 2^{(Q^*)}$ such that $\delta(q, a)$ is a regular string language over Q for every $a \in \Sigma$ and $q \in Q$.

To simplify notation, we sometimes also write $a(L) \to q$ for $\delta(q, a) = L$. A *run* of B on a tree t is a labeling $\lambda : \mathrm{Dom}(t) \to Q$ such that for every $v \in \mathrm{Dom}(t)$

with n children we have that $\lambda(v1)\cdots\lambda(vn) \in \delta(\lambda(v), \mathrm{lab}^t(v))$. Note that when v has no children, the criterion reduces to $\varepsilon \in \delta(\lambda(v), \mathrm{lab}^t(v))$. A run is *accepting* iff the root is labeled with an accepting state, that is, $\lambda(\varepsilon) \in F$. A tree is *accepted* if there is an accepting run. The set of all accepted trees is denoted by $L(B)$ and is called a *regular tree language*. A UTA is *bottom-up deterministic* if for all $q, q' \in Q$ with $q \neq q'$ and $a \in \Sigma$ we have that $\delta(q, a) \cap \delta(q', a) = \emptyset$.

When defining the *size* of a UTA, we have to fix a representation of the regular languages $\delta(q, a)$. As argued in the introduction, we represent $\delta(q, a)$ by a DFA since non-deterministic representations immediately make the minimization problem intractable (Theorem 1). We denote by DUTA the bottom-up deterministic UTAs where the transitions $\delta(q, a)$ are represented by DFAs. As DFAs are deterministic when reading a string from left to right, we also refer to DUTAs as *bottom-up left-to-right deterministic UTAs* . The *size* of a DUTA $B = (Q, \Sigma, \delta, F)$ is $|Q| + \sum_{(q,a)} |\delta(q, a)|$, where $|\delta(q, a)|$ is the number of states of the DFA accepting $\delta(q, a)$.

We mention the following basic result about DUTAs.

Theorem 3. *Containment and equivalence of DUTAs is in* PTIME.

Proof (Sketch). Given two DUTAs, we can translate them in PTIME into tree automata over a known binary encoding of unranked trees, such as the first-child next-sibling encoding. The canonical way to do this translates a DUTA into an *unambiguous tree automaton over binary trees*. Due to the work of Seidl [23], we can test containment and equivalence of these automata in PTIME. □

To the best of our knowledge, it is not known whether the standard containment test works in PTIME, since complementing a DUTA is *not* trivial (unless the DUTA is *complete*, then one just has to switch final and non-final states).

2.4   Are DUTAs Deterministic?

We raise the question whether the computation of a DUTA is truly deterministic or not. Informally, we assume that a *computation* of a DUTA proceeds in a bottom-up manner, reads every node of a tree only once and remembers only one state of an internal DFA while reading the states that are assigned to the children of a certain node. We show in a small example that under these conditions, the computation of a DUTA in fact still has a very limited form of non-determinism. In the next section we show that this is exactly what makes minimization hard.

Let A be the DUTA with transition function

$$\delta(q_a, a) = \delta(q_b, b) = \varepsilon$$

$$\delta(q_1, r) = \{q_a q_a\} \qquad \text{by}$$

$$\delta(q_2, r) = \{q_a q_b\} \qquad \text{by}$$

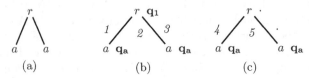

Fig. 1. A tree t, a successful run on t and a partially successful run on t

and final states $\{q_1, q_2\}$. This automaton accepts the language $\{r(aa), r(ab)\}$. When computing a bottom-up run for the tree in Figure 1(a), the state q_a will be assigned to both a-labeled leafs. At that point, it remains to assign a state to the r-labeled root. Here, we have the choice of starting to run the DFA for $\delta(q_1, r)$ or for $\delta(q_2, r)$. In Figure 1(b), we show the run that we obtain by choosing $\delta(q_1, r)$ (in which we also annotated the internal states 1, 2 and 3 of $\delta(q_1, r)$ in italic), and Figure 1(c) shows the partial run that is obtained when choosing $\delta(q_2, r)$, which cannot be completed to a successful run. So even though there is only one successful run, the computation of the run itself still has a limited choice. Intuitively, this corresponds to an *unambiguous* rather than completely deterministic automata model.

One could argue that this choice in the computation is implementation-dependent. When implementing the automaton A, one could e.g. choose to simulate $\delta(q_1, r)$ and $\delta(q_2, r)$ *in parallel*. But then, one actually obtains a different notion of UTAs, namely the *parallel UTAs* [6, 21] that we study in Section 4.4.

3   Minimizing UTAs

In this section we study the minimization problem on bottom-up left-to-right deterministic UTAs. We show two unexpected negative results: Given a regular tree language L, there does *not* exist an (up to isomorphism) unique minimal DUTA that accepts L. The minimization problem for DUTAs even turns out to be NP-complete.

3.1   Minimal Automata are Not Unique

We show the non-uniqueness by an example. Consider the regular languages L_1, L_2 and L_3 defined by regular expressions $(bbb)^*$, $b(bbbbbb)^*$ and $bb(bbbbbbbbb)^*$ respectively. Note that L_1, L_2 and L_3 are pairwise disjoint, and that the minimal DFAs A_1, A_2 and A_3 accepting L_1, L_2 and L_3 have 3, 6 and 9 states respectively. It is easy to verify that the minimal DFAs B_1 and B_2 accepting $L_1 \cup L_2$ and $L_1 \cup L_3$ have 6 and 9 states respectively. Let $L = L_1 \cup L_2 \cup L_3$ and consider the tree language $T := \{r(a(w)) \mid w \in L\}$.

There exist two minimal DUTAs for T. The first one, $N_1 = (Q_1, \Sigma, \delta_1, F_1)$ has accept state q_0 and transition function

$$\delta_1(q_0, r) = q_1 + q_2 \qquad \delta_1(q_1, a) = B_1 \qquad \delta_1(q_2, a) = A_3 \qquad \delta_1(b, b) = \varepsilon.$$

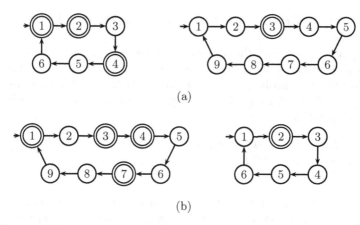

(a)

(b)

Fig. 2. Figure 2(a) contains the DFAs B_1 and A_3; and Figure 2(b) contains the DFAs B_2 and A_2. All transition arrows read the symbol b.

The size of N_1 is $|Q_1| + |\delta_1(q_0, r)| + |B_1| + |A_3| + |\delta_1(b, b)| = 4 + 2 + 6 + 9 + 1 = 22$. The DFAs B_1 and A_3 are sketched in Figure 2(a). The other automaton, $N_2 = (Q_2, \Sigma, \delta_2, F_2)$ has accept state q_0 and transition function

$$\delta_2(q_0, r) = q_1 + q_2 \qquad \delta_2(q_1, a) = B_2 \qquad \delta_2(q_2, a) = A_2 \qquad \delta_2(b, b) = \varepsilon.$$

The size of N_2 is $|Q_2| + |\delta_2(q_0, r)| + |B_2| + |A_2| + |\delta_2(b, b)| = 4 + 2 + 9 + 6 + 1 = 22$. The DFAs B_2 and A_2 are sketched in Figure 2(b).

Of course, there are other possibilities to write $L = L_1 \cup L_2 \cup L_3$ as a disjoint union of regular languages. The obvious combinations one can make with A_1, A_2 and A_3 lead to DUTAs of size 26 (using A_1, A_2 and A_3), 28 (using $(A_2 \cup A_3)$ and A_1) and 24 (one automaton for L).

We show that no other combination of splitting L into a union of regular languages will result in a smaller DUTA accepting T. First, observe that any DUTA defining T needs at least three states in its state set Q, since all trees in T have depth three. However, as argued above, the minimum size of such a DUTA with three states is $3 + 2 + 18 + 1 = 24$. The only way to obtain a smaller DUTA is then to define L as a union of DFAs, of which the sum of the number of states is strictly smaller than $9 + 6 = 15$. However, if we write L as a union of DFAs, there must be at least one DFA D_1 that accepts an infinite number of strings in L_2. It is easy to see that D_1 has at least 6 states, as D_1 may not accept strings *not* in L. Analogously, we can argue that there must be at least one DFA D_2 that accepts an infinite number of strings in L_3. If $D_1 = D_2$, it is easy to see that D_1 has at least 18 states. If $D_2 \neq D_1$, then it is easy to see that D_2 has at least 9 states. Therefore, the above automata are indeed minimal for T, and as Figure 2 shows, they are clearly not isomorphic.

3.2 Minimization Is NP-Complete

The minimization problem for DUTAs is defined analogously as the minimization problem for finite automata: Given a DUTA A and an integer m, decide whether there exists a DUTA B such that $L(B) = L(A)$ and the size of B is lesser than or equal to m.

As Section 3.1 illustrates, the problem of defining a regular string language as a small disjoint union of DFAs lies at the heart of the minimization problem for DUTAs. We call this problem GENERAL MINIMUM DISJOINT UNION and define it formally as follows: Given a DFA M and an integer ℓ, do there exist DFAs $M_1, \ldots, M_n$ such that

(1) $L(M) = L(M_1) \cup \cdots \cup L(M_n)$; and
(2) for every $i \neq j$, $L(M_i) \cap L(M_j) = \emptyset$; and
(3) $\sum_{i=1}^{n} |M_i| \leq \ell$?

It can be shown that GENERAL MINIMUM DISJOINT UNION is NP-complete by a reduction from VERTEX COVER. Actually, GENERAL MINIMUM DISJOINT UNION is even NP-complete when $n = 2$. The proof for this is not straightforward, and technically the hardest proof in the paper, but the reduction is interesting in its own right. The proof can be found in [15]. Although we do not go deeper on this in the paper, variations of the reduction can actually be used to show that the three open problems stated in the conclusion of [11] are NP-complete [12].

Theorem 4. DUTA MINIMIZATION *is* NP-*complete.*

Proof (Sketch). The upper bound follows from Theorem 3. Given a DUTA A and an integer m, the NP algorithm simply guesses an automaton B of size at most m and verfies in PTIME whether it is equivalent to A.

For the lower bound, we do a reduction from GENERAL MINIMUM DISJOINT UNION. Given a DFA $M = (Q_M, \Sigma_M, \delta_M, I_M, F_M)$ and integer ℓ, we have to construct a DUTA A and an integer m such that A has an equivalent DUTA of size m iff M can be written as a disjoint union of DFAs for which the size does not exceed ℓ. Intuitively, we construct A such that it accepts the trees of the form $r(w)$, where the root node is labeled with a special symbol r and the string w is in $L(M)$. For the full proof, we refer to [15]. $\square$

4   Solutions for Efficient Minimization

As we have shown, UTA minimization is unfeasible even when the horizontal languages are represented by DFAs. The problem is raised when using multiple rules for the same label, for recognizing these horizontal regular languages.

Three alternative notions of bottom-up deterministic tree automata for unranked trees were proposed recently, each of them yielding a solution to the problem. First, one can define notions of bottom-up determinism based on translations between unranked and ranked trees. *Stepwise tree automata* [4] are an algebraic notion of automata for unranked trees which also correspond to automata over binary trees by means of such a translation. Alternatively, one can use tree automata that operate on the *standard encoding* of unranked into binary trees (see, e.g. [7]).

Finally, *parallel UTAs (pUTAs)* alter the rule format of UTAs and have been independently proposed in [21] and [6]. All these automata yield notions of bottom-up determinism which lead to unique minimal automata and polynomial time minimization.

4.1   Automata on Binary Trees

We first treat the automata models which can also be defined on ranked trees. We therefore recall the notion of a traditional tree automaton.

Definition 5. A (traditional) *tree automaton (TA)* for a binary signature is a tuple $A = (Q, \Sigma, \delta, (I_a)_{a \in \Sigma}, F)$ where Q is a finite set of states, the signature $\Sigma = \Sigma_0 \uplus \Sigma_2$ consists of a finite set of constants Σ_0 and finite set of binary function symbols Σ_2, $F \subseteq Q$ is the set of final states, $I_a \subseteq Q$ is a set of initial states for every $a \in \Sigma_0$, and δ is a function $\delta : Q \times Q \times \Sigma_2 \rightarrow 2^Q$ mapping a pair of states and a function symbol to a set of possible new states.

A *run* of A on a tree t is a labeling $\lambda : \mathrm{Dom}(t) \rightarrow Q$ such that *(i)* for every leaf node u, $\lambda(u) \in I_{\mathrm{lab}(u)}$; and *(ii)* for all inner nodes u, $\lambda(u) \in \delta(\lambda(u1), \lambda(u2), \mathrm{lab}(u))$. A run is *accepting* iff the root is labeled with an accepting state, that is, $\lambda(\varepsilon) \in F$. A tree is *accepted* if there is an accepting run on t.

A binary tree automaton is *(bottom-up) deterministic* if for all $q, q' \in Q$ and $a \in \Sigma$, $\delta(q, q', a)$ contains at most one element. To simplify notation for TAs, we sometimes also write $a \rightarrow q$ and $a(q, q') \rightarrow p$ to say that $q \in I_a$ and $p \in \delta(q, q', a)$ respectively.

The *size* of a binary tree automaton $A = (Q, \Sigma, \delta, (I_a)_{a \in \Sigma}, F)$ is the number of elements in its state set Q. We denote the size of A by $|A|$.

4.2   Stepwise Tree Automata

Stepwise tree automata are an algebraic version of automata for unranked trees [4]. For the algebraic perspective, we refer to that paper.

A *stepwise tree automaton* over an unranked signature Σ is a (traditional) tree automaton over the binary signature $\Sigma \uplus \{@\}$ where all labels in Σ serve as constants and @ is a binary function symbol.

One of the nicest features of stepwise tree automata is that they are traditional tree automata, but can also run over *unranked trees*. Indeed, stepwisetree au-

initial states	$I_a = \{5\}$	$I_b = \{4\}$
rules	$@(5,4) \rightarrow 6$	$@(5,5) \rightarrow 6$
	$@(6,4) \rightarrow 6$	$@(6,5) \rightarrow 6$
final states	$\{5,6\}$	

Fig. 3. A deterministic stepwise tree automaton for $a((a|b)^*)$, equivalent to the pUTA in Figure 5

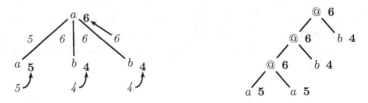

Fig. 4. Runs of the stepwise automaton from Figure 3. To the left, on the unranked tree and to the right, on its Curried binary encoding.

tomata can be understood as traditional tree automata that operate on Curried binary encodings of unranked trees. Currying the unranked tree

$$\text{plus}(4, 5, \text{plus}(6, 7, 8))$$

for instance yields plus@4@5@(plus@6@7@8) which (if we assume left associativity) is the binary tree

$$@\big(@\big(@(\text{plus}, 4), 5\big), @\big(@\big(@(\text{plus}, 6), 7\big), 8\big)\big),$$

but in infix notation. Figure 4 shows this correspondence. The italic states in the left tree correspond exactly to the bold states in the run on its Curried encoding, which is the tree on the right. On the unranked tree, the italic states can be seen as the explicit computation of the tree automaton. For every node, the state in bold is simply a copy of the rightmost italic state below. In Section 4.4, we show a run of an equivalent *parallel UTA* in Figure 5. There, the correspondence between the italic and the bold states is given by the *output function* of the automaton.

Myhill-Nerode Property. The Myhill-Nerode theorem yields an up to isomorphism unique representation for minimal deterministic automata for regular languages. The states of the minimal automaton correspond to the classes of the congruence induced by the language.

The Myhill-Nerode theorem holds generally for algebraic automata notions (see e.g. [5]) and thus for finite automata, standard tree automata [10, 27], and stepwise tree automata [4]. Myhill-Nerode inspired theorems for automata on unranked trees were shown for UTAs (Theorem G in [2]) and for *parallel UTAs* [6], which we treat in Section 4.4. Remarkably, in the former case the theorem does not lead to minimal automata and in the latter case the theorem uses two quite particular equivalence relations instead of a single canonical congruence, as in the ranked case. In this section, we formulate the Myhill-Nerode theorem, such that it holds both for traditional tree automata and stepwise tree automata interpreted over unranked trees.

In both cases, a *context* C is a function mapping trees to trees. In the case of binary trees over Σ, a context can be represented by a binary tree over the binary signature $\Sigma \uplus \{\bullet\}$ that contains a single occurence of the hole marker $\bullet$ at a leaf node. Context application $C(t)$ to a tree t replaces the hole marker in C by t. A *context* C for an unranked tree over Σ is a tree over the unranked signature $\Sigma \uplus \{\bullet\}$ that contains a single occurence of the hole marker, but this time possibly labeling an internal node. Given a context C and a tree $t = a(t_1 \cdots t_n)$, we define context application $C(t)$ inductively as follows:

- $\bullet(t'_1, \cdots, t'_m)(a(t_1, \cdots, t_n)) = a(t_1, \cdots, t_n, t'_1, \cdots, t'_m)$
- $a(t'_1, \cdots, t'_i, \cdots, t'_m)(t) = a(t'_1, \cdots, t'_i(t), \cdots, t'_m)$ where t'_i contains the $\bullet$.

A *congruence* on trees is an equivalence relation $\equiv$ that satisfies for every context C: if $t_1 \equiv t_2$ then $C(t_1) \equiv C(t_2)$. It is of *finite index* when there are only a finite number of equivalence classes. Given a tree language L, we define the congruence $\equiv_L$ induced by L through:

$$t_1 \equiv_L t_2 \text{ iff for every context } C: C(t_1) \in L \Leftrightarrow C(t_2) \in L.$$

Theorem 6 (Myhill-Nerode). *For any ranked or unranked tree language L it holds that L is a regular tree language iff its congruence $\equiv_L$ has finite index. Furthermore, there exists an (up to isomorphism) unique minimal bottom-up deterministic (stepwise) tree automaton for all regular languages L. The size of this automaton is equal to the index of $\equiv_L$.*

The proof of this theorem is immediate from the binary case [10]. It follows from the observation that the contexts we define for unranked trees are obtained by translating the contexts over binary trees through the inverse of the Curried encoding. We note that this theorem was partially proven in [2] (Theorem G). However, we feel that the present proof is simpler (as the theorem immediately carries over from the ranked case) and also leads to minimal automata, which is not the case in [2].

4.3 Standard Binary Encoding

Analogously as with stepwise tree automata, a tree automaton over the standard *first-child next-sibling* encoding of a tree can be seen as working directly over the unranked tree (see, e.g. [7]). In this encoding, an unranked tree is simply viewed as a binary tree over the first-child and next-sibling relation. Whenever a Σ-symbol has no left or no right child, a special symbol $\perp$ is inserted.

As in Section 4.2, a Myhill-Nerode theorem for unranked trees can also be obtained using the inverse of the standard first-child next-sibling encoding. However, in Section 5.1, we argue that the latter leads to exponentially more equivalence classes, and hence, exponentially larger minimal automata.

4.4 Parallel UTAs

The problem with UTAs bottom-up left-to-right determinism is that it may force the interpreter of the automaton to choose between several rules for the same label. The obvious solution is to run all automata for the same label in parallel, and thus unify them. This idea leads to the notion of parallel UTAs.

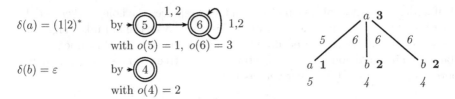

$\delta(a) = (1|2)^*$ by

with $o(5) = 1$, $o(6) = 3$

$\delta(b) = \varepsilon$ by

with $o(4) = 2$

Fig. 5. A deterministic pUTA $(Q, \Sigma, \delta, \{1, 3\}, o)$ for $a((a|b)^*)$, equivalent to the stepwise tree automaton in Figure 3, and its run on $a(abb)$, annotated in bold to the right of the alphabet symbols. The runs of the internal DFAs are annotated in italic.

A *parallel UTA (pUTA)* is a tuple $A = (Q, \Sigma, \delta, F, o)$ which consists of a finite set Q of states, a collection of horizontal regular languages $\delta(a) \subseteq Q^*$ represented by a finite automaton for each $a \in \Sigma$, a set of final states $F \subseteq Q$, and a collection of output functions $o(a)$ for all $a \in \Sigma$ that maps final states of the finite automaton recognizing $\delta(a)$ to states in Q.

Let $(Q_a, Q, \delta_a, I_a, F_a)$ be the finite automaton recognizing $\delta(a)$ for every $a \in \Sigma$. A run of A on a tree t is a labeling function $\lambda : \mathrm{Dom}(t) \to Q$ that satisfies for all nodes $u \in \mathrm{Dom}(t)$ with n children that $\lambda(u) = o(a)(\delta_a^*(\lambda(u1) \cdots \lambda(un)))$, where δ_a^* is the homomorphic extension of δ_a to strings in Q^*. An example for a pUTA is illustrated in Figure 5.

We call a pUTA *deterministic* if all subautomata for recognizing horizontal languages $\delta(a)$ are DFAs. The class of deterministic pUTAs has unique minimal automata and allows for efficient minimization [6, 21]. They can recognize all regular languages, as shown by the following transformations.

Every deterministic pUTA A can be transformed into an equivalent DUTA (Q, Σ, δ', F) so that for every $a \in \Sigma$ and $q \in Q$:

$$\delta'(q, a) = (Q_a, Q, \delta_a, I_a, o(a)^{-1}(q))$$

Conversely, any DUTA can be converted into an equivalent deterministic pUTA but possibly at the cost of an exponential blow-up. The first step is to unify the horizontal subautomata for the language $\cup_{q \in Q} \delta(q, a)$ for every label a, by constructing the product automaton (which can cause the exponential blow-up). The output function $o(a)$ maps every tuple in the product with a final state of the automaton recognizing $\delta(q, a)$ to q.

5   Size Comparison

5.1   Stepwise vs Standard Binary Encoding

Let $[\![t]\!]$ denote the standard binary *first-child next-sibling* encoding of an unranked Σ-tree t over $\Sigma \uplus \{\bot\}$. Let $\bar{t}$ denote the tree obtained from t by reversing for every node its list of children. For instance, if $t = a(b, c, d(e, f))$, then $\bar{t} = a(d(f, e)c, b)$. We extend these notations in the obvious way to tree languages.

To be able to compare stepwise tree automata to tree automata over the first-child next-sibling encoding, we need to study one of the two over these reversed trees. The reason is that deterministic stepwise tree automata read the children of a node from *left to right* whereas deterministic tree automata over the standard encoding read them from *right to left*, which leads to an exponential blow-up of the minimal size in both directions. The witness tree languages for this claim are based on the languages $L((a + b)^n a(a + b)^*)_{n \in \mathbb{N}}$, which cause an exponential blow-up for DFAs which read strings from right to left. Here we take the standard encoding over the reversed trees.

Lemma 7. *For all unranked trees t_1, t_2, if $\overline{[[t_1]]} \equiv_{\overline{[[L]]}} \overline{[[t_2]]}$ then $t_1 \equiv_L t_2$.*

Proof (Sketch). This follows from the definitions of the encoding and the contexts: any context for a tree in the standard encoding can be obtained by translating a context in the Curried encoding. □

Proposition 8. *The minimal bottom-up deterministic stepwise tree automaton for an unranked regular language L is never larger than the minimal bottom-up deterministic tree automaton for the inverted standard encoding $\overline{[[L]]}$.*

Proof. Due to the Myhill-Nerode Theorem 6 it is sufficient to compare the indexes of the congruences $\equiv_L$ and $\equiv_{\overline{[[L]]}}$. By Lemma 7, if two trees are in different equivalence classes of $\equiv_L$ then their encodings will be different equivalent classes of $\equiv_{\overline{[[L]]}}$, i.e., the index of L smaller or equal than the index of $\overline{[[L]]}$. □

Proposition 9. *There exists an infinite class of languages $(L_i)_{i \in \mathbb{N}}$ such that for every L_i, the minimal bottom-up deterministic stepwise tree automaton for L_i is exponentially more succinct than the minimal bottom-up deterministic tree automaton for the encoding $\overline{[[L_i]]}$.*

Proof (Sketch). The proof is based on the fact that the smallest DFA for the union of DFAs $A_1, \ldots, A_n$ can be exponentially larger than the sum of the sizes $|A_1| + \cdots + |A_n|$. □

5.2 Stepwise vs Parallel UTAs

We mention the following proposition without proof:

Proposition 10. *Minimal deterministic stepwise tree automata are always smaller or equal than minimal deterministic parallel UTAs for the same language.*

It is easy to see that translating a stepwise automaton to a pUTA gives at most a quadratic blow-up. This upper bound is also tight:

Proposition 11. *There exists an infinite class of languages $(L_i)_{i \in \mathbb{N}}$ such that for every L_i, the minimal bottom-up deterministic stepwise tree automaton is quadratically more succinct than the minimal deterministic pUTA.*

Proof. The lemma holds for $L_n = \{a_1(a^n), \ldots, a_n(a^n)\}$. pUTAs need n different automata of size n to accept the string a^n, so their minimal size is $\mathcal{O}(n^2)$. Stepwise automata can share the state sets of these, so their minimal size is $\mathcal{O}(n)$. □

6   Top-Down Deterministic UTAs

We briefly discuss a minimization result for top-down deterministic UTAs. According to the definition of Brüggemann-Klein, Murata and Wood, a UTA $A = (Q, \Sigma, \delta, F)$ is top-down deterministic if for all $q \in Q$, $a \in \Sigma$, and $n \geq 0$, $\delta(q, a)$ contains at most one string of length n [2]. We show that a more expressive form of top-down deteriminism still allows for *(i)* a PTIME minimization algorithm and *(ii)* uniqueness up to isomorphism of the minimal automaton. This notion of top-down determinism not only allows to take into account the number of siblings but also their labeling. It is very similar to the notion defined by Cristau, Löding and Thomas [6].

To define the notion of top-down determinism, we assume that there is a function $f : Q \to \Sigma$ that associates to each state the unique alphabet symbol it can be assigned to in a run of the automaton. The idea from this function stems from *specialized DTDs* [20], which are always provided by such a function. The results in this section therefore directly carry over onto specialized DTDs. We extend this function f in the obvious way to strings over Q.

The main motivation of this section lies in XML schema languages. Indeed, the proposed notion of top-down determinism is strictly more powerful than the notions of *single-type* and *restrained competition* specialized DTDs [16], which correspond to the expressive power of XML Schema [28] and 1-pass preorder typing [14] respectively. It is not hard to see that the proposed minimization algorithm preserves the single-type and restrained competition properties and hence, as a corollary, minimization of single-type and restrained competition specialized DTDs (in which the internal regular languages are represented by DFAs) is also in PTIME.

We call a UTA $A = (Q, \Sigma, \delta, F)$ *top-down deterministic* if every language defined by a DFA D representing $\delta(q, a)$ has the following property: if w and w' in $L(D)$ and $f(w) = f(w')$ then $w = w'$.

Theorem 12. *Every top-down deterministic UTA can be minimized in* PTIME. *This minimal top-down deterministic UTA is unique up to isomorphism.*

We briefly sketch the minimization algorithm. Let $A = (Q, \Sigma, \delta, F)$ be top-down deterministic with mapping $f : Q \to \Sigma$. Given a state $q \in Q$, we denote by $L(A, q)$ the language accepted by $(Q, \Sigma, \delta, \{q\})$. The following algorithm minimizes A:

(1) *Trim* A, that is, remove all unreachable states from Q, and remove all $q \in Q$ for which $L(A, q) = \emptyset$, and their corresponding transitions.

(2) Test, for each q_i and q_j in Q, $i \neq j$, whether $L(A, q_i) = L(A, q_j)$. If $L(A, q_i) = L(A, q_j)$, then replace all occurrences of q_j in the definition of δ by q_i, remove the transition $\delta(q_j, f(q_j))$, and remove q_j from Q.
(3) For each $q \in Q$, minimize the DFA representing $\delta(q, f(q))$.

7   Conclusions

We have shown that the minimization problem for DUTAs (bottom-up deterministic UTAs in which the languages in the transition function are represented by DFAs) is NP-complete. The reason behind this hardness result is that these DUTAs are not truly deterministic. Indeed, DUTAs still allow to represent regular languages over states by a *disjoint union of DFAs*, as exemplified in Section 3.1. Furthermore, the canonical translations of DUTAs over the known ranked encodings result in *unambiguous* rather than deterministic binary tree automata.

A second contibution of the paper is a comparison between several notions of determinism for unranked tree automata. We compared three different notions: parallel UTAs, which were defined independently in [6] and [21], stepwise tree automata [4], and ranked tree automata over the *first-child next-sibling* encoding. In general, the stepwise tree automata provide the smallest minimal automata. Moreover, since they have a direct connection to traditional ranked tree automata through an encoding based on currying, a PTIME minimization algorithm and a Myhill-Nerode theorem is immediate.

Acknowledgments

We thank Frank Neven and Thomas Schwentick for helpful discussions and comments on a previous version of the paper.

References

1. D. Angluin. Learning regular sets from queries and counterexamples. *Information and Computation*, 75(2):87–106, 1987.
2. A. Brüggemann-Klein, M. Murata, and D. Wood. Regular tree and regular hedge languages over unranked alphabets: Version 1, april 3, 2001. Technical Report HKUST-TCSC-2001-0, The Hongkong University of Science and Technology, 2001.
3. J. Carme, A. Lemay, and J. Niehren. Learning node selecting tree transducers from completely annotated examples. In *ICGI 2004*, pages 91–102, 2004.
4. J. Carme, J. Niehren, and M. Tommasi. Querying unranked trees with stepwise tree automata. In *RTA 2004*, pages 105–118, 2004.
5. B. Courcelle. On recognizable sets and tree automata. In *Resolution of equations in algebraic structures*, pages 93–126, 1989.
6. J. Cristau, C. Löding, and W. Thomas. Deterministic automata on unranked trees. In *FCT 2005*, 2005. To Appear.
7. M. Frick, M. Grohe, and C. Koch. Query evaluation on compressed trees (extended abstract). In *LICS 2003*, pages 188–197, 2003.

8. E.M. Gold. Complexity of automaton identification from given data. *Inform. Control*, 37:302–320, 1978.
9. T. Jiang and B. Ravikumar. Minimal NFA problems are hard. *SIAM Journal on Computing*, 22(6):1117–1141, 1993.
10. D. Kozen. On the Myhill-Nerode theorem for trees *Bulletin of the European Association for Theoretical Computer Science*, 147:170–173, 1992.
11. A. Malcher. Minimizing finite automata is computationally hard. *Theoretical Computer Science*, 327(3):375–390, 2004.
12. W. Martens. On minimizing finite automata with very little non-determinism. Manuscript, 2005.
13. W. Martens and F. Neven. Frontiers of tractability for typechecking simple XML transformations. In *PODS 2004*, pages 23–34, 2004.
14. W. Martens, F. Neven, and T. Schwentick. Which XML schemas admit 1-pass preorder typing? In *ICDT 2005*, pages 68–82, 2005.
15. W. Martens and J. Niehren. Minimizing Tree Automata for Unranked Trees. Full Version. http://www.uhasselt.be/wim.martens/pubs.html
16. M. Murata, D. Lee, M. Mani, and K. Kawaguchi. Taxonomy of XML schema languages using formal language theory. *ACM Transaction on Internet Technology*, 5(4), 2005. To Appear.
17. F. Neven and T. Schwentick. Expressive and efficient pattern languages for tree-structured data. In *PODS 2000*, pages 145–156, 2000.
18. F. Neven and T. Schwentick. Query automata on finite trees. *Theoretical Computer Science*, 275:633–674, 2002.
19. J. Oncina and P. Garcia. Inferring regular languages in polynomial update time. In *Pattern Recognition and Image Analysis*, pages 49–61, 1992.
20. Y. Papakonstantinou and V. Vianu. DTD inference for views of XML data. In *PODS 2000*, pages 35–46. ACM Press, 2000.
21. S. Raeymaekers and M. Bruynooghe. Minimization of finite unranked tree automata. Manuscript, 2004.
22. T. Schwentick. XPath query containment. *Sigmod Record*, 33(2):101–109, 2004.
23. H. Seidl. Deciding equivalence of finite tree automata. *SIAM Journal on Computing*, 19(3):424–437, 1990.
24. R. E. Stearns and H. B. Hunt III. On the equivalence and containment problems for unambiguous regular expressions, regular grammars and finite automata. *SIAM Journal on Computing*, 14(3):598–611, 1985.
25. L. J. Stockmeyer and A. R. Meyer. Word problems requiring exponential time: Preliminary report. In *STOC 1973*, pages 1–9, 1973.
26. D. Suciu. Typechecking for semistructured data. In *DBPL 2001*, pages 1–20, 2001.
27. J.W. Thatcher and J.B. Wright. Generalized finite automata theory with an application to a decision problem of second-order logic. *Mathematical Systems Theory*, 2(1):57–81, 1968.
28. World Wide Web Consortium. XML Schema http://www.w3.org/XML/Schema

Dependency-Preserving Normalization
of Relational and XML Data

Solmaz Kolahi

Department of Computer Science, University of Toronto
solmaz@cs.toronto.edu

Abstract. Having a database design that avoids redundant information
and update anomalies is the main goal of normalization techniques. Ideally, data as well as constraints should be preserved. However, this is not
always achievable: while BCNF eliminates all redundancies, it may not
preserve constraints, and 3NF, which achieves dependency preservation,
may not always eliminate all redundancies.

Our first goal is to investigate how much redundancy 3NF tolerates
in order to achieve dependency preservation. We apply an information-
theoretic measure and show that only prime attributes admit redundant
information in 3NF, but their information content may be arbitrarily
low.

Then we study the possibility of achieving both redundancy elimination and dependency preservation by a hierarchical representation of
relational data in XML. We provide a characterization of cases when an
XML normal form called XNF guarantees both.

Finally, we deal with dependency preservation in XML and show that
like in the relational case, normalizing XML documents to achieve non-
redundant data can result in losing constraints. By modifying the definition of XNF, we define another normal form for XML documents,
X3NF, that generalizes 3NF for the case of XML and achieves dependency preservation.

1 Introduction

Database design for relational data is defined as coming up with a "good" way
of grouping the attributes of interest into tables, yielding a database schema [1].
Here "good" refers to schemas that prevent the database from storing anomalies.
The notion of normalization has a key role in design theory and is a well-studied
subject (refer to [5] for a survey). Given a database schema together with a set
of dependencies defined over the attributes, normalization is the act of refining
the schema into a "better" schema, considering three criteria: preserving the
data, preserving the dependencies, and eliminating redundancy. In this paper,
we focus on the last two criteria: how do we represent data to have minimum
redundancy while preserving all the dependencies?

Normalization algorithms that produce schemas in BCNF guarantee to eliminate the possibility of redundancy. However, for some relational specifications

G. Bierman and C. Koch (Eds.): DBPL 2005, LNCS 3774, pp. 247–261, 2005.

it is not possible to achieve dependency-preserving BCNF relations. Normalizing into 3NF relations is guaranteed to be dependency-preserving; finding the price that we have to pay for this preservation, in terms of redundancy, is the first contribution of this paper. We apply a recently-introduced information-theoretic measure [4] to see where in a database and how much the normal form 3NF allows redundancy. We show that in a database instance of a 3NF schema, only positions corresponding to prime attributes (members of candidate keys) admit redundant information, but their information content may be arbitrarily low.

Then we study the possibility of achieving both redundancy elimination and dependency preservation by a hierarchical representation of relational data in XML. A paper [17] that addresses a similar problem shows that any arbitrary mapping of a relation into a hierarchical XML document is redundancy-free if and only if the relation is in BCNF. However, the authors do not provide a characterization of cases when a redundancy-free XML document is obtainable from non-BCNF relational data. As our second contribution, we provide a PTIME algorithm that given a relational schema and a set of functional dependencies defined over it, decides if there is a corresponding dependency-preserving XML representation, which does not allow redundant information, and outputs such an XML specification if there is any. There are also papers [8, 14] that address the problem of constraint-preserving transformations from XML to relational databases, which is not a subject of interest in this paper.

To do the above transformation, we need to study the design principles of XML documents as well. Defining dependency constraints over the schemas of XML documents, such as DTDs, has been a subject of interest over the past years. The semantics of key constraints [6, 7], foreign keys and inclusion constraints [10, 11, 12, 2], and functional dependencies [3, 16, 18, 15, 13, 19] and their inference, consistency, and complexity issues have been studied. The normalization of XML documents has also been addressed in three papers [3, 9, 19]. All of them define similar normal forms for XML that do not allow redundancy with respect to a set of dependency constraints. However, the concept of dependency preservation is not addressed in any of the proposed XML normalization techniques.

In this paper, we deal with the concept of dependency preservation in normalization of XML documents. Then by modifying the normal form XNF [3], we present another normal form X3NF that generalizes 3NF for the case of XML. This is our last contribution.

The rest of this paper is organized as follows: Section 2 reviews some basic concepts of relational and XML design theory. In Section 3 we apply an information-theoretic measure of information content to 3NF. In Section 4 we show how to represent relational data in dependency-preserving XML documents that have no redundancy. We introduce the normal form X3NF for XML documents in Section 5, and in Section 6 we bring concluding remarks and ideas of future research. Due to space limitations, most of the proofs are omitted in the paper but are available in the appendix, which can be found at: http://www.cs.toronto.edu/~solmaz/docs/dbpl05appendix.pdf.

2   Preliminaries

2.1   Relational Databases and Normal Forms

A relational specification $(\mathcal{R}, \Sigma)$ consists of an m-ary relational schema $\mathcal{R}$ and a set of integrity constraints Σ defined over $\mathcal{R}$, where m is the number of attributes associated with $\mathcal{R}$ denoted as $sort(\mathcal{R})$. An instance I of $(\mathcal{R}, \Sigma)$, written as $I \in inst(\mathcal{R}, \Sigma)$, is a finite set of m-tuples such that I satisfies the constraints in Σ.

In this paper, we focus on functional dependencies (FDs) and assume that all of the constraints in Σ are of the form $X \rightarrow Y$, where $X, Y \subseteq sort(R)$. An instance I satisfies $X \rightarrow Y$ iff for every two tuples $t_1, t_2 \in I$, $t_1[X] = t_2[X]$ implies $t_1[Y] = t_2[Y]$. A relational specification $(\mathcal{R}, \Sigma)$ is in BCNF iff for every nontrivial FD $X \rightarrow Y \in \Sigma$, we have $X \rightarrow sort(\mathcal{R}) \in \Sigma^+$ (X is a key), where Σ^+ is the set of all the FDs implied by Σ. A candidate key is a key whose proper subsets are not keys. Specification $(\mathcal{R}, \Sigma)$ is in 3NF iff for every nontrivial FD $X \rightarrow A$, X is a key, or A is a member of a candidate key (A is prime).

Given $(\mathcal{R}, \Sigma)$, there are known algorithms that decompose the schema into $(\mathcal{R}_1, \Sigma_1), \ldots, (\mathcal{R}_n, \Sigma_n)$, such that $\bigcup_{i \in [1,n]} sort(\mathcal{R}_i) = sort(\mathcal{R})$, and for each $i \in [1, n]$, $sort(\mathcal{R}_i) \neq \emptyset$, $\Sigma_i = \pi_{\mathcal{R}_i}(\Sigma^+)$, and $(\mathcal{R}_i, \Sigma_i)$ is in BCNF (or 3NF). BCNF decompositions guarantee to produce relations that do not store any redundant data, while 3NF decompositions may not produce non-redundant relations, but they guarantee to preserve all the FDs, i.e. Σ is equivalent to $\bigcup_{i \in [1,n]} \Sigma_i$.

2.2   XML Documents and Normal Forms

DTDs and XML Trees. For a formal definition of a DTD, assume that we have the following disjoint sets: El of element names, Att of attribute names, which start with the symbol @, Str of possible values of string-valued attributes.

A *DTD (Document Type Definition)* D is defined to be $D = (E, A, P, R, r)$, where $E \subseteq El$ is a finite set of element types, $A \subseteq Att$ is a finite set of attributes, P is a set of rules $\tau \rightarrow P_\tau$ for each $\tau \in E$, where P_τ is a regular expression over $E - \{r\}$, R assigns a subset of A to each element $\tau \in E$, and $r \in E$ is the root.

An *XML tree* is a finite rooted directed tree $T = (N, G)$, where N is the set of nodes, and G is the set of edges, together with a labeling function $\lambda : N \rightarrow El$ and an attribute function $\rho_@ : N \rightarrow Str$ for each @$a \in Att$. We say tree T conforms to DTD $D = (E, A, P, R, r)$, written as $T \models D$, if the root of T is labeled r, and for every $x \in N$ with $\lambda(x) = a$, the word $\lambda(x_1) \ldots \lambda(x_n)$ is in the language defined by P_a where $x_1, \ldots, x_n$ are children of x in order, @$l \in R(a)$ iff the function $\rho_@$ is defined on x.

Functional Dependencies for XML. Given a DTD $D = (E, A, P, R, r)$, an *element path* q is a word in the language E^*, and an *attribute path* is a word of the form $q.@l$, where $q \in E^*$ and @$l \in A$. An element path q is consistent with D if there is a tree $T \models D$ that contains a node reachable by q; if the nodes reachable by q have attribute @l, then the attribute path $q.@l$ is consistent with

D. The set of all paths consistent with a DTD D is denoted by $paths(D)$. The last element type that occurs on a path q is called $last(q)$.

Given an XML tree $T = (N, G)$ such that $T \models D$, a *tree tuple* [3] is a subtree of T rooted at r containing at most one occurrence of every path. Intuitively, the set of all tree tuples in T forms a relational representation of T. Formally, a tree tuple is a mapping $t : paths(D) \rightarrow N \cup Str \cup \{\perp\}$ such that if for an element path q whose last letter is a, we have $t(q) \neq \perp$, then $t(q) \in N$ and $\lambda(t(q)) = a$; if q' is a prefix of q, then $t(q') \neq \perp$ and $t(q')$ lies on the path from the root to $t(q)$ in T; if $@l$ is defined for $t(q)$ and its value is $v \in Str$, then $t(q.@l) = v$.

A *functional dependency* over a DTD D [3] is an expression of the form $\{q_1, \ldots, q_n\} \rightarrow q$, where $q, q_1, \ldots, q_n \in paths(D)$. A tree T satisfies an FD $\{q_1, \ldots, q_n\} \rightarrow q$ if for any two tree tuples t_1, t_2 in T, whenever $t_1(q_i) = t_2(q_i) \neq \perp$ for all $i \in [1, n]$, then $t_1(q) = t_2(q)$.

XNF: An XML Normal Form. Given a DTD D and a set Σ of FDs over D, $(D, \Sigma)^+$ is the set of all FDs implied by (D, Σ). An FD is called *trivial* if it belongs to $(D, \emptyset)^+$. We say that (D, Σ) is in *XML Normal Form (XNF)* [3] if for every nontrivial FD $X \rightarrow q.@l$ in $(D, \Sigma)^+$, the FD $X \rightarrow q$ is also in $(D, \Sigma)^+$. This normal form generalizes BCNF for XML documents and disallows any redundancy caused by FDs in the document.

3   Relational Third Normal Form Revisited

The amount of information provided by each cell of a relational database with respect to a set of integrity constraints can be determined using an information-theoretic measure that has been introduced recently [4]. Using this measure, it is known that the information content of every cell in an instance of a BCNF relational schema is maximum.

In this section, we characterize the relational 3NF using this measure and show that in an instance of a relational schema in 3NF, only for the cells corresponding to prime attributes the information content can be less than maximum, meaning that they store redundant information. However, the redundancy of such cells can be arbitrarily high. This is the price that we have to pay in 3NF decompositions to guarantee preservation of FDs.

3.1   Information-Theoretic Measure of Information Content

Here, we briefly review the information-theoretic measure that will be used in the rest of this section and refer the reader to [4] for more details. Intuitively, $\text{INF}_I(p|\Sigma)$ measures the average information provided by position p with respect to constraints Σ, given all possible ways of removing values in the instance I.

Let $\mathcal{R}$ be a relational schema, Σ a set of constraints, and $I \in inst(\mathcal{R}, \Sigma)$. The set of positions in I, $Pos(I)$, is defined as $\{(\mathcal{R}, t, A) \mid t \in I \text{ and } A \in sort(\mathcal{R})\}$. Let $n = |Pos(I)|$, and suppose each position in $Pos(I)$ is assigned a unique number $p \in [1, n]$. When the active domain of instance I is contained in $[1, k]$, the information content of a position $p \in Pos(I)$ with respect to the set of constraints Σ, written as $\mathrm{INF}_I^k(p|\Sigma)$, is informally defined as follows. Let $X \subseteq Pos(I) - \{p\}$. Suppose the values in those positions are lost, and someone restores them from the set $[1, k]$; we measure how much information this gives us about the value of p, by computing an entropy of a certain distribution. Then $\mathrm{INF}_I^k(p|\Sigma)$ is the average of such entropy over all sets $X \subseteq Pos(I) - \{p\}$.

To define the measure more formally, let $\Omega(I, p)$ be the set of 2^{n-1} vectors $(a_1, \ldots, a_{p-1}, a_{p+1}, \ldots, a_n)$ such that for every $i \in [1, n] - \{p\}$ a_i is either a variable v_i or the value in the i-th position of I. Given a vector $\bar{a} \in \Omega(I, p)$, the conditional entropy $P(a|\bar{a})$ characterizes how likely a is to occur in position p, if some values are removed from I according to the tuple $\bar{a}$. Let $I_{(a,\bar{a})}$ be a table obtained from I by putting a in position p and a_i in position i for $i \neq p$. Then $SAT_\Sigma^k(I_{(a,\bar{a})})$ is defined as the set of all substitutions $\sigma : \bar{a} \to [1, k]$ such that $\sigma(I_{(a,\bar{a})}) \models \Sigma$. The probability $P(a|\bar{a})$ is defined as:

$$P(a|\bar{a}) = \frac{|SAT_\Sigma^k(I_{(a,\bar{a})})|}{\sum_{b \in [1,k]} |SAT_\Sigma^k(I_{(b,\bar{a})})|}.$$

The measure of the amount of information in position p is then defined as:

$$\mathrm{INF}_I^k(p|\Sigma) = \sum_{\bar{a} \in \Omega(I,p)} \left(P(\bar{a}) \sum_{a \in [1,k]} P(a|\bar{a}) \log \frac{1}{P(a|\bar{a})} \right),$$

where $P(\bar{a}) = 1/2^{n-1}$ since we consider a uniform distribution on $\Omega(I, p)$. For the case of infinite domain, the measure $\mathrm{INF}_I(p|\Sigma)$ is defined as:

$$\lim_{k \to \infty} \frac{\mathrm{INF}_I^k(p|\Sigma)}{\log k}.$$

This measure of information content can be used to distinguish a good design from a bad one. A database specification $(\mathcal{R}, \Sigma)$ is defined as *well-designed* if for every $I \in inst(\mathcal{R}, \Sigma)$ and every $p \in Pos(I)$, $\mathrm{INF}_I(p|\Sigma) = 1$; this means every position of every instance should have the maximum information. It is also known that if $(\mathcal{R}, \Sigma)$ is in BCNF or 4NF, then it is well-designed.

3.2 Characterizing 3NF

We now apply the criterion of being well-designed to relational third normal form. We want to know where and to what extent 3NF allows a database to store redundant information.

The following theorem shows that only positions corresponding to prime attributes can store redundant information. Then using an example, we will see that 3NF does not impose an upper bound for this redundancy.

Theorem 1. *Let Σ be a set of FDs over a relational schema $\mathcal{R}$. The specification $(\mathcal{R}, \Sigma)$ is in 3NF if and only if for every $I \in inst(\mathcal{R}, \Sigma)$ and $p = (\mathcal{R}, t, A)$ in $Pos(I)$, $\mathrm{INF}_I(p|\Sigma) < 1$ implies A is a prime attribute.*

A	B	B_1	...	B_m
1	1	1	...	1
1	2	1	...	1
1	3	1	...	1
1	4	1	...	1
⋮	⋮	⋮		⋮
1	$|tup|$	1	...	1

Fig. 1. A database instance

Example 1. Consider the database instance shown in Fig. 1, which is an instance of $(\mathcal{R}, \Sigma)$, where $\mathcal{R} = (A, B, B_1, \ldots, B_m)$, $\Sigma = \{AB \rightarrow B_1 \ldots B_m, B_1 \rightarrow A, \ldots, B_m \rightarrow A\}$, and the domain of each attribute is $\mathbb{N}$. It is easy to see that $(\mathcal{R}, \Sigma)$ is in 3NF. Let p denote the position of the gray cell in the instance. If we lose this value, there are many other tuples that can help restore it considering the FDs. Our goal is to measure the amount of information that this cell provides and see if this amount can be arbitrarily close to zero.

Claim. The information content of position p in Example 1 can be obtained by the following equation:

$$\text{INF}_I(p|\Sigma) = \sum_{i=0}^{m} \frac{\binom{m}{i}(1 + 2^{-i})^{|tup|-1}}{2^{|tup|+m-1}}.$$

It can be seen that by choosing the number of attributes (dependencies) and number of tuples big enough, we could make the information content of position p in Example 1 arbitrarily small. Therefore, we have:

Theorem 2. *For every $\epsilon \in (0, 1]$, there exists a relational schema $\mathcal{R}$, a set of FDs Σ over $\mathcal{R}$, an instance $I \in inst(\mathcal{R}, \Sigma)$, and position $p \in Pos(I)$ such that $(\mathcal{R}, \Sigma)$ is in 3NF, and $\text{INF}_I(p|\Sigma) < \epsilon$.*

Proof. Consider again position p of the database instance of Fig. 1 and the constraints of Example 1. The following inequalities show that for $\text{INF}_I(p|\Sigma)$ to be less than ϵ, it is enough to have $m > -\log_2 \epsilon + 1$ and $|tup| > \log_{3/4} \epsilon/2 + 1$:

$$\sum_{i=0}^{m} \frac{\binom{m}{i}(1 + 2^{-i})^{|tup|-1}}{2^{|tup|+m-1}} < \epsilon.$$

$$2^{|tup|-1} + \sum_{i=1}^{m} \binom{m}{i}(1 + \frac{1}{2})^{|tup|-1} < 2^{|tup|+m-1}\epsilon.$$

$$2^{|tup|-1} + 2^m(1 + \frac{1}{2})^{|tup|-1} < 2^{|tup|+m-1}\epsilon.$$

$$\frac{2^{2|tup|-2} + 2^m 3^{|tup|-1}}{2^{|tup|-1}} < 2^{|tup|+m-1}\epsilon.$$

$$\left(\frac{1}{2}\right)^m + \left(\frac{3}{4}\right)^{|tup|-1} < \epsilon.$$

$$m > -\log_2 \epsilon + 1 \ , \ |tup| > \log_{3/4} \epsilon/2 + 1.$$

4 Dependency-Preserving Redundancy-Free Conversion of Relational Data into XML Documents

In designing relational databases, relations are sometimes decomposed to avoid redundancies and update anomalies. Losslessness, dependency preservation, and redundancy elimination are the three desired properties for each decomposition. However, it is not always possible to achieve all the three: while BCNF decomposition eliminates all redundancies, it may not preserve dependencies, and 3NF decomposition, which achieves dependency preservation, may produce relations that store data with high degrees of redundancy, as we have seen in Section 3.

In this section, we want to show that for some relational specifications, it is possible to produce an FD-preserving XML representation, which is in XNF and hence avoids redundancies and update anomalies. This way we can take advantage of good properties of BCNF and 3NF that are not achievable together in relational representation.

Example 2. Consider the relational schema $\mathcal{R}(A, B, C)$, with FDs $\mathcal{F} = \{AB \to C$ and $C \to B\}$. This is a classical example of a relational schema that does not have any FD-preserving BCNF decomposition. We can however convert it into a DTD $D = (E, A, P, R, r)$ and a set of FDs Σ such that (D, Σ) does not allow redundant data:

- $E = \{r, A, B, C\}$.
- $A = \{@a, @b, @c\}$.
- $P(r) = B^*, \ \ P(B) = A^*, \ \ P(A) = C^*, \ \ P(C) = \epsilon$.
- $R(r) = \emptyset, \ \ R(A) = \{@a\}, \ \ R(B) = \{@b\}, \ \ R(C) = \{@c\}$.
- $\Sigma = \{r.B.@b \to r.B,$
    $\{r.B, r.B.A.@a\} \to r.B.A,$
    $\{r.B.A, r.B.A.C.@c\} \to r.A.B.C,$
    $\{r.B.A.@a, r.B.@b\} \to r.B.A.C.@c,$
    $r.B.A.C.@c \to r.B.@b\}$.

This conversion is visualized in Fig. 2. Note that the first three FDs are the result of the nested structure of the document. The second FD for example means that given a B element, a value of attribute $@a$ uniquely determines one of the children, which is an A element. The last two FDs are the translations of relational FDs in $\mathcal{F}$. From the set of FDs Σ, we can easily infer the following two FDs: $\{r.B.A.@a, r.B.@b\} \to r.B.A.C$ and $r.B.A.C.@c \to r.B$. Thus, (D, Σ) is in normal form XNF and hence does not allow redundancy.

In the above example, the correct hierarchical ordering of elements in the DTD makes it possible to have an XML representation in XNF from a non-BCNF relation. Since for each relational FD there is a path in the DTD containing all the

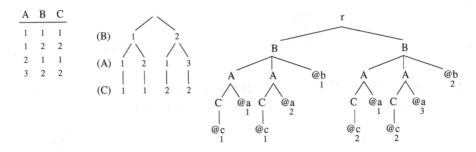

Fig. 2. Conversion of relational data into a redundancy-free XML document

participating attributes, the representation is also FD-preserving. We now formally define this hierarchical translation for an arbitrary relational specification and investigate the conditions that a relational specification needs to satisfy in order to have an XML representation in XNF.

Definition 1. (Hierarchical Translation of Relational Schema) *Let $\mathcal{R} = (A_1, \ldots, A_m)$ be a relational schema and $\mathcal{F}$ be a set of FDs defined over it. We define DTD $D = (E, A, P, R, r)$ and the set of XML FDs Σ as a hierarchical translation of $(\mathcal{R}, \mathcal{F})$ as follows:*

- *$E = \{\tau_1, \ldots, \tau_m\} \cup \{r\}$; each element τ_i corresponds to a relational attribute $A_i \in \mathcal{R}$.*
- *$A(r) = \emptyset$ and for $i \in [1, m]$, $A(\tau_i) = @l_i$; each element has an attribute to store a value.*
- *Elements in E form an ordering $\tau_{\pi_1}, \ldots, \tau_{\pi_m}$ such that $P(r) = \tau_{\pi_1}^*$, $P(\tau_{\pi_m}) = \epsilon$, and for every $i \in [1, m)$, $P(\tau_{\pi_i}) = \tau_{\pi_{i+1}}^*$.*
- *The FD $r.\tau_{\pi_1}.@l_{\pi_1} \to \tau_{\pi_1}$ is in Σ. Also for each $i \in [2, m]$, there is an FD $\{p, p.\tau_{\pi_i}.@l_{\pi_i}\} \to p.\tau_{\pi_i}$ in Σ, where p is the path from the root to the parent of τ_{π_i}.*
- *For every FD $X_1 \to X_2 \in \mathcal{F}$, there is a corresponding FD $S_1 \to S_2 \in \Sigma$, such that for every attribute A_i in X_1 (X_2), there is a path $p.\tau_i.@l_i$ in S_1 (S_2), where τ_i corresponds to A_i and p is the path from the root to the parent of τ_i.*

Let $\mathcal{R} = (A_1, \ldots, A_m)$ be a relational schema, $\mathcal{F}$ a set of FDs over $\mathcal{R}$, and (D, Σ) a hierarchical translation of $(\mathcal{R}, \mathcal{F})$. Then:

Theorem 3. *The XML specification (D, Σ) is in XNF iff for every FD $X \to p.@l \in (D, \Sigma)^+$ and every prefix q of path p, it is the case that $X \to q.@m \in (D, \Sigma)^+$, where $R(last(q)) = \{@m\}$.*

Corollary 1. *$(\mathcal{R}, \mathcal{F})$ has a redundancy-free XML representation iff we can put the attributes of $\mathcal{R}$ in order $A_{\pi_1}, \ldots, A_{\pi_m}$ such that for every nontrivial FD $X \to A_{\pi_i} \in \mathcal{F}^+$ and every $j < i$, the FD $X \to A_{\pi_j}$ is also in $\mathcal{F}^+$.*

Example 3. Consider the following functional dependencies over the relational schema $\mathcal{R} = (A, B, C, D, F)$:

$$ABCD \rightarrow F$$
$$FD \rightarrow A$$
$$FC \rightarrow B$$

Since none of the FDs $FC \rightarrow A$ or $FD \rightarrow B$ hold, we cannot put the attributes in the desired order, and the schema does not have an XNF hierarchical translation.

Let $\mathcal{F}_{min} = \{X_1 \rightarrow A_1, \ldots, X_k \rightarrow A_k\}$ denote the minimal cover of the FDs over the relational schema $\mathcal{R}$. In order to find the appropriate order of attributes, we shall first compute the intersection of the closures of all X_i's ($i \in [1, k]$). If the intersection is empty, there is no XML representation for this relational schema in XNF. If not, we output the attributes in the intersection in an arbitrary order as the first elements of the ordering. We remove from $\mathcal{F}_{min}$ the FDs whose right-hand sides are already in the output. Then we repeat computing the intersection of closures with the remaining FDs until there is no FD left or all the attributes are in the output. This procedure is described in Algorithm 1.

Some relational specifications do not satisfy the condition of Corollary 1. However, there might be an FD-preserving decomposition of them such that each of the decomposed schemas can be hierarchically translated into an XML specification in XNF. Suppose $(D_1, \Sigma_1), \ldots, (D_n, \Sigma_n)$ are the XML translations of the decomposed relations as described above. We can combine all the DTDs into a single DTD by concatenating all the regular expressions assigned to their roots and assign the resulting expression to the new root. Then we have to take the union of element types, attributes, and FDs. Note that we assume the sets of element types are disjoint. This can be seen in the following example and is formally described in Section 4.1.

Example 4. Consider the following functional dependencies over the relational schema $\mathcal{R} = (A, B, C, D, F)$:

$$ABC \rightarrow DF$$
$$DC \rightarrow A$$
$$F \rightarrow B$$

Consider a dependency-preserving decomposition for this schema as follows: $\mathcal{R}_1 = (A, B, C, D)$ with FDs $DC \rightarrow A$, $ABC \rightarrow D$, and $\mathcal{R}_2 = (A, B, C, F)$ with FDs $F \rightarrow B$, $ABC \rightarrow F$. A possible XML specification in XNF would include DTD $D = (E, A, P, R, r)$ as follows. The set of FDs Σ, omitted here, consists of the FDs resulting from the hierarchical translation and the FDs corresponding to the relational FDs. It can be easily verified that (D, Σ) is in XNF.

- $E = \{r, A, B, C, D, F, A', B', C'\}$.
- $A = \{@a, @b, @c, @d, @f\}$.
- $P(r) = A^*B'^*$, $P(A) = B^*$, $P(B) = C^*$, $P(C) = D^*$,
  $P(D) = \epsilon$, $P(B') = A'^*$, $P(A') = C'^*$, $P(C') = F^*$, $P(F) = \epsilon$.

- $R(r) = \emptyset$, $R(A) = R(A') = \{@a\}$, $R(B) = R(B') = \{@b\}$,
  $R(C) = R(C') = \{@c\}$, $R(D) = \{@d\}$, $R(F) = \{@f\}$.

Note that the original 3NF schema does not have a hierarchical translation in XNF since none of $DC \to B$ or $F \to A$ hold, so the decomposition is necessary.

Input: Relational schema $\mathcal{R}$ and set of FDs $\mathcal{F}$.
Output: Either (D, Σ) in XNF or "No XNF Representation".

Initialize (D, Σ) with only a root r ;
Compute $\mathcal{F}_{min}$ as a minimal cover of $\mathcal{F}$;
Decompose $(\mathcal{R}, \mathcal{F}_{min})$ into lossless 3NF $(\mathcal{R}_1, \mathcal{F}_1), \ldots, (\mathcal{R}_n, \mathcal{F}_n)$ based on $\mathcal{F}_{min}$;
for $i := 1$ *to* n **do**
    if *there is no FD in* $\mathcal{F}_i$ **then**
        $O_i :=$ an arbitrary order of attributes in $\mathcal{R}_i$;
    else
        Compute X_i^{j+} for all FD $X_i^j \to A_i^j$ in $\mathcal{F}_i$;
        $X :=$ attributes in $\mathcal{R}_i$;
        while $X \neq \emptyset$ **do**
            if *no FD in* $\mathcal{F}_i$ *has an attribute in* X *on the right-hand side* **then**
                $Y := X$;
            else
$$Y := \left(\bigcap_{A_i^j \in X} X_i^{j+} \right) \cap X ;$$
            if $Y = \emptyset$ **then**
                return "No XNF Representation" ;
            else
                Append attributes in Y to the ordering O_i ;
                $X := X - Y$;
    $(D, \Sigma) := attach \, ((D, \Sigma), O_i, \mathcal{F}_i)$;
return (D, Σ) ;

Algorithm 1. FD-preserving translation of relational data into redundancy-free XML documents

So far we have considered a special way of converting relational data into a tree-like XML document, namely hierarchical translation. When there is no redundancy-free hierarchical XML representation for a relational specification $(\mathcal{R}, \mathcal{F})$, one might think of other ways of translating $(\mathcal{R}, \mathcal{F})$ into an XML specification (D, Σ), such that (D, Σ) is in XNF and hence does not allow redundancy. Here we claim that in this case even a more general approach, named *semi-hierarchical translation*, does not help. In this approach each element type can represent more than one relational attribute.

Example 5. A semi-hierarchical representation of relational schema of Example 2 consists of DTD $D = (E, A, P, R, r)$ and a set of FDs Σ as follows:

- $E = \{r, AB, C\}$.
- $A = \{@a, @b, @c\}$.

- $P(r) = AB^*,\ \ P(AB) = C^*,\ \ P(C) = \epsilon.$
- $R(r) = \emptyset,\ \ R(AB) = \{@a, @b\},\ \ R(C) = \{@c\}.$
- $\Sigma = \{\{r.AB.@a, r.AB.@b\} \to r.AB,$
    $\{r.AB, r.AB.C.@c\} \to r.AB.C,$
    $\{r.AB.@a, r.AB.@b\} \to r.AB.C.@c,$
    $r.AB.C.@c \to r.AB.@b\}.$

Theorem 4. *A relational specification $(\mathcal{R}, \mathcal{F})$ has a redundancy-free hierarchical translation iff it has a redundancy-free semi-hierarchical translation.*

In other words, checking the conditions of Corollary 1 is enough to know whether or not a relational specification has a non-redundant semi-hierarchical XML representation. Since we believe that semi-hierarchical translation is the most natural way of representing relational data in XML documents, we interchangeably use the general term "XML representation" and the term "hierarchical translation" throughout this paper.

4.1   Algorithm

Given a relational specification $(\mathcal{R}, \mathcal{F})$, Algorithm 1 decides, in polynomial time in the size of $(\mathcal{R}, \mathcal{F})$, whether there is a redundancy-free XML representation for it and produces an XML specification (D, Σ) if there is one.

First, the minimal cover of the FD set is computed. Then a 3NF decomposition is done based on the minimal cover. This decomposition has to be FD-preserving and lossless, so we may add a relation containing attributes of a candidate key. The algorithm then finds the right ordering of attributes for each decomposed relation as described previously. Once an ordering is found, it should be attached to the DTD that is being constructed incrementally. This is done by the operator *attach*, which given an XML specification (D, Σ), an ordering of relational attributes O_i and a set of FDs $\mathcal{F}_i$ over it, updates (D, Σ) by performing the following steps:

- For each $j \in [1, |O_i|]$, create a fresh element type τ_j corresponding to jth attribute in O_i and a fresh attribute name $@l_j$. Then assign $R(\tau_j) := \{@l_j\}$.
- Update $P(r) := P(r).\tau_1^*$, and for each $j \in [1, |O_i|)$, assign $P(\tau_j) := \tau_{j+1}^*$. Assign $P(\tau_{|O_i|}) := \epsilon$.
- Add to Σ the FDs $r.\tau_1.@l_1 \to r.\tau_1$ and $\{p, p.\tau_j.@l_j\} \to p.\tau_j$ for each $j \in (1, |O_i|]$, where p is the path from the root to the parent of τ_j.
- Translate each FD in $\mathcal{F}_i$ into an XML FD by finding the corresponding DTD elements and add it to Σ.

5   XML Third Normal Form

Given an XML specification (D, Σ), there is a decomposition algorithm [3] that produces a lossless specification (D', Σ') in XNF. This decomposition sometimes results in losing some of the FDs as shown in Example 6. In this section we show that in fact for some (D, Σ), it is not possible to have an FD-preserving XNF decomposition. Then we introduce another normal form for XML documents, X3NF, that generalizes relational 3NF for XML.

5.1   Losing FDs in XNF Decomposition

Example 6. Consider the XML document in Fig. 3 that describes a company database. This document satisfies the following constraint: any two clients with the same postal code value must have the same city value. This can be expressed with the following XML FD:

$$company.branch.clients.client.@postal\_code \rightarrow \atop company.branch.clients.client.@city. \quad (1)$$

Since the value of postal code does not identify a node corresponding to a *client* element, this document does not satisfy XNF and stores redundant information caused by the FD. To avoid this, the normalization technique suggests to split the information of cities and postal codes by creating a new element type *city_info*. The restructured version of the document that reflects this decomposition is shown in Fig. 4.

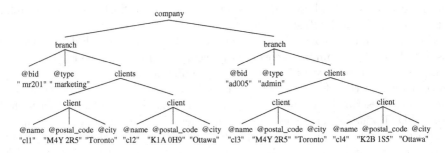

Fig. 3. An XML document containing redundant information

Now assume there is another constraint in the original document of Fig. 3: if two clients are in the same city and require a certain type of service, they are handled by the same branch; written as:

$$\{company.branch.clients.client.@city,\ company.branch.@type\} \rightarrow \atop company.branch. \quad (2)$$

By splitting the cities information in the restructured document of Fig. 4, we actually break the nesting of the element *branch* and the attribute *@city*, so this functional dependency no longer holds over the new document.

The above example shows that the XNF decomposition algorithm [3] is not dependency-preserving. We have also seen that using Algorithm 1, we cannot give an FD-preserving XML representation in XNF for some relational specifications, like the one in Example 3. In general, the concept of dependency

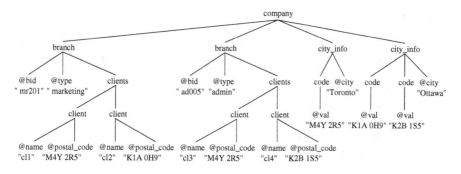

Fig. 4. A redundancy-free XML document

preservation seems to be more involved for the case of XML due to the fact that the implication problem of FDs is not even known to be decidable in presence of DTDs. However, these observations can lead us to the conjecture that like its relational counterpart, BCNF, the normal form XNF cannot be achieved for some XML specifications without losing some FDs. To prove that this conjecture is in fact true, we consider a DTD representation for the relational schema of Example 3 and show that if there is a decomposition (or restructured version) of this representation that satisfies XNF, then some of the FDs are lost or some spurious FDs are imposed[1].Thus:

Theorem 5. *There are XML specifications* (D, Σ), *for which there is no dependency-preserving XNF decomposition.*

5.2   X3NF

In order to avoid the problem of losing FDs in XNF decomposition, we now define another normal form that accepts redundancy to some extent and generalizes the relational 3NF for XML documents.

Let D be a DTD and Σ a set of FDs defined over it. Then:

Definition 2. (Prime Attribute Path) *Attribute path* $p.@l \in paths(D)$ *is called prime if there is a nontrivial FD* $S' \rightarrow p' \in (D, \Sigma)^+$ *such that* $p.@l \in S'$, p' *is an element path, and* S' *is minimal* $(S' - \{p.@l\} \rightarrow p' \notin (D, \Sigma)^+)$.

Definition 3. (X3NF) (D, Σ) *is in XML third normal form (X3NF) iff for every nontrivial FD* $S \rightarrow p.@l \in (D, \Sigma)^+$, *the FD* $S \rightarrow p$ *is also in* $(D, \Sigma)^+$, *or* $p.@l$ *is prime.*

Example 7. Consider the document of Fig. 3 and FDs (1) and (2) that it satisfies. The conditions of X3NF are not violated by FD (1) since the attribute path *company.branch.clients.client.@city* is on the left-hand side of FD (2), whose right-hand side is an element path.

---

[1] For more details, please refer to the appendix available at:http://www.cs.toronto. edu/~solmaz/docs/dbpl05appendix.pdf .

5.3   3NF and X3NF

There is an easy way to map a relational schema $\mathcal{R} = (A_1, \ldots, A_m)$ and FDs $\mathcal{F}$ over it into a DTD $D_\mathcal{R} = (E, A, P, R, r)$ and a set of XML FDs $\Sigma_\mathcal{F}$ [3]:

- $E = \{r, G\}$.
- $A = \{@a_1, \ldots, @a_m\}$.
- $P(r) = G^*$ and $P(G) = \epsilon$.
- $R(r) = \emptyset$, $R(G) = \{@a_1, \ldots, @a_m\}$.
- For each FD $A_{i_1} \ldots A_{i_k} \rightarrow A_i \in \mathcal{F}$, $\{r.G.@a_{i_1}, \ldots, r.G.@a_{i_k}\} \rightarrow r.G.@a_i$ is in Σ.
- $\{r.G.@a_1, \ldots, r.G.@a_m\} \rightarrow r.G$ is in Σ.

Proposition 1. *Given a relational schema $\mathcal{R} = (A_1, \ldots, A_m)$ and FDs $\mathcal{F}$ over $\mathcal{R}$, $(\mathcal{R}, \mathcal{F})$ is in 3NF (BCNF) iff $(D_\mathcal{R}, \Sigma_\mathcal{F})$ is in X3NF (XNF).*

There is another way of mapping relational data into XML documents, which was introduced as hierarchical translation in Section 4. We have seen that by choosing the right order of attributes, we can produce an XML specification in XNF from a relational specification that might not even be in 3NF. The following proposition says if the relational schema is already in 3NF (or BCNF), we can produce an XML specification in X3NF (or XNF) by putting the relational attributes in any arbitrary order.

Proposition 2. *Let $(\mathcal{R}, \mathcal{F})$ be a relational specification in 3NF (BCNF) and (D, Σ) be a hierarchical translation of it obtained from an arbitrary ordering of attributes in $\mathcal{R}$. Then (D, Σ) is in X3NF (XNF).*

6   Conclusions

We looked at the problem of designing dependency-preserving XML documents. We showed that for some relational specifications, for which there is no FD-preserving BCNF decomposition, it is possible to have a dependency-preserving XML design that is in normal form XNF [3] and hence eliminates all redundancies. This can be done by a hierarchical mapping of relational attributes to XML elements defined by a DTD. This transformation of data was justified by showing the fact that to guarantee dependency preservation, relational 3NF allows high degrees of redundancy in positions of database that store values for prime attributes. This was shown using an information-theoretic measure [4].

For some XML specifications however, there is no dependency-preserving XNF decomposition. By modifying the definition of XNF, we proposed a new normal form, X3NF, that generalizes 3NF and allows redundancy to some extent.

A formal definition of dependency preservation for XML using DTD paths is the next step. Then we plan to prove that applying XNF decomposition algorithm [3], with the new definition of anomalous FDs as the ones that violate X3NF, never results in losing an FD.

Acknowledgments. The author is very grateful to Leonid Libkin for his great advices and helpful comments.

References

1. S. Abiteboul, R. Hull, and V. Vianu. Foundations of Databases. Addison-Wesley, 1995.
2. M. Arenas, W. Fan, and L. Libkin. On Verifying Consistency of XML Specifications. In *PODS'02*, pages 259–270.
3. M. Arenas and L. Libkin. A Normal Form for XML Documents. In *PODS'02*, pages 85–96.
4. M. Arenas and L. Libkin. An Information-Theoretic Approach to Normal Forms for Relational and XML Data. *J. ACM*, 52(2): 246–283, ACM Press, 2005.
5. C. Beeri, P. A. Bernstein, and N. Goodman. A Sophisticate's Introduction to Database Normalization Theory. In *VLDB'78*, pages 113–124.
6. P. Buneman, S. Davidson, W. Fan, C. S. Hara, and W. Tan. Reasoning about Keys for XML. *Inf. Syst.*, 28(8): 1037–1063, 2003.
7. P. Buneman, S. B. Davidson, W. Fan, C. S. Hara, and W. Tan. Keys for XML. In *WWW'01*, pages 201–210.
8. Y. Chen, S. Davidson, C. Hara, and Y. Zheng. RRXS: Redundancy Reducing XML Storage in Relations. In *VLDB'03*, pages 189–200.
9. D. W. Embley and W. Yin Mok. Developing XML Documents with Guaranteed "Good" Properties. In *ER'01*, pages 426–441.
10. W. Fan, G. M. Kuper, and J. Siméon. A Unified Constraint Model for XML. In *WWW'01*, pages 179–190.
11. W. Fan and L. Libkin. On XML Integrity Constraints in the Presence of DTDs. In *PODS'01*, pages 114–125.
12. W. Fan and J. Siméon. Integrity Constraints for XML. In *PODS'00*, pages 23–34.
13. S. Hartmann and S. Link. More Functional Dependencies for XML. In *ADBIS'03*, pages 355–369.
14. D. Lee and W. W. Chu. Constraints-Preserving Transformation from XML Document Type Definition to Relational Schema. In *ER'00*, pages 323–338.
15. M. Lee, T. Wang Ling, and W. Lup Low. Designing Functional Dependencies for XML. In *EDBT'02*, pages 124–141.
16. M. Vincent and J. Liu. Functional Dependencies for XML. In *APWEB'03*, pages 22–34.
17. M. W. Vincent, J. Liu, and C. Liu. Redundancy Free Mappings from Relations to XML. In *WAIM'04*, pages 346–356.
18. M. W. Vincent, J. Liu, and C. Liu. Strong Functional Dependencies and Their Application to Normal Forms in XML. *ACM TODS*, 29(3): 445–462, ACM Press, 2004.
19. J. Wang and R. W. Topor. Removing XML Data Redundancies Using Functional and Equality-Generating Dependencies. In *Australian Database Conference*, pages 65–74, 2005.

Complexity and Approximation of Fixing Numerical Attributes in Databases Under Integrity Constraints[*]

Leopoldo Bertossi[1], Loreto Bravo[1],
Enrico Franconi[2], and Andrei Lopatenko[2],[**]

[1] Carleton University, School of Computer Science, Ottawa, Canada
{bertossi, lbravo}@scs.carleton.ca
[2] Free University of Bozen–Bolzano, Faculty of Computer Science, Italy
{franconi, lopatenko}@inf.unibz.it

Abstract. Consistent query answering is the problem of computing the answers from a database that are consistent with respect to certain integrity constraints that the database as a whole may fail to satisfy. Those answers are characterized as those that are invariant under minimal forms of restoring the consistency of the database. In this context, we study the problem of repairing databases by fixing integer numerical values at the attribute level with respect to denial and aggregation constraints. We introduce a quantitative definition of database fix, and investigate the complexity of several decision and optimization problems, including *DFP*, i.e. the existence of fixes within a given distance from the original instance, and *CQA*, i.e. deciding consistency of answers to aggregate conjunctive queries under different semantics. We provide sharp complexity bounds, identify relevant tractable cases; and introduce approximation algorithms for some of those that are intractable. More specifically, we obtain results like undecidability of existence of fixes for aggregation constraints; *MAXSNP*-hardness of *DFP*, but a good approximation algorithm for a relevant special case; and intractability but good approximation for *CQA* for aggregate queries for one database atom denials (plus built-ins).

1 Introduction

Integrity constraints (ICs) are used to impose semantics on a database with the purpose of making the database an accurate model of an application domain. Database management systems or application programs enforce the satisfaction of the ICs by rejecting undesirable updates or executing additional compensating actions. However, there are many situations where we need to interact with databases that are inconsistent in the sense that they do not satisfy certain desirable ICs. In this context, an important problem in database research consists in characterizing

---

[*] Dedicated to the memory of Alberto Mendelzon. Our research on this topic started with conversations between Loreto Bravo and him. Alberto was always generous with his time, advice and ideas; our community is already missing him very much.

[**] Also: University of Manchester, Department of Computer Science, UK.

G. Bierman and C. Koch (Eds.): DBPL 2005, LNCS 3774, pp. 262–278, 2005.

and retrieving consistent data from inconsistent databases [4], in particular consistent answers to queries. From the logical point of view, consistently answering a query posed to an inconsistent database amounts to evaluating the truth of a formula against a particular *class of first-order structures* [2], as opposed to the usual process of truth evaluation in a single structure (the relational database).

Certain database applications, like census, demographic, financial, and experimental data, contain quantitative data, usually associated to nominal or qualitative data, e.g. number of children associated to a household identification code (or address); or measurements associated to a sample identification code. Usually this kind of data contains errors or mistakes with respect to certain semantic constraints. For example, a census form for a particular household may be considered incorrect if the number of children exceeds 20; or if the age of a parent is less than 10. These restrictions can be expressed with denial integrity constraints, that prevent some attributes from taking certain values [11]. Other restrictions may be expressed with aggregation ICs, e.g. the maximum concentration of certain toxin in a sample may not exceed a certain specified amount; or the number of married men and married women must be the same. Inconsistencies in numerical data can be resolved by changing individual attribute values, while keeping values in the keys, e.g. without changing the household code, the number of children is decreased considering the admissible values.

We consider the problem of fixing integer numerical data wrt certain constraints while (a) keeping the values for the attributes in the keys of the relations, and (b) minimizing the quantitative global distance between the original and modified instances. Since the problem may admit several global solutions, each of them involving possibly many individual changes, we are interested in characterizing and computing data and properties that remain invariant under any of these fixing processes. We concentrate on denial and aggregation constraints; and conjunctive queries, with or without aggregation.

Database repairs have been studied in the context of consistent query answering (CQA), i.e. the process of obtaining the answers to a query that are consistent wrt a given set of ICs [2] (c.f. [4] for a survey). There, consistent data is characterized as invariant under all minimal forms of restoring consistency, i.e. as data that is present in all minimally repaired versions of the original instance (the *repairs*). Thus, an answer to a query is consistent if it can be obtained as a standard answer to the query from *every possible* repair. In most of the research on CQA, a repair is a new instance that satisfies the given ICs, but differs from the original instance by a minimal set, under set inclusion, of (completely) deleted or inserted tuples. Changing the value of a particular attribute can be modelled as a deletion followed by an insertion, but this may not correspond to a minimal repair. However, in certain applications it may make more sense to correct (update) numerical values only in certain attributes. This requires a new definition of repair that considers: (a) the quantitative nature of individual changes, (b) the association of the numerical values to other key values; and (c) a quantitative distance between database instances.

Example 1. Consider a network traffic database D that stores flow measurements of links in a network. This network has two types of links, labelled 0 and 1, with maximum capacities 1000

Traffic	Time	Link	Type	Flow
1.1	a	0	1100
1.1	b	1	900
1.3	b	1	850

and 1500, resp. Database D is inconsistent wrt this IC. Under the tuple and set oriented semantics of repairs [2], there is a unique repair, namely deleting tuple $Traffic(1.1, a, 0, 1100)$. However, we have two options that may make more sense than deleting the flow measurement, namely updating the violating tuple to $Traffic(1.1, a, 0, 1000)$ or to $Traffic(1.1, a, 1, 1100)$; satisfying an implicit requirement that the numbers should not change too much.   □

Update-based repairs for restoring consistency are studied in [25]; where changing values in attributes in a tuple is made a primitive repair action; and semantic and computational problems around CQA are analyzed from this perspective. However, peculiarities of changing numerical attributes are not considered, and more importantly, the distance between databases instances used in [25, 26] is based on set-theoretic homomorphisms, but not quantitative, as in this paper. In [25] the repaired instances are called *fixes*, a term that we keep here (instead of *repairs*), because our basic repair actions are also changes of (numerical) attribute values. In this paper we consider fixable attributes that take integer values and the quadratic, Euclidean distance L_2 between database instances. Specific fixes and approximations may be different under other distance functions, e.g. the "city distance" L_1 (the sum of absolute differences), but the general (in)tractability and approximation results remain. However, moving to the case of real numbers will certainly bring new issues that require different approaches; they are left for ongoing and future research. Actually it would be natural to investigate them in the richer context of constraint databases [18].

The problem of attribute-based correction of census data forms is addressed in [11] using disjunctive logic programs with stable model semantics. Several underlying and implicit assumptions that are necessary for that approach to work are made explicit and used here, extending the semantic framework of [11].

We provide semantic foundations for fixes that are based on changes on numerical attributes in the presence of key dependencies and wrt denial and aggregate ICs, while keeping the numerical distance to the original database to a minimum. This framework introduces new challenging decision and optimization problems, and many algorithmic and complexity theoretic issues. We concentrate in particular on the "Database Fix Problem" (*DFP*), of determining the existence of a fix at a distance not bigger than a given bound, in particular considering the problems of construction and verification of such a fix. These problems are highly relevant for large inconsistent databases. For example, solving *DFP* can help us find the minimum distance from a fix to the original instance; information that can be used to prune impossible branches in the process of materialization of a fix. The *CQA* problem of deciding the consistency of query answers is studied wrt decidability, complexity, and approximation under several alternative semantics.

We prove that *DFP* and *CQA* become undecidable in the presence of aggregation constraints. However, *DFP* is *NP*-complete for linear denials, which are enough to capture census like applications. CQA belongs to Π_2^P and becomes Δ_2^P-hard, but for a relevant class of denials we get tractability of CQA to non aggregate queries, which is again lost with aggregate queries. Wrt approximation, we prove that DFP is $MAXSNP$-hard in general, and for a relevant subclass of denials we provide an approximation within a constant factor that depends on the number of atoms in them. All the algorithmic and complexity results, unless otherwise stated, refer to data complexity [1], i.e. to the size of the database that here includes a binary representation for numbers. For complexity theoretic definitions and classical results we refer to [21].

This paper is structured as follows. Section 2 introduces basic definitions. Sections 3 presents the notion of database fix, several notions of consistent answer to a query; and some relevant decision problems. Section 4 investigates their complexity. In Section 5 approximations for the problem of finding the minimum distance to a fix are studied, obtaining negative results for the general case, but good approximation for the class of local denial constraints. Section 6 investigates tractability of CQA for conjunctive queries and denial constraints containing one database atom plus built-ins. Section 7 presents some conclusions and refers to related work. Proofs and other auxiliary, technical results can be found in [5].

2 Preliminaries

Consider a relational schema $\Sigma = (\mathcal{U}, \mathcal{R}, \mathcal{B}, \mathcal{A})$, with domain $\mathcal{U}$ that includes $\mathbb{Z}^1$, $\mathcal{R}$ a set of database predicates, $\mathcal{B}$ a set of built-in predicates, and $\mathcal{A}$ a set of attributes. A database instance is a finite collection D of *database tuples*, i.e. of ground atoms $P(\bar{c})$, with $P \in \mathcal{R}$ and $\bar{c}$ a tuple of constants in $\mathcal{U}$. There is a set $\mathcal{F} \subseteq \mathcal{A}$ of all the *fixable* attributes, those that take values in $\mathbb{Z}$ and are allowed to be fixed. Attributes outside $\mathcal{F}$ are called *rigid*. $\mathcal{F}$ need not contain all the numerical attributes, that is we may also have rigid numerical attributes.

We also have a set $\mathcal{K}$ of key constraints expressing that relations $R \in \mathcal{R}$ have a primary key K_R, $K_R \subseteq (\mathcal{A} \smallsetminus \mathcal{F})$. Later on (c.f. Definition 2), we will assume that $\mathcal{K}$ is satisfied both by the initial instance D, denoted $D \models \mathcal{K}$, and its fixes. Since $\mathcal{F} \cap K_R = \emptyset$, values in key attributes cannot be changed in a fixing process; so the constraints in $\mathcal{K}$ are *hard*. In addition, there may be a separate set IC of *flexible* ICs that may be violated, and it is the job of a fix to restore consistency wrt them (while still satisfying $\mathcal{K}$).

A *linear denial constraint* [18] has the form $\forall \bar{x} \neg (A_1 \wedge \ldots \wedge A_m)$, where the A_i are database atoms (i.e. with predicate in $\mathcal{R}$), or built-in atoms of the form $x\theta c$, where x is a variable, c is a constant and $\theta \in \{=, \neq, <, >, \leq, \geq\}$, or $x = y$. If $x \neq y$ is allowed, we call them *extended* linear denials.

Example 2. The following are linear denials (we replace $\wedge$ by a comma): (a) No customer is younger than 21: $\forall Id, Age, Income, Status \neg (Customer(Id, Age, Income, Status), Age < 21)$. (b) No customer with income less than 60000 has "silver" status: $\forall Id, Age, Income, Status \neg (Customer(Id, Age, Income, Status),$

---

[1] With simple denial constraints, numbers can be restricted to, e.g. $\mathbb{N}$ or $\{0,1\}$.

Income < 60000, *Status* $=$ *silver*). (c) The constraints in Example 1, e.g. $\forall T, L,$ *Type, Flow* $\neg($ *Traffic*$(T, L,$ *Type, Flow*$)$, *Type* $= 0$, *Flow* > 1000). $\qquad\square$

We consider aggregation constraints (ACs) [23] and aggregate queries with *sum, count, average*. *Filtering* ACs impose conditions on the tuples over which aggregation is applied, e.g. $sum(A_1 : A_2 = 3) > 5$ is a sum over A_1 of tuples with $A_2 = 3$. *Multi-attribute* ACs allow arithmetical combinations of attributes as arguments for *sum*, e.g. $sum(A_1 + A_2) > 5$ and $sum(A_1 \times A_2) > 100$. If an AC has attributes from more than one relation, it is *multi-relation*, e.g. $sum_{R_1}(A_1) = sum_{R_2}(A_1)$, otherwise it is *single-relation*.

An *aggregate conjunctive query* has the form $q(x_1, \ldots x_m; agg(z)) \leftarrow B(x_1, \ldots, x_m, z, y_1, \ldots, y_n)$, where *agg* is an aggregation function and its *non-aggregate matrix* (NAM) given by $q'(x_1, \ldots x_m) \leftarrow B(x_1, \ldots, x_m, z, y_1, \ldots, y_n)$ is a usual first-order (FO) conjunctive query with built-in atoms, such that the *aggregation attribute* z does not appear among the x_i. Here we use the set semantics. An aggregate conjunctive query is *cyclic* (*acyclic*) if its NAM is cyclic (acyclic) [1].

Example 3. $q(x, y, sum(z)) \leftarrow R(x, y), Q(y, z, w), w \neq 3$ is an aggregate conjunctive query, with aggregation attribute z. Each answer (x, y) to its NAM, i.e. to $q(x, y) \leftarrow R(x, y), Q(y, z, w), w \neq 3$, is expanded to $(x, y, sum(z))$ as an answer to the aggregate query. $sum(z)$ is the sum of all the values for z having a w, such that (x, y, z, w) makes $R(x, y), Q(y, z, w), w \neq 3$ true. In the database instance $D = \{R(1, 2), R(2, 3), Q(2, 5, 9), Q(2, 6, 7), Q(3, 1, 1), Q(3, 1, 5), Q(3, 8, 3)\}$ the answer set for the aggregate query is $\{(1, 2, 5 + 6), (2, 3, 1 + 1)\}$. $\qquad\square$

An *aggregate comparison query* is a sentence of the form $q(agg(z)), agg(z)\theta k$, where $q(agg(z))$ is the head of a scalar aggregate conjunctive query (with no free variables), θ is a comparison operator, and k is an integer number. For example, the following is an aggregate comparison query asking whether the aggregated value obtained via $q(sum(z))$ is bigger than 5: $Q : q(sum(z)), sum(z) > 5$, with $q(sum(z)) \leftarrow R(x, y), Q(y, z, w), w \neq 3$.

3   Least Squares Fixes

When we update numerical values to restore consistency, it is desirable to make the smallest overall variation of the original values, while considering the relative relevance or specific scale of each of the fixable attributes. Since the original instance and a fix will share the same key values (c.f. Definition 2), we can use them to compute variations in the numerical values. For a tuple $\bar{k}$ of values for the key K_R of relation R in an instance D, $\bar{t}(\bar{k}, R, D)$ denotes the unique tuple $\bar{t}$ in relation R in instance D whose key value is $\bar{k}$. To each attribute $A \in \mathcal{F}$ a fixed numerical weight α_A is assigned.

Definition 1. For instances D and D' over schema Σ with the same set $val(K_R)$ of tuples of key values for each relation $R \in \mathcal{R}$, their *square distance* is

$$\Delta_{\bar{\alpha}}(D, D') = \sum_{\substack{R \in \mathcal{R}, A \in \mathcal{F} \\ \bar{k} \in val(K_R)}} \alpha_A (\pi_A(\bar{t}(\bar{k}, R, D)) - \pi_A(\bar{t}(\bar{k}, R, D')))^2,$$

where π_A is the projection on attribute A and $\bar{\alpha} = (\alpha_A)_{A \in \mathcal{F}}$. $\qquad\square$

Definition 2. For an instance D, a set of fixable attributes $\mathcal{F}$, a set of key dependencies $\mathcal{K}$, such that $D \models \mathcal{K}$, and a set of flexible ICs IC: A *fix* for D wrt IC is an instance D' such that: (a) D' has the same schema and domain as D; (b) D' has the same values as D in the attributes in $\mathcal{A} \setminus \mathcal{F}$; (c) $D' \models \mathcal{K}$; and (d) $D' \models IC$. A *least squares fix* (LS-fix) for D is a fix D' that minimizes the square distance $\Delta_{\bar{\alpha}}(D, D')$ over all the instances that satisfy (a) - (d). □

In general we are interested in LS-fixes, but (non-necessarily minimal) fixes will be useful auxiliary instances.

Example 4. (example 1 cont.) $\mathcal{R} = \{Traffic\}$, $\mathcal{A} = \{Time, Link, Type, Flow\}$, $\mathcal{K}_{Traffic} = \{Time, Link\}$, $\mathcal{F} = \{Type, Flow\}$, with weights $\bar{\alpha} = (10^{-5}, 1)$, resp. For original instance D, $val(\mathcal{K}_{Traffic}) = \{(1.1, a), (1.1, b), (1.3, b)\}$, $\bar{t}((1.1, a),$ $Traffic, D) = (1.1, a, 0, 1100)$, etc. Fixes are $D_1 = \{(1.1, a, 0, 1000), (1.1, b, 1, 900),$ $(1.3, b, 1, 850)\}$ and $D_2 = \{(1.1, a, 1, 1100), (1.1, b, 1, 900), (1.3, b, 1, 850)\}$, with distances $\Delta_{\bar{\alpha}}(D, D_1) = 100^2 \times 10^{-5} = 10^{-1}$ and $\Delta_{\bar{\alpha}}(D, D_2) = 1^2 \times 1$, resp. Therefore, D_1 is the only LS-fix. □

The coefficients α_A can be chosen in many different ways depending on factors like relative relevance of attributes, actual distribution of data, measurement scales, etc. In the rest of this paper we will assume, for simplification, that $\alpha_A = 1$ for all $A \in \mathcal{F}$ and $\Delta_{\bar{\alpha}}(D, D')$ will be simply denoted by $\Delta(D, D')$.

Example 5. The database D has relations $Client(ID, A, M)$, with key ID, attributes A for age and M for amount of money; and $Buy(ID, I, P)$, with key $\{ID, I\}$, I for items, and P for prices. We have denials $IC_1 : \forall ID, P, A, M \neg$ $(Buy(ID, I, P), Client(ID, A, M), A < 18, P > 25)$ and $IC_2 : \forall ID, A, M \neg($ $Client(ID, A, M), A < 18, M > 50)$, requiring that people younger than 18 can-

not spend more than 25 on one item nor spend more than 50 in the store. We added an extra column in the tables with a label for each tuple. IC_1 is violated by $\{t_1, t_4\}$ and $\{t_1, t_5\}$; and IC_2 by $\{t_1\}$ and $\{t_2\}$. We have two LS-fixes (the modified version of tuple t_1 is t_1',

D:

Client	ID	A	M	
	1	15	52	t_1
	2	16	51	t_2
	3	60	900	t_3
Buy	ID	I	P	
	1	CD	27	t_4
	1	DVD	26	t_5
	3	DVD	40	t_6

D':

Client'	ID	A	M	
	1	15	50	t_1'
	2	16	50	t_2'
	3	60	900	t_3
Buy'	ID	I	P	
	1	CD	25	t_4'
	1	DVD	25	t_5'
	3	DVD	40	t_6

D'':

Client''	ID	A	M	
	1	18	52	t_1''
	2	16	50	t_2''
	3	60	900	t_3
Buy''	ID	I	P	
	1	CD	27	t_4
	1	DVD	26	t_5
	3	DVD	40	t_6

etc.), with distances $\Delta(D, D') = 2^2 + 1^2 + 2^2 + 1^2 = 10$, and $\Delta(D, D'') = 3^2 + 1^2 = 10$. We can see that a global fix may not be the result of applying "local" minimal fixes to tuples. □

The built-in atoms in linear denials determine a solution space for fixes as an intersection of semi-spaces, and LS-fixes can be found at its "borders" (c.f. previous example and Proposition A.1 in [5]). It is easy to construct examples with an exponential number of fixes. For the kind of fixes and ICs we are considering, it is possible that no fix exists, in contrast to [2,3], where, if the set of ICs is consistent as a set of logical sentences, a fix for a database always exist.

Example 6. $R(X,Y)$ has key X and fixable Y. $IC_1 = \{\forall X_1 X_2 Y \neg (R(X_1,Y), R(X_2, Y)), X_1 = 1, X_2 = 2), \forall X_1 X_2 Y \neg (R(X_1, Y), R(X_2,Y)), X_1 = 1, X_2 = 3), \forall X_1 X_2 Y \neg (R(X_1,Y), R(X_2,Y)), X_1 = 2, X_2 = 3), \forall XY \neg (R(X,Y), Y > 3), \forall XY \neg (R(X,Y), Y < 2)\}$ is consistent. The first three ICs force Y to be different in every tuple. The last two ICs require $2 \leq Y \leq 3$. The inconsistent database $R = \{(1,-1), (2,1), (3,5)\}$ has no fix. Now, for IC_2 with $\forall X, Y \neg (R(X,Y), Y > 1)$ and $sum(Y) = 10$, any database with less than 10 tuples has no fixes. □

Proposition 1. If D has a fix wrt IC, then it also has an LS-fix wrt IC.   □

4   Decidability and Complexity

In applications where fixes are based on changes of numerical values, computing concrete fixes is a relevant problem. In databases containing census forms, correcting the latter before doing statistical processing is a common problem [11]. In databases with experimental samples, we can fix certain erroneous quantities as specified by linear ICs. In these cases, the fixes are relevant objects to compute explicitly, which contrasts with CQA [2], where the main motivation for introducing repairs is to formally characterize the notion of a consistent answer to a query as an answer that remains under all possible repairs. In consequence, we now consider some decision problems related to existence and verification of LS-fixes, and to CQA under different semantics.

Definition 3. For an instance D and a set IC of ICs:

(a) $Fix(D, IC) := \{D' \mid D'$ is an LS-fix of D wrt $IC\}$, the *fix checking problem.*
(b) $Fix(IC) := \{(D, D') \mid D' \in Fix(D, IC)\}$.
(c) $NE(IC) := \{D \mid Fix(D, IC) \neq \emptyset\}$, for *non-empty* set of fixes, i.e. the problem of *checking existence of LS-fixes.*
(d) $NE := \{(D, IC) \mid Fix(D, IC) \neq \emptyset\}$.
(e) $DFP(IC) := \{(D, k) \mid$ there is $D' \in Fix(D, IC)$ with $\Delta(D, D') \leq k\}$, the *database fix problem,* i.e. the problem of checking existence of LS-fixes within a given positive distance k.
(f) $DFOP(IC)$ is the optimization problem of finding the minimum distance from an LS-fix wrt IC to a given input instance.   □

Definition 4. Let D be a database, IC a set ICs, and Q a conjunctive query[2].

(a) A ground tuple $\bar{t}$ is a *consistent answer* to $Q(\bar{x})$ under the: (a1) *skeptical semantics* if for every $D' \in Fix(D, IC)$, $D' \models Q(\bar{t})$. (a2) *brave semantics* if there

---

[2] Whenever we say just "conjunctive query" we understand it is a non aggregate query.

exists $D' \in Fix(D, IC)$ with $D' \models Q(\bar{t})$. (a3) *majority semantics* if $|\{D' \mid D' \in Fix(D, IC)$ and $D' \models Q(\bar{t})\}| > |\{D' \mid D' \in Fix(D, IC)$ and $D' \not\models Q(\bar{t})\}|$.
(b) That $\bar{t}$ is a consistent answer to Q in D under semantics $\mathcal{S}$ is denoted by $D \models_{\mathcal{S}} Q[\bar{t}]$. If Q is ground and $D \models_{\mathcal{S}} Q$, we say that *yes* is a consistent answer, meaning that Q is true in the fixes of D according to semantics S. $CA(Q, D, IC, \mathcal{S})$ is the set of consistent answers to Q in D wrt IC under semantics $\mathcal{S}$. For ground Q, if $CA(Q, D, IC, \mathcal{S}) \neq \{yes\}$, $CA(Q, D, IC, \mathcal{S}) := \{no\}$.
(c) $CQA(Q, IC, \mathcal{S}) := \{(D, \bar{t}) \mid \bar{t} \in CA(Q, D, IC, \mathcal{S})\}$ is the decision *problem of consistent query answering*, of checking consistent answers.   □

Proposition 2. $NE(IC)$ can be reduced in polynomial time to the complements of $CQA(False, IC, Skeptical)$ and $CQA(True, IC, Majority)$, where *False, True* are ground queries that are always false, resp. true.   □

In Proposition 2, it suffices for queries *False, True* to be false, resp. true, in all instances that share the key values with the input database. Then, they can be represented by $\exists Y R(\bar{c}, Y)$, where $\bar{c}$ are not (for *False*), or are (for *True*) key values in the original instance.

Theorem 1. Under extended linear denials and complex, filtering, multi-attribute, single-relation, aggregation constraints, the problems NE of existence of LS-fixes, and CQA under skeptical or majority semantics are undecidable.   □

The result about NE can be proved by reduction from the undecidable Hilbert's problem on solvability of diophantine equations. For CQA, apply Proposition 2. Here we have the original database and the set of ICs as input parameters. In the following we will be interested in data complexity, when only the input database varies and the set of ICs is fixed [1].

Theorem 2. For a fixed set IC of linear denials: (a) Deciding if for an instance D there is an instance D' (with the same key values as D) that satisfies IC with $\Delta(D, D') \leq k$, with positive integer k that is part of the input, is in NP. (b) $DFP(IC)$ is NP-complete. (c.f. Definition 3(e))   □

By Proposition 1, there is a fix for D wrt IC at a distance $\leq k$ iff there is an LS-fix at a distance $\leq k$. Part (b) of Theorem 2 follows from part (a) and a reduction of *Vertex Cover* to $DFP(IC_0)$, for a fixed set of denials IC_0. By Theorem 2(a), if there is a fix at a distance $\leq k$, the minimum distance to D for a fix can be found by binary search in $log(k)$ steps. Actually, if an LS-fix exists, its square distance to D is polynomially bounded by the size of D (c.f. proof of Theorem 3 in [5]). Since D and a fix have the same number of tuples, only the size of their values in a fix matter, and they are constrained by a fixed set of linear denials and the condition of minimality.

Theorem 3. For a fixed set IC of extended linear denials: (a) The problem $NE(IC)$ of deciding if an instance has an LS-fix wrt IC is NP-complete, and (b) CQA under the skeptical and the majority semantics is $coNP$-hard.   □

For hardness in (a), (b) in Theorem 3, linear denials are good enough. Membership in (a) can be obtained for any fixed finite set of extended denials. Part (b) follows from part (a). The latter uses a reduction from *3-Colorability*.

Theorem 4. For a fixed set IC of extended linear denials: (a) The problem $Fix(IC)$ of checking if an instance is an LS-fix is $coNP$-complete, and (b) CQA under skeptical semantics is in Π_2^P, and, for ground atomic queries, Δ_2^P-hard. $\square$

Part (a) uses $3SAT$. Hardness in (b) is obtained by reduction from a Δ_2^P-complete decision version of the problem of searching for the lexicographically *Maximum 3-Satisfying Assignment (M3SA)*: Decide if the last variable takes value 1 in it [17–Theo. 3.4]. Linear denials suffice. Now, by reduction from the *Vertex Cover Problem*, we obtain.

Theorem 5. For aggregate comparison queries using *sum*, CQA under linear denials and brave semantics is $coNP$-hard. $\square$

5   Approximation for the Database Fix Problem

We consider the problem of finding a good approximation for the general optimization problem $DFOP(IC)$.

Proposition 3. For a fixed set of linear denials IC, $DFOP(IC)$ is *MAXSNP*-hard. $\square$

This result is obtained by establishing an L-reduction to $DFOP(IC)$ from the *MAXSNP*-complete [22, 21] *B-Minimum Vertex Cover Problem*, i.e. the vertex cover minimization problem for graphs of bounded degree [16–Chapter 10]. As an immediate consequence, we obtain that $DFOP(IC)$ cannot be uniformly approximated within arbitrarily small constant factors [21].

Corollary 1. Unless $P = NP$, there is no *Polynomial Time Approximation Schema* for *DFOP*. $\square$

This negative result does not preclude the possibility of finding an efficient algorithm for approximation within a constant factor for *DFOP*. Actually, in the following we do this for a restricted but still useful class of denial constraints.

5.1   Local Denials

Definition 5. A set of linear denials IC is *local* if: (a) Attributes participating in equality atoms between attributes or in joins are all rigid; (b) There is a built-in atom with a fixable attribute in each element of IC; (c) No attribute A appears in IC both in comparisons of the form $A < c_1$ and $A > c_2$.[3] $\square$

In Example 5, IC is local. In Example 6, IC_1 is not local. Local constraints have the property that by doing local fixes, no new inconsistencies are generated, and there is always an LS-fix wrt to them (c.f. Proposition A.2 in [5]). Locality is a sufficient, but not necessary condition for existence of LS-fixes as can be seen from the database $\{P(a,2)\}$, with the first attribute as a key and non-local denials $\neg(P(x,y), y < 3), \neg(P(x,y), y > 5)$, that has the LS-fix $\{P(a,3)\}$.

---

[3] To check condition (c), $x \leq c$, $x \geq c$, $x \neq c$ have to be expressed using $<,>$, e.g. $x \leq c$ by $x < c+1$.

Proposition 4. For the class of local denials, *DFP* is *NP*-complete, and *DFOP* is *MAXSNP*-hard. □

This proposition tells us that the problem of finding good approximations in the case of local denials is still relevant.

Definition 6. A set I of database tuples from D is a *violation set* for $ic \in IC$ if $I \not\models ic$, and for every $I' \subsetneq I$, $I' \models ic$. $\mathcal{I}(D, ic, t)$ denotes the set of violation sets for ic that contain tuple t. □

A violation set I for ic is a minimal set of tuples that simultaneously participate in the violation of ic.

Definition 7. Given an instance D and ICs *IC*, a *local fix* for $t \in D$, is a tuple t' with: (a) the same values for the rigid attributes as t; (b) $S(t, t') := \{I \mid \text{there is } ic \in IC, I \in \mathcal{I}(D, ic, t) \text{ and } ((I \smallsetminus \{t\}) \cup \{t'\}) \models ic\} \neq \emptyset$; and (c) there is no tuple t'' that simultaneously satisfies (a), $S(t, t'') = S(t, t')$, and $\Delta(\{t\}, \{t''\}) \leq \Delta(\{t\}, \{t'\})$, where Δ denotes quadratic distance. □

$S(t, t')$ contains the violation sets that include t and are solved by replacing t' for t. A local fix t' solves some of the violations due to t and minimizes the distance to t.

5.2 Database Fix Problem as a Set Cover Problem

For a fixed set *IC* of local denials, we can solve an instance of *DFOP* by transforming it into an instance of the *Minimum Weighted Set Cover Optimization Problem* (*MWSCP*). This problem is *MAXSNP*-hard [20, 21], and its general approximation algorithms are within a logarithmic factor [20, 9]. By concentrating on local denials, we will be able to generate a version of the *MWSCP* that can be approximated within a constant factor (c.f. Section 5.3).

Definition 8. For a database D and a set *IC* of local denials, $\mathcal{G}(D, IC) = (T, H)$ denotes the *conflict hypergraph* for D wrt *IC* [8], which has in the set T of vertices the database tuples, and in the set H of hyperedges, the violation sets for elements $ic \in IC$. □

Hyperedges in H can be labelled with the corresponding ic, so that different hyperedges may contain the same tuples. Now we build an instance of *MWSCP*.

Definition 9. For a database D and a set *IC* of local denials, the instance $(U, \mathcal{S}, w)$ for the *MWSCP*, where U is the underlying set, $\mathcal{S}$ is the set collection, and w is the weight function, is given by: (a) $U := H$, the set of hyperedges of $\mathcal{G}(D, IC)$. (b) $\mathcal{S}$ contains the $S(t, t')$, where t' is a local fix for a tuple $t \in D$. (c) $w(S(t, t')) := \Delta(\{t\}, \{t'\})$. □

It can be proved that the $S(t, t')$ in this construction are non empty, and that $\mathcal{S}$ covers U (c.f. Proposition A.2 in [5]).

If for the instance $(U, \mathcal{S}, w)$ of *MWSCP* we find a minimum weight cover $\mathcal{C}$, we could think of constructing a fix by replacing each inconsistent tuple $t \in D$ by a local fix t' with $S(t,t') \in \mathcal{C}$. The problem is that there might be more than one t' and the key dependencies would not be respected. Fortunately, this problem can be circumvented.

Definition 10. Let $\mathcal{C}$ be a cover for instance $(U, \mathcal{S}, w)$ of the $MWSCP$ associated to D, IC. (a) $\mathcal{C}^*$ is obtained from $\mathcal{C}$ as follows: For each tuple t with local fixes $t_1, \ldots, t_n$, $n > 1$, such that $S(t, t_i) \in \mathcal{C}$, replace in $\mathcal{C}$ all the $S(t, t_i)$ by a single $S(t, t^*)$, where t^* is such that $S(t, t^*) = \bigcup_{i=1}^{n} S(t, t_i)$. (b) $D(\mathcal{C})$ is the database instance obtained from D by replacing t by t' if $S(t, t') \in \mathcal{C}^*$. $\square$

It holds (c.f. Proposition A.3 in [5]) that such an $S(t, t^*) \in \mathcal{S}$ exists in part (a) of Definition 10. Notice that there, tuple t could have other $S(t, t')$ outside $\mathcal{C}$. Now we can show that the reduction to $MWSCP$ keeps the value of the objective function.

Proposition 5. If $\mathcal{C}$ is an optimal cover for instance $(U, \mathcal{S}, w)$ of the $MWSCP$ associated to D, IC, then $D(\mathcal{C})$ is an LS-fix of D wrt IC, and $\Delta(D, D(\mathcal{C})) = w(\mathcal{C}) = w(\mathcal{C}^*)$. $\square$

Proposition 6. For every LS-fix D' of D wrt a set of local denials IC, there exists an optimal cover $\mathcal{C}$ for the associated instance $(U, \mathcal{S}, w)$ of the $MWSCP$, such that $D' = D(\mathcal{C})$. $\square$

Proposition 7. The transformation of $DFOP$ into $MWSCP$, and the construction of database instance $D(\mathcal{C})$ from a cover $\mathcal{C}$ for $(U, \mathcal{S}, w)$ can be done in polynomial time in the size of D. $\square$

We have established that the transformation of $DFOP$ into $MWSCP$ is an L-reduction [21]. Proposition 7 proves, in particular, that the number of violation sets $S(t, t')$ is polynomially bounded by the size of the original database D.

Example 7. (example 5 continued) We illustrate the reduction from $DFOP$ to $MWSCP$. The violation sets are $\{t_1, t_4\}$ and $\{t_1, t_5\}$ for IC_1 and $\{t_1\}$ and $\{t_2\}$ for IC_2. The figure shows the hypergraph. For the $MWSCP$ instance, we need the local fixes. Tuple t_1 has two local fixes $t'_1 = (1, 15, 50)$, that solves the violation set $\{t_1\}$ of IC_2 (hyperedge B), and $t''_1 = (1, 18, 52)$, that solves the violation sets $\{t_1, t_4\}$ and $\{t_1, t_5\}$ of IC_1, and $\{t_1\}$ of IC_2 (hyperedges A,B, C), with weights 4 and 9, resp. t_2, t_4 and t_5 have one local fix each corresponding to: $(2, 16, 50)$, $(1, CD, 25)$ and $(1, DVD, 25)$, resp. The consistent tuple t_3 has no local fix.

The $MWSCP$ instance is shown in the table, where the elements are rows and the sets (e.g. $S_1 = S(t_1, t'_1)$), columns. An entry 1 means that the set contains

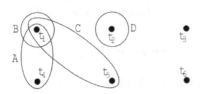

Set	S_1	S_2	S_3	S_4	S_5
Local Fix	t_1'	t_1"	t_2'	t_4'	t_5'
Weight	4	9	1	4	1
Hyperedge A	0	1	0	1	0
Hyperedge B	1	1	0	0	0
Hyperedge C	0	1	0	0	1
Hyperedge D	0	0	1	0	0

the corresponding element; and a 0, otherwise. There are two minimal covers, both with weight 10: $C_1 = \{S_2, S_3\}$ and $C_2 = \{S_1, S_3, S_4, S_5\}$. $D(C_1)$ and $D(C_2)$ are the two fixes for this problem. $\qquad \square$

If we apply the transformation to Example 6, that had non-local set of ICs and no repairs, we will find that instance $D(C)$, for C a set cover, can be constructed as above, but it does not satisfy the flexible ICs, because changing inconsistent tuples by their local fixes solves only the initial inconsistencies, but new inconsistencies are introduced.

5.3   Approximation Via Set Cover Optimization

Now that we have transformed the database fix problem into a weighted set cover problem, we can apply approximation algorithms for the latter. We know, for example, that using a greedy algorithm, $MWSCP$ can be approximated within a factor $log(N)$, where N is the size of the underlying set U [9]. The approximation algorithm returns not only an approximation $\hat{w}$ to the optimal weight w^o, but also a -non necessarily optimal- cover $\hat{C}$ for problem (U, S, w). As in Definition 10, $\hat{C}$ can be used to generate via $(\hat{C})^\star$, a fix $D(\hat{C})$ for D that may not be LS-minimal.

Example 8. (examples 5 and 7 continued) We show how to to compute a solution to this particular instance of $DFOP$ using the greedy approximation algorithm for $MWSCP$ presented in [9]. We start with $\hat{C} := \emptyset$, $S_i^0 := S_i$; and we add to C the S_i such that S_i^0 has the maximum *contribution ratio* $|S_i^0|/w(S_i^0)$. The alternatives are $|S_1|/w(S_1) = 1/4$, $|S_2|/w(S_2) = 3/9$, $|S_3|/w(S_3) = 1$, $|S_4|/w(S_4) = 1/4$ and $|S_5|/w(S_5) = 1$. The ratio is maximum for S_3 and S_5, so we can add any of them to $\hat{C}$. If we choose the first, we get $\hat{C} = \{S_3\}$. Now we compute the $S_i^1 := S_i^0 \setminus S_3^0$, and choose again an S_i for $\hat{C}$ such that S_i^1 maximizes the contribution ratio. Now S_5 is added to $\hat{C}$, because S_5^1 gives the maximum. By repeating this process until we get all the elements of U covered, i.e. all the S_i^k become empty at some iteration point k, we finally obtain $\hat{C} = \{S_3, S_5, S_1, S_4\}$. In this case $\hat{C}$ is an optimal cover and therefore, $D(\hat{C})$ is exactly an LS-fix, namely D' in Example 5. Since this is an approximation algorithm, in other examples the cover obtained might not be optimal. $\qquad \square$

Proposition 8. Given database instance D with local ICs IC, the database instance $D(\hat{C})$ obtained from the approximate cover $\hat{C}$ is a fix and it holds $\Delta(D, D(\hat{C})) \leq log(N) \times \Delta(D, D')$, where D' is any LS-fix of D wrt IC and N is the number of of violation sets for D wrt IC. $\qquad \square$

In consequence, for any set IC of local denials, we have a polynomial time approximation algorithm that solves $DFOP(IC)$ within an $O(log(N))$ factor, where N is the number of violation sets for D wrt IC. As mentioned before, this number N, the number of hyperedges in $\mathcal{G}$, is polynomially bounded by $|D|$ (c.f. Proposition 7). N may be small if the number of inconsistencies or the number of database atoms in the ICs are small, which is likely the case in real applications.

However, in our case we can get even better approximations via a cover $\hat{C}$ obtained with an approximation algorithms for the special case of the *MWSCP* where the number of occurrences of an element of U in elements of S is bounded by a constant. For this case of the *MWSCP* there are approximations within a constant factor based on "linear relaxation" [16–Chapter 3]. This is clearly the case in our application, being $m \times |\mathcal{F}| \times |IC|$ a constant bound (independent from $|D|$) on the frequency of the elements, where m is the maximum number of database atoms in an IC.

Theorem 6. There is an approximation algorithm that, for a given database instance D with local ICs *IC*, returns a fix $D(\hat{C})$ such that $\Delta(D, D(\hat{C})) \leq c \times \Delta(D, D')$, where c is a constant and D' is any LS-fix of D. □

6   One Atoms Denials and Conjunctive Queries

In this section we concentrate on the common case of *one database atom denials* (1AD), i.e. of the form $\forall\neg(A, B)$, where atom A has a predicate in $\mathcal{R}$, and B is a conjunction of built-in atoms. They capture range constraints; and census data is usually stored in single relation schemas [11].

For 1ADs, we can identify tractable cases for *CQA* under LS-fixes by reduction to *CQA* for (tuple and set-theoretic) repairs of the form introduced in [2] for key constraints. This is because each violation set (c.f. Definition 6) contains one tuple, maybe with several local fixes, but all sharing the same key values; and then the problem consists in choosing one from different tuples with the same key values (c.f. proof in [5] of Theorem 7). The transformation preserves consistent answers to both ground and open queries.

The "classical" -tuple and set oriented- repair problem as introduced in [2] has been studied in detail for functional dependencies in [8, 12]. In particular, for tractability of *CQA* in our setting, we can use results and algorithms obtained in [12] for the classical framework.

The *join graph* $\mathcal{G}(Q)$ [12] of a conjunctive query Q is a directed graph, whose vertices are the database atoms in Q. There is an arc from L to L' if $L \neq L'$ and there is a variable w that occurs at the position of a non-key attribute in L and also occurs in L'. Furthermore, there is a self-loop at L if there is a variable that occurs at the position of a non-key attribute in L, and at least twice in L.

When Q does not have repeated relations symbols, we write $Q \in \mathcal{C}_{Tree}$ if $\mathcal{G}(Q)$ is a forest and every non-key to key join of Q is full i.e. involves the whole key. Classical *CQA* is tractable for queries in $\mathcal{C}_{Tree}$ [12].

Theorem 7. For a fixed set of 1ADs and queries in $\mathcal{C}_{Tree}$, consistent query answering under LS-fixes is in *PTIME*. □

We may define that a aggregate conjunctive query belongs to $\mathcal{C}_{Tree}$ if its underlying non-aggregate conjunctive query, i.e. its NAM (c.f. Section 2) belongs to $\mathcal{C}_{Tree}$. Even for 1ADs, with simple comparison aggregate queries with *sum*, tractability is lost under the brave semantics.

Proposition 9. For a fixed set of 1ADs, and for aggregate queries that are in C_{Tree} or acyclic, CQA is NP-hard under the brave semantics.   □

For queries Q returning numerical values, which is common in our framework, it is natural to use the *range semantics* for CQA, introduced in [3] for scalar aggregate queries and functional dependencies under classical repairs. Under this semantics, a consistent answer is the pair consisting of the *min-max* and *max-min* answers, i.e. the supremum and the infimum, resp., of the set of answers to Q obtained from LS-fixes. The CQA decision problems under range semantics consist in determining if a numerical query Q, e.g. an aggregate query, has its answer $\leq k_1$ in every fix (*min-max* case), or $\geq k_2$ in every fix (*max-min* case).

Theorem 8. For each of the aggregate functions *sum, count distinct*, and *average*, there is a fixed set of 1ADs and a fixed aggregate acyclic conjunctive query, such that CQA under the range semantics is NP-hard.   □

For the three aggregate functions one 1AD suffices. The results for *count distinct* and *average* are obtained by reduction from $MAXSAT$ [21] and $3SAT$, resp. For *sum*, we use a reduction from the *Independent Set Problem* with bounded degree 3 [14]. The general *Independent Set Problem* has bad approximation properties [16–Chapter 10]. The *Bounded Degree Independent Set* has efficient approximations within a constant factor that depends on the degree [15].

Theorem 9. For any set of 1ADs and conjunctive query with *sum* over a non-negative attribute, there is a polynomial time approximation algorithm with a constant factor for CQA under *min-max* range semantics.   □

The factor in this theorem depends upon the ICs and the query, but not on the size of the database. The acyclicity of the query is not required. The algorithm is based on a reduction of our problem to satisfying a subsystem with maximum weight of a system of weighted algebraic equations over the Galois field with two elements $GF[2]$ (a generalization of problems in [13, 24]), for which a polynomial time approximation similar to the one for $MAXSAT$ can be given [24].

7   Conclusions

We have shown that fixing numerical values in databases poses many new computational challenges that had not been addressed before in the context of consistent query answering. These problems are particularly relevant in census like applications, where the problem of *data editing* is a common and difficult task (c.f. http://www.unece.org/stats/documents/2005.05.sde.htm). Also our concentration on aggregate queries is particularly relevant for this kind of statistical applications. In this paper we have just started to investigate some of the many problems that appear in this context, and several extensions are in development. We concentrated on integer numerical values, which provide a useful and challenging domain. Considering real numbers in fixable attributes opens many new issues, requires different approaches; and is a subject of ongoing research.

The framework established in this paper could be applied to qualitative attributes with an implicit linear order given by the application. The result we have presented for fixable attributes that are all equally relevant ($\alpha_A = 1$ in Definitions 1 and 2) should carry over without much difficulty to the general case of arbitrary weighted fixes. We have developed (but not reported here) extensions to our approach that consider *minimum distribution variation* LS-fixes that keep the overall statistical properties of the database. We have also developed optimizations of the approximation algorithm presented in Section 5; and its implementation and experiments are ongoing efforts. More research on the impact of aggregation constraints on LS-fixes is needed.

Of course, if instead of the L_2 distance, the L_1 distance is used, we may get for the same database a different set of (now L_1) fixes. The actual approximations obtained in this paper change too. However, the general complexity and approximability results should remain. They basically depend on the fact that distance functions are non-negative, additive wrt attributes and tuples, computable in polynomial time, and monotonically increasing. Another possible semantics could consider an epsilon of error in the distance in such a way that if, for example, the distance of a fix is 5 and the distance to another fix is 5.001, we could take both of them as (minimal) LS-fixes.

Other open problems refer to cases of polynomial complexity for linear denials with more that one database atom; approximation algorithms for the *DFOP* for non-local cases; and approximations to CQA for other aggregate queries.

For related work, we refer to the literature on consistent query answering (c.f. [4] for a survey and references). Papers [25] and [11] are the closest to our work, because changes in attribute values are basic repair actions, but the peculiarities of numerical values and quantitative distances between databases are not investigated. Under the set-theoretic, tuple-based semantics, [8, 7, 12] report on complexity issues for conjunctive queries, functional dependencies and foreign key constraints. A majority semantics was studied in [19] for database merging. Quite recent papers, but under semantics different than ours, report research on fixing numerical values under aggregation constraints [10]; and heuristic construction of repairs based on attribute values changes [6].

Acknowledgments. Research supported by NSERC, CITO/IBM-CAS Student Internship Program, and EU projects: Sewasie, Knowledge Web, and Interop. L. Bertossi is Faculty Fellow of IBM Center for Advanced Studies (Toronto Lab.).

References

[1] Abiteboul, S., Hull, R. and Vianu, V. *Foundations of Databases.* Addison-Wesley, 1995.

[2] Arenas, M, Bertossi, L. and Chomicki, J. Consistent Query Answers in Inconsistent Databases. In *Proc. ACM Symposium on Principles of Database Systems (PODS 99)*, 1999, pp. 68-79.

[3] Arenas, M, Bertossi, L. and Chomicki, J., He, X., Raghavan, V., and Spinrad, J. Scalar aggregation in inconsistent databases. *Theoretical Computer Science*, 2003, 296:405–434.

[4] Bertossi, L. and Chomicki, J. Query Answering in Inconsistent Databases. In *Logics for Emerging Applications of Databases*, J. Chomicki, G. Saake and R. van der Meyden (eds.), Springer, 2003.

[5] Bertossi, L., Bravo, L., Franconi, E. and Lopatenko, A. Fixing Numerical Attributes Under Integrity Constraints. Corr Archiv paper cs.DB/0503032; March 15, 2005.

[6] Bohannon, P., Michael, F., Fan, F. and Rastogi, R. A Cost-Based Model and Effective Heuristic for Repairing Constraints by Value Modification. In *Proc. ACM International Conference on Management of Data (SIGMOD 05)*, 2005, pp. 143-154.

[7] Cali, A., Lembo, D., Rosati, R. On the Decidability and Complexity of Query Answering over Inconsistent and Incomplete Databases. In *Proc. ACM Symposium on Principles of Database Systems (PODS 03)*, 2003, pp. 260-271.

[8] Chomicki, J. and Marcinkowski, J. Minimal-Change Integrity Maintenance Using Tuple Deletions. *Information and Computation*, 2005, 197(1-2):90-121.

[9] Chvatal, V. A Greedy Heuristic for the Set Covering Problem. *Mathematics of Operations Research*, 1979, 4:233-235.

[10] Flesca, S., Furfaro, F. and Parisi, F. Consistent Query Answers on Numerical Databases under Aggregate Constraints. In *Proc. Tenth International Symposium on Database Programming Languages (DBPL 05)*, 2005.

[11] Franconi, E., Laureti Palma, A., Leone, N., Perri, S. and Scarcello, F. Census Data Repair: a Challenging Application of Disjunctive Logic Programming. In *Proc. Logic for Programming, Artificial Intelligence, and Reasoning (LPAR 01)*. Springer LNCS 2250, 2001, pp. 561-578.

[12] Fuxman, A. and Miller, R. First-Order Query Rewriting for Inconsistent Databases. In *Proc. International Conference on Database Theory (ICDT 05)*, Springer LNCS 3363, 2004, pp. 337-354.

[13] Garey, M.R. and Johnson, D.S. Computers and Intractability: A Guide to the Theory of NP-Completeness. W.H. Freeman and Co., 1979.

[14] Garey, M., Johnson, D. and Stockmeyer, L. Some Simplified NP-Complete Graph Problems. *Theoretical Computer Science*, 1976, 1(3):237-267.

[15] Halldorsson, M. and Radhakrishnan, J. Greed is Good: Approximating Independent Sets in Sparse and Bounded-degree Graphs. In *Proc. ACM Symposium on Theory of Computing (SToC 94)*, 1994, pp. 439-448.

[16] Hochbaum, D.(ed.) *Approximation Algorithms for NP-Hard Problems*. PWS, 1997.

[17] Krentel, M. The Complexity of Optimization Problems. *J. Computer and Systems Sciences*, 1988, 36:490-509.

[18] Kuper, G., Libkin, L. and Paredaens, J.(eds.) *Constraint Databases*. Springer, 2000.

[19] Lin, J. and Mendelzon, A.O. Merging Databases under Constraints. *International Journal of Cooperative Information Systems*, 1996, 7(1):55-76.

[20] Lund, C. and Yannakakis, M. On the Hardness of Approximating Minimization Problems. *J. of the Association for Computing Machinery*, 1994, 45(5):960-981.

[21] Papadimitriou, Ch. *Computational Complexity*. Addison-Wesley, 1994.

[22] Papadimitriou, Ch. and Yannakakis, M. Optimization, Approximation and Complexity Classes. *J. Computer and Systems Sciences*, 1991, 43:425-440.

[23] Ross, K., Srivastava, D., Stuckey, P., and Sudarshan, S.. Foundations of Aggregation Constraints. *Theoretical Computer Science*, 1998, 193(1-2):149–179.

[24] Vazirani, V. Approximation Algorithms. Springer, 2001.

[25] Wijsen, J. Condensed Representation of Database Repairs for Consistent Query Answering. In *Proc. International Conference on Database Theory (ICDT 03)*, Springer LNCS 2572, 2003, pp. 378-393.

[26] Wijsen, J. Making More Out of an Inconsistent Database. In *Proc. East-European Conference on Advances in Databases and Information Systems (ADBIS 04)*, Springer LNCS 3255, 2004, pp. 291-305.

Consistent Query Answers on Numerical Databases Under Aggregate Constraints

Sergio Flesca, Filippo Furfaro, and Francesco Parisi

DEIS - Università della Calabria,
Via Bucci - 87036 Rende (CS) ITALY
Fax: +39 0984 494713
{flesca, furfaro, parisi}@si.deis.unical.it

Abstract. The problem of extracting consistent information from relational databases violating integrity constraints on numerical data is addressed. In particular, aggregate constraints defined as linear inequalities on aggregate-sum queries on input data are considered. The notion of repair as consistent set of updates at attribute-value level is exploited, and the characterization of several data-complexity issues related to repairing data and computing consistent query answers is provided.

1 Introduction

Research has deeply investigated several issues related to the use of integrity constraints on relational databases. In this context, a great deal of attention has been devoted to the problem of extracting reliable information from databases containing pieces of information inconsistent w.r.t. some integrity constraints. All previous works in this area deal with "classical" forms of constraint (such as keys, foreign keys, functional dependencies), and propose different strategies for updating inconsistent data reasonably, in order to make it consistent by means of minimal changes. Indeed these kinds of constraint often do not suffice to manage data consistency, as they cannot be used to define algebraic relations between stored values. In fact, this issue frequently occurs in several scenarios, such as scientific databases, statistical databases, and data warehouses, where numerical values of tuples are derivable by aggregating values stored in other tuples.

In this work we focus our attention on databases where stored data violates a set of *aggregate constraints*, i.e. integrity constraints defined on aggregate values extracted from the database. These constraints are defined on numerical attributes (such as sales prices, costs, etc.) which represent measure values and are not intrinsically involved in other forms of constraints.

Example 1. Table 1 represents a two-years *cash budget* for a firm, that is a summary of cash flows (receipts, disbursements, and cash balances) over the specified periods. Values '*det*', '*aggr*' and '*drv*' in column *Type* stand for *detail*, *aggregate* and *derived*, respectively. In particular, an item of the table is *aggregate* if it is obtained by aggregating items of type *detail* of the same section, whereas

G. Bierman and C. Koch (Eds.): DBPL 2005, LNCS 3774, pp. 279–294, 2005.

Table 1. A cash budget

Year	Section	Subsection	Type	Value
2003	Receipts	beginning cash	drv	20
2003	Receipts	cash sales	det	100
2003	Receipts	receivables	det	120
2003	Receipts	total cash receipts	aggr	250
2003	Disbursements	payment of accounts	det	120
2003	Disbursements	capital expenditure	det	0
2003	Disbursements	long-term financing	det	40
2003	Disbursements	total disbursements	aggr	160
2003	Balance	net cash inflow	drv	60
2003	Balance	ending cash balance	drv	80
2004	Receipts	beginning cash	drv	80
2004	Receipts	cash sales	det	100
2004	Receipts	receivables	det	100
2004	Receipts	total cash receipts	aggr	200
2004	Disbursements	payment of accounts	det	130
2004	Disbursements	capital expenditure	det	40
2004	Disbursements	long-term financing	det	20
2004	Disbursements	total disbursements	aggr	190
2004	Balance	net cash inflow	drv	10
2004	Balance	ending cash balance	drv	90

a *derived* item is an item whose value can be computed using the values of other items of any type and belonging to any section.

A cash budget must satisfy the following integrity constraints:

1. for each section and year, the sum of the values of all *detail* items must be equal to the value of the *aggregate* item of the same section and year;
2. for each year, the net cash inflow must be equal to the difference between total cash receipts and total disbursements;
3. for each year, the ending cash balance must be equal to the sum of the beginning cash and the net cash balance.

Table 1 was acquired by means of an OCR tool from two paper documents, reporting the cash budget for 2003 and 2004. The original paper document was consistent, but some symbol recognition errors occurred during the digitizing phase, as constraints 1) and 2) are not satisfied on the acquired data for year 2003, that is:

i) in section *Receipts*, the aggregate value of *total cash receipts* is not equal to the sum of detail values of the same section.
ii) the value of *net cash inflow* is not to equal the difference between *total cash receipts* and *total disbursements*.

In order to exploit the digital version of the cash budget, a fundamental issue is to define a reasonable strategy for locating OCR errors, and then "repairing" the acquired data to extract reliable information.   □

Most of well-known techniques for repairing data violating either key constraints or functional dependencies accomplish this task by performing deletions and insertions of tuples. Indeed this approach is not suitable for contexts analogous to that of Example 1, that is of data acquired by OCR tools from paper documents. For instance, repairing Table 1 by either adding or removing rows means hypothesizing that the OCR tool either jumped a row or "invented" it when acquiring the source paper document, which is rather unrealistic. The same issue arises in other scenarios dealing with numerical data representing pieces of information acquired automatically, such as sensor networks. In a sensor network with error-free communication channels, no reading generated by sensors can be lost, thus repairing the database by adding new readings (as well as removing collected ones) is of no sense. In this kind of scenario, the most natural approach to data repairing is updating directly the numerical data: this means working at attribute-level, rather than at tuple-level. For instance, in the case of Example 1, we can reasonably assume that inconsistencies of digitized data are due to symbol recognition errors, and thus trying to re-construct actual data values is well founded. Likewise, in the case of sensor readings violating aggregate constraints, we can hypothesize that inconsistency is due to some trouble occurred at a sensor while generating some reading, thus repairing data by modifying readings instead of deleting (or inserting) them is justified.

1.1   Related Work

First theoretical approaches to the problem of dealing with incomplete and inconsistent information date back to 80s, but these works mainly focus on issues related to the semantics of incompleteness [14]. The problem of extracting reliable information from inconsistent data was first addressed in [1], where an extension of relational algebra (namely *flexible algebra*) was proposed to evaluate queries on data inconsistent w.r.t. key constraints (i.e. tuples having the same values for key attributes, but conflicting values for other attributes). The first proof-theoretic notion of *consistent query answer* was introduced in [9], expressing the idea that tuples involved in an integrity violation should not be considered in the evaluation of consistent query answering. In [2] a different notion of consistent answer was introduced, based on the notion of *repair*: a repair of an inconsistent database D is a database D' satisfying the given integrity constraints and which is minimally different from D. Thus, the consistent answer of a query q posed on D is the answer which is in every result of q on each repair D'. In particular, in [2] the authors show that, for restricted classes of queries and constraints, consistent answers can be evaluated without computing repairs, but by looking only at the specified constraints and rewriting the original query q into a query q' such that the answer of q' on D is equal to the consistent answer of q on D. Based on the notions of repair and consistent query answer introduced in [2], several works investigated more expressive classes of queries and constraints. In [3] extended disjunctive logic programs with exceptions were used for the computation of repairs, and in [4] the evaluation of aggregate queries on inconsistent data was investigated. A further generalization was proposed in [13], where the authors defined a technique based on the rewriting of constraints into extended disjunctive rules with two different forms of negation (negation as failure and classical negation). This technique was shown to be sound and complete for universally quantified constraints.

All the above-cited approaches assume that tuple insertions and deletions are the basic primitives for repairing inconsistent data. More recently, in [12] a repairing strategy using only tuple deletions was proposed, and in [7, 19, 20] repairs consisting of also value-update operations were considered. The latter are the first approaches performing repairs at the attribute-value level, but are not well-suited in our context, as they do not consider any form of aggregate constraint.

The first work investigating aggregate constraints on numerical data is [18], where the consistency problem of very general forms of aggregation is considered, but no issue related to data-repairing is investigated. In [6] the problem of repairing databases by fixing numerical data at attribute level is investigated. The authors show that deciding the existence of a repair under both denial constraints (where built-in comparison predicates are allowed) and a non-linear form of multi-attribute aggregate constraints is undecidable. Then they disregard aggregate constraints and focus on the problem of repairing data violating denial constraints, where no form of aggregation is allowed in the adopted constraints.

1.2 Main Contribution

We investigate the problem of repairing and extracting reliable information from data violating a given set of aggregate constraints. These constraints consist of linear inequalities on aggregate-sum queries issued on measure values stored in the database. This syntactic form enables meaningful constraints to be expressed, such as those of Example 1 as well as other forms which often occur in practice.

We consider database repairs consisting of "reasonable" sets of value-update operations aiming at re-constructing the correct measure values of inconsistent data. We adopt two different criteria for determining whether a set of update operations repairing data can be considered "reasonable" or not: *set*-minimal semantics and *card*-minimal semantics. Both these semantics aim at preserving the information represented in the source data as much as possible. They correspond to different repairing strategies which turn out to be well-suited for different application scenarios.

We provide the complexity characterization of three fundamental problems:

i. *repairability*: is there at least one repair for the given database w.r.t. the specified constraints?

ii. *repair checking*: given a set of update operations, is it a "reasonable" repair?

iii. *consistent query answer*: is a given boolean query true in every "reasonable" repair?

2 Preliminaries

We assume classical notions of database scheme, relational scheme, and relations. In the following we will also use a logical formalism to represent relational databases, and relational schemes will be represented by means of sorted predicates of the form $R(A_1 : \Delta_1, \ldots, A_n : \Delta_n)$, where $A_1, \ldots, A_n$ are attribute names and $\Delta_1, \ldots, \Delta_n$ are the corresponding domains. Each Δ_i can be either $\mathbb{Z}$ (infinite domain of integers), $\mathbb{R}$ (reals), or $\mathbb{S}$ (strings). Domains $\mathbb{R}$ and $\mathbb{Z}$ will be said to be *numerical domains*, and attributes defined over $\mathbb{R}$ or $\mathbb{Z}$ will be said to be *numerical attributes*. Given a ground atom t denoting a tuple, the value of attribute A of t will be denoted as $t[A]$.

Given a database scheme $\mathcal{D}$, we will denote as $\mathcal{M}_{\mathcal{D}}$ (namely, *Measure attributes*) the set of numerical attributes representing measure data. That is, $\mathcal{M}_{\mathcal{D}}$ specifies the set of attributes representing measure values, such as weights, lengths, prices, etc. For instance, in Example 1, $\mathcal{M}_{\mathcal{D}}$ consists of the only attribute *Value*.

2.1 Aggregate Constraints

Given a relational scheme $R(A_1 : \Delta_1, \ldots, A_n : \Delta_n)$, an *attribute expression* on R is defined recursively as follows:

- a numerical constant is an attribute expression;
- each A_i (with $i \in [1..n]$) is an attribute expression;
- $e_1 \psi e_2$ is an attribute expression on R, if e_1, e_2 are attribute expressions on R and ψ is an arithmetic operator in $\{+, -\}$;
- $c \times (e)$ is an attribute expressions on R, if e is an attribute expression on R and c a numerical constant.

Let R be a relational scheme and e an attribute expression on R. An *aggregation function* on R is a function $\chi : (\Lambda_1 \times \cdots \times \Lambda_k) \to \mathbb{R}$, where each Λ_i is either $\mathbb{Z}$, or $\mathbb{R}$, or $\mathbb{S}$, and it is defined as follows:

$$\chi(x_1, \ldots, x_k) = \texttt{SELECT sum(e)}$$
$$\texttt{FROM} \quad \texttt{R}$$
$$\texttt{WHERE} \quad \alpha(x_1, \ldots, x_k)$$

where $\alpha(x_1, \ldots, x_k)$ is a boolean formula on $x_1, \ldots, x_k$, constants and attributes of R.

Example 2. The following aggregation functions are defined on the relational scheme *CashBudget(Year, Section, Subsection, Type, Value)* of Example 1:

$\chi_1(x, y, z) = $ SELECT sum(Value)
               FROM   CashBudget
               WHERE   Section=x
                    AND Year=y AND Type=z

$\chi_2(x, y) = $ SELECT   sum(Value)
              FROM   CashBudget
              WHERE   Year = x
                  AND Subsection=y

Function χ_1 returns the sum of *Value* of all the tuples having *Section* x, *Year* y and *Type* z. For instance, $\chi_1($'Receipts', '2003', 'det'$)$ returns $100 + 120 = 220$, whereas χ_1('Disbursements', '2003', 'aggr') returns 160. Function χ_2 returns the sum of *Value* of all the tuples where *Year*=x and *Subsection*=y. In our running example, as the pair *Year, Subsection* is a key for the tuples of *Cash-Budget*, the sum returned by χ_2 is an attribute value of a single tuple. For instance, χ_2('2003', 'cash sales') returns 100, whereas χ_2('2004', 'net cash inflow') returns 10.   □

Definition 1 (Aggregate constraint). *Given a database scheme $\mathcal{D}$, an aggregate constraint on $\mathcal{D}$ is an expression of the form:*

$$\forall x_1, \ldots, x_k \ \left(\phi(x_1, \ldots, x_k) \implies \sum_{i=1}^{n} c_i \cdot \chi_i(X_i) \leq K \right) \tag{1}$$

where:

1. $c_1, \ldots, c_n, K$ *are constants;*
2. $\phi(x_1, \ldots, x_k)$ *is a conjunction of atoms containing the variables $x_1, \ldots, x_k$;*
3. *each $\chi_i(X_i)$ is an aggregation function, where X_i is a list of variables and constants, and variables appearing in X_i are a subset of $\{x_1, \ldots, x_k\}$.*

Given a database D and a set of aggregate constraints $\mathcal{AC}$, we will use the notation $D \models \mathcal{AC}$ [resp. $D \not\models \mathcal{AC}$] to say that D is consistent [resp. inconsistent] w.r.t. $\mathcal{AC}$.

Observe that aggregate constraints enable equalities to be expressed as well, since an equality can be viewed as a pair of inequalities. For the sake of brevity, in the following equalities will be written explicitly.

Example 3. Constraint 1 defined in Example 1 can be expressed as follows:

$$\forall x, y, s, t, v \ \ CashBudget(y, x, s, t, v) \implies \chi_1(x, y, 'det') - \chi_1(x, y, 'aggr') = 0$$

□

For the sake of simplicity, in the following we will use a shorter notation for denoting aggregate constraints, where universal quantification is implied and variables in ϕ which do not occur in any aggregation function are replaced with the symbol '_'. For instance, the constraint of Example 3 can be written as:

$$CashBudget(y, x, \_, \_, \_) \implies \chi_1(x, y, 'det') - \chi_1(x, y, 'aggr') = 0$$

Example 4. Constraints 2 and 3 of Example 1 can be expressed as follows:

Constraint 2: $CashBudget(x, \_, \_, \_, \_) \implies$
$\chi_2(x, 'net\ cash\ inflow') - (\chi_2(x, 'total\ cash\ receipts') - \chi_2(x, 'total\ disbursements')) = 0$

Constraint 3: $CashBudget(x, \_, \_, \_, \_) \implies$
$\chi_2(x, 'ending\ cash\ balance') - (\chi_2(x, 'beginning\ cash') + \chi_2(x, 'net\ cash\ balance')) = 0$

Consider the database scheme consisting of relation *CashBudget* and relation *Sales(Product, Year, Income)*, containing pieces of information on annual product sales. The following aggregate constraint says that, for each year, the value of *cash sales* in *CashBudget* must be equal to the total incomes obtained from relation *Sales*:

$$CashBudget(x, \_, \_, \_, \_) \wedge Sales(\_, x, \_) \implies \chi_2(x, \text{'cash sales'}) - \chi_3(x) = 0$$

where $\chi_3(x)$ is the aggregation function returning the total income due to products sales in year x:

$$\chi_3(x) = \texttt{SELECT sum(Income)}$$
$$\texttt{FROM}\quad \texttt{Sales}$$
$$\texttt{WHERE}\quad \texttt{Year = x} \qquad \qquad \qquad \square$$

2.2   Updates

Updates at attribute-level will be used in the following as the basic primitives for repairing data violating aggregate constraints. Given a relational scheme R in the database scheme $\mathcal{D}$, let $\mathcal{M}_R = \{A_1, \ldots, A_k\}$ be the subset of $\mathcal{M}_\mathcal{D}$ containing all the attributes in R belonging to $\mathcal{M}_\mathcal{D}$.

Definition 2 (Atomic update). *Let $t = R(v_1, \ldots, v_n)$ be a tuple on the relational scheme $R(A_1 : \Delta_1, \ldots, A_n : \Delta_n)$. An atomic update on t is a triplet $< t, A_i, v_i' >$, where $A_i \in \mathcal{M}_R$ and v_i' is a value in Δ_i and $v_i' \neq v_i$.*

Update $u = < t, A_i, v_i' >$ replaces $t[A_i]$ with v_i', thus yielding the tuple $u(t) = R(v_1, \ldots, v_{i-1}, v_i', v_{i+1}, \ldots, v_n)$.

Observe that atomic updates work on the set $\mathcal{M}_R$ of measure attributes, as our framework is based on the assumption that data inconsistency is due to errors in the acquisition phase (as in the case of digitization of paper documents) or in the measurement phase (as in the case of sensor readings). Therefore our approach will only consider repairs aiming at re-constructing the correct measures.

Example 5. Update $u = < t, Value, 130 >$ issued on the following tuple:

$$t = CashBudget(2003, \text{'Receipts'}, \text{'cash sales'}, \text{'det'}, 100)$$

returns the tuple:

$$u(t) = CashBudget(2003, \text{'Receipts'}, \text{'cash sales'}, \text{'det'}, 130).$$

$\qquad\qquad\qquad\qquad\qquad\qquad\qquad\qquad\qquad\qquad\qquad\qquad\qquad\qquad\qquad\square$

Given an update u, we denote the attribute updated by u as $\lambda(u)$. That is, if $u = < t, A_i, v >$ then $\lambda(u) = < t, A_i >$.

Definition 3 (Consistent database update). *Let D be a database and $U = \{u_1, \ldots, u_n\}$ be a set of atomic updates on tuples of D. The set U is said to be a consistent database update iff $\forall j, k \in [1..n]$ if $j \neq k$ then $\lambda(u_j) \neq \lambda(u_k)$.*

Informally, a set of atomic updates U is a consistent database update iff for each pair of updates $u_1, u_2 \in U$, u_1 and u_2 do not work on the same tuples, or they change different attributes of the same tuple.

The set of pairs $< tuple, attribute >$ updated by a consistent database update U will be denoted as $\lambda(U) = \cup_{u_i \in U} \lambda(u_i)$.

Given a database D and a consistent database update U, performing U on D results in the database $U(D)$ obtained by applying all atomic updates in U.

3   Repairing Inconsistent Databases

Definition 4 (Repair). *Let $\mathcal{D}$ be a database scheme, $\mathcal{AC}$ a set of aggregate constraints on $\mathcal{D}$, and D an instance of $\mathcal{D}$ such that $D \not\models \mathcal{AC}$. A repair ρ for D is a consistent database update such that $\rho(D) \models \mathcal{AC}$.*

Example 6. A repair ρ for *CashBudget* w.r.t. constraints 1), 2) and 3) consists in decreasing attribute *Value* in the tuple:

$$t = CashBudget(2003, \text{'Receipts'}, \text{'total cash receipts'}, \text{'aggr'}, 250)$$

down to 220; that is, $\rho = \{ < t, Value, 220 > \}$.   □

We now characterize the complexity of the repair-existence problem. All the complexity results in the paper refer to data-complexity, that is the size of the constraints is assumed to be bounded by a constant.

The following lemma is a preliminary result which states that potential repairs for an inconsistent database can be found among set of updates whose size is polynomially bounded by the size of the original database.

Lemma 1. *Let $\mathcal{D}$ be a database scheme, $\mathcal{AC}$ a set of aggregate constraints on $\mathcal{D}$, and D an instance of $\mathcal{D}$ such that $D \not\models \mathcal{AC}$. If there is a repair ρ for D w.r.t. $\mathcal{AC}$, then there is a repair ρ' for D such that $\lambda(\rho') \subseteq \lambda(\rho)$ and ρ' has polynomial size w.r.t. D.*

Theorem 1 (Repair existence). *Let $\mathcal{D}$ be a database scheme, $\mathcal{AC}$ a set of aggregate constraints on $\mathcal{D}$, and D an instance of $\mathcal{D}$ such that $D \not\models \mathcal{AC}$. The problem of deciding whether there is a repair for D is NP-complete (w.r.t. the size of D).*

Proof. Membership. A polynomial size witness for deciding the existence of a repair is a database update U on D: testing whether U is a repair for D means verifying $U(D) \models \mathcal{AC}$, which can be accomplished in polynomial time w.r.t. the size of D and U. If a repair exists for D, then Lemma 1 guarantees that a polynomial size repair for D exists too.

Hardness. We show a reduction from CIRCUIT SAT to our problem. Without loss of generality, we consider a boolean circuit C using only NOR gates. The inputs of C will be denoted as $x_1, \ldots, x_n$. The boolean circuit C can be represented by means of the database scheme:

$gate(\underline{IDGate}, norVal, orVal),$
$gateInput(\underline{IDGate}, IDIngoing}, Val),$
$input(\underline{IDInput}, Val).$

Therein:

1. each gate in C corresponds to a tuple in *gate* (attributes *norVal* and *orVal* represent the output of the corresponding NOR gate and its negation, respectively);
2. inputs of C correspond to tuples of *input*: attribute *Val* in a tuple of *input* represents the truth assignment to the input $x_{IDInput}$;
3. each tuple in *gateInput* represents an input of the gate identified by *IDGate*. In particular, *IDIngoing* refers to either a gate identifier or an input identifier; attribute *Val* is a copy of the truth value of the specified ingoing gate or input.

We consider the database instance D where the relations defined above are populated as follows. For each input x_i in C we insert the tuple $input(id(x_i), -1)$ into D, and for each gate g in C we insert the tuple $gate(id(g), -1, -1)$, where function $id(x)$ assigns a unique identifier to its argument (we assume that gate identifiers are distinct from input identifiers, and that the output gate of C is assigned the identifier 0). Moreover, for each edge in C going from g' to the gate g (where g' is either a gate or an input of C), the tuple $gateInput(id(g), id(g'), -1)$ is inserted into D. Assume that $\mathcal{M}_{gate} = \{norVal, orVal\}$, $\mathcal{M}_{gateInput} = \{Val\}$, $\mathcal{M}_{input} = \{Val\}$. In the following, we will define aggregate constraints to force measure attributes of all tuples to be assigned either 1 or 0, representing the truth value *true* and *false*, respectively. The initial assignment (where every measure attribute is set to -1) means that the truth values of inputs and gate outputs is undefined.

Consider the following aggregation functions:

$NORVal(X) = $ `SELECT Sum(norVal)`
`FROM gate`
`WHERE (IDGate=X)`

$ORVal(X) = $ `SELECT Sum(orVal)`
`FROM gate`
`WHERE (IDGate=X)`

$IngoingVal(X, Y) = $ `SELECT Sum(Val)`
`FROM gateInput`
`WHERE (IDGate=X)`
`AND (IDIngoing=Y)`

$IngoingSum(X) = $ `SELECT Sum(Val)`
`FROM gateInput`
`WHERE (IDGate=X)`

$InputVal(X) = $ `SELECT Sum(Val)`
`FROM Input`
`WHERE (IDInput=X)`

$ValidInput( ) = $ `SELECT Sum(1)`
`FROM input`
`WHERE (Val≠0)`
`AND (Val≠1)`

$ValidGate( ) = $ `SELECT Sum(1)`
`FROM gate`
`WHERE (orVal≠0 AND orVal≠1)`
`OR (norVal≠0 AND norVal≠1)`

Therein: $NORVal(X)$ and $ORVal(X)$ return the truth value of the gate X and its opposite, respectively; $IngoingVal(X, Y)$ returns, for the gate with identifier X, the truth value of the ingoing gate or input having identifier Y; $IngoingSum(X)$ returns the sum of the truth values of the inputs of the gate X; $InputVal(X)$ returns the truth assignment of the input X; $ValidInput( )$ returns 0 iff there is no tuple in relation *input* where attribute Val is neither 0 nor 1, otherwise it returns a number greater than 0; likewise, $ValidGate( )$ returns 0 iff there is no tuple in relation *gate* where attributes $norVal$ or $orVal$ are neither 0 nor 1 (otherwise it returns a number greater than 0).

Consider the following aggregate constraints on $\mathcal{D}$:

1. $ValidInput( ) + ValidGate( ) = 0$, which entails that only 0 and 1 can be assigned either to attributes $orVal$ and $norVal$ in relation *gate*, and to attribute Val in relation *input*;
2. $gate(X, \_, \_) \Rightarrow ORVal(X) + NORVal(X) = 1$, which says that for each tuple representing a NOR gate, the value of $orVal$ must be complementary to $norVal$;
3. $gate(X, \_, \_) \Rightarrow ORVal(X) - IngoingSum(X) \leq 0$, which says that for each tuple representing a NOR gate, the value of $orVal$ cannot be greater than the sum of truth assignments of its inputs (i.e. if all inputs are 0, $orVal$ must be 0 too);
4. $gateInput(X, Y, \_) \Rightarrow IngoingVal(X, Y) - ORVal(X) \leq 0$, which implies that, for each gate g, attribute $orVal$ must be 1 if at least one input of g has value 1;
5. $gateInput(X, Y, \_) \Rightarrow IngoingVal(X, Y) - NORVal(Y) - InputVal(Y) = 0$, which imposes that the attribute Val in each tuple of $gateInput$ is the same as the truth value of either the ingoing gate or the ingoing input.

Observe that D does not satisfy these constraints, but every repair of D corresponds to a valid truth assignment of C.

Let $\mathcal{AC}$ be the set of aggregate constraints consisting of constraints 1-5 defined above plus constraint $NORVal(0) = 1$ (which imposes that the truth value of the output gate must be *true*). Therefore, deciding whether there is a truth assignment which evaluates C to *true* is equivalent to asking whether there is a repair ρ for D w.r.t. $\mathcal{AC}$.   □

Remark. Theorem 1 states that the repair existence problem is decidable. This result, together with the practical usefulness of the considered class of constraints, makes the complexity analysis of finding consistent answers on inconsistent data interesting. Basically decidability results from the linear nature of the considered constraints. If products between two attributes were allowed as attribute expressions, the repair-existence problem would be undecidable (this can be proved straightforwardly, since this form of non-linear constraints is more expressive than those introduced in [6], where the corresponding repair-existence problem was shown to be undecidable). However, observe that occurrences of products of the form $A_i \times A_j$ in attribute expressions can lead to undecidability only if both A_i and A_j are measure attribute. Otherwise, this case is equivalent to products of the form $c \times A$, which can be expressed in our form of aggregate constraints.

3.1   Minimal Repairs

Theorem 1 deals with the problem of deciding whether a database D violating a set of aggregate constraints $\mathcal{AC}$ can be repaired. If this is the case, different repairs can be performed on D yielding a new database consistent w.r.t. $\mathcal{AC}$, although not all of them can be considered "reasonable". For instance, if a repair exists for D changing only one value in one tuple of D, any repair updating all values in all tuples of D can be reasonably disregarded. To evaluate whether a repair should be considered "relevant" or not, we introduce two different ordering criteria on repairs, corresponding to the comparison operators '$\leq_{set}$' and '$\leq_{card}$'. The former compares two repairs by evaluating whether one of the two performs a subset of the updates of the other. That is, given two repairs ρ_1, ρ_2, we say that ρ_1 precedes ρ_2 ($\rho_1 \leq_{set} \rho_2$) iff $\lambda(\rho_1) \subseteq \lambda(\rho_2)$. The latter ordering criterion states that a repair ρ_1 is preferred w.r.t. a repair ρ_2 ($\rho_1 \leq_{card} \rho_2$) iff $|\lambda(\rho_1)| \leq |\lambda(\rho_2)|$, that is if the number of changes issued by ρ_1 is less than ρ_2.

Observe that $\rho_1 <_{set} \rho_2$ implies $\rho_1 <_{card} \rho_2$, but the vice versa does not hold, as it can be the case that repair ρ_1 changes a set of values $\lambda(\rho_1)$ which is not a subset of $\lambda(\rho_2)$, but whose cardinality is less than that of $\lambda(\rho_2)$.

Example 7. Another repair for *CashBudget* is:

$$\rho' = \{\langle t_1, Value, 130\rangle, \langle t_2, Value, 70\rangle, \langle t_3, Value, 190\rangle\},$$

where:

$t_1 = CashBudget(\ 2003,\ 'Receipts',\ cash\ sales',\ 'det',\ 100),$
$t_2 = CashBudget(\ 2003,\ 'Disbursements',\ 'long-term\ financing',\ 'det',\ 40),$
$t_3 = CashBudget\ (\ 2003,\ 'Disbursements',\ 'total\ disbursements',\ 'aggr',\ 160).$

Observe that $\rho <_{card} \rho'$, but not $\rho <_{set} \rho'$ (where ρ is the repair defined in Example 6). $\qquad\square$

Definition 5 (Minimal repairs). *Let $\mathcal{D}$ be a database scheme, $\mathcal{AC}$ a set of aggregate constraints on $\mathcal{D}$, and D an instance of $\mathcal{D}$. A repair ρ for D w.r.t. $\mathcal{AC}$ is a* set-*minimal repair [resp.* card-*minimal repair] iff there is no repair ρ' for D w.r.t. $\mathcal{AC}$ such that $\rho' <_{set} \rho$ [resp. $\rho' <_{card} \rho$].*

Example 8. Repair ρ of Example 6 is minimal under both the *set*-minimal and the *card*-minimal semantics, whereas ρ' defined in Example 7 is minimal only under the *set*-minimal semantics.

Consider the repair $\rho'' = \{\langle t_1, Value, 110\rangle, \langle t_2, Value, 110\rangle, \langle t_3, Value, 220\rangle\}$ where:

$t_1 = CashBudget(\ 2003,\ 'Receipts',\ 'cash\ sales',\ 'det',\ 100),$
$t_2 = CashBudget(\ 2003,\ 'Receipts',\ 'receivables',\ 'det',\ 120),$
$t_3 = CashBudget(\ 2003,\ 'Receipts',\ 'total\ cash\ receipts',\ 'aggr',\ 250).$

The strategy adopted by ρ'' can be reasonably disregarded, since the only atomic update on tuple t_3 suffices to make D consistent. In fact, ρ'' is not minimal neither under the *set*-minimal semantics (as $\lambda(\rho) \subset \lambda(\rho'')$ and thus $\rho <_{set} \rho''$) nor under the *card*-minimal one. $\qquad\square$

Given a database D which is not consistent w.r.t. a set of aggregate constraints $\mathcal{AC}$, different *set*-minimal repairs (resp. *card*-minimal repairs) can exist on D. In our running example, repair ρ of Example 6 is the unique *card*-minimal repair, and both ρ and ρ' are *set*-minimal repairs (where ρ' is the repair defined in Example 7). The set of *set*-minimal repairs and the set of *card*-minimal repairs will be denoted, respectively, as ρ_M^{set} and ρ_M^{card}.

Theorem 2 (Minimal-repair checking). *Let $\mathcal{D}$ be a database scheme, $\mathcal{AC}$ a set of aggregate constraints on $\mathcal{D}$, and D an instance of $\mathcal{D}$ such that $D \not\models \mathcal{AC}$. Given a repair ρ for D w.r.t. $\mathcal{AC}$, deciding whether ρ is minimal (under either the card-minimality and set-minimality semantics) is coNP-complete (w.r.t. the size of D and ρ).*

Set-minimality vs card-minimality

Basically, both the *set*-minimal and the *card*-minimal semantics aim at considering "reasonable" repairs which preserve the content of the input database as much as possible. The notion of repair minimality based on the number of performed updates has been discussed in the context of relational data violating "non-numerical" constraints (such as keys, foreign keys, and functional dependencies) in [5], where only tuple deletions were considered. Indeed, most of the proposed approaches consider repairs consisting of deletions and insertions of tuples, and preferred repairs are those consisting of minimal sets of insert/delete operations. In fact, the *set*-minimal semantics is more natural than the *card*-minimal one when no hypothesis can be reasonably formulated to "guess" how data inconsistency occurred, which is the case of previous works on database-repairing. As it will be clear in the following, in the general case, the adoption of the *card*-minimal semantics could make reasonable sets of delete/insert operations to be not considered as candidate repairs, even if they correspond to error configurations which cannot be excluded.

For instance, consider the relational scheme:

$$Department(Name,\ Area,\ Employees,\ Category)$$

and the relation:

Department	Area	Employees	Category	
D_1	100	24	A	$\longrightarrow t_1$
D_2	100	30	B	$\longrightarrow t_2$
D_3	100	30	B	$\longrightarrow t_3$

where the following functional dependencies are defined:

FD_1: *Area → Employees*   (i.e. departments having the same area must have the same number of employees)

FD_2: *Employees → Category* (i.e. departments with the same number of employees must be of the same category)

The above-reported relation does not satisfy FD_1, as the three departments occupy the same area but do not have the same number of employees. Suppose we are using a repairing strategy based on deletions and insertions of tuples. Different repairs can be adopted. For instance, if we suppose that the inconsistency arises as tuple t_1 contains wrong information, *Department* can be repaired by only deleting t_1. Otherwise, if we assume that t_1 is correct, a possible repair consists of deleting t_2 and t_3. If the *card*-minimal semantics is adopted, the latter strategy will be disregarded, as it performs two deletions, whereas the former deletes only one tuple. On the contrary, if the *set*-minimal semantics is adopted, both the two strategies define minimal repairs (as the sets of tuples deleted by each of these strategies are not subsets of one another). In fact, if we do not know how the error occurred, there is no reason to assume that the error configuration corresponding to the second repairing strategy is not possible. Indeed, inconsistency could be due to integrating data coming from different sources, where some sources are not up-to-date. However, there is no good reason to assume that the source which contains the smallest number of tuples is the one that is up to date. See [15] for a survey on inconsistency due to data integration.

Likewise, the *card*-minimal semantics could disregard reasonable repairs also in the case that a repairing strategy based on updating values instead of deleting/inserting whole tuples is adopted [1]. For instance, if we suppose that the inconsistency arises as the value of attribute *Area* is wrong for either t_1 or both t_2 and t_3, *Department* can be repaired by replacing the *Area* value for either t_1 or both t_2 and t_3 with a value different from 100. Otherwise, if we assume that the *Area* values for all the tuples are correct, *Department* can be repaired w.r.t. FD_1 by making the *Employees* value of t_1 equal to that of t_2 and t_3. Indeed this update yields a relation which does not satisfy FD_2 (as $t_1[Category] \neq t_2[Category]$) so that another value update is necessary in order to make it consistent. Under the *card*-minimal semantics the latter strategy is disregarded, as it performs more than one value update, whereas the former changes only the *Area* value of one tuple. On the contrary, under the *set*-minimal semantics both the two strategies define minimal repairs (as the sets of updates issued by each of these strategies are not subsets of one another). As for the case explained above, disregarding the second repairing strategy is arbitrary, if we do not know how the error occurred.

Our framework addresses scenarios where also *card*-minimal semantics can be reasonable. For instance, if we assume that integrity violations are generated while acquiring data by means of an automatic or semi-automatic system (e.g. an OCR digitizing a paper document, a sensor monitoring atmospheric conditions, etc.), focusing on error configurations which can be repaired with the minimum number of updates is well founded. Indeed this corresponds to the case that the acquiring system made the minimum number of errors (e.g. bad symbol-recognition for an OCR, sensor troubles, etc.), which can be considered the most probable event.

---

[1] Value updates cannot be necessarily simulated as a sequence deletion/insertion, as this might not be minimal under set inclusion.

In this work we discuss the existence of repairs, and their computation under both *card*-minimal and *set*-minimal semantics. The latter has to be preferred when no warranty is given on the accuracy of acquiring tools, and, more generally, when no hypothesis can be formulated on the cause of errors.

3.2   Consistent Query Answers

In this section we address the problem of extracting reliable information from data violating a given set of aggregate constraints. We consider boolean queries checking whether a given tuple belongs to a database, and adopt the widely-used notion of consistent query answer introduced in [2].

Definition 6 (Query). *A query over a database scheme $\mathcal{D}$ is a ground atom of the form $R(v_1, \ldots, v_n)$, where $R(A_1, \ldots, A_n)$ is a relational scheme in $\mathcal{D}$.*

Definition 7. (Consistent query answer). *Let $\mathcal{D}$ be a database scheme, D be an instance of $\mathcal{D}$, $\mathcal{AC}$ be a set of aggregate constraints on $\mathcal{D}$ and q be a query over $\mathcal{D}$. The consistent query answer of q on D under the* set-*minimal semantics [resp.* card-*minimal semantics] is true iff $q \in \rho(D)$ for each $\rho \in \rho_M^{set}$ [resp. for each $\rho \in \rho_M^{card}$].*

The consistent query answers of a query q issued on the database D under the *set*-minimal and *card*-minimal semantics will be denoted as $q^{set}(D)$ and $q^{card}(D)$, respectively. The following theorems characterize data-complexity of the consistent query answering problem under both the *set*-minimal and *card*-minimal semantics.

Theorem 3 (Consistent query answer under *set*-minimal semantics). *Let $\mathcal{D}$ be a database scheme, D be an instance of $\mathcal{D}$, $\mathcal{AC}$ a set of aggregate constraints on $\mathcal{D}$ and q a query over D. Deciding whether $q^{set}(D) = true$ is Π_2^p-complete (w.r.t. the size of D).*

Theorem 4 (Consistent query answer under *card*-minimal semantics). *Let $\mathcal{D}$ be a database scheme, D an instance of $\mathcal{D}$, $\mathcal{AC}$ a set of aggregate constraints on $\mathcal{D}$ and q be a query over D. Deciding whether $q^{card}(D) = true$ is $\Delta_2^p[\log n]$-complete (w.r.t. the size of D).*

4   Conclusions and Future Work

We have addressed the problem of repairing and extracting reliable information from numerical databases violating aggregate constraints, thus filling a gap in previous works dealing with inconsistent data, where only traditional forms of constraints (such as keys, foreign keys, etc.) were considered. In fact, aggregate constraints frequently occur in many real-life scenarios where guaranteeing the consistency of numerical data is mandatory. In particular, we have considered aggregate constraints defined as sets of linear inequalities on aggregate-sum queries on input data. For this class of constraints we have characterized the complexity of several issues related to the computation of consistent query answers.

Some related issues remain still open. For instance, it would be interesting to get a tight characterization of the combined complexity of the consistent-query-answer problem. Another interesting issue is the identification of decidable cases when more expressive forms of constraint are adopted, where products between attribute values are allowed to be expressed.

References

1. Agarwal, S., Keller, A. M., Wiederhold, G., Saraswat, K., Flexible Relation: An Approach for Integrating Data from Multiple, Possibly Inconsistent Databases, *Proc. International Conference on Data Engineering (ICDE)*, 495–504, 1995.
2. Arenas, M., Bertossi, L. E., Chomicki, J., Consistent Query Answers in Inconsistent Databases, *Proc. Symposium on Principles of Database Systems (PODS)*, 68–79, 1999.
3. Arenas, M., Bertossi, L. E., Chomicki, J., Specifying and Querying Database Repairs using Logic Programs with Exceptions *Proc. International Conference on Flexible Query Answering Systems (FQAS)*, 27–41,2000.
4. Arenas, M., Bertossi, L. E., Chomicki, J., He, X., Raghavan, V., Spinrad, J., Scalar aggregation in inconsistent databases, *Theoretical Computer Science (TCS)*, Vol. 3(296), 405-434, 2003.
5. Arenas, M., Bertossi, L. E., Chomicki, J., Answer sets for consistent query answering in inconsistent databases, *Theory and practice of logic programming (TPLP)*, Vol. 3(4-5), 393–424, 2003.
6. Bertossi, L., Bravo, L., Franconi, E., Lopatenko, A., Fixing Numerical Attributes Under Integrity Constraints, *Proc. 10th International Symposium on Database Programming Languages (DBPL)* (These proceedings), 2005.
7. Bohannon, P., Flaster, M., Fan, W., Rastogi, R., A Cost-Based Model and Effective Heuristic for Repairing Constraints by Value Modification, *Proc. ACM SIGMOD International Conference on Management of Data (SIGMOD)*, 143–154, 2005.
8. Borosh, I., Treybig, L. B., Bounds on positive integral solutions of linear diophantine equations, *Proc. American Mathematical Society*, Vol. 55(2), 299-304, 1976.
9. Bry, F., Query Answering in Information Systems with Integrity Constraints, *IFIP WG 11.5 Working Conference on Integrity and Control in Information Systems (IICIS)*, 113–130, 1997.
10. Cadoli, M., Donini, F. M., Liberatore, P., Schaerf, M., Feasibility and unfeasibility of off-line processing. *Proc. 4th Israeli Symposium on Theory of Computing and Systems (ISTCS'96)*, 100–109, 1996.
11. Chomicki, J., Marcinkowski, J., Staworko, S., Computing consistent query answers using conflict hypergraphs, *Proc. 13th International Conference on Information and Knowledge Management (CIKM)*, 417–426, 2004.
12. Chomicki, J., Marcinkowski, J., Minimal-Change Integrity Maintenance Using Tuple Deletions, *Information and Computation (IC)*, Vol. 197(1-2), 90–121, 2005.
13. Greco, G., Greco, S., Zumpano, E., A Logical Framework for Querying and Repairing Inconsistent Databases, *IEEE Transactions on Knowledge and Data Engineering (TKDE)*, Vol. 15(6), 1389–1408, 2003.
14. Imielinski, T., Lipski, W., Incomplete Information in Relational Databases, *Journal of the Association for Computing Machinery (JACM)*, Vol. 31(4), 761–791, 1984.

15. Lenzerini, M., Data Integration: A Theoretical Perspective, *Proc. Symposium on Principles of Database Systems (PODS)*, 233–246, 2002.
16. Papadimitriou, C. H., On the complexity of integer programming, *Journal of the Association for Computing Machinery (JACM)*, Vol. 28(4), 765–768, 1981.
17. Papadimitriou, C. H., Computational Complexity, Addison-Wesley, 1994.
18. Ross, K. A., Srivastava, D., Stuckey, P. J., Sudarshan, S., Foundations of Aggregation Constraints, *Theoretical Computer Science (TCS)*, Vol. 193(1-2), 149–179, 1998.
19. Wijsen, J., Condensed Representation of Database Repairs for Consistent Query Answering, *Proc. International Conference on Database Theory (ICDT)*, 378–393, 2003.
20. Wijsen, J., Making More Out of an Inconsistent Database, *Proc. International Conference on Advances in Databases and Information Systems (ADBIS)*, 291–305, 2004.

Author Index

Lecture Notes in Computer Science

For information about Vols. 1–3735

please contact your bookseller or Springer